Big Data at Work

The amount of data in our world has been exploding, and analyzing large data sets—so called big data—will become a key basis of competition in business. Statisticians and researchers will be updating their analytic approaches, methods, and research to meet the demands created by the availability of big data. The goal of this book is to show how advances in data science have the ability to fundamentally influence and improve organizational science and practice. This book is primarily designed for researchers and advanced undergraduate and graduate students in psychology, management, and statistics.

Scott Tonidandel is Associate Professor, Department of Psychology, Davidson College, NC. He received his PhD in Industrial Organizational Psychology from Rice University in 2001. He teaches courses in Psychological Research, Design and Analysis, and Research Methods and Issues in Psychology. His research includes issues related to computerized testing, and statistical and methodological issues.

Eden B. King is Associate Professor of Industrial Organizational Psychology at George Mason University. She earned her PhD from Rice University in 2006. Her research is mostly in the area of diversity, inclusion, and women in business. She is currently the Associate Editor of the *Journal of Management* and the *Journal of Business and Psychology*. She is also on the Editorial Board of the *Academy of Management Journal*.

Jose M. Cortina, Professor of Industrial Organizational Psychology at George Mason University, is President Elect of SIOP. He received his PhD in Psychology from Michigan State University. He serves as Editor of the I-O research methods journal *Organizational Research Methods*. He has an outstanding publication record and a tremendously high level of visibility in this field.

SIOP Organizational Frontiers Series

The Organizational Frontiers Series is sponsored by the Society for Industrial and Organizational Psychology (SIOP). Launched in 1983 to make scientific contributions accessible to the field, the series publishes books addressing emerging theoretical developments, fundamental and translational research, and theory-driven practice in the field of Industrial-Organizational Psychology and related organizational science disciplines including organizational behavior, human resource management, and labor and industrial relations.

Books in this series aim to inform readers of significant advances in research; challenge the research and practice community to develop and adapt new ideas; and promote the use of scientific knowledge in the solution of public policy issues and increased organizational effectiveness.

The Series originated in the hope that it would facilitate continuous learning and spur research curiosity about organizational phenomena on the part of both scientists and practitioners.

The Society for Industrial and Organizational Psychology (SIOP) is an international professional association with an annual membership of more than 8,000 industrial-organizational (I-O) psychologists who study and apply scientific principles to the workplace. I-O psychologists serve as trusted partners to business, offering strategically focused and scientifically rigorous solutions for a number of workplace issues. SIOP's mission is to enhance human well-being and performance in organizational and work settings by promoting the science, practice, and teaching of I-O psychology. For more information about SIOP, please visit www.siop.org.

The Organizational Frontiers Series

SIOP Organizational Frontiers Series

Series Editor

Richard Klimoski
George Mason University

De Dreu/Gelfand: (2008) *The Psychology of Conflict and Conflict Management in Organizations*

Ostroff/Judge: (2007) *Perspectives on Organizational Fit*

Baum/Frese/Baron: (2007) *The Psychology of Entrepreneurship*

Weekley/Ployhart: (2006) *Situational Judgment Tests: Theory, Measurement and Application*

Dipboye/Colella: (2005) *Discrimination at Work: The Psychological and Organizational Bases.*

Griffin/O'Leary-Kelly: (2004) *The Dark Side of Organizational Behavior.*

Hofmann/Tetrick: (2003) *Health and Safety in Organizations.*

Jackson/Hitt/DeNisi: (2003) *Managing Knowledge for Sustained Competitive Knowledge.*

Barrick/Ryan: (2003) *Personality and Work.*

Lord/Klimoski/Kanfer: (2002) *Emotions in the Workplace.*

Drasgow/Schmitt: (2002) *Measuring and Analyzing Behavior in Organizations.*

Feldman: (2002) *Work Careers.*

Zaccaro/Klimoski: (2001) *The Nature of Organizational Leadership.*

Rynes/Gerhart: (2000) *Compensation in Organizations.*

Klein/Kozlowski: (2000) *Multilevel Theory, Research and Methods in Organizations.*

Ilgen/Pulakos: (1999) *The Changing Nature of Performance.*

Earley/Erez: (1997) *New Perspectives on International I-O Psychology.*

Murphy: (1996) *Individual Differences and Behavior in Organizations.*

Guzzo/Salas: (1995) *Team Effectiveness and Decision Making.*

Howard: (1995) *The Changing Nature of Work.*

Schmitt/Borman: (1993) *Personnel Selection in Organizations.*

Zedeck: (1991) *Work, Families and Organizations.*

Schneider: (1990) *Organizational Culture and Climate.*

Goldstein: (1989) *Training and Development in Organizations.*

Campbell/Campbell: (1988) *Productivity in Organizations.*

Hall: (1987) *Career Development in Organizations.*

Big Data at Work

The Data Science Revolution and Organizational Psychology

Edited by Scott Tonidandel,
Eden B. King, and Jose M. Cortina

Routledge
Taylor & Francis Group

NEW YORK AND LONDON

First published 2016
by Routledge
605 Third Avenue, New York, NY 10017
4 Park Square, Milton Park, Abingdon, Oxon OX14 4RN

Routledge is an imprint of the Taylor & Francis Group, an informa business

Library of Congress Cataloging-in-Publication Data
Big data at work : the data science revolution and organizational psychology / edited by
   Scott Tonidandel, Eden B. King, & Jose M. Cortina.
     pages cm. — (The organizational frontiers series)
   Includes bibliographical references and index.
 1. Organizational behavior. 2. Big data. 3. Organizational sociology. 4. Psychology,
Industrial. I. Tonidandel, Scott. II. King, Eden. III. Cortina, Jose M.
  HD58.7.B534 2016
  302.3'5—dc23
  2015010678

ISBN: 978-1-84872-581-2 (hbk)
ISBN: 978-1-84872-582-9 (pbk)
ISBN: 978-1-31578-050-4 (ebk)

Typeset in Minion
by Apex CoVantage, LLC

For the questions, scientists, and loved ones who inspire us.

Contents

Foreword

It is difficult to come up with a better example of a topic that addresses the needs of both scientists and practitioners who are interested in the human condition in work organizations than the one that is central to this volume. As pointed out by the editors, our field is already affected by the work of others claiming expertise in big data analytics. Policy and managerial decisions are being made based on the analysis of enormous pools of data recently available to us as a result of information technology that allows us to capture and store judgments and choices being made by millions of people on a daily basis. But there remains a major gap between what we know and don't know about the best approaches to such things as human data acquisition, data storage and analysis, the most appropriate conceptual frameworks to be used, mitigating the weaknesses inherent in post hoc interpretations, or how best to scope out the ethical challenges (and limits) inherent to big data analytics. This gap is especially problematic when it comes to understanding the potential role of big data analytics in promoting the welfare of people working in organizations or the success of the company that employs them. The chapters of this volume have been written with these in mind. For those who have an immediate need to apply what we do know, there is still much to glean from a close reading of this volume. On the other hand, for those who seek better answers (or who may even be skeptical about the benefits of the big data analytic movement), the book's contributors provide much to build on. Finally for those who choose to interpret or intermediate the data analytics efforts of those in other, related disciplines (e.g., labor economics), there is much by way of excellent guidance provided. Indeed, even if only some of the goals for the volume as set out by the editors in their introductory chapter are achieved, our field in the future will be substantially better off. In this regard, I am reminded of the saying: "The best way to predict the future is to shape it." Along these lines I hope that this volume stimulates the reader to accept such a premise and play a position when it comes to shaping the science and methods of big data people analytics.

Richard Klimoski
Series Editor January 9, 2015

1

Building Understanding of the Data Science Revolution and I-O Psychology

Eden B. King, Scott Tonidandel, Jose M. Cortina, and Alexis A. Fink

> "The amount of data in our world has been exploding, and analyzing large data sets—so-called big data—will become a key basis of competition, underpinning new waves of productivity growth, innovation, and consumer surplus . . ."
> —James Manyika et al., McKinsey Global Institute (2011)

> "Work-force science, in short, is what happens when big data meets H.R. . . . In the past, studies of worker behavior were typically based on observing a few hundred people at most. Today, studies can include thousands or hundreds of thousands of workers, an exponential leap ahead."
> —Steve Lohr, New York Times (2013)

> "We're seeing a revolution in measurement, and it will revolutionize organizational economics and personnel economics."
> —Erik Brynjolfsson, MIT (2013)

These quotes exemplify the profuse conversations about the intersection of big data and business in newspapers, blogs, and popular books. Markedly absent from this discourse is the voice of industrial-organizational (I-O) psychologists. This book, purposefully and permanently, brings I-O psychologists into this important discussion.

It is our view that I-O psychologists are poised at an opportune moment in history to leverage our knowledge of people, work, and quantitative methods to serve as ambassadors, interpreters, and translators between computer scientists and business clients. We are uniquely trained to help decipher and make sense of business-related data patterns from the lens of psychological science. We further argue that organizational psychologists may also be uniquely suited to address questions of privacy, ethics, and "dustbowl empiricism" that emerge in discussions of big data. Thus, this volume strives to accomplish two important goals: (1) to review critical issues in collecting, analyzing, communicating, and theorizing about big data, and (2) to ignite rigorous scholarship on big data in organizations.

To fulfill these objectives, this book is organized into two primary sections. The first section deals with technical and methodological aspects of big data (e.g., collecting, analyzing, warehousing, integrating, and visualizing) and the second addresses topical content areas where big data might be well positioned to contribute to paths of future inquiry (e.g., selection, teamwork, and diversity). Here we set the stage for these ideas by introducing a general definition of big data and generating ideas about opportunities for its integration in I-O psychology. We also describe potential practical and conceptual challenges that are brought about by big data. In the context of these descriptions, we foreshadow the chapters that follow; we briefly summarize the ways in which each chapter responds to the practical, conceptual, and substantive challenges and opportunities of big data. Altogether, these chapters will describe how advances in data science have the ability to fundamentally influence and improve organizational science and practice.

WHAT ARE BIG DATA?

Big data can be understood with regard to three primary characteristics (the "three V's"; Laney, 2001): (1) *volume*—large number of data points, (2) *velocity*—both the throughput of the data (amount being added constantly) and the latency in using this information, and (3) *variety*—multiple sources of data being integrated. Organizational psychologists may encounter data that fulfill all three of these key factors, but our interpretation is broader—big data in organizational sciences might not necessarily include all three of these characteristics. Moreover, we don't believe that any particular amount of each V defines big data. Rather, data become big data when the different V's force you to think about and interact with your data differently. For example, the most central component of big data in most peoples' minds is volume. But there is no single sample size that qualifies as big data. The volume of data that we might deal with would most likely not reach the level of computer science applications (hundreds of terabytes), but high volume instead might be data sets that overwhelm commonly available computing resources and require nontraditional analytic procedures. Similarly, the actual sample size itself might not be very large, but there is big data volume because data for a large number of variables are being collected for each individual (think moment by moment performance or location data) that can't be analyzed using traditional data reduction techniques. Or the volume of the data could be manageable, but the high velocity of the data forces us to abandon our theories and methods that were developed for more static studies. In each of these instances, we enter the realm of big data because the situation created by the V's requires us to reconsider our science, to apply new theories and methods, and to ask new and different questions of the data that were not previously possible. Further, the emergence of these statistical and data management approaches allows us to apply new methods to old problems and potentially gain additional insight. That is, we may find novel and useful insights by applying new techniques to data sets that could be analyzed using standard methods—thus expanding overall the universe of insights we can bring to bear on the world of work.

WHAT ARE THE EMERGING OPPORTUNITIES FOR SCIENCE AND PRACTICE?

What could it mean for the study and practice of organizational psychology if we had access to varied and dynamic data? How can we apply new analytic strategies to understand workplace dynamics in more nuanced ways? What could we learn and how could we enhance organizational effectiveness and employee wellness? This is the world of big data, which represents an opportunity to build our science and expand the impact of our discipline. Here we hope to ignite interest in this topic by brainstorming about the major areas of scholarship and practice in organizational psychology that could be explored, expanded, and impacted though big data. Testing of models in these areas—a small sample of which are listed in Table 1 and discussed in the second section of the book—might be facilitated through new data and techniques.

Emerging Tools and Potential Applications

In this section, we describe several new tools and sources of data that can be leveraged to build big data and organizational science: sociometric sensors, social media data and sentiment analyses, microexpression analyses, and psychophysiological measures. This is not an exhaustive list, but rather

TABLE 1.1

Areas of opportunity at the intersection of big data and I-O psychology

Area	Example New Topics
Selection	- Targeted recruitment (targeted marketing efforts) - Limitless biodata to increase validity and inspire new theory
Training	- Genuinely adaptive training environments - Individually tailored training experiences - Objective indicators of transfer of training
Performance Management	- Visualization of individual, team, and organizational performance over time - Real-time, continuous monitoring and feedback
Leadership	- Neural networks of effective leaders - Live assessment of leadership behaviors for succession planning - Modeling of leader-member exchange relationships for leader development - Data-driven decision making
Teams	- Identification of effective communication and coordination patterns across team types - Tracking and visualizing team development over time - Deducing effective physical space designs for teams that vary with regard to type and interdependence
Occupational Health	- Preventative identification of health or safety risk factors or behaviors - Adaptive gamification to motivate employee health behavior
Work-Family	- Genuine time-use studies with intervention designs - Exploration of policies, practices, signals, and traditions that comprise family-friendly cultures
Diversity	- Assessing inclusion through geospatial shapes of communication, coordination, and friendship networks - Identifying barriers through sentiment or microexpression analysis of intergroup communication
Future Horizons	- The influence of global or community factors/events on employees and organizations

a preliminary set of data sources that (especially in combination) might offer new insights into I-O psychology. These and other tools, through complementary inductive and deductive approaches, allow new questions and ideas to be generated.

Sociometric sensors. Sociometric sensors are wearable technology that can collect a wide range of information automatically from users and individuals around them. These devices exploit the fact that many people are already comfortable with wearable electronics, such as cell phones, digital watches, pedometers, and the emerging device category around personal biometrics such as Fitbit and Google Glass. These devices have a number of benefits over traditional observational data collection methods and can replace costly human observation, which is susceptible to subjective biases and memory errors. A variety of highly accurate data can be available such as nonlinguistic social signals (e.g., interest, excitement, influence) and relative location monitoring. Indeed, such sensors are being used to investigate a host of phenomena in organizational behavior. For example, activity and number of team interactions have been shown to be related to creativity (Tripathi & Burleson, 2012). Similarly, Olguín-Olguín and Pentland (2010) found that activity level and interaction patterns as measured by sociometric sensors predicted success by teams in an entrepreneurship competition. These same sensors have also been used in field studies to measure inter-team collaboration patterns as well as integration processes in multicultural teams (Kim, McFee, Olguín, Waber, & Pentland, 2012). In their chapter on teamwork, Kozlowski Chao, Chang, and Fernandez describe the initial stages of team-based research that leverages this kind of technology to assess team process dynamics.

Social media data, text analysis, and sentiment analyses. An obvious area of focus in the world of big data is social media. Social media include websites and applications that enable users to create and share content or participate in social networking. The content of this electronic communication is a treasure trove of psychologically relevant information about people, their relationships, and their behavior. Analyses might involve simply tracking patterns of viewing or clicking, time spent in different virtual spaces, or social network patterns such as who is interacting with whom. According to IBM (2015), social media analytics are designed to "help organizations understand and act upon the social media impact of their products, services, markets, campaigns, employees and partners." For employers, of course, social media can take on a different importance. Social media activity can give clues to employee engagement and warn of exit behavior. Recruiters can and do review social media information to find and vet candidates. Reviews on sites like Glassdoor affect employment branding and thereby influence the recruiting process of organizations.

Social media may be particularly informative through the lens of sentiment analyses. Sentiment analyses go beyond simple counts of frequency of clicks to analyze the content of what is spoken or written. For example, sentiment analysis could be used to examine the positive or negative content of tweets or to analyze an email to determine whether its author is happy, frustrated, or sad. More sophisticated forms of sentiment analyses use deep learning models to represent full sentences and capture the contexts around which particular language is used. The potential of big data sentiment analyses on business-relevant constructs is further evidenced by the chapter on Twitter analysis (Hernandez, Newman, & Jeon), which develops and applies a word count dictionary representing job satisfaction to a Twitter feed of over one million tweets per day. This is an exciting area, with emerging firms applying real-time methodologies like natural language processing that can recognize sarcasm and emotional nuances (e.g., Kanjoya) and connecting specific text strings and properties to outcomes (e.g., Textio). The leading players in this space are combining sophisticated algorithms with powerful computing and elegant visualization, and they are driving specific, measurable business outcomes.

Microexpression analyses. Another exciting tool with a range of potential applications involves microexpression analyses. Microexpressions can be understood as representations of brief and unconscious reactions to stimuli that cannot be masked but can be detected through careful observation (Ekman, 2009). The original facial action coding system was first published in 1978 and involved intensive ongoing training procedures and coding schemes. Technology has advanced to the point that these codings can be programmed and used to automatically assess genuine reactions and responses to stimuli (Shreve, Godavarthy, Goldgof, & Sarkar, 2011). This advancement has clear applications for law enforcement (i.e., detection of lies, hostility, and dangerous demeanor), but being able to objectively assess genuine human emotion can also be useful to phenomena relevant to I-O such as selection, decision-making, and leadership (see Barsade, Ramarajan, & Westen, 2009). The ability to link microexpression measurement to specific organizational stimuli may lead to insights into effective manager behavior and change management strategies, or to new approaches to measuring and managing employee engagement.

Neuro/psychophysiological tools. A wide set of tools has been developed to detect subtle changes in physiological reactions to stimuli such as brain activation, heart rate, and hormonal variation. This might include EEGs, blood pressure or heart rate monitors, automatic hormone testers, and FMRI imaging (see Becker, Cropanzano, & Sanfey, 2011). This emerging set of technologies has much to tell us about the inner workings of the brain as well as indicators of health and fitness that have relevance for occupational health psychology. These are not new but are growing in production, shrinking in size and cost, and increasing in their potential applications for understanding workplace dynamics. The rise in personal biometrics systems opens the door to scalable data capture and enables fascinating new analyses. As offerings in this segment evolve to include biometric measurements and connectivity to smartphones and other devices, new opportunities emerge for real-time linkage analyses.

Novel Questions Enabled by Big Data

Perhaps the most highly touted advantage of big data is that it will allow us to answer old questions in more comprehensive ways. We must not forget, however, that big data may also allow (or force) us to reconceptualize phenomena that we have been studying for decades. Consider the findings of Ilies, Scott, and Judge (2006) that citizenship varies substantially within person, and that this variance can be explained in part by job attitudes (again, within person). Regardless of whether one considers the experience sampling approaches used in their study to be big data or not, there is no denying that the results suggest an entirely different citizenship phenomenon (i.e., some days I'm a good citizen, some days I'm not) from the one that appears in previous work (i.e., I'm a good citizen, you aren't). As Cortina and Landis (2008) put it, ". . . these results call into question almost all of the previous research on this topic" (p. 303). Which phenomena might we understand in a completely different way after focusing big data approaches on them?

In this section, we briefly describe knowledge that might be gained through the lens of big data—using the methods described above—across topics in organizational science. We chose three examples from a broader list of potential topics (see Table 1) that are not covered elsewhere in the book but nonetheless exemplify the potential of big data to inspire scholarship.

Example 1: Work-family. The intersection of work and family, and the ways in which involvement in both spheres can be mutually enhancing or depleting, is inherently a phenomenon that takes place in dynamic times and places. Scholars have begun to employ event- and time-contingent experience sampling methods (e.g., daily diaries) to questions about the ongoing decisions that people make to prioritize work or family and the immediate affective and physical consequences (e.g., Shockley & Allen, 2013). The tools and sources of big data could take this approach—and with it, our understanding—substantially further. Sensors with geospatial and relational trackers or health monitoring devices, for example, could provide incredibly rich, detailed, and objective observations of the behavioral patterns and corresponding physical consequences for men and women across work and family divides. Knowing where and with whom men and women with different family and work obligations spend their time may allow us to isolate the individual behaviors and decisions that lead to work-family conflict and balance, which in turn could have transformative effects on describing, predicting, and preventing work/life conflict more generally.

Example 2: Training. The proliferation of Internet- and/or computer-based training systems opens up the possibility for genuinely adaptive training systems. Algorithms could be constructed that—like computer adaptive testing—adapt automatically to the needs of learners and tailor their experiences appropriately. To the extent that these adaptive responses are consistent with empirically supported theories of learning, and potentially even tailored to individual differences such as goal orientation, training outcomes could be maximized. This could be accomplished through adaptations in the delivery modality or on the actual content delivered. That is, big data analyses could use techniques such as random forests analysis (see Chapter 3 by Oswald and Putka, this volume) to identify and automatically generate effective combinations of content, form, practice, and assessment that generate optimal training outcomes. In essence, big data give us the opportunity to move from rigid, prescriptive approaches to more agile strategies that capitalize on equifinality. These approaches may expand the absolute quantity of talent available in the marketplace by creating a greater development in a larger population of workers.

Example 3: Performance management. There are also real areas of potential in performance management, a context wherein real-time, continuous monitoring and automated feedback can be particularly useful. Current theories of performance tend to reflect the reality that formal performance appraisal, where it exists, occurs quite seldom (e.g., twice per year), and is necessarily general in nature. What would we learn about performance, its prediction, and its management if it were measured at a much more molecular level on an ongoing basis? In one study using wearable sociometric sensors, co-located and distributed team members were provided visual cues that represent the relative contributions of each team member to the task discussion (Kim, Chang, Holland, & Pentland, 2008). These cues motivated behavioral changes: teams engaged in more collaborative interactions and communication balance after the visual cues than before. Thus, the immediate feedback enabled by big data (its collection, computation, and visualization) enabled higher performance teams. And of course, this raises new questions about the tradeoffs between resource allocation to the task and resource allocation to the processing of feedback, a question that seems irrelevant when feedback only occurs once or twice per year.

These examples complement the much more detailed descriptions of big data applications in selection and assessment (Illingworth, Lippstreu, & Deprez-Sims), teams (Kozlowski et al.), turnover (Hausknecht & Li), and diversity (Botsford Morgan, Dunleavy, & DeVries) that comprise the second half of this book.

Finally, it is worth noting that one of the significant promises of big data is the opportunity for many small improvements, rather than a few larger ones. When data collection is laborious, sample sizes are small, many relevant variables remain unmeasured, and computational power is a scarce resource, a conservative approach focusing on just a few sure bets was important. As we evolve to a world where data are ubiquitous, sample sizes are enormous, a nearly infinite variety of variables are measured, and computational power is abundant, it becomes efficient to pursue many small improvements, in essence building a mountain out of pebbles (see Schumpeter, 2014).

What Are the Dominant Challenges?

The world of big data, though full of opportunity, is not a panacea. Our enthusiasm must be tempered in light of practical and conceptual concerns that cannot be overlooked. We briefly describe some of the most common challenges that big data engenders below.

Practical Concerns

Analysis. The rise of big data poses significant challenges to traditional analytic methods that were developed for single shot studies with a limited set of variables and a relatively small number of subjects. With samples sizes increasing by orders of magnitude, our customary reliance on statistical significance testing becomes obsolete. Increased volume in terms of larger sets of variables creates a need for nonstandard data reduction techniques, as established methods become intractable with many, many columns of data. Standard regression practices that typically rely on a well-defined set of variables or attempt to identify the best model from a larger set of variables are outmoded, as they fail to leverage all of the information available. Despite these obstacles, numerous advances in computer science and other domains can be successfully applied to the organizational sciences to provide better answers. Oswald and Putka review a number of these modern techniques.

A related problem arises from the variety of data now available. Simple quantifiable metrics like test scores, responses to survey items, or supervisor ratings of behavior are being replaced by more varied and complex forms of data. These data may consist of textual data, location data, auditory information, or social network graphs. Two chapters in the current volume illustrate applications of these new forms of data to traditional organizational science research questions. Hernandez, Newman, and Jeon describe the challenges associated with the novel use of Twitter data to index job satisfaction while Kozlowski et al. describe using wearable sensors to investigate team dynamics.

The sheer size and complexity of big data demand these new techniques. However, many of these techniques can be applied beneficially to smaller, less complex data sets as well, allowing new insights. For example, machine learning and random forests can be applied where previously we may have used regression. These techniques will yield additional insights. As the systems that apply insights become more sophisticated, some of these more nuanced findings become practical to investigate and apply.

The analysis of big data also necessitates a new look at the quality of our data. Another less common V sometimes mentioned as a defining feature of big data is *veracity*—to which I-O psychologists would refer as validity. Clearly, validity, defined as the degree to which data allow for appropriate inferences regarding objects of measurement, is crucial regardless of the size of data. In other words, veracity is not a problem unique to big data, which is why we omitted it from our definition. Nevertheless, when data contain substantial volume, velocity, and especially variety, it may be particularly challenging to ensure veracity. The appropriate use of big data requires making use of new statistical techniques to identify and correct (or discard) questionable data points and to translate those that remain into something that allows appropriate inferences regarding variables and phenomena of interest.

Moreover, our prior notions of measurement quality may need to be expanded or modified for big data applications. Concepts such as test-retest reliability are irrelevant for phenomena that vary from moment to moment, but we as a field may have overrated its relevance for such phenomena because we study them at a more temporally molar level. In contrast, more emphasis may need to be placed on errors specific to the measurement instrument. While surveys are identical instruments across individuals, big data measurement technology may not be. Take wearable sensors as an example. It is highly probable that these devices are manufactured such that variability exists in their baseline sensitivity. Furthermore, the sensitivity of any given device may vary with changes in the environment (e.g., walking through a doorway, sitting down at a desk). If these devices were used to identify team centrality, the individual with the most sensitive device, either as a matter of technology or as a matter of environment, may be identified as being most central in the network. Their device would pick up more team member signals on more occasions, not because the person is actually more central, but because their device is more successful at measuring the variable of interest than are the devices of others in the network. However, we believe that, as I-O psychologists, we are ideally situated to contribute to the big data movement because of our expertise with measurement issues. While measurement quality is seldom mentioned in most big data applications, we can bring to bear numerous theories of measurement, such as generalizability theory, that incorporate error from different sources into overall evaluation of measurement quality.

Integration. Another challenge posed by the variety of data sources comprising big data is integration. Employee survey data, human resource information system data, performance management data, and employee social interaction data represent some of the data variety that organizations may wish to leverage in a data analytics application. Unfortunately, these different types of data are often housed in completely separate systems with incompatible interfaces. Moreover, the volume of this data further exacerbates the difficulties of bringing together these disparate sources into a single data system. As discussed earlier in this chapter, much of the most exciting work in big data is in integrating data from multiple data sources, such as biometric sensors, or from entirely separate databases, such as financial systems, click data from websites, and so forth. Significant challenges are encountered in terms of just accessing the data necessary for a big data project. The chapter by Ryan discusses the myriad issues related to integrating disparate big data sources along with some proposed solutions for overcoming these difficulties.

Interpretation. The volume, velocity, and variety of big data also make attempts to interpret trends over time, individuals, and geospatial indicators incredibly complex. Traditional approaches to data interpretation are insufficient in describing big data; new interpretative lenses are essential. Two of the current chapters highlight strategies for data interpretation from the perspective of its visualization (Sinar), sonification, and multi-modal displays (Stanton). Visualization is another element of analysis that has evolved dramatically with the rise of big data and that holds significant promise for driving impact. Good visualization is more than pretty pictures; good visualization will efficiently display multidimensional data and can either complement more traditional numerical data displays or stand alone to display data purely graphically. Additionally, many data visualization tools are navigable (they allow drill down within the visualization), and many display data as they change in real time. There are a dizzying variety of tools to generate data visualizations; one of the best known is Tableau. Data visualization presents a powerful new, efficient approach to rapidly assessing information. The description of these strategies will aid in the sense-making of business-related data patterns from the lens of psychological science. This is a critical and often overlooked area, and one where I-O psychologists can make a differential impact. A significant risk with big data is that findings will be highlighted without adequate or appropriate interpretation or contextualization, leading perhaps to counterproductive "solutions." Deep content expertise can help in structuring analytic problems in such a way that findings are likely to be meaningful and actionable and can help identify whether findings are causal or attributable to an unmeasured third variable.

Conceptual Concerns

The question of novelty. Although the popular conception is that these approaches have just evolved since about 2010, in truth, applying science to data from work is old news. We have been doing data analytics about workplace dynamics for over a century. Clearly, the act of using data to inform the science of work is not new. Yet another chapter in the book (Illingworth et al.) details the ways in which big data approaches to selection and assessment differ from traditional lenses. We have moved from gigabytes to terabytes, from real-time capture to real-time analysis, and from structured to unstructured data. Together, these chapters suggest that while data science is indeed old, big data science is quite new.

The death of theory. A fear that scholars often raise is whether big data are simply technologically sophisticated forms of dustbowl empiricism; the mantra "correlation does not imply causation" is nearly shouted from soapboxes. A less cynical reaction to big data is that an iterative combination of inductive and deductive approaches can be supported by the voluminous data now available (see chapters in this volume by Putka &

Oswald; Kozlowski et al.) Rather than the death of theory, big data can be leveraged to improve and enhance our current theories. Some would argue that many of our theories are somewhat limited and lack relevant variables. Moreover, we may not even know what those missing variables might be. The big data analytic approach permits us to test a wider variety of variables that could lead to the identification of new variables that should be part of our theories but currently aren't. Thus, while we improve our predictive capabilities, we simultaneously improve our theory by incorporating new variables, testing out alternative models, and replicating our results. Robust methods such as (massive) field experiments like the one Facebook recently conducted on its members to determine whether moods can be contagious through social media (Kramer, Guillory, & Hancock, 2014) are now available as a compelling approach to testing meaningful theories. We would argue that theory is not necessarily dead, but rather that it must be applied thoughtfully to designing methods and interpreting findings from big data. Further, many organizations currently have nearly inconceivable volumes of data, but finite time and energy to devote to culling through it all. As a practical matter, simply choosing a starting place requires some level of working theory. As big data analytics evolve as an organizational practice, we are seeing depth of content expertise (which is to say, application of theory) as a critical differentiator between those internal research teams that produce the most consistent actionable insights and that struggle more to create impact.

Ethics. An important boundary condition of the potential of big data is the set of ethical issues unique to it. Questions around the use of personal information, privacy of individuals, informed consent, and integrity of analysis are often raised in discussions of big data. Indeed, backlash from the general public to the Facebook study described in the previous section was immense (Goel, 2014). These are real and undeniable concerns that can constrain the opportunities available. In the final chapter of this book, Guzzo discusses initial ethical guidance for I-O psychologists dealing with big data that builds on principles developed by the Society for Industrial-Organizational Psychology. Ultimately, big data analytics must be held to the same standards of morality as traditional methods to be (1) viable and (2) supported in the long term. There are two significant challenges with this, however. First, the realities of current data management make this more difficult and demand more sophistication than we have required in the past. Cloud-based storage and reams of individual-level data, even if anonymized, create inherent privacy risks, and therefore introduce risk of harm that simply did not exist a decade ago. Second, the vast majority of people conducting big data research today have come to the work via engineering, mathematics, and computer science channels, rather than psychology. Data science as a field is still maturing, and consistent standards for ethics and privacy protections have not yet emerged. I-O psychology as a discipline can play a critical role in articulating a set of practical standards in in this area.

CONCLUSION

As quantitatively minded scientist-practitioners, organizational psychologists are ideally situated to help drive the questions and analytics behind big data. Yet few scholars in our field have discussed the specific ways in which the lens of our science should be brought to bear on or might benefit from big data. We hope that this book encourages I-O psychologists to raise new questions, use novel tools, design new courses and curricula, build new partnerships, and fully engage in the world of big data.

REFERENCES

Barsade, S. G., Ramarajan, L., & Westen, D. (2009). Implicit affect in organizations. *Research in Organizational Behavior, 29*, 135–162.

Becker, W. J., Cropanzano, R., & Sanfey, A. G. (2011). Organizational neuroscience: Taking organizational theory inside the neural black box. *Journal of Management, 37*(4), 933–961.

Cortina, J. M., & Landis, R. S. (2008). When small effect sizes tell a big story, and when large effect sizes don't. In C. E. Lance & R. J. Vandenberg (Eds.), *Statistical and Methodological Myths and Urban Legends: Received Doctrine, Verity, and Fable in the Organizational and Social Sciences* (pp. 287–308). Malwah, NJ: Erlbaum.

Ekman, P. (2009). *Telling lies: Clues to deceit in the marketplace, politics, and marriage (revised edition)*. New York, NY: WW Norton & Company.

Goel, V. (2014, June 29). Facebook tinkers with users' emotions in news feed experiment, stirring outcry. *New York Times.*

IBM (2015). Retrieved from http://www.ibm.com

Ilies, R., Scott, B. A., & Judge, T. A. (2006). The interactive effects of personal traits and experienced states on intraindividual patterns of citizenship behavior. *Academy of Management Journal, 49*(3), 561–575.

Kim, T., Chang, A., Holland, L., & Pentland, A. (2008). Meeting mediator: Enhancing group collaboration using sociometric feedback. In *Proceedings of the 2008 ACM Conference on Computer Supported Cooperative Work*, 457–466. Retrieved from http://dl.acm.org/citation.cfm?id=1460563&picked=prox&CFID=523388114&CFTOKEN=38029144

Kim, T., McFee, E., Olguín, D. O., Waber, B., & Pentland, A. (2012). Sociometric badges: Using sensor technology to capture new forms of collaboration. *Journal of Organizational Behavior, 33*(3), 412–427.

Kramer, A. D., Guillory, J. E., & Hancock, J. T. (2014). Experimental evidence of massive-scale emotional contagion through social networks. *Proceedings of the National Academy of Sciences, 111*(24), 8788–8790.

Laney, D. (2001). 3-D data management: Controlling data volume, velocity and variety. *META Group Research Note.* Retrieved from http://goo.gl/Bo3GS

Lohr, S. (2013, April 20). Big data, trying to build better workers. *The New York Times.*

Manyika, J., Chui, M., Brown, B., Bughin, J., Dobbs, R., Roxburg, C., & Byers, A. H. (2011). Big data: The next frontier for innovation and productivity. *McKinsey Global Institute.* Retrieved from http://www.mckinsey.com/insights/business_technology/big_data_the_next_frontier_for_innovation

Olguín-Olguín, D., & Pentland, A. (2010). Sensor-based organisational design and engineering. *International Journal of Organisational Design and Engineering, 1*(1), 69–97.

Schumpeter (July 19, 2014). Little things mean a lot: Businesses should aim for lots of small wins from 'big data' that add up to something big. *The Economist.*

Shockley, K. M., & Allen, T. D. (2013). Episodic work- family conflict, cardiovascular indicators, and social support: An experience sampling approach. *Journal of Occupational Health Psychology, 18*(3), 262–275.

Shreve, M., Godavarthy, S., Goldgof, D., & Sarkar, S. (2011). Macro- and micro-expression spotting in long videos using spatio-temporal strain. In *Automatic Face & Gesture Recognition and Workshops (FG 2011), 2011 IEEE International Conference* 51–56.

Tripathi, P., & Burleson, W. (2012). Predicting creativity in the wild: experience sample and sociometric modeling of teams. In *Proceedings of the ACM 2012 Conference on Computer Supported Cooperative Work*, 1203–1212. Retrieved from http://dl.acm.org/citation.cfm?id=2145204

Part I

Big Issues for Big Data Methods

2

A Big Data Platform for Workforce Analytics

Jacqueline Ryan and Hailey Herleman

Industrial and organizational psychologists are very familiar with statistical techniques to find patterns in data that either support or fail to support a hypothesis. The field is less familiar with mining large datasets for patterns; however, the growth and variety of big data are causing researchers to take an interest in what can be learned from these datasets. One of the main challenges to progress in the academic literature relates to gaining access to the organizational datasets required to mine for patterns and/or test hypotheses. In fact at the 2014 SIOP conference many presenters in sessions on big data stated, and restated, that their largest challenge to really understanding the implications of big data in the field was finding big data to analyze.

Organizations, however, have the opposite problem. They have so much data available from both internal and external sources such as transactional systems, events, emails, social media, and sensors (to name a few) that they are challenged to figure out how to find patterns and insights in the inherent complexity of data. Applied I-O psychologists struggle to supply data for research because figuring out where it is, how to get to it, and how to put it together in some meaningful form is quite a challenge. In order to advance the field and truly understand what can be learned from big data, more knowledge is needed about the basics of big data management and accessibility from both a methodology and software perspective.

The goal of this chapter is to share best practices in managing an information supply chain with I-O psychologists and other readers so that they can get the most value out of big data. These practices originated in big data analytics disciplines outside of the realm of human resources and while the HR space creates some unique challenges, many of the techniques and lessons learned from other disciplines apply. The following sections will first define big data in the workforce, and then discuss the challenges around managing and accessing these data. Following this, the core capabilities required of a big data platform are discussed along with considerations for cloud based and local hosting.

BIG DATA IN THE WORKFORCE

Big data in the realm of workforce management are not new; however, it is being created and stored in volumes we could not have imagined even ten years ago. What is new is the availability of technology to get value out of the breadth of data that exist about employees for use in workforce analytics. Let's look at one perspective of big data in HR.

Data about employees can be categorized into at least five different subgroups: demographic data, compensation data, performance data, behavioral data, and social interaction data. Business results data could arguably also be included to create a sixth category for those roles where revenue can be directly attributed to a job role. Sources for employee data can include survey responses, systems of record, social business platforms, and learning systems, to name a few. Taken all together, a complete view of the employee (Figure 2.1) can start to be seen.

Comprehensive View of the Employee

Demographic Data
- Demographic Data
- Employee contact and identification
- Education
- Credentials
- Diversity
- Credentials
- Employment history

Compensation Data
- Job description
- Compensation
- Benefits
- Rewards

Behavioral Data
- Skills, competencies, expertise
- Attitudes and personality traits
- Preferences
- Collaboration indicators
- Aptitudes

Performance Data
- Position
- Performance evaluations
- Experiences
- Leadership assignments
- Classes and training
- Learning styles
- Retention indicators
- Top performer indicators

Social Interaction Data
- Social network influence
- Thought leadership
- Self-identified and network tagged skills
- Engagement indicators
- Areas of interest

FIGURE 2.1
Employee data from different interactions within the workforce

Having a complete view of an employee is important because it allows for new patterns and insights to be discovered that are not possible when individual data points about an employee are taken in isolation.

Demographic data are unique to a candidate or employee and are transferable through an employee's career. Typically these data are captured during the job application process and the onboarding process and managed within a human resources information system (HRIS). Employee demographic data are essential for employers to understand their diversity and compliance profile. Examples include:

- Employee identification (name, social security number, title)
- Employee contact information (address, phone, email)
- Education (highest educational level, school, degree, graduation year)
- Diversity (gender, age, ethnicity, marital status, birth date & country, veteran status—US, disability)
- Skills/credentials (languages, credentials, certifications)
- Employment history (within company, external to company).

Demographic data, while generally available on all employees, can be some of the most sensitive information to use as there is an expectation, and in certain countries a legal requirement, to maintain and validate security compliance of personally identifiable information such as a social security numbers. When demographic data security is properly managed, these data can provide important workforce segmentation insights when combined with other data such as social interaction data.

Compensation data are specific to an employee's job and employment within a company. These data reflect information about salary and benefits for the work an employee performs. Data in this category are typically quantitative; however, there are also qualitative attributes such as work flexibility, developmental opportunities, etc. Examples include:

- Job description (job title, responsibilities, functions)
- Compensation (base pay, commissions, overtime pay, bonus, stock)
- Benefits (dental, insurance, medical, vacation, leaves of absence, retirement)
- Rewards (awards, stock options, vacation).

Compensation data, like demographic data, are usually maintained in an HRIS and are also very sensitive in nature. In order to conduct employee research at the individual level, information such as compensation has to be carefully governed. Although, as employee compensation often represents the most significant cost to an organization (Society for Human Resource Management, 2008), the data patterns surrounding compensation can be critical to understand in conjunction with other data such as employee performance and employee engagement.

Performance data are accumulated over the lifespan of an employee and describe their business impact and objectives achieved relative to their roles within the business. Examples include:

- Position (role, level)
- Performance (evaluation scores, advancement history)
- Experiences (job history, role history)
- Leadership assignments (temporary assignments, projects, role)
- Classes and training (seminars, higher education, classes)
- Retention indicators (employee engagement scores, employee attitudes, loyalty, workplace climate)
- Top performer indicators (upward mobility, relative ranking, business impact).

Performance data in I-O research often represent the criterion variable. A key goal in the field is to discover the factors that influence employee performance and retention. However, in big data research, performance data can be defined in many different ways and represent different types of information. While this information is somewhat sensitive, especially performance ratings, it doesn't carry nearly the expectation of privacy that demographic and compensation data carry. These data, however, carry their own set of challenges. They are often not consistently measured, recorded, or stored. Performance data could be stored in a performance management system, onboarding system, learning software system, HRIS, or in all of the above. Reconciling data across all these systems to get a clear view of an employee's performance profile can be challenging.

Behavioral data represent information about an employee's or candidate's cognitive ability, personality, preferences, and behavioral style. It is typically obtained from psychometric testing such as assessments, or rated by supervisors. Examples of data collected include:

- Knowledge, skills, and abilities
- Attitudes and personality traits
- Preferences (culture, engagement)
- Motivational attributes

- Values
- Collaboration indicators (e.g., networks).

Behavioral data are essential to understanding an employee's (or applicant's) potential. Where performance data record how a person actually performs in his/her job, these data points provide information on individual knowledge, skills, abilities, and other characteristics (KSAOs) and traits that may indicate what an employee or candidate is capable of doing even if not currently given the opportunity to display these traits in his/her current job. These data are more difficult to measure, although I-O psychologists and psychometricians have focused great energy to ensure there are sound methods available for measuring such characteristics. In addition these data, like performance data, are often scattered in various applicant tracking systems, assessment systems, performance management software, and/or social software. While these can be key predictors of future behavior and success, finding and compiling these data can be tricky for most organizations today.

Social interaction data describe employee presence and interaction on social business platforms both internal and external to an organization and are increasingly common in today's workplace. As work arrangements shift to more work from home arrangements and away from traditional office spaces, employees are finding new ways to connect with each other and with customers (Society for Human Resource Management, 2012). Digital social interactions create a mass of data which more and more companies are tapping in to for business and employee engagement insights (Schroeck, Shockley, Smart, Romero-Morales, & Tufano, 2012). These data are typically generated through normal business interactions and have impact beyond collaboration to encompass a representation of collective knowledge, expertise, and accelerate learning within networks. Examples include:

- Scope of influence (network profile)
- Thought leadership (influencer, follower)
- Skills (self-identified and network tagged)
- Engagement (passion, sentiment, contribution level, loyalties)
- Areas of interest

Social business collaboration platforms such as Connections, Yammer, and SharePoint amass large amounts of social interaction data each day as employees conduct normal business creating activities, loading files, commenting in communities and blogs, and forming subgroups for collaboration. Employee interactions with other employees and with customers also occur on external social platforms such as Twitter, Facebook, and LinkedIn. Advances in social analytics technology that facilitate employee sentiment analysis, identification of trending topics and issues, etc. have enabled HR leaders to engage in some of the same activities in which marketing has been involved for several years.

Social interaction data are typically text based and therefore pose unique data storage challenges given the volume of data generated in social interactions. Security and compliance requirements from the country of origin of these data also have to be understood and acted on.

CHARACTERISTICS OF WORKFORCE BIG DATA

As was explained earlier in the chapter, big data refers to all data in workforce analytics and can be characterized by four traits: volume, variety, velocity, and veracity (Zikopoulos et al., 2013).

FIGURE 2.2
Workforce big data characteristics

Let's look at each trait relative to the employee data types that were just described.

Volume refers to the size of data. There are more sources of data available to organizations today than ever before in our history. This is due in part to the world becoming much more instrumented and interconnected, thereby generating data well beyond petabyte ranges. Data on this scale pose real management and cost challenges that are relevant for the functioning of workforce analytics. Consider employee network analysis, employee sentiment analysis, and trending topic analysis as links to employee engagement, employee impact, and employee retention. These types of analysis operate using social media data, which are oftentimes extremely voluminous.

Consider as well data exhaust, which represents the breadcrumb trails that potential applicants leave behind when researching an employer on a company web site and applying for a job online. This type of data, collected over long periods of time and used for trend analysis and analysis of abandoned application processes, is another example of highly voluminous data.

Variety refers to the many types of data available: structured, semi-structured, and unstructured. Employee demographic data are an example of structured data, where data are typically stored and managed using relational data store methods. Employee social interaction data is an example of unstructured data typically represented as text data. XML and email are examples of semi-structured data. Historically, quantitative and qualitative techniques have been applied to different sorts of questions by different people with different training. The difference with big data is that now researchers must consider the overall picture created from analytic processes applied to a variety of data. As an example, combining insights from a predictive retention analysis applied over structured data with predictive analysis applied over social media data provides a stronger signal on retention risk factors but requires skill in large sample, longitudinal, quantitative and qualitative textual analysis, and the means by which one combines the previous two.

Velocity refers to the rate at which data are made available. As an example, data can be made available at specific points in time such as yearly employee engagement survey results, ad hoc points in time such as candidate applications, or in streaming real time such as employee social interactions over social platforms. While as a field I-O research has always appreciated the depth of insight that can be created by longitudinal studies, data velocity is a relatively new challenge for the field. The discussion is no longer only about insight gained from a single dataset. It is now also about the decision making rhythm on a particular topic, how often data are made available and updated so that they can be analyzed for insight to inform a given decision, and how to pull it together in those

timeframes. High velocity big data are critical to support ongoing, data driven decision making at the point in time in which an event is occurring.

Veracity refers to the quality or trustworthiness of data. Veracity has always been a concern for I-O psychologists.

A great amount of time and effort has been devoted to careful psychometric measurement and standardization of scales. We know that putting garbage data into any type of analysis will yield results that are, well, garbage. In the realm of big data, however, the data are often automatically generated by software applications, downloaded in different forms, and compiled across various systems. What is the quality of the data that are coming in? What are the rules and governance processes that determine which data are used for business insight and which are not of sufficient quality for such analysis? What do we do with data that are suspect? All of these are unique challenges for researchers created by the variability in the veracity of big data.

CHALLENGES MANAGING AND ACCESSING BIG DATA FOR WORKFORCE ANALYTICS

Finding and Understanding Data

With over 90% of the world's data created in the last two years (Kleyman, 2012), this makes the challenge of understanding the value of data that much more difficult. What amount of these data are noise as opposed to data that are relevant for finding useful patterns that provide insights? Over 20% of the amount of available data today exists in traditional systems, whereas 80% of the world's data is unstructured such as text, images, video, etc.

One of the most common questions that arise in workforce analytics is "What data do I have and is it useful?" As seen in the previous section, data are stored in many different locations and originate from execution of business processes, transactions, events, or as an outcome of the way in which we do work. However, not all data are considered relevant.

There are a number of issues that need to be considered when looking at the value of data:

1. Confidence in data—low quality data (so-called dirty data) lead to unreliable workforce analysis, which casts doubt on the insights produced.
2. Data freshness—although important for trend analysis, data that are captured in the past will yield less current or "point in time" insights than data captured in the present.

3. Data availability—access to data across lines of business within an organization varies to such a degree that, although data may exist, it may not always be possible to utilize based on company policies, authorization level, and even country, region, and industry security and privacy restrictions.
4. Completeness of data—data that are missing key elements such as those required for an employee profile typically compromise the ability to uncover relevant patterns.

A major cause of failure in finding unique insights from workforce analysis is inaccurate or incomplete data. Over 25% of time is spent resolving bad quality data. If not addressed at the source, it typically costs 10 to 100 times as much to fix upstream. Research has shown that data quality degrades at a predictable rate of about 2% per month. This can have a substantial impact on outcomes from predictive workforce modeling.

Governing Data Access and Security

The cost and ramifications of using unsecure data for workforce analysis, typical of non-production environments such as a sandbox or test environment, can be significant. Over 70% of organizations use live customer data in non-production environments (Feravich, 2011). Upwards of 50% of organizations have no way of knowing if data used in analysis was compromised (Ponemon, 2007), which can result in an average cost of $194 per record due to a data breach (Mckendrick, 2012).

As workforce analysis increases in complexity requiring additional data sources, the issues surrounding information governance needs to be considered more carefully. Key questions to assess include:

1. Are there regulatory compliance requirements for data access and data sharing within the country and/or region that need to be adhered to?
2. Are there operational and business rules in place that guide data sharing across business units?
3. Are there restrictions within the organization governing who can access certain data sources based on their role or need to know?
4. Are there ethical use considerations in place to govern using employee data deemed personal data that are created for one purpose but used for another? Are there practices in place to gain employee consent for use such that transparency with employees is maintained on the intent of use for these data?

Information governance practices provide a holistic approach to managing, improving, and using data in workforce analytics. The end goal is having confidence in the insights learned from analytical processes that are defendable and reliable. Data governance models typically include disciplines covering data quality management, information life-cycle management, and information security and privacy management.

There are two schools of thought on the use of big data in analytics projects as it relates to governance: some believe that data need to be maintained in their original raw form and that any modifications to data through governance processes reduce the resulting insights. The other school of thought is that, given the cost of compliance and increased security risks, big data must be governed. In reality, both points of view can be achieved today with advances in both big data technologies to manage data in their raw form and governance processes applied to big data platforms.

Provisioning Trusted Data for Workforce Analytics

Workforce analytics that use a single data source are rare, if not non-existent, today given the advances and application of behavioral science analytical processes. The diversity of data that are used today originating from on-premises systems, cloud applications, web services, etc. results in a number of challenges that I-O researchers have to face including:

- Location of data
- Protocols for accessing data
- Format of data
- Authorization and security requirements
- Availability and timeliness of data
- Integration methodology to use all required data sources.

Another factor that comes into play even after all of these requirements are addressed is provisioning data for multiple analysts who all have different studies underway. This can become a job in itself and, in fact, is multiple jobs requiring skills found in an information architect, database administrator (DBA), ETL (extract, transform, and load) developer, and data analyst to manage the data supply chain requirements.

Costs Associated with Managing Big Data

Big data are growing by 40% per year (Manyika et al., 2011). The characteristics of big data that were described earlier in terms of volume, variety, velocity, and veracity put new challenges on traditional systems particularly as they relate to cost.

Operational and storage costs are the biggest cost factors typically measured as operational expenses (OPEX) and capital expenses (CAPEX). Along with workload performance requirements, these have both driven development of new approaches to manage data to reduce these cost factors. This is relevant to workforce analytics processes as it impacts the overall costs that need to be considered associated with deriving insights and results.

The challenges described here associated within finding, understanding, managing, governing, and provisioning big data become more acute as multiple workforce analytics projects are undertaken. If every researcher and workforce data scientist within an organization has to track down their own data and deal with each of these challenges individually at the scale of big data, the costs, time, and effort associated with workforce analytics becomes unmanageable. These are the challenges that a big data platform addresses.

BIG DATA PLATFORM CORE CAPABILITIES

Let's take an example of a typical globally integrated business. In this example, survey data reside external to the organization, managed by a third party survey vendor. Employee demographic data reside in an HRIS system managed by HR operations. Historical employee performance data reside in a performance management system managed by HR talent management. Employee salary and compensation data reside in yet additional systems managed by the compensation group within HR. Social interaction data are managed within the enterprise's social business platform managed by IT. Business results data are located in financial systems managed within finance. Figure 2.3 illustrates the numerous systems where all these data would reside across the organization.

In this example, each I-O researcher would need to independently manage interactions with each organization for data set extracts and manage their own local copies of data. This proliferation of data does nothing to help with data security or data quality as different versions of the truth for data begin to surface causing analytic outcomes to be challenging if not impossible to defend or trace. The I-O researcher is also left to manage the integration of all required data sets and any subsequent updates that would be needed (daily, weekly, monthly, quarterly, etc.) as data change due to the normal course of business.

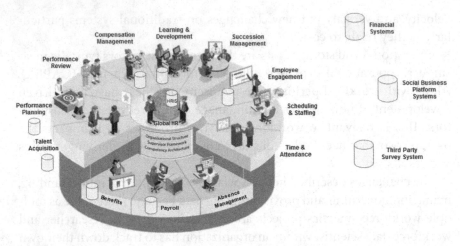

FIGURE 2.3
Employee data represented in silo systems across the organization

In those cases where an I-O researcher has sourced data from centralized IT resources either by an HRIT group or the enterprise's IT group, a traditional approach would typically entail an enterprise data management architecture (Zikopoulos, deRoos, Bienko, Buglio, & Andrews, 2015) such as shown in figure 2.4.

In this scenario, data from operational systems are loaded into a staging area, typically an FTP server, and then prepared and cleansed for loading in to an enterprise data warehouse (EDW). A subset of the data from the

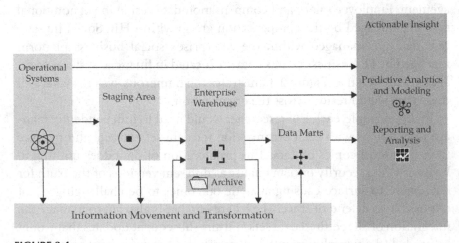

FIGURE 2.4
A traditional approach to enterprise data management

EDW data may be loaded into a data mart, which manages data represented through a dimensional model oriented to a specific line of business. The enterprise data warehouse becomes the central resource for data. Over time though, as new data sources that are voluminous in nature, such as the examples described earlier, are stored in the warehouse, costs can sky rocket when EDW software charges by amount of data stored. The other issues that have surfaced over time revolve around the fact that the very benefit an EDW provides by requiring a common data model for easier access to data is that finer grain details of data are lost, such as the example of click through data and social data that are actually required in certain workforce analytics processing. Data stored in an EDW is typically time-bound, meaning a certain amount of data within a given date range is stored and then eventually moved out of the warehouse to a data repository for archiving. This makes it difficult to do certain long term historical analysis such as historical hire trend analysis or operational workforce planning, as a couple of examples.

To get around this, I-O researchers and workforce data scientists have taken the route of sourcing workforce data from the EDW and operational systems, storing this data on their local systems. This approach compounds the issues of multiple versions of the truth for data and data security and governance.

Big data platform services address these challenges with the end goal of creating a reliable and trusted information supply chain that manages, integrates, and governs data for workforce analysis enabling:

- Big data to be responsibly combined for new uses
- Discovering and exploring data with visualizations that are intuitive
- Supporting multiple analytical techniques (e.g., cognitive, predictive, statistics, operational BI)
- Optimizing multiple analytical processes
- Minimizing IT costs
- Managing, governing, and securing information.

To enable these capabilities, a big data platform performs several core functions:

1. Governs data quality and manages the information lifecycle, which includes the following services:

    a. Cleanse, manage, and monitor the state of data quality over time and integrate with other data sources

   b. Manage and maintain a comprehensive view of the employee that can be virtually referenced across multiple workforce analytics projects
   c. Secure monitoring of data access and data usage based on roles and access authority
   d. Manage data throughout its lifecycle—from creation to retirement of analytics processes—to ensure regulatory and business process compliance.

2. Manage big data in a cost effective manner that provide the following services:

   a. Reliably manage massive amounts of data—both structured and unstructured
   b. Reduce operational costs by augmenting data warehouses that may currently be in place
   c. Support data exploration to determine which data is the most valuable and extract that data in a cost-effective manner for further workforce analysis
   d. Provision governed data to workforce analytics projects that is transparent to users.

These services are delivered through zones (Chessell & Smith, 2013) that set up an information supply chain, as illustrated with the workforce analytics example in figure 2.5.

Zones represent separate areas for storing, processing, and accessing data based on the data characteristics and type of workforce analytics processing being deployed. Let's look at each zone within the big data platform.

Landing Zone

The landing zone extends existing data warehouses to store high volume data in its raw format, both structured (e.g., HRIS data) and unstructured (e.g., social business platform data) in a cost effective manner using Hadoop technology. Hadoop was originally pioneered by Google and Yahoo! and is an open source software framework for storing and processing extremely large data sets at low cost with dramatic performance gains. In short, Hadoop makes big data easier to manage. By distributing the processing of large data sets across clusters of commodity servers, Hadoop is designed to scale to thousands of systems. Hadoop also provides high fault

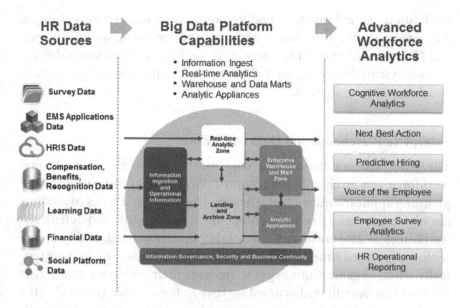

FIGURE 2.5

An information supply chain delivers trusted and governed data for workforce analytics.

tolerance, which means that the system can continue to function correctly even during failures of individual components. One of the many advantages of Hadoop is cost savings in data storage since commodity systems, including storage devices, are used. Another advantage is faster processing time over large data sets. The time to read 1TB from a single disk is about six hours at 50MB/second. As data sets get big, traditional approaches no longer work, which is why distributed systems are used.

Data stored in their raw format in Hadoop can be analyzed using data discovery and analysis tools to reveal initial patterns and insights. Detailed information is also managed and provisioned here for statistical, predictive, and prescriptive analysis. Data are typically maintained for a longer period of time after analysis to enable investigation into outliers and unexpected results. All of this is possible due to the economics and processing capabilities of Hadoop.

Information Ingestion Zone

The information ingestion zone integrates information across all workforce and business data sources for validation, correlation, cleansing, and transformation. Data are received in the landing zone, which has minimal verification and reformatting modifications. Using our previous example, data integration tools are used to connect to the systems across HR, finance, and IT to access data according to security and access permissions defined by each system. Data continue to be managed by the original group from which the data are sourced.

Enterprise Warehouse and Data Mart Zone

The enterprise warehouse and data mart zone is where traditional workforce reporting and applications, such as operational workforce planning applications, are typically run. Data for these types of analysis are highly governed to ensure compliance, auditability, and defensibility. Historical data are usually consolidated, summarized, and bounded within a specified timeframe within a data warehouse. This zone is typically where organizations begin to manage their employee data across the business. As will be discussed further in the chapter, this is also the zone where more and more services are becoming commercially available and provisioned through cloud software as a service (SaaS) form factors to address the skills and costs associated with managing data warehouses.

Real Time Analytics Zone

Real time analytics enable in-line analytic processing over raw data that are arriving too quickly to store then analyze, such as employee social data. Unlike the other zones, data are not managed and maintained in this zone. Rather, this is a processing zone where data are consumed and analyzed as they are being created. An example is analyzing click stream data as an applicant is transitioning through a business's web site and applying for a job—understanding and analyzing points where the application process is abandoned and how and why the process completes.

Complex event processing engines have traditionally been used for performing real time analytics processing; however, their costs, complexity, and limitations make it more difficult to adopt. New technologies have emerged around stream processing that operate over all types of data (structured, semi-structured, and unstructured data) providing nearly instantaneous and reliable delivery of extremely large volumes of data. Data such as click stream data can be processed as it's generated and trends and patterns can be identified at the point in time the event is occurring instead of analyzing after all data has been copied or landed.

Analytic Appliances Zone

Workforce analytics workloads that contain complex models, more advanced analytics, and/or require processing multiple models in parallel require the functionality of a relational database management system (RDBMS), but with consideration around minimizing the impact to existing workforce reporting and performance management applications. The analytic appliances zone supports these types of workloads by using dedicated appliances that manage high volume and highly complex data co-located with the analytics processes. Analytics appliances have unique approaches to optimize analytical workloads such as no indexing. Data are stored in a manner that is more suitable for parallel processing. Analytical functions are embedded into the core of the processing engines to improve processing performance. Quite often hardware accelerators are used to further improve analytics workload processing performance.

Together, these zones enable a whole paradigm shift in the approach to workforce analytics. We'll look at five examples that compare traditional workforce analytics approaches to new approaches that are possible with big data platform services.

Use More of the Available Employee and Business Data

Traditional approaches typically use a subset of data that is statistically relevant as the sample set to model and test against. Employee retention models, as an example, historically use a subset of employee data to identify key attributes that are drivers for employees voluntarily leaving a company. With a big data approach, all employee information can be analyzed without imposed sample size restrictions. Additional

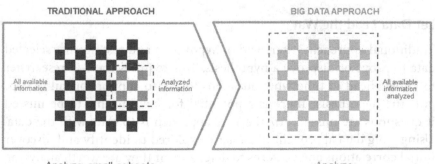

TRADITIONAL APPROACH   BIG DATA APPROACH

All available information   Analyzed information   All available information analyzed

Analyze small subsets of information   Analyze *all* information data about employees can also be pulled in to model without the costs of data management outweighing the benefits of increased model precision.

Make It Easier to Use Data

As mentioned earlier, one of the biggest challenges in workforce analytics is the time and effort required to collect and prepare data for use—and for good reason. With traditional approaches, data had to be cleansed before performing any type of analysis. Using a big data approach, all available data are used as-is and data are cleansed as needed and in some cases analyzed as raw information. This allows initial analysis to be performed to discover patterns, test initial hypotheses, and identify additional data that ought to be brought in before major efforts are undertaken to cleanse and normalize data for deeper analysis.

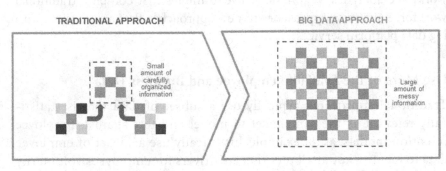

TRADITIONAL APPROACH — Small amount of carefully organized information

BIG DATA APPROACH — Large amount of messy information

Carefully cleanse information *before* any analysis

Analyze information as is, cleanse as needed

Let Data Lead the Way

Traditional approaches start with a hypothesis and test against selected data to prove or disprove a hypothesis. This requires the I-O researcher to know ahead of time what questions to ask to support or fail to support the hypothesis. There is a potential for key insights to be missed if questions are missed. An alternate approach is to start with the data. Using a big data approach, all data are explored to identify and discover initial correlations and patterns to determine if they are worth analyzing further.

TRADITIONAL APPROACH   BIG DATA APPROACH

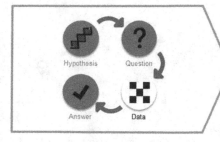 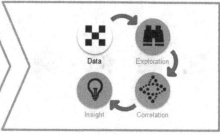

Start with hypothesis and   Explore *all* data and
test against selected data   identify correlations

Use Data as They Are Captured

Traditional approaches analyze data only after they have been processed and stored, typically in a data warehouse and/or data mart. This effectively causes a delay in getting at insights that may need to be acted on sooner rather than later. Using a big data approach, data are analyzed *as they are created* to get insights in real time as an event is occurring. This can be incredibly valuable to respond to events as they are occurring, such as identifying employee fraud through transactional system data analysis, guided instructional opportunities at the point of interaction, or trending issues discovered through employee interaction on social business platforms.

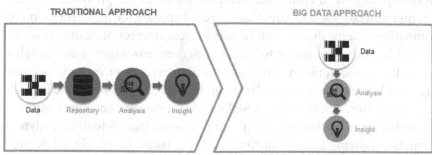

TRADITIONAL APPROACH   BIG DATA APPROACH

Analyze data *after* it's been   Analyze data *in motion* as it's
processed and landed in a warehouse   generated, in real time
or mart

Combine Analysis from Data in Motion and Data at Rest for Stronger Signals

Data at rest and in motion can be analyzed in parallel using analytics processes that operate best within each zone. Structured data such as employee

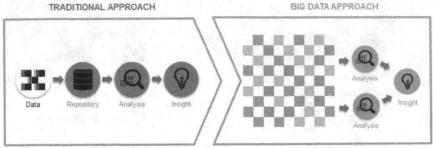

TRADITIONAL APPROACH

BIG DATA APPROACH

Analyze data *after* it's been processed and landed in a warehouse or mart

Combine analysis from data in motion & data at rest for stronger signals

demographic and performance data are examples of data that are sourced for predictive retention models. Social data is sourced for social network and interaction analysis. The combined outcomes of these two analytics processes provide stronger signals and validation of an employee attrition score.

CLOUD BIG DATA PLATFORM SERVICES

Cloud technology, combined with the advent of cognitive computing, creates a whole new opportunity to simplify workforce analytics. Cloud computing is the delivery of on-demand computing resources covering anything from applications to entire data centers. Resources are provided over the internet on a pay-for-use basis. Cognitive systems are the next generation of computing systems that combine cloud services, data services, analytics, and natural language processing to quickly discover new patterns and insights from all data. Cognitive systems learn from interactions over time, becoming more knowledgeable as the language and terminology of a domain, such as human resources, is acquired. Skills, lack of time, and costs are examples of the typical obstacles preventing business users from adopting analytics. Cognitive systems address all three of these issues by enabling HR professionals and I-O researchers to pose questions in natural language with statistical and predictive analysis automatically managed through cloud services. Insights are returned through visualizations that are based on the question, which helps simplify storytelling. IBM Watson is an example of commercially available cognitive system offered as a cloud service.

Entire components of the big data platform described in the previous section can be provided as a service. The advantage is that costs and complexity associated with buying and managing the underlying hardware, software, provisioning, and hosting are all provided as a service. This allows the I-O researcher to more focus on workforce analysis rather than managing the underlying information supply chain.

There are multiple cloud computing deployment models, each intended to address different aspects of data ownership, security, and resource management. These styles can be adopted for different workforce analytical projects depending on the nature of use and security and access requirements.

Public Cloud

Public cloud services are owned and managed by companies that provide access to computing resources. There's no need to purchase hardware, software, or supporting infrastructure, as the cloud provider manages all of these. Resources are shared through a multi-tenant environment.

Private Cloud

Private cloud services are owned and managed by companies that manage the virtualization and provisioning of customizable resources. More control over the environment is possible with private cloud, as use of resources is in a dedicated environment that is not multi-tenant in nature.

Hybrid Cloud

Hybrid cloud services use a private cloud foundation and provisions services using the public cloud approach. Sensitive data are managed in a traditional data center environment or private cloud while applications are provisioned in a multi-tenant approach.

Workforce analytic processes can also be provisioned as a service within a cloud environment. These services are typically known as software as a service (SaaS) solutions. SaaS analytic solutions take data as input and return the results of statistical analysis or other analytical methods such as predictive and prescriptive through the service or directly to a cloud application.

SUMMARY

Big data provide a tremendous opportunity to identify a comprehensive view of employees and expand the impact and outcomes from workforce analytics. Big data in the workforce can include employee demographic data, performance data, compensation data, behavioral data, and social interaction data. Workforce big data have characteristics relating to the variety, velocity, volume, and veracity of data that pose new challenges for I-O researchers. Technologies and best practices from other fields of study can be directly applied to human resources to help address these challenges to gain access to organizational datasets, govern data access and security, manage and provision trusted data, and minimize costs associates with workforce big data.

In addition to addressing the challenges of managing workforce big data, a big data platform creates a whole new paradigm shift in the approach to workforce analytics. All employee information can be used in analysis instead of only a subset of data. The effort required to use data is reduced. Insights discovered from examining data first can guide the amount of additional workforce analysis that may or may not be required. Real time analysis is made possible, enabling insights to be surfaced at the time of an event such as detecting employment branding issues through social media sources. In addition, stronger signals can be identified by running multiple workforce analytical workloads in parallel.

Technologies such as Not only SQL (NoSQL) databases, Hadoop, and RDBMS support information management zones. Zones provide fit-for-purpose services that are used depending on the specific data and workforce analytics processing that are being performed by an I-O researcher or workforce data scientist. The landing zone, information ingestion zone, enterprise data warehouse and data mart zone, real time analytics zone, and analytic appliance zone all together enable an effective and trusted information supply chain.

The availability of cognitive systems delivered through a cloud form factor is driving a powerful transformational effect on the availability of advanced analytics for I-O researchers and workforce data scientists, as well as HR professionals. Data and analytical services historically delivered as on-premises services requiring specialized skills and knowledge to manage and maintain are now being delivered as a subscription service in the cloud. The information supply chain instantiated through a cloud big data platform is the way of the future.

REFERENCES

Chessell, M., & Smith H. (2013). *Patterns of information management.* Retrieved from http://www.redbooks.ibm.com/Redbooks.nsf/ibmpressisbn/9780133155501

Feravich, S. (2011, December 21). Ensuring protection for sensitive test data. Retrieved from http://www.dbta.com/Articles/Editorial/Trends-and-Applications/Ensuring-Protection-for-Sensitive-Test-Data—79145.aspx

Kleyman, B. (2012, September 12). The big data battleground: Analyzing the big picture. Retrieved from http://www.datacenterknowledge.com/archives/2012/09/12/a-look-into-the-big-data-battleground-analyzing-the-market/

Manyika, J., Chui, M., Brown, B., Bughin, J., Dobbs, R., Roxburgh, C., & Byers, A.H. (2011). *Big data: The next frontier for innovation, competition, and productivity.* Retrieved from http://www.mckinsey.com/insights/business_technology/big_data_the_next_frontier_for_innovation

Mckendrick, J. (2012, March 20). Cost of a data breach: $194 per record. Retrieved from http://www.smartplanet.com/blog/business-brains/cost-of-a-data-breach-194-per-record/

Ponemon, L. (2007, November 27). The insecurity of test data: The unseen crisis. Retrieved from http://download.101com.com/pub/esj/files/TestDataReport.pdf

Schroeck, M., Shockley, R., Smart, J., Romero-Morales, D., & Tufano, P. (2012). Analytics: The real-world use of big data. Retrieved from http://www.ibm.com/systems/hu/resources/the_real_word_use_of_big_data.pdf

Society for Human Resource Management. (2008, November 1). Salaries as a percentage of operating expense. Retrieved from http://www.shrm.org/research/articles/articles/pages/metricofthemonthsalariesaspercentageofoperatingexpense.aspx

Society for Human Resource Management. (2012, December 5). Managing and leveraging workplace use of social media. Retrieved from *http://www.shrm.org/templatestools/toolkits/pages/managingsocialmedia.aspx*

Zikopoulos, P., deRoos, D., Bienko, C., Buglio, R., & Andrews, M. (2015). *Big data beyond the hype*. Retrieved from http://www.ibmbluhub.com/big-data-ebook/

Zikopoulos, P., Deutsch, T., Deroos, D., Corrigan, D., Parasuraman, K., & Giles, J. (2013). *Harness the power of big data, the IBM big data platform*. Retrieved from https://www14.software.ibm.com/webapp/iwm/web/signup.do?source=sw-info mgt&S_PKG=ov8257&S_CMP=is_bdebook3

3

Statistical Methods for Big Data

A Scenic Tour

Frederick L. Oswald and Dan J. Putka

Organizational psychologists are armed with the dual talents of scientific knowledge and a practical bent: they identify important phenomena found within organizations and employees; they connect those phenomena conceptually to existing theories of work; they develop data-driven research or applications; and they analyze and interpret data in ways that further advance science and practice. Indeed, one may say that organizational psychologists have been data-driven "workforce scientists" for over a century (Koppes & Vinchur, 2012). Despite this rich history, recent popular press sentiment is that workforce science is an exciting new area tied to the advent and influx of big data (see Bersin, 2013; Lohr, 2013). It is certainly true that many aspects of big data in organizations are new, and to that end, this chapter is dedicated to reviewing new analysis methods. Thus, it is important for organizational psychology to apply its hard-won experience and expertise to new big data considerations, and it is also important for the big data movement itself to appreciate and learn from the data- and theory-driven approaches that organizational psychologists have applied to work phenomena for over a century (one day, the popular press might pick up on this latter point as well).

MOVING BEYOND SMALL DATA

Organizational psychology—like most of psychology—has been beset with a history of small data, or samples with data that may not generalize to other settings and samples. This has led to the strident complaint that research in psychology has been statistically underpowered for decades (see Cohen, 1992; Maxwell, 2004; Sedlmeier & Gigerenzer, 1989), meaning that practically significant effects in the world often get overlooked (creating type II errors) and potentially not published. Or sometimes when such underpowered effects get published, they are overstated because the magnitude of the observed effect has to be biased upward enough to become statistically significant (creating publication bias).

Historically, the solution to this problem in organizational research has been by taking one of three paths. The first path has been to make use of *large-sample studies* such as data available in military settings (e.g., "Project A," a massive army selection and classification project; see Campbell, 1990), or data obtained from larger organizations, industries, or agencies (e.g., Fortune 100 companies, the Department of Labor, public utility companies). The second path has been through *meta-analysis*, where weighting study effect sizes by their precision (inverse sampling error variance) provided average effect sizes that were more stable and informative than any small-sample study taken alone, and this has also enabled insights into study-level moderators of effect size. Here, we see something of a trade-off between these two paths: whereas large-sample studies tend to focus on refined hypotheses and local settings, meta-analyses tend to focus on more simple effects (e.g., *d*-values, zero-order correlations) derived across multiple studies, where samples and settings can serve as moderators provided there are enough studies available. A third path has been *synthetic validity* (Scherbaum, 2005), which can be viewed as a hybrid approach in that correlations relevant to KSAs and criteria are ideally obtained from large and relevant samples, and they are combined in a meta-analytic (synthetic) manner to obtain validity information on a wide variety of jobs or occupations – even those that typically have small samples. The synthetic approach has demonstrated accurate validities within families of jobs (Johnson & Carter, 2010), and the approach also allows for validity estimation even for jobs of the future that do not exist yet but where the KSAs and criteria are known.

Whichever route that is taken, large sample sizes are the desirable end result so that statistical significance issues can give way to more substantive discussion about practical significance. The movement from statistical to practical significance can be witnessed in the current shifts in psychological research, which can be said to be seismic. The cultures of statistical estimation, study replication, open access, and research transparency have, singly or in combination, given rise to new journals (e.g., *Archives of Scientific Psychology*, registered replication reports in *Perspectives on Psychological Science*), new editorial policies (e.g., Cumming, 2014; Eich, 2014;

Landis, Cortina, & Rogelberg, 2014), and new projects (e.g., the "Many Labs" project; Klein et al., 2014). Statistical significance is de-emphasized under these new paradigms and instead is subsumed by accurate estimation of effect sizes that can then be judged in context for their practical significance (Aguinis et al., 2010). Large sample sizes are required to detect statistically significant effects; differences between effects require even larger sample sizes (e.g., Hsu, 1993; Trattner & O'Leary, 1980); and the sample-size requirements are larger still when hypotheses and their statistical models are even more complex (e.g., moderator effects, structural equation models). One might think that data sets that one might call big data would alleviate this concern, yet big data models are able to fit complex relationships where they exist, and therefore they too are very hungry for data.

Up to this point, we have provided the reader with some of the historical context and conceptual issues that are pertinent to the future for big data in organizational research. The remainder of this chapter provides a scenic tour of big data methods. As with most scenic tours, we highlight some of the major landmarks and skip some others in order to obtain a useful and non-technical appreciation of the overall landscape. After taking this tour, it is our hope that the reader will book a more serious and more technical vacation with big data methods to explore some of them in greater detail. We provide an array of up-to-date resources that might serve this latter purpose (see the *Resources* section).

BIG DATA METHODS

We have organized our discussion around two sets of big data methods. The first set focuses on what are known as *supervised learning* methods in the machine learning literature. These methods are primarily concerned with prediction of some criterion. That is, one has a criterion and a set of predictors, and an algorithm attempts to "learn" a rule or set of rules for predicting that criterion based on observed data. These algorithms are using data to learn relationships between predictors and criteria in the same spirit (but in a very different way) that regression or ANOVA learns underlying relationships. The second set focuses on what are known as *unsupervised learning* methods. These methods do not involve prediction of a criterion per se, but rather focus on reducing the dimensionality of data, essentially providing modern variants on factor analysis and cluster analysis concepts. An organizational example might further illustrate this difference: whereas a supervised learning big data method might show how employees characteristics relate to the risk of turnover (i.e., a prediction problem), an unsupervised method might provide insights into the distinctions among different types or classes of turnover (i.e., a grouping or clustering problem), which may in turn be used to help hone and refine a supervised learning method (i.e., focusing it on predicting different types of turnover, rather than turnover in general).

Supervised Learning Methods

Support vector machines. The support vector machine (SVM) is a statistical approach that allows for nonlinear prediction of the sort that our traditional analyses do not permit. Imagine that SVM is used to classify cases into one of two values on a criterion variable (e.g., salespersons staying versus voluntarily leaving the company) based on a set of predictors (e.g., salespersons' job satisfaction, performance ratings, current salary). SVM will consider each person in the sample as having a vector of p predictors, and then it will try to separate the vectors that belong to each value of the criterion as mathematically cleanly as possible using what is called a *hyperplane*. The amount of separation is called a *margin*, where a wider margin is better so long as errors in classification are optimized (e.g., classification errors are minimized in future samples). Support vectors are those vectors (cases) that lie along the margin and serve to define it. The approach to SVM using *soft margins* allows the final solution to have some errors in classification. This in fact might have to be done in many cases because separation cannot be done entirely cleanly. The SVM approach can be extended to more than two categories; it can be modified to reduce the negative influence of outliers, and it can be applied to data that undergo nonlinear transformation (e.g., a polynomial kernel) with the hope of improving separation and therefore classification efficiency.

Artificial neural networks. Artificial neural networks (ANN) are similar in spirit to multiple regression, where relationships between multiple predictors and a single criterion are determined. However, rather than using a linear model, the model for ANN is more complex in that relationships between predictors and criteria are based on a model, the components of which resemble neurons in the brain. More specifically, the "neurons" are hidden nodes between the predictors and the criterion, where the user has a lot of latitude in determining their number, how they are connected, and how many layers of connection there are. In this sense, ANN is a black box method because, although the predictors and criterion are observed, the nodes (neurons) are hidden and there is no single correct way to specify their number or configuration.

But let's assume the user specifies an ANN for the purposes of prediction, and then each neuron receives activation, which is some function of the incoming activity (usually a weighted sum) from connected neurons. Once the activation received exceeds a certain threshold, the neuron then "fires," or transmits, its own activation to other connected neurons in the neural network that themselves function similarly. Typically, neurons only transmit forward across neuronal layers, although some models allow for backward transmission as well. ANNs use iterative methods to achieve the appropriate set of weights in the neural network; in doing so, they also often incorporate backpropagation, part of the iteration procedure in ANN that examines discrepancies between predicted and actual criterion values, looks back into the network and adjusts the neural weights to reduce those discrepancies before starting the next iteration of prediction by the model.

Even an ANN containing a small handful of connected neurons will allow for complex predictions. More neurons might be appropriate for a more complex phenomenon, but as with any complex model, when there are too many neurons, there is the concern that the model will be over-trained and not predict as well in new data sets. The typical levels of reliability and sample sizes in psychological data do not support ANN models that are too complex. In addition, even with stable prediction, the weights for ANNs are typically not interpretable due to the arbitrariness of how the neural network is set up. Nonetheless, we hold hope that the continued use of ANN in organizational research would give rise to at least some cases of theoretically motivated modeling that leads to substantively interpretable weights.

ANNs have appeared in different organizational research applications: In a large sample of managers, about two-thirds of whom were incarcerated for white-collar crime, neural network models have been found to predict criminality at levels similar to discriminant analysis models, even after the models were cross-validated in independent data sets (Collins & Clark, 2006). Likewise, neural network models have demonstrated the same predictive power as linear regression models for personality predicting work performance in large samples of professionals, police recruits and bus drivers (Minbashian, Bright, & Bird, 2010). So long as the linear regression models contained relevant interaction and quadratic terms, these simple models performed equally as well as artificial neural networks—sometimes better and usually no worse.

Note that the comparable performance for linear models was reached because the researcher actually knew what the relevant interaction and quadratic terms were *a priori*. When little theory exists in a given domain, and when limited empirical investigation has been conducted, then having access to big data and flexible modeling techniques such as ANN can help researchers inductively discover reliable interactions and non-linearities more readily because, using ANN, these do not have to be specified *a priori*. However, note that ANN models are somewhat arbitrary such that an ANN based on different quantity and connection of neurons may be revealing of different nonlinearities for the same data set (Somers & Casal, 2009). Thus, like all big data methods discussed here, ANNs that appear to hold out promise for practical prediction (Scarborough & Somers, 2006) should be subjected to high levels of scrutiny, such as by testing alternative models, cross-validation on independent samples of data, and attempting substantive interpretation to build organizational theory.

Decision trees and random forests. Imagine that you successfully walk from the beginning to the end of a maze without hitting a dead end. To do this, you started at the entrance, you had to make decisions to turn left or right whenever you were at a juncture, and eventually you reached the exit. Decision trees treat each case in a data set similarly: At each juncture there is a predictor, and which way the case "turns" depends on whether its predictor score is above or below a cut-point. If the junctures (predictors) and turns (cut-points) are selected appropriately, then cases will reach the correct classification (exit). Decision trees can flexibly detect interactions between predictors where they exist, but those interactions are intended to generalize to other samples, so there are statistical rules for when to stop branching or how to prune the tees to their predictive essence.

Random forests is an example of the *model ensemble* technique because it makes use of collections of decision tree models to make classification decisions (Breiman, 2001). Each tree in the forest has a vote on prediction (or classification) for each case in the data set, and there are methods for growing each tree to ensure that the random forest contains diverse trees and therefore makes robust classification decisions that avoid overfitting (e.g., selection from the training set without replacement; random selection of predictors and cut-points). Another benefit of random forests is to determine predictor variable importance, where more important predictors and their interactions result in more successful classification (Friedman & Popescu, 2008). Sometimes reducing overall prediction is not the only goal; sometimes the goal also is to reduce errors within one specific category (e.g., serious on-the-job errors versus minor ones), and decision trees and random forests can be adjusted to strike the appropriate balance between global and local optimization.

Naïve Bayes. Naïve Bayes can be used in a variety of settings, but it is most often used when classifying text based on words extracted from them; for instance, Naïve Bayes has been used as a tool for effectively detecting and filtering out spam e-mail. This is accomplished by training the model to learn which words work singly or in combination to distinguish spam versus normal e-mail (e.g., spam e-mail might be more likely to contain the word "free" or the phrase "click here," and normal e-mail might be more likely to contain words such as your first name and the word "meeting").

Overall, spam is less frequent than normal e-mail, no matter what the content of the e-mail may be, and thus Naïve Bayes takes these base rate differences into account when predicting outcomes. Using Bayes' theorem, essentially the formula for e-mail classification with a single word would be $p(\text{spam}|\text{word}) = [p(\text{word}|\text{spam})*p(\text{spam})] / p(\text{word})$. Naïve Bayes extends Bayes' theorem by incorporating multiple words; most words are not in any given text, so the algorithm is handling very sparse matrices (i.e., lots of zero-frequency cells). To make computation much easier, Naïve Bayes makes the deliberately naïve assumption that multiple words are independent of one another, once category membership is assumed. Despite this assumption being decidedly wrong in most cases, the accuracy of the Naïve Bayes classifier is remarkably accurate and in line with other big data methods.

Naïve Bayes could be used in organizational research to classify whether people decide to apply versus not apply for a job based on detailed information they learn about the organization, the job and the benefits offered (see Murphy & Tam, 2004, for a Bayesian perspective on job applicants). As another example, applicants could be classified into hireable versus not hireable, say, based on the text of resumes; this in line with recent research that has focused on personality trait information contained in the text of resumes being related to hireability (Burns, Christiansen, Morris, Periard, & Coaster, 2014). For example, resume language pertaining to high levels of interpersonal skills, supervisory experience, and attention to detail might classify an applicant as being hireable, whereas a resume lacking this information and/or having unimportant or undesirable information could classify an applicant as being unhireable.

Note that Naïve Bayes could also incorporate resume features other than language into classifying applicants into hireable/unhireable categories. For example, how well organized and formatted the resume is and whether it was turned in on time could be quantified and incorporated into the model. As with the spam e-mail example, a set of resumes that are labeled as hireable or unhireable would be needed as training data to estimate the Naïve Bayes model; then the estimated model would be used to apply hireable/unhireable labels to a test data set of resumes; finally, accuracy could be determined on the basis of the performance of hired employees (taking range restriction due to selection into account).

LASSO and elastic net. The regression method of the LASSO (least absolute shrinkage and selection operator; see Tibshirani, 1996) is the same as the familiar method of linear regression analysis, but it adds an important extension. The extension is a requirement that the sum of the absolute values of the regression coefficients not exceed a specified value. This value is called a *tuning parameter*, and LASSO can vary this value to be very large or very small. When the tuning parameter is very large, then essentially there is no constraint on the sum and LASSO produces exactly the same results as linear regression. But conversely, when the tuning parameter is small, the magnitudes of the regression coefficients tend to shrink toward zero compared with their linear regression counterparts (in order to keep the sum of these magnitudes small).

In fact, when there are many predictors in the formula, the LASSO will shrink many if not most of the predictor coefficients to zero, meaning these predictors are not used at all in the LASSO regression model. Therefore, the tuning parameter in LASSO can end up performing predictor selection, which gives one a sense of the importance of each predictor: when the tuning parameter is varied continuously from zero to a very large number, the predictors that enter into the LASSO regression model with non-zero coefficients earlier should be considered more important than predictors that enter later when the value of the tuning parameter increases. And unlike linear regression, LASSO can also provide valid solutions when the initial correlation matrix is not positive definite, such as when there are a large number of predictors and even when the number of predictors exceeds the sample size as might happen with big data.

The LASSO is limited in some ways, one important way being that LASSO will focus on one predictor among a group of correlated predictors and tend to ignore the rest. The elastic net (Zou & Hastie, 2005) is a method that will consider all predictors within a correlated group because its constraint is a mathematical balance (convex weighting) between the LASSO constraint (sum of absolute regression coefficients) and the ridge regression constraint (sum of squared regression coefficients). The elastic net also performs predictor selection by forcing some coefficients to zero, particularly when a large number of predictors is involved.

Avoiding Capitalizing on Chance

In reviewing the section above, one might get the impression that the sole goal of supervised learning methods is maximizing prediction within the data set on which the algorithm is trained. However, that would not be correct. The applied statistics and machine learning community have been quite concerned with identifying ways to cross-validate predictions produced by these techniques and avoid simply capitalizing on chance by overfitting their data (James, Witten, Hastie, & Tibshirani, 2014).

To illustrate, say that you have obtained organizational data indicating which salespeople get promoted along with other data that are imperfect but seemingly related to promotion decisions: job performance ratings, peer ratings of teamwork, number of sales calls made and percentage of successful conversions of those call into sales. You would like to predict the promotion criterion from these other data that serve as predictors. To do so, a *training* data set is identified that contains a set of predictors and a criterion. You then apply a supervised learning method (such as one of the ones discussed above) to determine underlying relationships between the predictors and the criterion, namely how well each case can predict a criterion score (or be classified into a criterion category) given its respective predictor values.

Although modern supervised learning methods can be used to model relationships that are more complex than might be found with traditional statistical methods (e.g., ordinary least squares regression), the number of variables involved with big data can be huge relative to the amount of data in the multivariate space. In many instances, the number of variables in the data set might far exceed the number of cases (e.g., team dynamics being captured with real-time biometric sensors, Kozlowski, Chang, & Biswas, 2014; eye-tracking data in test-takers that might capture 50 eye movements per second; van Hooft & Born, 2012). Even with 100 variables, a trillion data points may not cover a complex multivariate space adequately (Domingo, 2012), leading to what is known as the curse of dimensionality: when there are many highly correlated variables, it can become difficult to distinguish cases from one another (an extension of the multicollinearity problem in linear regression), and yet when there are many irrelevant variables, then it can be impossible to find signals in the sea of noise.

The issues above all lead to a situation where the likelihood of capitalizing on chance when attempting to predict an outcome of interest with powerful, modern supervised learning methods are very high—unless steps are taken to avoid overfitting one's local data. It is critically important that steps be taken so these algorithms do not fool us with their sample-specific findings: A glove that is custom-made to your hand will fit very nicely, but how well will it fit on another hand? It likely will fit many other hands, but it is virtually guaranteed that it will not fit as well. Likewise, the fit of a modern supervised learning algorithm to a training data set will be custom-fit to some extent. Thus, the challenge is to optimize prediction in one's local sample in a way that also optimizes prediction in other independent samples of data.

Supervised learning methods typically achieve this via sophisticated model fitting and cross-validation strategies, where models are tuned and selected to strike a balance between local optimization and generalization (James et al., 2014). At their simplest level, these strategies may take the form of initially training the algorithm on a training set of data, and then applying it to an independent test set of data. In the organizational sciences, this would be akin to fitting a regression model and generating regression coefficients based on one sample of data, and then applying those parameters to predictors in another independent set of data (a cross-validation data set) to see how well predictions made by that model cross-validate. This is done because the R^2 for the regression model in the sample in which its parameters are estimated is an overly optimistic estimate of the R^2 if those parameters were applied to a new, independent set of data. This happens because the regression coefficients comprising a simple OLS regression model are optimized to the data on which the model is fit.

Typically, in the organizational sciences, cross-validation is done either formulaically (see Schmitt & Ployhart, 1999), or via independent samples as described above. Although a formula-based approach works well for simple OLS regression models, as one gets into the complexity of modern supervised learning methods, more sophisticated approaches to cross-validation are required (e.g., k-fold validation, bootstrapping), and as such the machine learning and applied statistics literature has devoted much attention to the topic (again, see the instructional book of James et al., 2014, for a review). Another key feature of these techniques was just mentioned, how—unlike simple OLS regression where regression coefficients are fully optimized based on local data—there are mechanisms built into many modern supervised learning methods that effectively allow one to control (or tune) the degree to which model parameters are optimized based on one's local data. This allows the researcher to take more control of the tradeoff between local optimization of prediction and future generalization of prediction, rather than simply settling for full local optimization offered by OLS and other common modeling approaches (e.g., traditional logistic regression and SEM). The aforementioned LASSO and elastic net techniques are two examples of this, where the constraints they put on the regression coefficients during the model estimation process effectively strike a balance between a fully optimized, sample-specific set of regression coefficients and a more constrained set of coefficients that does not result in a optimal least-squares prediction in the sample at hand but, as a result, its predictions hold up better upon cross-validation.

Unsupervised Learning Methods

In the sections below, we discuss several unsupervised learning methods. Recall that these are methods for which prediction of some criterion is not the goal per se, but rather the goal is a reliable grouping or clustering of the data. Sometimes this might be done to reduce the dimensionality of a set of data (e.g., reduce the number of predictors of a phenomenon), to understand the dimensionality or structure of a set of data (e.g., different types of turnover, different sets of work values), or to simply understand similarity between different types of objects (e.g., employees, teams, jobs). As with the supervised methods just discussed, these unsupervised methods are generally more flexible than traditional analytic approaches.

k-means. The purpose of a *k*-means analysis is to identify meaningful clusters or groupings of cases (often rows) in a data set. For example, let's say a researcher works for a large organization that has taken a job-analysis approach to profile all of its jobs according to a common competency framework; now the organization wants to take the jobs data and create groups of jobs that are empirically similar in terms of their competency requirements. *k*-means would select a subset of *m* cases (jobs) that serve as initial centroids, or centers, for each of *m* clusters. Next, *k*-means assigns each data point (job) to the nearest centroid in multivariate space. After creating these new clusters (i.e., sets of related jobs), the centroids are re-estimated as the means of the members within each cluster. This ends up creating new distances between the data points and the centroids, meaning that some of the data (jobs) will be reassigned to a different centroid or cluster that is closer. The procedure iterates between cluster assignment and centroid estimation until convergence is reached.

k-nearest neighbors. The k-nearest neighbors (kNN) algorithm is similar to k-means, except that it begins with a set of training data that is already associated with cluster labels applied to them (e.g., jobs in the

O*NET data base that already contain job family labels or perhaps labels from a previous analysis, such as the k-means above). To continue the previous example, say that the organization in our k-means illustration above acquired a new operating unit and decided to profile all new jobs with that unit according to its existing competency framework. Bear in mind that they already have a set of job families identified via their k-means analyses described above. For the new unit, they could use kNN to identify which existing job family each job from the new unit is most similar to. The method would assign each job to the job family that is the most frequent among the k-nearest neighbors in the training data set. The question then becomes what is nearest and what number k is best to choose. Euclidean distance often determines nearest, which is the sum of squared distances across variables, although different distances to neighbors are certainly justifiable (e.g., all neighbors could be included, weighted by their distance). The number of neighbors to choose is a trade-off between over- and under-fitting the model to the data: When k is too many, then underlying distinctions might be overlooked, but when k is too few, then important influences of nearby cases will be ignored.

Density-based clustering and Ward's hierarchical clustering. Hierarchical clustering represents a given data set as a tree, where the optimal number of clusters that summarizes the data lies somewhere between the trunk (all data are in one group) and the leaves (each data point stands is on its own). Branches of the tree are determined by splits in the data that ideally improve the balance between within-cluster homogeneity and between-cluster heterogeneity (similar to the goal of k-means, or even a high F-test in ANOVA).

Density-based clustering (DeBaCl) is a hierarchical clustering algorithm that implements the idea of level sets (Hartigan, 1975), where essentially branches in hierarchy are determined in a way that corresponds to the hierarchy of modes in how the data are presumed to be distributed (i.e., their estimated probability density function). The hierarchy established by DeBaCl reveals how clusters of data are separated or nested within one another. Available software also contains graphics for interactively exploring the tree hierarchy (called a dendogram) and clusters located at given levels in the tree (Kent, Rinaldo, & Verstynen, 2013).

Ward's method is a traditional hierarchical clustering technique that builds from the bottom up in an ANOVA-like manner, clustering pairs of clusters together at each stage so that the between-cluster variance is maximized and the within-cluster variance is minimized. The clustering continues until a single group captures all the data; however, at each stage of the clustering, one can estimate the resulting error (ESS, Euclidean sum of squares) to determine which level of clustering appears to best represent the data. Appropriate clustering generally occurs when error does not increase much; conversely, if error increases a great deal, then that suggests the more refined clusters in the previous stage were a more appropriate representation of the data. To our knowledge, there is no widespread application of the DeBaCl algorithms due to their novelty.

Organizational psychologists have made use of both k-means (see Aziz & Zickar, 2006; Kossek, Ruderman, Braddy, & Hannum, 2012) and Ward's method (see Converse & Oswald, 2004), but they could benefit from exploring k-nearest neighbor and DeBaCl algorithms. All clustering methods can be tested for sensitivity or robustness by considering outliers, cluster member reassignment and re-estimation during iterations of cluster estimation (see Steinley, 2003). Additionally, in the organizational context, one could imagine that validity estimation might also inform the appropriate level of clustering in a hierarchy, as might the types of data involved such as job analyst, incumbent or employee data informing the same constructs (Converse & Oswald, 2004).

Market basket analysis. Market basket analysis (MBA) is also called *affinity analysis*, where rules of association are induced from available categorical data and can be used to determine profiles of people. For example, Aguinis, Forcum, and Joo (2013) used MBA to illustrate the types of benefits that employees indicated they valued in a nationwide survey (e.g., holiday pay, health care reimbursement, retirement plans). There are three indices reported by MBA. The first is *lift*, which reflects the strength of association between A and B and whether this relationship is statistically significant. Lift is non-negative and is greater than one for a positive association (A and B co-occur) and less than one for a negative association (A and B tend to appear separately). The second index is *support*, which is the probability that A and B occur together relative to the rest of the data set. When the number of variables is very large, support values will tend to be very small, where the relative size of the support value across associations may be more important than the absolute magnitude. The third index is *confidence*, reflecting the probability that A is chosen given that B is chosen (or vice-versa). These are conditional probabilities, so even when there are a large number of variables, confidence can be high because it is limited to the variables in question (e.g., A and B) no matter how big the pool of variables may be. Rule-of-thumb benchmarks have been established for appropriate levels of lift, support and confidence to indicate meaningful levels of association, but we defer to the statistical program that you may use for running MBA because better benchmarks evolve quickly in the domain of big data analyses.

(WHEN) WILL BIG DATA METHODS YIELD BIG DATA INSIGHTS?

The big data movement promises greater empirical insights through statistical methods that can be applied to more data (e.g., modeling more variables and/or time points than employees being analyzed); messy and missing data (e.g., analyzing unstructured text from websites, resumes, or blog posts; non-random missing data patterns); multilevel and cross-classified data (e.g., longitudinal real-time data nested within employees, teams, occupations, organizations, industries and regions); and cross-functional data (e.g., data cutting across recruiting and selection, employee and team performance evaluation, compensation and benefits, customer relations, and internal promotions/exits/transfers).

Figure 3.1 emphasizes how sample data are used to estimate models, and how these sample-based data and models can be conceptually compared to their respective population data and models, the latter usually being unobserved. The discrepancy between sample and population modeling is not new; in fact this figure is an extension of a similar model in the structural equation modeling (SEM) literature, offered by Cudeck and Henly (1991) in the specific context of estimating population SEMs. Here, we are considering the numerous discrepancies between samples and populations in big data, and between data and models that arise in big data analyses.

Sampling discrepancies represent gaps between the sample data and the population of interest. Understanding these discrepancies requires defining ones population well, which often is challenging to do, even when the population data come from the same company as the sample: Do samples change over time? What if the company opens new divisions, restructures itself, merges with another company (and its data) or downsizes? Reducing sampling discrepancy is as much a substantive effort (defining the population carefully albeit imperfectly) as a statistical one (obtaining large samples that qualify as big data). Good samples are not only unbiased with respect to the population (i.e., they sample randomly); they are also large enough to fairly represent key aspects of the population that ideally can be defined *a priori* (e.g., age, gender, job type, job experience). Observed data are based on imperfect measures or surveys; they also involve range-restricted samples (most obviously when inferences are to be made to job applicants who

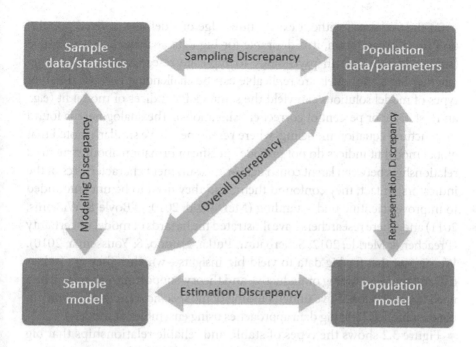

were not selected and criterion data are unavailable). These issues might be considered, if not somehow statistically corrected for (Schmidt & Hunter, 2014), in big data measurement, data collection and data analyses.

Modeling discrepancy happens because big data models (like any models) reflect attempts to summarize data and statistics that, as just noted, are themselves imperfect. For example, a cluster analysis summarizes distances between data points, and random forests summarize decision trees that themselves select nodes that summarize the data for the purpose of making predictions. Furthermore, there is *estimation discrepancy* because coefficients in a sample model are estimating the population coefficients in a parallel model based on population data. Finally, we want to remember that "[e]ssentially, all models are wrong, but some are useful" (Box & Draper, 1987, p. 424), meaning that even population models are representations of the population data. If there is a "true model" in the population, it is likely unknown and probably unknowable. Hence, there will always be some form of *representation discrepancy* between the population data and the model that attempts to summarize those data. Even though representation discrepancy is unknowable, it is one of the four sources of discrepancy that contributes indirectly to *overall discrepancy* between the data in the population that we'd like to represent via the sample model that we hope suffices in doing so.

At the very least, without exact knowledge of a definite or fixed population in an organization, it is desirable for big data analyses to be replicable (similar to the push in psychology to replicate research effects). Judging whether big data models are replicable can be challenging because different types of model solutions can yield the same global indices of model fit (e.g., an R^2 statistic or percent of correct classifications). The analog here is found in structural equation modeling, where researchers have similarly noted that global model fit indices do not provide specific information about structural relationships between latent constructs or measurement characteristics of the indicators; in fact, they confound them, and they need to be unconfounded to improve scientific understanding (McDonald, 2010; O'Boyle & Williams, 2011) and where researchers have illustrated the hazards of model uncertainty (Preacher & Merkle, 2012; Scherbaum, Putka, Naidoo, & Youssefina, 2010). We suspect that for big data to yield big insights—whether they are inductive and theory-building or deductive and theory-supporting—there will be a need to gain a substantive understanding of the specific sources of stability in big data models (and big data approaches using ensembles of models).

Figure 3.2 shows the types of stable and reliable relationships that big data methods—as completely exploratory tools—might uncover. First, stable and generalizable patterns of estimated relationships might be discovered *between latent constructs*, and those findings would have a natural psychological interpretation. For example, dependability has been a predictor construct found to correlate negatively with counterproductive work behavior (Dudley, Orvis, Lebiecki, & Cortina, 2006). Second, stable and generalizable patterns of relationships might be estimated *between scales*, where each scale might be a commercial measure that claims to measure a construct of interest (e.g., there are commercial personality scales that measure dependability, and there are also commercial performance evaluation measures). These relationships might be discussed from a psychological perspective, to the extent they align with latent constructs (e.g., have high factor loadings in Figure 3.1). They may also be discussed from a practical perspective, in that companies typically only administer one measure of a given construct (not several measures of a single construct, as a researcher might when conducting SEM), and organizations are interested in the validity for observed measures when the interest is in prediction.[1] Conceptually, the content of psychological measures ought to be content relevant while minimizing construct deficiencies and irrelevancies; empirically, such measures ought to demonstrate high reliability in measuring constructs of interest across whatever facets are deemed irrelevant (e.g., different items, alternate forms or over time).

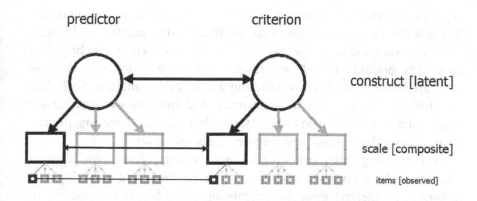

Third, stable and generalizable patterns of relationships might exist *between items*, above and beyond relationships found between the respective scales to which the items contribute. Here is where big data methods might serve to improve prediction at the item level, but potentially without any commensurate gain in practical or theoretical understanding of these relationships. Thus, even if model R^2 values improved by finding stable item-level relationships using any of the family of big data methods, any sound justification for item-level improvements in prediction might be near-impossible. Then again, we hope for a future where, at least in some cases, such findings could signal systematic and substantively interpretable relationships that remain robust across independent samples. This phenomenon might encourage one to incorporate new measures that amplify this signal (i.e., to generate more good data to be incorporated into one's big data), and it also could encourage expanding theory beyond the bounds of what was originally established inductively through the measurement of constructs specified *a priori*. In general, stable item-level relationships that defy interpretation might be problematic for researchers and practitioners who generally seek theoretical understanding and not solely increases in prediction; moreover, it could be especially problematic in the legal setting when measures showing adverse impact need to demonstrate interpretable validities that support business necessity. Item-level relationships, no matter how stable and generalizable, may seem quite esoteric in the legal context unless there is also a substantive interpretation that is also generalizable across settings.

All of this is to support the notion that the expertise of I-O psychologists will not disappear when big data methods are incorporated into our analytic repertoire. In fact, our expertise will become more important because theory-driven measures ensure that big data analyses and results are based on good data, not just big data. Data offered by psychological measures should be reliable and substantive, the latter meaning that the data are at the level of scales reflecting a construct of interest. Such data are then more closely related to constructs and therefore are substantively interpretable in the context of big data analyses tied to clustering, prediction, structural modeling, Bayesian networks and so on.

In concluding this scenic tour, we hope you appreciate how big data methods—those reviewed and, those that continue to be developed—demonstrate themselves to be promising, accessible and applicable in organizational research and practice. More generally, we hope you will join us in a future (if not a revolution) that brings together extensive sources of organizational data (e.g., connected widely across functions of the organization, sampled intensively at the employee or team levels), flexible modeling approaches that are sensitive to cross-validation and generalizability concerns, and an improved inductive-deductive cycle of analysis and theorizing on the basis of big data that integrate across macro- and micro-level organizational phenomena. This chapter avoided the curmudgeonly notion that traditional methods are to be preferred until big data methods convincingly demonstrate their superiority. Instead, we offer big data methods as a useful addition to the toolbox for addressing organizational problems, as well as a point of entry into a much larger data analysis community. Like all analysis methods, big data methods are most informative when they have high-quality data on which to operate, and to risk repeating ourselves, they will not supplant our substantive expertise as I-O psychologists to achieve their full potential. Critically, they will require it.

RESOURCES

Organization-oriented Material

Foreman, J. W. (2014). *Data smart: Using data science to transform information into insight.* Indianapolis, IN: Wiley.

Miller, T. M. (2014). *Modeling techniques in predictive analytics: Business problems and solutions with R.* Upper Saddle River, NJ: Pearson Education.

O'Neil C., & Schutt, R. (2014). *Doing data science: Straight talk from the frontline.* Sebastopol, CA: O'Reilly Media, Inc.

Provost, F., & Fawcett, T. (2013). *Data science for business: What you need to know about data mining and data-analytic thinking.* Sebastopol, CA: O'Reilly Media, Inc.

Stanton, J. M. (2012). *An introduction to data science.* Retrieved from http://ischool.syr.edu/media/documents/2012/3/DataScienceBook1_1.pdf

Stanton, J. M. (2013). Data mining: A practical introduction for organizational researchers. In J. M. Cortina & R. S. Landis (Eds.), *Modern research methods for the study of behavior in organizations* (199–232). New York, NY: Routledge Academic.

General Material

Bishop, C. M. (2006). *Pattern recognition and machine learning.* New York, NY: Springer.

Breiman, L., & Cutler, A. (n.d.). Retrieved from https://www.stat.berkeley.edu/~breiman/RandomForests/

James, G., Witten, D., Hastie, T., & Tibshirani, R. (2014). *An introduction to statistical learning with applications in R.* New York: Springer.

Witten, I. H., Frank, E., & Hall, H. A. (2011). *Data mining: Practical machine learning tools and techniques* (3rd ed.). Burlington, MA: Morgan Kaufmann.

Programming Material

CRAN task view: Machine learning & statistical learning. Retrieved from http://cran.r-project.org/web/views/MachineLearning.html

Lantz, B. (2013). *Machine learning with R.* Birmingham, UK: Packt Publishing Ltd.

Machine Learning Group at the University of Waikato (2014, October 28). Weka3: Data mining software in Java. Retrieved from http://www.cs.waikato.ac.nz/ml/weka/

NOTE

1. We are also well aware of *operational validity,* which reflects an estimated correlation between an observed predictor and a criterion corrected for measurement error variance (see Binning & Barrett, 1989). In the current illustration, operational validity is a side issue, but incidentally, the current framework would reflect operational validity if each criterion scale were a latent factor with items as indicators.

REFERENCES

Aguinis, H., Forcum, L. E., & Joo, H. (2013). Using market basket analysis in management research. *Journal of Management, 39,* 1799–1824.

Aguinis, H., Werner, S., Abbott, J. L., Angert, C., Park, J. H., & Kohlhausen, D. (2010). Customer-centric science: Reporting significant research results with rigor, relevance, and practical impact in mind. *Organizational Research Methods, 13,* 515–539.

Aziz, S., & Zickar, M. J. (2006). A cluster analysis investigation of workaholism as a syndrome. *Journal of Occupational Health Psychology, 11,* 52–62.

Bersin, J. (2013, February 27). Big data in human resources: Talent analytics comes of age. *Forbes.* Retrieved from http://www.forbes.com.

Binning, J. F., & Barrett, G. V. (1989). Validity of personnel decisions: A conceptual analysis of the inferential and evidential bases. *Journal of Applied Psychology, 74*, 478–494.

Box, G. E. P., & Draper, N. R. (1987). *Empirical model-building and response surfaces.* New York, NY: Wiley.

Breiman, L. (2001). Random forests. *Machine Learning, 45*, 5–32.

Burns, G. N., Christiansen, N. D., Morris, M. B., Periard, D. A., & Coaster, J. A. (2014). Effects of applicant personality on resume evaluations. *Journal of Business and Psychology, 29*, 573-591.

Campbell, J. P. (1990). Overview of the Army selection and classification project (Project A). *Personnel Psychology, 43*, 231-239.

Cohen, J. (1992). A power primer. *Psychological Bulletin, 112*, 155–159.

Collins, J. M., & Clark, M. R. (2006). An application of the theory of neural computation to the prediction of workplace behavior: An illustration and assessment of network analysis. *Personnel Psychology, 46*, 503–524.

Converse, P. D., & Oswald, F. L. (2004). The effects of data type on job classification and its purposes. *Psychology Science, 46*, 99–127.

Cudeck, R., & Henly, S. J. (1991). Model selection in covariance structures and the "problem" of sample size: A clarification. *Psychological Bulletin, 109*, 512–519.

Cumming, G. (2014). The new statistics: Why and how. *Psychological Science, 25*, 7–29.

Domingos, P. (2012). A few useful things to know about machine learning. *Communications of the ACM, 55*, 79–87.

Dudley, N. M., Orvis, K. A., Lebiecki, J. E., & Cortina, J. M. (2006). A meta-analytic investigation of conscientiousness in the prediction of job performance: Examining the intercorrelations and the incremental validity of narrow traits. *Journal of Applied Psychology, 91*, 40–57.

Eich, E. (2014). Business not as usual. *Psychological Science, 25*, 3–6.

Friedman, J. H., & Popescu, B. E. (2008). Predictive learning via rule ensembles. *The Annals of Applied Statistics, 2*, 916–954.

Hartigan, J. (1975). *Clustering algorithms.* New York, NY: Wiley.

Hsu, L. M. (1993). Using Cohen's tables to determine the maximum power attainable in two-sample tests when one sample is limited in size. *Journal of Applied Psychology, 2*, 303–305.

James, G., Witten, D., Hastie, T., & Tibshirani, R. (2014). *An introduction to statistical learning with applications in R.* New York, NY: Springer.

Johnson, J. W., & Carter, G. W. (2010) Validating synthetic validation: Comparing traditional and synthetic validity coefficients. *Personnel Psychology, 63*, 755–795.

Kent, B. P., Rinaldo, A., & Verstynen, T. (2013, July 30). DeBaCl: A Python package for interactive DEnsity-BAsed CLustering. Retrieved from http://arxiv.org/abs/1307.8136

Klein, R. A., Ratliff, K. A., Vianello, M., Adams Jr., R. B., Bahník, S., Bernstein, M. J., . . . & Nosek, B. A. (2014). Investigating variation in replicability: A "many labs" project. *Social Psychology, 45*, 142–152.

Koppes, L. L., & Vinchur, A. J. (2012). A history of industrial and organizational psychology. In S. W. J. Kozlowski (Ed.), *The Oxford handbook of organizational psychology, Volume 1* (pp. 22–75). New York, NY: Oxford University Press.

Kossek, E., Ruderman, M., Braddy, P., & Hannum, K. (2012). Work-nonwork boundary management profiles: A person-centered approach. *Journal of Vocational Behavior, 81*, 112–128.

Kozlowski, S. W. J., Chang, C. H., & Biswas, S., (2014, February). Capturing the dynamics of teamwork. Presented at the NASA Human Research Program Investigators' Workshop, Galveston, TX.

Landis, R. S., Cortina, J. M., & Rogelberg, S. G. (2014). Provisional acceptance based on a peer-reviewed proposal: An alternative publication model in search for scientific truth. *Journal of Business and Psychology*. Retrieved from https://jbp.uncc.edu/

Lohr, S. (2013, April 20). Big data, trying to build better workers. *The New York Times*. Retrieved from http://www.nytimes.com

Maxwell, S. E. (2004). The persistence of underpowered studies in psychological research: Causes, consequences, and remedies. *Psychological Methods, 9*, 147–163.

McDonald, R. (2010). Structural models and the art of approximation. *Perspectives on Psychological Science, 5*, 675–686.

Minbashian, A., Bright, J. E. H., & Bird, K. D. (2010). A comparison of artificial neural networks and multiple regression in the context of research on personality and work performance. *Organizational Research Methods, 13*, 540–561.

Murphy, K. R., & Tam, A. P. (2004). The decisions job applicants must make: Insights from a Bayesian perspective. *International Journal of Selection and Assessment, 12*, 66–74.

O'Boyle Jr., E. H., & Williams, L. J. (2011). Decomposing model fit: Measurement vs. theory in organizational research using latent variables. *Journal of Applied Psychology, 96*, 1–12.

Preacher, K. J., & Merkle, E. C. (2012). The problem of model uncertainty in structural equation modeling. *Psychological Methods, 17*, 1–14.

Scarborough, D., & Somers, M. (2006). *Neural networks in organizational research: Applying pattern recognition to the analysis of organizational behavior*. Washington, DC: American Psychological Association.

Scherbaum, C. A. (2005). Synthetic validity: Past, present, and future. *Personnel Psychology, 58*, 481–515.

Scherbaum, C., Putka, D. J., Naidoo, L., & Youssefina, D. (2010). Key driver analyses: Current trends, problems, and alternative approaches. In S. Albrecht (Ed.), *Handbook of employee engagement: Models, measures, and practice* (pp. 182–196). Cheltenham, UK: Edward-Elgar Publishing House.Schmidt, F. L., & Hunter, J. E. (2014). *Method of meta-analysis: Correcting error and bias in research findings*. Thousand Oaks, CA: Sage.

Schmitt, N., & Ployhart, R. E. (1999). Estimates of cross-validity for stepwise-regression and with predictor selection. *Journal of Applied Psychology, 84*, 50–57.

Sedlmeier, P., & Gigerenzer, G. (1989). Do studies of statistical power have an effect on the power of studies? *Psychological Bulletin, 105*, 309–316.

Somers, M. J., & Casal, J. C. (2009). Using artificial neural networks to model nonlinearity: The case of the job-satisfaction-job performance relationship. *Organizational Research Methods, 12*, 403–417.

Steinley, D. (2003). Local optima in K-means clustering: What you don't know may hurt you. *Psychological Methods, 8*, 294–304.

Tibshirani, R. (1996). Regression shrinkage and selection via the lasso. *Journal of the Royal Statistical Society, Series B, 58*, 267-288.

Trattner, M. H., & O'Leary, B. S. (1980). Sample sizes for statistical power in testing for differential validity. *Journal of Applied Psychology, 65*, 127–134.

van Hooft, E. A., Born, M. P. (2012). Intentional response distortion on personality tests: Using eye-tracking to understand response processes when faking. *Journal of Applied Psychology, 97*, 301–316.

Zou, H., & Hastie, T. (2005). Regularization and variable selection via the elastic net. *Journal of the Royal Statistical Society B, 67*, 301–320.

4

Twitter Analysis

Methods for Data Management and a Word Count Dictionary to Measure City-level Job Satisfaction

Ivan Hernandez, Daniel A. Newman, and Gahyun Jeon

METHODOLOGICAL BENEFITS OF BIG DATA FOR STUDYING PSYCHOLOGY

The advent of big data presents both opportunities and challenges for studying behavior and psychological processes. There are three features often used to characterize big data: volume, velocity, and variety (Laney, 2001). That is, big data provide an abundance of information, at a faster pace, and about more concepts than previously possible. However, these characteristics also mean that previous data analytic methods might become less feasible. Instead, methods are needed that address the specific defining features of big data. In this chapter, we offer an example of how massive information allows us to reveal new phenomena and discover answers to new psychological questions. Specifically, we will discuss how big data can be used to measure popular psychological constructs (e.g., job satisfaction) at the city level of analysis, which can then be used to predict related city-level concepts, as well as offer insight into new multi-level and macro-level hypotheses.

Much psychological research relies on data taken from small convenience samples measured at one point in time (Gosling, Vazire, Srivastava, & John, 2004). For example, in the *Journal of Personality and Social Psychology*, the premier journal in social psychology, 67% of the American samples (and 80% of the samples from other countries) were composed solely of undergraduates in psychology courses (Arnett, 2008). This tendency for social psychologists to rely on small undergraduate samples has not decreased overtime (Gallander Wintre, North, & Sugar, 2001). Reliance on small samples that are restricted in terms of demographics, education, college major, or other variables can be problematic. Meta-analyses show that effects based on college samples do not often replicate when examined in non-student samples (Peterson, 2001; Henrich, Heine, & Norenzayan, 2010). Further, even if the samples were representative, the small number of participants limits the size of effects researchers can study due to low statistical power (Cohen, 1992). For example, the average effect size in social psychology is $r = 0.21$ (Richard, Bond, & Zoota, 2003). To have even an 80% chance of detecting that effect size with the standard false positive rate of 5%, researchers would need at least 194 participants in each study. However, in an analysis of one of psychology's leading journals, *Cognition*, the median sample sizes were 80 total participants for regular articles and 52 participants for brief articles (Bertamini & Munafò, 2012). Fraley and Vazire (2014) further showed that the average sample size for studies in journals from the field of social psychology were greatly underpowered (e.g., median $N = 73$ for *Psychological Science*, median $N = 90$ for *Journal of Personality and Social Psychology*). Therefore, currently popular data collection methods make it difficult to understand human behavior, and like an astronomer using too small of a telescope, small sample sizes render researchers unable to detect a vast array of phenomena, both big and small, in the world (Simonsohn, 2013).

Incorporating big data into our analyses can solve many of the issues facing the field of psychology. The characteristics of big data—volume, velocity, and variety—can directly address the limitations of generalizability and statistical power. Because of its scale, researchers using big data have the statistical power to study phenomena with much smaller effect sizes. Thus, big data have the potential to enable examination of a broader variety of behaviors. Additionally, the velocity of big data allows studies to easily go beyond the single time-point (cross-sectional) designs typically employed. Researchers can more easily generate a longer history of their data, enabling them to examine change over time (Kelly & McGrath, 1988; Mitchell & James, 2001). The variety of big data also allows researchers to explore new situations, topics, and people. Groups and settings not easily found in the lab can be reached *en masse* via the internet. Similarly, researchers are potentially provided the opportunity to take findings from the lab and replicate them in different populations.

TWO EASY WAYS TO MANAGE BIG DATA: FILTERING AND AGGREGATING

Given computational limits (e.g., speed, memory), when a researcher is potentially faced with millions (or even millions of millions) of data points, there are several preprocessing strategies that could be implemented to handle the massive dataset. For the current paper, we mention three strategies: (a) filtering—only attending to part of the data, (b) aggregating—combining or averaging the data units to obtain a smaller number of units, and (c) segmenting—partitioning the data into pieces that fit within computational limits that can then be processed separately and combined later. Whereas filtering and aggregating procedures are much more familiar to psychologists and will be discussed further below, segmenting is a topic better described to an audience of computer scientists. For a useful example of segmenting, we refer the reader to Google's MapReduce (Dean & Ghemawhat, 2004). Fortunately, segmenting is not typically necessary for the moderately sized datasets we use in Twitter analysis. Below, we briefly review the major fallacies to be avoided when undertaking the two primary approaches for preprocessing big data—filtering and aggregating.

Fallacies of Filtering: The Missing Data Problem

Data filtering involves selecting part of the data for further analysis, while ignoring, excluding, or discarding the remainder of the data. Although filtering has the advantage of reducing the dataset to a manageable size, it suffers the distinct disadvantage of potentially creating *missing data bias* in one's parameter estimates (e.g., bias in correlations, regression coefficients, etc.) The risk of missing data bias emerges whenever the filtering process is not completely random. To elaborate, incomplete data are considered missing completely at random (MCAR; Rubin, 1976) when the probability that data are ignored or missing does not depend upon any of the observed data or upon any of the ignored or missing data (i.e., MCAR means that p(missing|complete) = p(missing); see Schafer & Graham, 2002; Newman, 2003). When missing or ignored data are not MCAR, then missing data bias is a multiplicative function of the amount of missing data (e.g., response rate or amount of data filtered), and the extent to which the data are missing systematically (not randomly) (see Newman, 2014; Newman & Cottrell, in press for examples and formulae that describe the expected amount of missing data bias in the Pearson correlation under missing data). In short, data filtering makes sense only if the filtering can be completely random (MCAR; e.g., flipping a coin or rolling a die), and if the amount of data that remains post-filtering is large enough to provide reasonable statistical power (Cohen, 1992).

Fallacies of Aggregating: The Levels of Analysis Problem

Data aggregation usually involves averaging the data from one level of analysis (e.g., individual level) up to a higher level of analysis (e.g., group level). It is important to note that any time data are aggregated (e.g., averaging individual-level responses up to the group level or averaging daily, within-person responses up to the individual, between-person level), then the basic phenomena being studied can change (Ostroff, 1993; Robinson, 1950). This is illustrated in Figure 4.1, where we see that the within-group correlations of x with y (i.e., the slopes of the lines within the ovals—within groups) are positive relationships, whereas the between-group correlation of x with y (i.e., the slope of the line across the different ovals—between groups) is a negative relationship. In Robinson's (1950) classic example, the individual-level correlation between being born outside the US and illiteracy (r_{within}) was small and positive, while the state-level correlation between foreign birth and illiteracy ($r_{between}$) was large and negative. Likewise, in the example shown in Figure 4.1, aggregating from the individual level up to the group level completely changes the observed x-y correlation from a positive relationship into a negative relationship.

As such, drawing an inference about individuals on the basis of correlations between groups, as well as drawing an inference about groups on the basis of correlations between individuals, will typically result in a fallacy. Drawing an inference about lower-level units (e.g., individuals) on the basis of relationships among higher-level units (e.g., groups) is called an *ecological fallacy*, and has chronically plagued cross-cultural researchers who seek to make statements about individuals on the basis of correlations between country-level variables. In contrast, drawing inferences about higher-level units (e.g., groups) on the basis of relationships among lower-level units (e.g., individuals) is called an *atomistic fallacy* (Kozlowski & Klein, 2000), and has chronically plagued HR researchers who seek to make statements about organization-level performance on the basis of correlations between individual-level variables (Schmidt, Hunter, McKenzie, & Muldrow, 1979).

A typical type of aggregation that we expect would be quite common in big data applications would be aggregating over time. That is, if data come in continuously (e.g., at multiple times throughout each day), then the researcher might decide to aggregate these data temporally into daily, weekly, monthly, quarterly, or annual measures. Similar to what we illustrate in Figure 4.1, the choice of a temporal aggregation period (e.g., daily versus quarterly) can fundamentally alter the basic phenomenon under investigation. As such, we warn big data researchers to make considered and

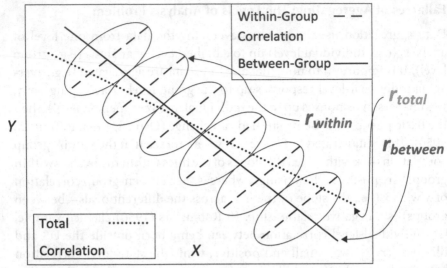

Note. In the example above, the within-group (individual-level) correlation (r_{within}) is positive, but the between-group (group-level) correlation ($r_{between}$) is negative. The total correlation is a weighted average of the within-group correlation and the between-group correlation,

$$r_{total} = r_{between}(\eta_x \eta_y) + r_{within}\sqrt{(1-\eta_x^2)(1-\eta_y^2)} \text{, where } \eta_x^2 = SS_{between} / SS_{total} \text{ (see Robinson, 1950).}$$

FIGURE 4.1

Aggregation Fallacy: Illustration That Correlation Between and Correlation Within Can Differ.

theoretically-appropriate choices for temporal aggregation periods (e.g., Harrison & Martocchio, 1998).

INTRODUCTION TO LINGUISTIC ANALYSIS OF MASSIVE TEXT-BASED DATASETS

One way to incorporate big data into psychological research is by finding openly available sources of data that reflect human behavior. Currently, the predominant source of data in psychology is overtly surveying people to self-report their thoughts, emotions, and attitudes. However, implementing surveys can be time consuming, can lead to limited sample sizes and time frames, and is expensive when seeking samples with thousands of respondents.

There exist alternative—albeit less common—ways to assess the thoughts, feelings, and attitudes people have. Psychological research on language finds that the words we use mirror our thoughts and feelings at that moment (Pennebaker, 2011). For example, people with depression are much more likely to have a self-focus and to use first person pronouns (Rude, Gortner, & Pennebaker, 2004). Similarly, people who are romantically interested in others are more likely to focus on these others and to match their language (e.g., use pronouns at a similar rate) (Ireland, Slatcher, Eastwick, Scissors, Finkel, & Pennebaker, 2011). As a third example, Christians are more likely to talk about religious terms, and atheists are more likely to talk about analytic processes (Ritter, Preston, & Hernandez, 2014). Therefore, another approach to studying psychological processes is to examine the concepts occurring in people's language, or *linguistic content analysis*. The central goal of linguistic content analysis is to classify words, phrases, or other units of text that people have written into a limited num ber of meaningful categories that are relevant to the researcher's hypothesis. Content analysis allows researchers to make use of the large quantity of text sources freely available over the internet and in established corpora. Forums, letters, speeches, e-mails, and blog posts all provide a wealth of information about the mindset of the speaker. Therefore, in the age of big data, text rep-resents an important source of information. Rather than analyzing a small sample of information from a selected group of participants, thousands (and even millions) of data points are now available to a researcher.

Although text analysis methods have been used for many decades, the popularity of the internet means that massive amounts of text data can be analyzed, and challenges arise due to its scale. Traditionally, content analy-sis involved performing case-by-case qualitative coding of conversations by a trained expert (Weber, 1990; Schamber, 2000). Whereas this quali-tative approach allows for an in-depth understanding of a small sample of conversations, the method was not designed to get a comprehensive picture of an entire culture or geographic region. Over the past decade, however, computer-based methods of text analysis have addressed these issues by enabling the coding of a larger amount of text in a faster, broader, more cost-efficient, and more quantitative way.

WORD COUNTING AS WAY TO STUDY PEOPLE

One of the most widely used computer programs in text analysis is linguis-tic inquiry and word count (LIWC; Pennebaker, Francis, & Booth, 2001). LIWC analyzes text samples (e.g., a news story, a blog, an e-mail) on a word-by-word basis and compares each word to an internal dictionary of over 2,000 words divided into different linguistic categories (e.g., positive affect/ emotions, money-related, personal pronouns). The output displays the per-centage of total words in the text that reflect each category. For example, if the four word text sample, "I am happy today," is given to LIWC, it would output a value of 0.25 for positive emotion (i.e., "happy" is 25% of the text), and 0.25 for first person pronouns (i.e., "I" is 25% of the text), and would give a value of 0 for categories like "money." Although LIWC is proprietary software that researchers would need to purchase, its underlying algorithm is a simple word counter. Provided the user already has a dictionary of terms, s/he can easily replicate the basic functionality of LIWC in any scripting language. Below is a simple LIWC clone written in Python that examines two psychological dimensions: positive and negative emotions.

```python
positiveemotions = ["good", "happy","fun", "love"]
negativeemotions = ["bad", "sad", "boring", "hate"]
file = open("documents.txt", "rb")
output = open("outputfile.txt", "wb")
line_number=0
for line in file:
    line_number+=1
    positive_count=0;
    negative_count=0
    words=line.split()
    for word in words:
        if word in positiveemotions:
            positive_count+=1
        if word in negativeemotions:
            negative_count+=1
        doc_length = len(words)
        positive_percent = str(float(positive_count)/
        float(doc_length))
        negative_percent = str(float(positive_
        count)/float(doc _length))
        line_info = ",".join([str(line_
        number),positive_percent,negative_percent]
        output.write(line_info + "\n")
file.close()
output.close()
```

In the code above, the user provides a list of key terms for each dictionary. This example uses a condensed version of the positive and negative affect dictionary (Pennebaker, Chung, Ireland, Gonzales, & Booth, 2011). The program then opens the file containing the text documents, each on a separate line. Next, it opens the output file where it will write the results. Then, for every line in the document file, the document is broken into separate words. Each word is compared against the words in the dictionaries. When a word matches a keyword in the dictionary, the counter for that dictionary increments by one. After all the words in the document have been searched, the percentage of the document containing dictionary-relevant keywords is calculated by dividing the number of keyword matches by the total number of words in the document. These values are then written to the output file on a new line. The process is then repeated for each document in the document file.

Although the algorithm is simple, the method opens the door to a wide array of opportunities not possible with human-based text coding methods. Entire corpora that would have taken years to read and code now take only seconds to analyze. Additionally, new dictionaries and constructs are able to be included by simply changing a few lines of code, whereas traditional methods of content analysis would have required an in-depth training for each new coding scheme.

Although some LIWC dictionaries are based on parts-of-speech (e.g., pronouns, prepositions), certain dictionary categories represent more psychological processes (e.g., anger, cognitive mechanisms, social engagement). These dictionaries are what make LIWC distinct from other word counting software, and they allow researchers to study latent constructs just as psychologists do with survey-based scales. By creating a dictionary containing a set of words related to a concept, LIWC can index various aspects of the mindset of the speaker. Questions pertaining to mood, thoughtfulness, certainty, and sociability can be addressed quickly and efficiently.

One might be skeptical that computational word count methods can serve as a proxy for conducting psychological research using surveys or human-supervised content analysis. The volume, velocity, and variety of massive data should seemingly come at the expense of being able to ascertain the meaning of the text in a consistent and valid manner. Indeed, the usefulness and improvement of this method over human coding definitely cannot be assumed. Rather, word count methods must be empirically validated. Therefore, it is necessary to evaluate these methods and show that they have an acceptable level of reliability and validity. The following section discusses basic ideas related to assessing a word count measure's psychometric properties.

Pennebaker's Approach to Establishing Reliability and Validity

To establish the reliability and validity of a word count approach for measuring psychological constructs, Pennebaker et al. (2001, 2007) conducted a multi-step process. He first began by brainstorming a list of emotional and cognitive dimensions often studied in social, health, and personality psychology to create a list of four basic psychological processes: social, cognitive, emotional, and sensory/perceptual. From those four dimensions, sub-dimensions were generated in a similar fashion that describe the various attributes of the higher-level dimensions (e.g., the sub-dimensions for emotional are anger, sadness, etc.) These four dimensions and their sub-dimensions are listed in Table 4.1. After target constructs were identified, Pennebaker derived potential words that could match those dimensions, using reference books, past psychological scales, and subjective opinion.

TABLE 4.1

Pennebaker's LIWC Dimensions

Psychological Process Dimensions	Sub-dimensions	Examples
Emotional processes		happy, hate, cry
	Positive emotions	happy, pretty, good
	Negative emotions	hate, worthless, enemy
	Sadness	grief, cry, sad
Cognitive processes		cause, know, ought
	Causation	because, effect, hence
	Insight	think, know, consider
	Discrepancy	should, would, could
	Tentativeness	maybe, perhaps, guess
	Inhibition	block, constrain
	Certainty	always, never
Sensory and perceptual processes		see, touch, listen
	Seeing	view, saw, look
	Hearing	heard, listen, sound
	Feeling	touch, hold, felt
Social processes		talk, us, friend
	Communication	talk, share, converse
	References to people	you, he, them
	Family	mom, brother, cousin
	Friends	pal, buddy, coworker
	Humans	boy, woman, group

Once the researcher has developed candidates for dictionary keywords, s/he has established face validity. In Pennebaker et al.'s (2001, 2007) method, three independent judges rated the words' acceptability for the category, with majority opinion deciding which words remained. These judges could also add their own ideas for words not already included in the list. Words would then be rated by the other judges in the same fashion. A second rating phase established the face discrimination of the individual words. The judges were given a word list for a dimension (e.g., cognitive processes), and were asked to indicate if each word on the list should be included in the higher dimension. They were then asked to which (if any) of the sub-dimension lists the word should belong. Agreement levels between the judges were recorded, and ranged from 93% to 100%.

After this second rating phase, Pennebaker et al. (2001, 2007) now had a tentative list of keywords, forming a preliminary dictionary with sub-dictionaries. The researchers examined the reliability of these dictionaries by applying them to a corpus of text collected from several dozen previous studies containing over eight million words. Because rare (low base-rate) words are unlikely to be useful for practical purposes and unlikely to show high retest reliabilities, words used less than 0.005% of the time or not listed in Francis and Kucera's (1982) book *Frequency Analysis of English Usage* were removed from the potential dictionary. After assuring that the base-rate frequency for each word was sufficiently high, the researchers calculated the internal consistency of these libraries. Internal consistency assesses how well scores on part of the scale correlate to the other part (e.g., split the test in half and see how the two halves correlate). One way to assess internal consistency reliability is by calculating Cronbach's alpha on each dictionary. To score the words, the authors ran the text through the dictionaries and, if a word in a category was present in the text, that text unit was assigned a score of 1 (and a 0 if the word was absent). This resulted in a binary, rectangular data matrix (text units × words). The authors also used a scoring system where a word's score was its percentage of frequency in the text. The average Cronbach's alpha for the word categories was $\alpha = 0.83$ (SD = 0.15) if using a binary coding, but was only $\alpha = 0.40$ (SD = 0.16) if using percentage coding.

Following the assessment of each dictionary's reliability, the researchers then assessed validity. First-year college students were brought into a study to write about different topics pertaining to the experience of coming to college. The topic was randomly assigned and corresponded to one of the psychological process dimensions. Some students, however, were assigned to a control condition and were asked to describe any particular object or event of their choosing in an unemotional way. After the writing phase of the study was completed, four judges rated the participants' essays on various emotional and cognitive content. The scores on each dimension in the dictionary were compared to the scores given by the four judges. Most dictionaries had a correlation of 0.4 or greater with judges' ratings of text on the respective dimension. These findings suggest that LIWC successfully measures positive and negative affect, several cognitive strategies, several types of thematic content, and various language composition elements.

CREATING A NEW TEXT-BASED CONSTRUCT FOR BIG DATA: TWITTER ANALYSIS

Next, we present a general set of psychometric guidelines for creating and validating word count dictionaries for the purpose of measuring text-based constructs.

1. Generate a large list of candidate key words or phrases

    a. Acquire corpus of text
    b. Apply judgment to create a word count dictionary

2. Examine the reliability of these dictionaries

    a. Test-retest
    b. Internal consistency (if possible)

3. Validate these dictionaries by predicting related concepts

    a. Convergent validity
    b. Discriminant validity

When creating a new word count dictionary, a list of candidate words or phrases must first be compiled. These words can come from a variety of sources. One option is to use prior text, established survey scales, reference books, and other pieces of information relevant to the construct as the basis for words. This approach is bottom-up. However, there may not be enough prior data or theory on the construct. Therefore, subjective judgment is typically necessary when creating a list of potential words for a word count dictionary. This process is more top-down, as it depends on one's expectations and intuition. Most likely a combination of the two is preferred because at this stage, there is little cost associated with including more keywords. Additionally, this stage sets the upper-limit on the number of possible words in the final dictionary, and the number of words in the final dictionary is related to reliability (which itself sets the upper-bound on the validity possible; see Allen & Yen, 2001).

Following the generation of preliminary words for the word count dictionary, the reliability of the dictionary must be assessed. As previously mentioned, there are a variety of ways to determine reliability. One method would be to examine retest reliability—how consistent the dictionary is over time. One could measure a group of text samples from participants or groups and then measure them again at another (or over several) point(s) in time. The dictionary would have high reliability if the participants' scores at one time point correlate with their scores at other time points. Another way to assess reliability would be to examine the internal consistency of the dictionary. That is, researchers can examine how much the individual parts of the dictionary correlate among themselves. This could be done by performing a word/phrase count on the individual words/phrases for each participant and then calculating the Cronbach's alpha coefficient across all of the words/phrases in the dictionary. It is important to note that a typical reliability often computed in content analysis—inter-rater reliability—is not possible in this case. Because word count methods are completely automated and deterministic, any two judges using the software and the same word count dictionary on the same text will always get the same results.

After reliability is established, the dictionary for the construct must demonstrate validity. One type of validity is nomological validity. That is, the construct must correlate to theoretically related concepts (Cronbach & Meehl, 1955). The researcher should consult past theory to determine which concepts are related to the word count dictionary construct. A second form of validity is convergent validity. To assess convergent validity, it would be ideal if researchers could get additional measures of the same construct. For example, if a researcher wishes to establish the validity of a Twitter dictionary construct measuring negative emotion, the researcher could obtain a survey measure of depression from the participants whose texts are being analyzed, and show the two are correlated to some degree. Yet another way to assess convergent validity would be to see whether two largely overlapping constructs (e.g., positive emotion and job satisfaction) are strongly correlated. Finally, another type of validity is discriminant validity. Establishing discriminant validity requires showing that a construct is distinct from other constructs. For example, if a researcher wants to establish discriminant validity for a negative emotion construct, s/he should demonstrate that it is *not* perfectly (nor near-perfectly) correlated with conceptually distinct measures, such as swearing or self-deprecation.

EXAMPLE OF USING BIG DATA TO CREATE A NEW TEXT-BASED MEASURE OF JOB SATISFACTION

To illustrate the process of creating a word count dictionary based on a psychological construct, as well as how it can then be applied to understanding human attitudes and behavior, we detail the creation of a new job satisfaction word count dictionary.

Acquire Corpus of Text

In order to identify the words and phrases for our job satisfaction word count dictionary, we first needed to obtain a corpus of text to develop preliminary statements for our dictionary. We used the microblogging website Twitter as our source of text. Twitter is currently the seventh most popular website in the world (Alexa, 2013) and allows users to post short-form messages (tweets) that describe their thoughts, sentiments, and concerns at a given moment. Studying Twitter data offers several methodological advantages for this project. By using Twitter, we can capture users' mindsets as they occur over a longer period of time and in an unprompted, casual setting (compared to standard surveys). Therefore, Twitter data is—in some ways—more suited for studying a person's state of mind on a day-to-day basis. Recent research has found convergent results from linguistic analysis on Twitter and psychological studies (Ritter, Preston, & Hernandez, 2014). Further, the magnitude of the data is significantly greater than in traditional contexts, allowing for a higher-powered analysis of a population as well as for studies of group-level and longitudinal phenomena. Twitter thus provides a unique opportunity to study psychological constructs on a large scale that is not possible through traditional survey and laboratory methods (Lazer et al., 2009).

For Twitter, we wanted to acquire as many tweets as possible from large metropolitan areas so that their job satisfaction could be correlated with other indices from those places. Therefore, we selected the 200 most populated cities in the United States (based on the city population as of July 1, 2012, as estimated by the United States Census Bureau, 2012). A list of these cities as well as the latitude and longitude coordinates of their centers can also be obtained from Wikipedia (List of United States cities by population, 2012). Latitude and longitude were recorded in decimal format (rather than the degree/minute/second format), which is the required format for the Twitter application programming interface (API) and represent the geographic center of the city. We also cross-referenced the coordinates with those provided by the Google Maps API via ITouch-Map (2007) to verify that they were accurate. It is important to note that the unit of analysis we chose was a city because it provides a large sample of data points (about 200 cities for our study). However, the researcher could also select to study the county- or state-level, but that might involve different theory (see Rentfrow, Gosling, Jokela, Stillwell, Kosinski, & Potter, 2013; Cohen, 1996, 1998; Harrington & Gelfand, 2014) and would reduce the number of data points possible (e.g., there are only 50 states in the US).

We collected data from Twitter using the scripting language Python to connect to Twitter. To facilitate communication with the API, we used Twython (McGrath, 2012), a third-party library that contains a collection of functions that are simpler to type and use than sending HTTP requests directly. It is important to note that researchers can collect social media data with most programming and scripting languages (e.g., Python, Ruby, PHP, Perl, etc.); however, we used Python because of its prevalence in the scientific community, ease of use, and readability of code.

Once the social media platform is determined, a programming or scripting language is chosen, and the API commands (or commands from API simplifier libraries) are understood, the user then creates a file in a text editor that contains the instructions for the API and what to do with each response. In *Appendix A*, we have placed a simple example of a Python file that connects to Twitter and downloads a set of tweets (see Code Sample 1).

When collecting social media data, this process of connecting to the API and saving the results is subsequently automated. That is, the user simply creates a series of loops that repeat a process (i.e., for commands) and handles events depending on conditions (i.e., if commands). The most basic case is to create a loop that runs infinitely, where the commands are sent, the data are received, the data are then saved in a text file or a database as a new entry, and the loop repeats. More complicated collection routines involve iterating through some variable of interest (e.g., location, user, phrase) and separating the data based on those variables. The data can then be analyzed later by comparing the results between instances or groups of the variable.

In our project, we want to automate the process of collecting tweets from a list of cities to assess differences between those cities on job satisfaction. The program will first read a text file containing a list of the cities and their latitude and longitude. These values will be saved to an array. This array will then be iterated through, and the coordinates passed onto the

Twython object. A basic search will be performed where all tweets from that city will be collected and written to a file containing the city's name. The program will consistently monitor the time, and at midnight, a new folder is created where the data from that day are saved. This process will repeat itself indefinitely, collecting data from cities perpetually until the program is terminated. After the collection period ends, you should have many folders in a common directory, each with a number of text files equal to the number of cities. These text files contain all of the tweets for that city for that day. This automation can be as simple as nesting the Twitter collection code in a "while True:" statement in Python, which repeats the commands indefinitely. Also, using the time.sleep() function of Python, a user can pause the script from running for a set interval of time to accommodate instances where the number of requests might exceed the rate limit of the API.

Our data collection period lasted 29 days, from December 21, 2013 until January 18, 2014. To maximize the number of tweets collected given the rate limits (see *Appendix A*), the authors had separate accounts, and two different desktop computers were set up to continuously collect tweets (every 15 minutes for 24 hours a day) from all 200 cities. Because we collected data from multiple servers, we merged the tweets collected from each into a single common file and removed duplicate tweets that may have been recorded by both computers. In *Appendix A*, we provide an example of a script that merges text files from two separate directories (one for each server) into a single directory (Code Sample 2). We also provide an example of how to remove duplicate tweets from a text file (Code Sample 3).

In total we collected 61,399,135 unique tweets from across 200 cities, with an average of 306,995 tweets per city and a standard deviation of 91,794. Once the data were collected, we generated a list of tweets that might be relevant examples of our construct. This required isolating the tweets that could potentially pertain to job satisfaction. To do so, we ran a script that goes through every tweet in every city file, and if the word "job" was in the tweet, then the tweet was saved to a separate file containing job tweets.

Apply Judgment to Create a Word Count Dictionary

Now that we had a corpus of potentially relevant text, we needed to further isolate tweets that could pertain to our construct of interest: *job satisfaction*. Due to the large number of unique tweets that contained the word

TABLE 4.2

Two judges' subjective categorization of job-related tweets to identify job satisfaction categories ("Love My Job" and "Hate My Job")

Judge #1 Category	#	Examples	Judge #2 Category	#	Examples
"Job Offer/Ad"	381	We're hiring—Amazing Perks, Constant Learning, Delighted Customers—check out this job PHX Job posting: Female Voice Talent wanted for various commercials (Arizona)	"Job Opening"	393	I'm hiring for this job: CDL Driver—Class A in Tucson, AZ Entry Level Job Opportunities Java /. NET / Python/ Ruby at Tekforce at Fremont, CA, US:
"Want/Looking for Job"	106	I need a job. . . . Or a trust fund . . . Something really praying I get this job	"Job Search"	30	Job hunting it's been 6 years since I had to do this Gonna go turn in my resume and try to get a job now. Byeee.
			"Hoping for Job"	39	I cant wait till i get my job I think I got the job #SoExcited
			"Vocational Interests"	6	Why does the future job I want require me to take such gross classes If true, I wish I would've known. That would've been an amazing job for me.
"News"	53	Florida online job demand hits all-time high Forbes: TX cities clearly the place to be in terms of job creation, wealth formation and overall growth	"News/Article/ Show"	59	How's your job? Detroit's Quicken Loans named top-5 best place to work. 11thstraight year Find out why NFL coordinator Rob Ryan is being denied a head coaching job due to his hair
			"Polls, Surveys"	1	Did Your Job Exist in 1984? [Poll and Infographic] http://t.co/vCkLHRQ9RM via @wonderoftech

(Continued)

TABLE 4.2 (Continued)

Judge #1 Category	#	Examples	Judge #2 Category	#	Examples
"Praise"	133	I have been to Rome They sure did a great job building it in a day Woke up this morning with no hangover, good job me	"Praise"	133	Great Job guys! I was thinking the same thing, they did a great job!
"Love My Job"	20	I really love my job. haha my job is way more respectable than yours.	"Love My Job"	12	I'm really starting to like my job Jk I love my job
			"Love, but. . ."	1	I Love My Job, But I'm Tired Af
"Hate My Job/ Dissatisfaction"	33	I hate my job. I'm not excited to get up in the morning. So sick of my job yo	"Hate My Job"	21	And it's days like this when I hate my job.#snow The thought of someone else telling me what to do and disrespecting me actually makes me nauseous so idk about the whole "job" thing
			"Turnover, Intention Planning"	6	Can't wait to leave my current job yo #Oh @1Lovee_GiAna: I need a really good reason to NOT Quit my job rn!!" ##00t
"Got a Job"	12	yesss! e i finllly got a job! Got my first big girl job! Il b a professional starting January 6th!	"Received a Job"	23	I'm stoked to start my new job today. I GOT THE JOB.
"Bad Job"	5	This Chiefs/Chargers telecast sucks. Terrible production job you are doing a bad job	"Derogatory"	1	You better take advantage of the good cigars. You don't get much else in that job. ~ Thomas P. O'Neill #tcot #tiot #tlot #gop

Category	N	Example
"Sarcastic"	8	These women today work a club like a job. All night in the club & have kids! How are you in the club all night? Who's watchin your kids? The only good thing about that job is that you HAVE TO talk to fine ass people
"Job as Metaphor/ Task"	55	Mess with me? I'll let karma do its job I mean it runs, just gotta get a new paint job & interior
"Job as Task"	26	RT @JayKingzz_: As a 3rd wheel, your job is to take pictures Being tall, handsome, and fit is tough job. but somebody has got to do it!!!
"Wisdom/ Advice/Saying"	26	RT @AprilOSimons: Happiness is an inside job. Bark less. Wag more. Stop letting your job interfere with your week. Look at this . . . you want be sorry!
"Job in General"	32	A man's job is to provide, protect, and be patient with his loved one. You don't deserve anyone the moment you screw up. Fuck that, I'm getting a job and moving out.
"Cursing/Sexual"	21	Ain't nuffin like a good blow job I fck w people who do their job.
"Job as Function"	2	Nyquil isn't doing its job.. :(@EarthPix: The kitten color printer ran out of ink mid job.

(*Continued*)

TABLE 4.2 (Continued)

Judge #1 Category	#	Examples	Judge #2 Category	#	Examples
"Own Job Related"	57	My family has no type of hope that imma have this job for a long time. Casual Fridays at my job	"My Job Description"	8	I feel extremely unqualified at my job. Don't people get degrees in computer science/ statistics to do this stuff???? #help Put some good work into the book this morning, now, time for a workout before the day job. Lovely day in FoCo.
			"Workplace"	10	@Emmz_hearts_Ken I'm gon send u a basket to yo job Just saw mache and jessica at my job awwwhhh I miss the team so much
			"Not Current/ Old Job"	6	I miss my old job low key I knew I should have kept the dss research job man
			"Concerns, Fear of Losing Job"	4	Big news this morning, the company I work for just announced it was merging with another company. Hopefully I can keep my job. #sarcasim101 Just finished my last test! I feel . . . eh . . . about it. But I'm done with this semester! Too bad I won't have a job after friday tho.
			"Objects"	1	RT @SialeGang: Im using the work computer to look for a better job
			"Pros—Cons"	8	Having a job. Being part of a group. Having "coworkers" . . . doing something productive. Being independent. HAVING MONEY. Only downside to this job is the lack of a walk in fridge. My go to cry spot.

Category	n	Example tweets
"Other People's Job"	70	I'm the one you be texting, when you at your job. Everybody has their dream job, its just the plan isn't always their.
"Biblical Figure"	4	Today's reading is: Job 38–39 "Job 1:22In all this, Job did not sin by charging God with wrongdoing.
"Get a Job"	7	Tell her to get a job On the real I feel as if anybody can slang I done did it before, let's see if you can handle getting a real mf job.
"Someone Else's Job"	106	@AdiDewey um. Ok you have a great job @EdCarrillo05 @Lilly_Fresh98 very true. And you're already a freshman, gotta get a job soon if you gonna save uo 10k.
"Proud"	5	We are proud of the work that we do and it shows in every job. There's nothing I dread after 5 beautiful days off more than a closing shift.Well, at least I have a job and it is payday! #blessed
"OCB," "CWB"	2	ll@KirbysLeftEye Same question asked of anyone who doesn't report workplace harassment immediately. Fear of losing job not a small thing. And after I canceled my morning job, almost went online to order other DL I found it in my jeans pocket. #notnice

Note. Results suggest ~1–2% of job-related tweets fall into "Love My Job" category, whereas ~2–3% of job-related tweets fall into "Hate My Job" category.

TABLE 4.3
Job satisfaction dictionary ("Love My Job")

love my work

loving my work

loove my work

looove my work

loooove my work

looooove my work

like my work

appreciate my work

favorite thing about my work

favorite part about my work

best thing about my work

best part about my work

can't complain about my work

my work is chill

my work is more respectable

love my job

loving my job

loove my job

looove my job

loooove my job

looooove my job

like my job

have the best job ever

appreciate my job

favorite thing about my job

favorite part about my job

best thing about my job

best part about my job

cant complain about my job

my job is chill

its an okay job

it is an okay job

good feeling about this job

thankful for this job

doin the job I wanna do in life

doing the job I want to do in life

my job is more respectable

best job Ive ever had

best job I have ever had

TABLE 4.4
Job dissatisfaction dictionary ("Hate My Job")

hate my work

hateeeee my work

hateeee my work

hateee my work

hatee my work

hate my work

h8 my work

going to quit my work

I hate customers

want to quit my work

sick of my work

my work sucks

my work makes me want to strangle

wish I was off today

dread going to my work

I would enjoy my work

I'd enjoy my work

hateeeee working

hateeee working

hateee working

hatee working

hate working

h8 working

(Continued)

TABLE 4.4 (Continued)

hate my job
hateeeee my job
hateeee my job
hateee my job
hatee my job
hate my job
h8 my job
going to quit my job
I hate customers
want to quit my job
wish I had a better paying job
wish I had a better job
this job has ruined
considering quitting this job
I want a fun job

"job" ($N = 301,595$), it would have been extremely time consuming to individually go through all tweets to code whether they directly pertain to the construct. Therefore, we selected a random smaller sample of job tweets to individually inspect. Specifically, we randomly sampled two separate sets of approximately 1,000 job-related tweets from a text file containing all of the tweets mentioning the word "job."

One set of 1,000 tweets was given to judge #1 (the first author) and another set of 1,000 different tweets was given to judge #2 (the third author). These judges then read each of the 1,000 individual tweets and independently attempted to assign them into subjective categories. The result was that both judges created similar categories of tweets (see Table 4.2). Roughly 1%–2% of job-related tweets fell into the "Love My Job" category (for both judges), whereas roughly 2% 3% of job-related tweets fell into the "Hate My Job" category (for both judges). Once the tweets were separated into categories, lists of tweets pertaining to job satisfaction ("Love My Job") and job dissatisfaction ("Hate My Job") were created.[1]

Now with phrases pertaining to job satisfaction and job dissatisfaction identified, an initial dictionary could be constructed using those phrases as templates. Each phrase was examined, and the general structure of the expression was identified and added to the dictionary. This step requires making many subjective decisions because each phrase is unique and no single rule can be applied universally. Rather, the researcher must balance between having the phrase be short enough that it can generalize to other similar sentiments, while having it be long enough that it won't match unrelated sentiments. To make the phrases more general, any statement that said "job" was also duplicated with the word "work" substituted. From this process, a preliminary *job satisfaction* dictionary and *job dissatisfaction* dictionary were created (see Tables 4.3 and 4.4). The job satisfaction dictionary contained 39 unique phrases, and the job dissatisfaction dictionary contained 38 unique phrases. We have now completed the first steps of the word count dictionary building process.

EXAMINE THE RELIABILITY OF THE WORD COUNT DICTIONARIES

Now that our dictionary of phrases is constructed, we can build a script to apply it to text. Similar to Pennebaker's LIWC program previously described, we will build a script that reads in a dictionary text file containing each target phrase on a separate line. Then the script will go through all the day folders and read each file. In each file, it will analyze every line to see if the line contains one of our target phrases. If it does, then the line will receive a score of 1, and if it does not, then it receives a score of 0. The program then repeats the process for the rest of the 200 cities and for the rest of the 29 days. The resulting file will contain 200*29 = 5,800 lines. These 5,800 lines can be transposed into a 200 (cities) × 29 (days) matrix containing the cities as the rows and the days as the columns, with the percentage of tweets matching the dictionary as entries. This matrix will allow us to analyze the dictionary's reliability and validity more easily.

The current approach differs from LIWC, because our scoring system is dichotomous (a tweet either contains the phrase or not), whereas LIWC assigns a percentage score (% of words in the tweet). However, our dictionary relies on using phrases as the unit of analysis, and therefore the text is considered as a whole. The complete script that applies the "Love My Job" and "Hate My Job" dictionary to the collected tweets, and that generates a data matrix, is found in *Appendix A* (Code Sample 4).

To assess reliability, we mentioned that there are two options: test-retest and internal consistency. Pennebaker et al. (2007) noted that, for text analysis, retest reliability is a useful and meaningful index of consistency. To measure test-retest reliability, we need to compute a correlation between

TABLE 4.5

Correlation matrix (city-level of analysis, 200 largest cities in the US)

Variable	M	SD	1	2	3	4	5	6	7	8	9
1. Job Satisfaction (% of tweets that are *Love My Job*)	0.0051	0.0043	—								
2. Job Dissatisfaction (% of tweets that are *Hate My Job*)	0.0057	0.000	0.05	—							
Discriminant Validity Variables											
3. Positive Affect (LIWC; % of words)	5.05	0.36	0.04	0.02	—						
4. Negative Affect (LIWC; % of words)	7.18	0.65	0.05	0.05	0.95*	—					
Frame of Reference Variables											
5. Duncan Socioeconomic Index (DSEI)	43.81	9.63	−0.19*	−0.02	−0.34*	−0.39*	—				
6. Occupational Prestige	37.45	12.48	−0.29*	0.04	−0.16	−0.19*	0.14	—			
7. Unemployment	6.93	1.93	−0.11	0.00	0.29*	0.35*	−0.20*	−0.04	—		
Work Variables											
8. Absenteeism	0.54	0.12	0.05	0.04	−0.13	−0.18*	0.05	0.05	−0.19*	—	
9. Travel Time to Work	22.26	7.11	−0.29*	−0.04	−0.44*	−0.42*	0.32*	0.19*	0.00	−0.02	—
10. Total Tweets	306995.68	92024.98	−0.17*	0.06	−0.37*	−0.41*	0.27*	0.26*	0.02	−0.01	0.50*

* $p < 0.05$. $N = 200$ cities (for job satisfaction, job dissatisfaction, LIWC variables, unemployment, and total tweets). $N = 137$ for IPUMS variables (DSEI, occupational prestige, absenteeism, and travel time).

the dictionary matches a city has on one day to the dictionary matches a city has on another day. As one option, we can load the 200 × 29 matrix into R or another statistics package and compute the correlation matrix directly, specifying each column (i.e., day) as a variable.

If the reliabilities are sufficiently high, then we can take the average of the data points across all days to represent the average level of our construct for that city. From the data that we collected, the city-level average correlation between one day's total and the next was $r = 0.12$ for the job satisfaction "Love My Job" dictionary, and $r = 0.34$ for the job dissatisfaction "Hate My Job" dictionary. We can also compute a measure of internal consistency across days. This involves estimating the standardized Cronbach's alpha, treating each day as a separate item (note that reliability should increase as the number of days in the observation window increases; see Cortina, 1993). The alpha across 29 days of tweets for the job satisfaction dictionary was $\alpha = 0.57$, and the alpha for the job dissatisfaction dictionary was $\alpha = 0.93$.

Thus, the job satisfaction dictionary has a relatively lower reliability compared the dissatisfaction dictionary, but across 29 days, they have reliability that is similar to that of many psychological scales. Therefore, we can take the average percentage of job satisfaction tweets, and of job dissatisfaction tweets, for each city and use those as our measures of city-level job satisfaction and city-level job dissatisfaction. City-level correlations among the variables in the current study are given in Table 4.5.

Convergent and Discriminant Validity

When merged into the same file, we find that the two dictionaries (job satisfaction and job dissatisfaction) are uncorrelated $r = -0.05$ ($p > 0.05$; *n.s.*) Thus, Twitter job satisfaction and Twitter job dissatisfaction seem to represent two distinct constructs and should be examined separately. To further examine the construct validity of the job satisfaction and job dissatisfaction dictionaries, we next identified key constructs that should be conceptually related to each of our measures.

As for discriminant validity (Campbell & Fiske, 1959), we first wanted to demonstrate that our Twitter job satisfaction and job dissatisfaction measures differ from Pennebaker's LIWC measures of positive affect and negative affect, respectively. That is, we wanted to see that our word count measure of job satisfaction correlated far less than 1.0 with Pennebaker's word count measure of positive affect, while our word count measure of job dissatisfaction correlated far less than 1.0 with Pennebaker's word count measure of negative affect. Both of these hypotheses were supported ($r_{jobsat,positiveaffect} = 0.04$; $r_{jobdissat,negativeaffect} = 0.05$; both $p > 0.05$, *n.s.*)

However, these near-zero correlations also fail to support convergent validity for our job satisfaction and job dissatisfaction word count dictionaries. That is, for convergent validity evidence we would have expected a sizeable nonzero relationship between job satisfaction and positive affect, as well as a sizeable nonzero relationship between job dissatisfaction and negative affect—but we found neither. At this point, the convergent validity evidence for our job satisfaction measures is extremely weak.

As an interesting aside, discriminant validity does not appear to be supported between Pennebaker's two LIWC affect measures (i.e., $r_{positiveaffect,negativeaffect} = 0.95$; $p < 0.05$), which raises the possibility that Pennebaker's two LIWC affect measures are actually measuring the same construct, rather than two separate constructs of positive and negative affect. The fact that this near-unity correlation has a positive sign also calls into question the construct validity of Pennebaker's positive and negative affect measures in the current Twitter sample.

Nomological Validity

As for nomological validity, there are five external variables to which we would expect city-level job satisfaction and job dissatisfaction to relate.

Hulin's (1966) frame of reference effect. First, we draw upon the frames of reference explanation for job satisfaction, which says that people's job satisfaction is based in part on how their work-related circumstances compare to the work-related circumstances of others to whom they compare themselves (i.e., the Cornell model; Smith, Hulin, & Kendall, 1969). Compared to other models of job satisfaction, the Cornell model predicts that two people could have the same objective, absolute placement on a variety of work-related factors, but still have differing levels of job satisfaction depending on how well or poorly those around them are doing on those factors. Thus, the Cornell model draws on social comparison theory (Festinger, 1954) suggesting that people's downward or upward comparisons to those around them affect their own perceived job satisfaction. This explanation predicts, for example, that in areas or times with low unemployment, people would be exposed to a large number of job alternatives and peers with jobs, many of which are probably better than the target individual's present position. These circumstances tend to produce upward social comparisons, which can lead people to experience lower job satisfaction with their present position.

Supporting this frame of reference hypothesis, past research finds a negative correlation between community prosperity and job satisfaction (Kendall, 1963). Also, research has found a negative correlation between economic conditions in communities and job satisfaction, and a positive correlation between percentage of sub-standard housing in a community and job satisfaction (Hulin, 1966). In other words, the worse the conditions faced by one's peers, the more satisfied one becomes with her/his own job situation due to the frame of reference effect. This theory would therefore predict a positive correlation between undesirable community character-istics (e.g., unemployment) and job satisfaction, such that people who are around others with poor or no jobs would become more satisfied with the jobs they themselves have. We thus set out to test Hulin's (1966) frame of reference effect, using Twitter data aggregated to the city level of analysis. For this set of hypotheses, we collected data on three city-level variables: socioeconomic status (SES), occupational prestige, and unemployment. We expected the first two variables (SES and occupational prestige) to be negatively related to city-level job satisfaction, while the third variable (unemployment) should be positively related to city-level job satisfaction.

In order to assess SES and occupational prestige at the city level, we used data from the Integrated Public Use Microdata Series (IPUMS) database, which is a publically funded organization that compiles US census data (Ruggles et al., 2010). The census data we used came from the American Community Survey (ACS), which is an ongoing statistical survey by the US Census Bureau sent to approximately 250,000 addresses monthly for a total N of three million per year). It provides individual-level data on a variety of variables, which we aggregated up to the city level. The majority of the IPUMS data used here were collected in 2012. The IPUMS dataset also reports the Duncan sociometric index (DSEI), which is the weighted sum of average occupational education and average occupational income for a city/metro area. For city-level occupational prestige, we used the Siegel occupational prestige score for each participant from the IPUMS data, which we averaged for all participants in the same city to compute city-level occupational prestige. This variable is based upon the series of surveys conducted at National Opinion Research Center during the 1960s. One important note is that only 137 cities in the IPUMS data matched cit-ies from which we had collected Twitter data, so the city-level sample size for IPUMS variables was only $N = 137$.

When we assessed the city-level correlations of both SES and occu-pational prestige with job satisfaction and job dissatisfaction, we found mixed results. Consistent with our hypothesized frame of reference effect, we found statistically significant negative correlations of Twitter job satisfaction with both Duncan SES ($r = -0.19$, p < 0.05) and occupational prestige ($r = -0.29$, p < 0.05). These findings reveal that as community circumstances improve, one's own job satisfaction suffers, as expected (see Hulin, 1966). These negative correlations lend support to the nomological validity of our word count dictionary measure of job satisfaction. On the other hand, our Twitter measure of job dissatisfaction did not correlate with either SES nor occupational prestige ($r = -0.02$, $r = 0.04$; both $p > 0.05$, n.s.), so we do not find evidence of nomological validity for the "Hate My Job" measure of city-level job dissatisfaction.

To collect the unemployment data for each city, we used the Wolfram Alpha API library for Python (Wolfram Alpha, 2015). We provide an example of the code used to collect data from the Wolfram Alpha API in *Appendix A* (Code Sample 5). We then examined the correlation between unemployment at the city-level and our job satisfaction measure. We found a small negative correlation of $r = -0.11$ ($p > 0.05$, n.s.) Thus our data show that cities with higher unemployment rates do not have higher levels of job satisfaction, contrary to our hypothesized frame of reference effect. Likewise, our hypothesized negative relationship between unemployment and job dissatisfaction ("Hate My Job") was not supported either ($r = 0.00$; $p > 0.05$, n.s.)

Work-related variables: Absenteeism and travel time. One construct that meta-analysis shows has a modest individual-level relationship to job satisfaction is how often people are absent from work, or absenteeism (Scott & Taylor, 1985). Specifically, the average uncorrected meta-analytic correlation at the individual level is $r = -0.15$. We also examined self-reported travel time to work, which we expected would relate positively to job dissatisfaction and negatively to job satisfaction. To test these ideas at the city level of analysis, we examined the correlation of each city's measure of job satisfaction and job dissatisfaction from our Twitter dictionaries with the most recent city-level measure of absenteeism and distance to work available to us.

The absenteeism data came from the IPUMS database and were aggregated up to the city level of analysis. For absenteeism, participants were asked to report, "Were you temporarily absent or on layoff from a job or business last week?" Their response options were "N/A," "No," "Yes, laid off," and "Yes, other reason (vacation, illness, labor dispute, etc.)" Because we are only interested in people who miss work intentionally, we only included in our analysis people who indicated in their survey that they were employed and who either said, "No" or "Yes, other reason." People who did not miss work were coded as a 0, and people saying they missed worked were coded as a 1. The IPUMS data also contained a variable related to travel time to work. Participants were asked, "How many minutes did it usually take you to get from home to work LAST WEEK?" Answers were given in terms of minutes and did not need to be recoded.

We then computed the average of the responses for each city in the IPUMS data file using the city where the participant reported working. We entered these city-level averages of absenteeism and transit time into the data file containing the city-level averages of Twitter job satisfaction and dissatisfaction. The correlation between absenteeism and our measure of job satisfaction was $r = 0.05$, and the correlation with our measure of job dissatisfaction was $r = 0.04$ (both $p > 0.05$, *n.s.*) Therefore, we did not find nomological validity evidence for our job satisfaction and job dissatisfaction word count dictionaries when inspecting the absenteeism correlations. Likewise, the correlation between our measure of job dissatisfaction and transit time was only $r = -0.04$ ($p > 0.05$, *n.s.*) In contrast, the correlation between job satisfaction and transit time at the city-level was $r = -0.29$ ($p < 0.05$), which confirmed our hypothesis that longer transit times would impair job satisfaction, thus lending support to the nomological validity of the Twitter job satisfaction measure.

In sum, our nomological validity results provided some support for the Twitter-based measure of job satisfaction (i.e., negative correlations with city-level SES, occupational prestige, and travel time to work; as expected). However, no support was found for the expected correlations of city-level job satisfaction with unemployment and absenteeism, and no support whatsoever was found for the nomological validity of the job dissatisfaction word count dictionary, with regard to either frame of reference variables (SES, occupational prestige, unemployment) or work-related variables (absenteeism, travel time to work). The null results for job dissatisfaction might be due in part to the extremely low variance between cities for the Twitter job dissatisfaction measure (SD = 0.000; see Table 4.5).

Spatial Network Autocorrelation

To examine whether people's expressions of positivity and negativity toward their jobs (at the city-level) are similar to the expressions found in nearby cities, we can use the spatial autocorrelation statistic Moran's I (Moran, 1950). Moran's I evaluates whether the observed data are clustered in some spatial area, and this statistic is often used in geographic and social network analyses.

To elaborate, Moran's I is like a Pearson correlation between individual actors' scores and the average scores across each actor's neighbors, where each neighbor's score is weighted by that neighbor's distance from the focal actor. Thus, in the current study, Moran's I tells us the correlation between a city's job satisfaction and the job satisfaction of nearby cities (i.e., spatial autocorrelation). Moran's I varies from −1 to +1 and is negative when dissimilar values (job satisfaction levels) occur near one another. Positive Moran's I indicates similar job satisfaction values occurring near one another. A Moran's I of 0 is the null hypothesis and suggests spatial randomness of the dependent variable.

For our current data, we already had geographic coordinates for each city, as those were used in the geolocation parameter for the Twitter search. These geographic coordinates were represented in decimal format, where the first number indicates the longitude and the second number the latitude. Because the US is west of the Greenwich prime meridian and north of the equator (i.e., the point of 0 longitude and 0 latitude), the longitudes were all negative numbers and the latitudes were all positive. With these latitude and longitude values entered as two separate columns in a data file, we applied the dist function in R, which computes the Euclidean distance between pairs of cities (as the crow flies) to produce a city × city proximity matrix of distances. This similarity matrix was entered as the weight matrix for the Moran's I routine using the spdep R package (Bivand et. al., 2005). We conducted two separate calculations of Moran's I at the city-level—one for the average percentage of

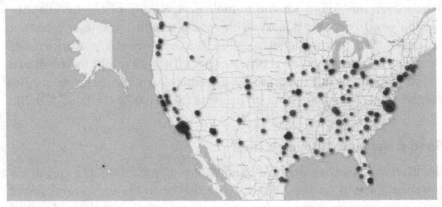

Note. The sizes of the circles represent the proportion of all tweets that were job satisfaction (e.g., "Love My Job") tweets for that city.

FIGURE 4.2
Average job satisfaction for the 200 most populated cities in the US.

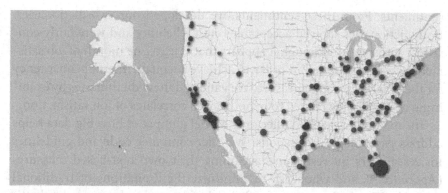

Note. The sizes of the circles represent the proportion of all tweets that were job dissatisfaction (e.g., "Hate My Job") tweets for that city.

FIGURE 4.3
Average job dissatisfaction for the 200 most populated cities in the US.

tweets that were job satisfaction tweets, and one for the average percentage of tweets that were job dissatisfaction tweets.

For job satisfaction, Moran's I = −0.02 ($p > 0.05$, *n.s.*), which means there was no appreciable spatial autocorrelation for city-level job satisfaction (see Figure 4.2). For job dissatisfaction, Moran's I = 0.20 ($p < 0.05$), which means that cities with higher job dissatisfaction tended to have nearby cities that also exhibited higher job dissatisfaction. In other words, city-level job dissatisfaction exhibits spatial clustering, suggesting that a dissatisfied city tends to be nearby to other dissatisfied cities (see Figure 4.3).

SUMMARY

In this chapter we described how big data can benefit psychological research. Specifically, it allows us to get a different perspective on already existing problems, while also providing a larger amount of information than is commonly garnered via traditional methods, making it well-suited to research questions involving higher levels of analysis and longer time frames. Massive text-based sources, such as Twitter, are able to be analyzed with computational word count methods. This automated content analysis has the potential to provide insight into people's attitudes. To demonstrate, we developed both a job satisfaction and a job dissatisfaction word count dictionary for computerized content analyses.

Using a sample of tweets collected from the 200 most populous cities in the United States, we extracted positive and negative work-related sentiments. From these sentiments, we developed our two dictionaries. Both dictionaries showed acceptable retest reliability and were fairly consistent across days, although it appears that at least one month of job satisfaction tweets is needed in order to achieve adequate internal consistency for the time-aggregated measure. We validated these dictionaries by examining how well they related to hypothesized correlates of job satisfaction.

The methods discussed offer only a brief glimpse at how big data helps address psychological questions. We offer computer code and guidelines for researchers interested in developing their own text-based measures (*Appendix A*) and who wish to minimize the limitations of traditional methods. Many other ways of utilizing big data to study macro-level attitudes and behavior exist, and more methods are being developed every day. The current work seeks to underscore the importance of learning how to utilize the potential of massive datasets in order to answer macro-level research questions that were not previously feasible to ask.

NOTE

1. Our phrase dictionary approach to measuring job satisfaction efficiently and accurately is only one of the many options available to researchers. *Supervised machine learning* routines are another method researchers can use to automatically identify tweets relevant to a construct (e.g., job satisfaction). We describe the machine learning approach in more detail (and contrast it to our phrase dictionary method) in *Appendix B*.

REFERENCES

Alexa (2013). Retrieved from http://www.alexa.com/siteinfo/twitter.com

Allen, M. J., & Yen, W. M. (2002). *Introduction to measurement theory*. Prospect Heights, IL: Waveland Press.

Arnett, J. J. (2008). The neglected 95%: Why American psychology needs to become less American. *American Psychologist, 63*(7), 602–614.

Bertamini, M., & Munafò, M. R. (2012). Bite-size science and its undesired side effects. *Perspectives on Psychological Science, 7*(1), 67–71.

Bivand, R., Bernat, A., Carvalho, M., Chun, Y., Dormann, C., Dray, S., . . . & Sparse, M. S. (2005). The spdep package. *Comprehensive R Archive Network*, version 0.3–13.

Campbell, D. T., & Fiske, D. W. (1959). Convergent and discriminant validation by the multitrait-multimethod matrix. *Psychological Bulletin, 56*, 81.

Cohen, D. (1996). Law, social policy, and violence: The impact of regional cultures. *Journal of Personality and Social Psychology, 70*, 961.

Cohen, D. (1998). Culture, social organization, and patterns of violence. *Journal of Personality and Social Psychology, 75*, 408.

Cohen, J. (1992). A power primer. *Psychological Bulletin, 112*(1), 155.

Cortina, J. M. (1993). What is coefficient alpha? An examination of theory and applications. *Journal of Applied Psychology, 78*(1), 98.

Cronbach, L. J., & Meehl, P. E. (1955). Construct validity in psychological tests. *Psychological Bulletin, 52*(4), 281.

Dean, J., & Ghemawat, S. (2008). MapReduce: simplified data processing on large clusters. *Communications of the ACM, 51*(1), 107–113.

Festinger, L. (1954). A theory of social comparison processes. *Human Relations, 7*(2), 117–140.

Fraley, R. C., & Vazire, S. (2014). The N-pact factor: Evaluating the quality of empirical journals with respect to sample size and statistical power. *PLoS ONE, 9*(10).

Francis, W. N., & Kurcera, H. (1982). *Frequency analysis of English usage: Lexicon and grammar.* Boston, MA: Houghton Mifflin.

Gallander Wintre, M., North, C., & Sugar, L. A. (2001). Psychologists' response to criticisms about research based on undergraduate participants: A developmental perspective. *Canadian Psychology/Psychologie Canadienne, 42*(3), 216.

Gosling, S. D., Vazire, S., Srivastava, S., & John, O. P. (2004). Should we trust Web-based studies? A comparative analysis of six preconceptions about Internet questionnaires. *American Psychologist, 59*, 93–104.

Harrington, J. R., & Gelfand, M. J. (2014). Tightness–looseness across the 50 United States. *Proceedings of the National Academy of Sciences, 111*, 7990–7995.

Harrison, D. A., & Martocchio, J. J. (1998). Time for absenteeism: A 20-year review of origins, offshoots, and outcomes. *Journal of Management, 24*(3), 305–350.

Henrich, J., Heine, S. J., & Norenzayan, A. (2010). The weirdest people in the world? *Behavioral and Brain Sciences, 33*(2–3), 61–83.

Hulin, C. L. (1966). The effects of community characteristics on measures of job satisfaction. *Journal of Applied Psychology, 50*, 185–192.

Ireland, M. E., Slatcher, R. B., Eastwick, P. W., Scissors, L. E., Finkel, E. J., & Pennebaker, J. W. (2011). Language style matching predicts relationship initiation and stability. *Psychological Science, 22*(1), 39–44.

ITouchMap (2007). Latitude and longitude of a point. Retrieved from http://itouchmap.com

Kelly, J. R. (1988). *On time and method.* Newbury Park, CA: Sage Publications.

Kendall, L. M. (1963). *Canonical analysis of job satisfaction and behavioral, personal background, and situational data* (Unpublished doctoral dissertation). Cornell University, Ithaca, NY.

Kozlowski, S. W., & Klein, K. J. (2000). A multilevel approach to theory and research in organizations: Contextual, temporal, and emergent processes.

Laney, D. (2001). 3D data management: Controlling data volume, velocity and variety. *META Group Research Note.*

Lazer, D., Pentland, A. S., Adamic, L., Aral, S., Barabasi, A. L., Brewer, D., . . . & Van Alstyne, M. (2009). Life in the network: The coming age of computational social science. *Science, 323*(5915), 721.

McGrath, R. (2012). Twython 2.5.4. Retrieved from http://pypi.python.org/pypi/twython/

Mitchell, T. R., & James, L. R. (2001). Building better theory: Time and the specification of when things happen. *Academy of Management Review, 26*(4), 530–547.

Moran, P. A. P. (1950). Notes on continuous stochastic phenomena. *Biometrika, 37*, 17–23.

Newman, D. A. (2003). Longitudinal modeling with randomly and systematically missing data: A simulation of ad hoc, maximum likelihood, and multiple imputation techniques. *Organizational Research Methods, 6*, 328–362.

Newman, D.A. (2014). Missing data: Five practical guidelines. *Organizational Research Methods, 17*(4), 372–411.

Newman, D.A., & Cottrell, J.M. (in press). Missing data bias: Exactly how bad is pairwise deletion? In C.E. Lance & R.J. Vandenberg (Eds.), *More statistical and methodological myths and urban legends.* New York, NY: Routledge.

Ostroff, C. (1993). The effects of climate and personal influences on individual behavior and attitudes in organizations. *Organizational Behavior and Human Decision Processes, 56*(1), 56–90.

Pennebaker, J.W. (2011). The secret life of pronouns. *New Scientist, 211,* 42–45.

Pennebaker, J.W., Chung, C.K., Ireland, M., Gonzales, A., & Booth, R.J. (2007). The development and psychometric properties of LIWC2007. Austin, TX: LIWC.

Pennebaker, J.W., Francis, M.E., & Booth, R.J. (2001). Linguistic inquiry and word count: LIWC 2001. Mahway, NJ: Lawrence Erlbaum Associates.

Peterson, R.A. (2001). On the use of college students in social science research: Insights from a second-order meta-analysis. *Journal of Consumer Research, 28*(3), 450–461.

Rentfrow, P.J., Gosling, S.D., Jokela, M., Stillwell, D.J., Kosinski, M., & Potter, J. (2013). Divided we stand: Three psychological regions of the United States and their political, economic, social, and health correlates. *Journal of Personality and Social Psychology, 105,* 996–1012.

Richard, F.D., Bond, C.F., & Stokes-Zoota, J.J. (2003). One hundred years of social psychology quantitatively described. *Review of General Psychology, 7*(4), 331–363.

Ritter, R.S., Preston, J.L., & Hernandez, I. (2014). Happy tweets: Christians are happier, more socially connected, and less analytical than atheists on Twitter. *Social Psychological and Personality Science, 5*(2), 243–249.

Robinson, W. (1950). Ecological correlations and the behavior of individuals. *American Sociological Review, 15*(3), 351–357.

Rude, S., Gortner, E.M., & Pennebaker, J. (2004). Language use of depressed and depression-vulnerable college students. *Cognition & Emotion, 18*(8), 1121–1133.

Ruggles S., Alexander, J.T., Genadek, K., Goeken, R., Schroeder, M.B., & Sobek, M. (2010). *Integrated public use microdata series: Version 5.0.* Minneapolis, MN: University of Minnesota.Schafer, J.L., & Graham, J.W. (2002). Missing data: Our view of the state of the art. *Psychological Methods, 7*(2), 147.

Schamber, L. (2000). Time-line interviews and inductive content analysis: Their effectiveness for exploring cognitive behaviors. *Journal of the American Society for Information Science, 51,* 734–744.

Schmidt, F.L., Hunter, J.E., McKenzie, R.C., & Muldrow, T.W. (1979). Impact of valid selection procedures on work-force productivity. *Journal of Applied Psychology, 64*(6), 609.

Scott, K.D., & Taylor, G.S. (1985). An examination of conflicting findings on the relationship between job satisfaction and absenteeism: A meta-analysis. *Academy of Management Journal, 28*(3), 599–612.

Simonsohn, U. (2015). Small telescopes: Detectability and the evaluation of replication results. *Psychological Science, 26(5),* 559-569.

Smith, P.C., Kendall, L.M., & Hulin, C.L. (1969) *The measurement of satisfaction in work and retirement.* Chicago, IL: Rand McNally.

Wikipedia (2012). List of United States cities by population. Retrieved from http://en.wikipedia.org/wiki/List_of_United_States_cities_by_population

Weber, R.P. (1990). *Basic content analysis.* Beverly Hills, CA: Sage.

APPENDIX A

Data Collection Details and Code Samples

Before we delve into the example, we briefly mention how data collection and filtering are done for Twitter data. Collection of data through social media usually happens through API access. Rather than trying to configure a script to download and parse the needed information directly from many different webpages (e.g., scraping), an API is a specification of remote calls that a server (e.g., Twitter) documents so that developers can request information to be sent to an application (e.g., a smartphone application, a web browser, a computer program). After a developer sends a request, the Twitter API returns the information requested in JavaScript Object Notation (JSON) containing the tweet and the parameters associated with each tweet (e.g., username of the author, date created, location, number of retweets, etc.) The Python language can read the returned JSON and save the various pieces of information as objects that the user can access in a programming language (e.g., strings, integers, Boolean). This process is similar to how a web browser sends a request (e.g., an address) to a website, the server of which then returns the information requested in hypertext markup language (HTML) that a web browser can then parse into something meaningful for the end-user. For our purposes, the Python programming language serves as the browser, and the Twitter API serves as the website server.

One API option is to use the streaming API (i.e., the "firehose"), which provides a real-time sample of all tweets and is indifferent to location. Using the streaming API in this way provides quasi-random sampling of 1% of all tweets sent from the population at a given point in time, but the sampling is still potentially nonrandom with regard to the time of day (e.g., if all tweets are collected in the morning, they might not generalize to the afternoon). One solution to this is to collect the Twitter data continuously for many days—although even this alternative does not offer random sampling with regard to time of year (e.g., the current data collection took place over 29 days at the end of the year, which included the winter holiday period). Another option is to use the Twitter representational state transfer (REST) API, which allows developers to search information (e.g., tweets that users have made publicly visible) matching a set of parameters. Compared to the streaming API, the REST API has more restrictions. Developers interested in using Twitter's APIs must register on the Twitter developer website (https://dev.twitter.com/) to receive an access token. This access token has a request limit of 180 requests for each 15-minute interval for the REST API. When a developer submits a query to the API, the account associated with the access token has her/his request limit reduced by one for the next 15 minutes. After all 180 requests have been used in a single 15-minute window, the Twitter API no longer returns requests until the 15 minutes have elapsed, restarting the request limit for that user. Therefore, this API is best suited for researchers who have a predetermined target population and want to filter out users outside of that population at the time of collection. Despite these limits, there are various options researchers have to mitigate them. If collaborating with another author with a separate IP address, the two could each set up their own account on a respective computer/server, and then each collect an independent set of tweets. After a pre-determined stopping point, the authors would combine their files to a single drive and have their data processing scripts refer to both files. Any potential duplicate tweets can be removed later.

For this project, because we wanted tweets from specific cities (and hence location is important), we used the Twitter REST API version 1.1 (rather than the streaming API). The REST API is better suited for the goals of the current project because it is able to return tweets that originated from specific regions of the US and therefore will provide a larger sample of users in each specific area compared to what the streaming API could provide. The REST API accepts latitude and longitude coordinates and a maximum search radius. It then returns the 100 most recent tweets from the time of the request (although the 100 most retweeted tweets can also be returned if requested) that are within that radius. To determine the user's location, Twitter first queries users who have voluntarily enabled their exact location to be displayed with their tweets. It then queries users based on their profile location information. When the user makes another API request, Twitter returns the 100 most recent tweets again from the time the second request was made. If that location has not made 100 new tweets within the past 15 minutes, then there will be overlap between the tweets returned from newest request and the previous request. Thus it is important to save the unique tweet information so that duplicate entries can be later removed by the user before analysis. For our project, we sent hypertext transfer protocol (HTTP) get requests, with the relevant location parameters (using the Python programming language) to the Twitter application programming interface (API).

Our study design examines 200 US cities. Querying the 100 most recent tweets from a city counts as one API request. Because the API limit is 180 requests per 15-minute interval, we queried the 100 most recent Tweets with a 15 km radius (the suggested default radius on the REST API) from the city's latitude and longitude coordinates for 180 cities. After 15 minutes had passed, we queried the remaining 20 cities, plus 160 randomly selected cities. Then after 15 minutes had elapsed again, the 20 cities not queried in the previous sample were queried as well as 160 randomly selected cities. This sampling process ensures that the maximum difference in number of queries between cities will only be one, and the maximum difference in time between city queries is 15 minutes.

Nonetheless, our inferences are naturally limited to only those individuals who used Twitter during the time period we sampled, who had also enabled Twitter to know their location, and who were within 15 kilometers of the city center. As such, to the extent that Twitter usage/nonusage is correlated with variables in the current study (e.g., job satisfaction), we would expect some degree of missing data bias (Newman, 2014; Newman & Cottrell, 2015). More information about the REST API can be found in their developer documentation.[1]

Code Sample 1: Python code to connect to Twitter API using the Twython library, search for English tweets containing the phrase "big data" within a geographic location, an saves the results to the text file

```
from twython import Twython, TwythonError
APP_KEY="Enter APP KEY HERE"
APP_SECRET="ENTER APP SECRET ID HERE"
Access_TOKEN="ENTER YOUR TWITTER ACCESS TOKEN HERE"
Access_TOKEN_SECRET="ENTER YOUR TWITTER ACCESS
TOKEN SECRET HERE"
twitter = Twython(APP_KEY,APP_SECRET,ACCESS_
TOKEN,ACCESS_TOKEN_SECRET)
search_results=twitter.search(q="BigData",geoc
ode="36.77,-119.4,15km",lang="en")
with open("tweets.txt", "ab") as f:
    for tweet in search_results['statuses']:
        message=tweet['text'].encode
        ('ascii', 'ignore')
        f.write(str(message)+"\n")
```

The first line loads the Twython library into Python. The next four lines are the personal access information you receive from Twitter when you sign up for a developer's account. These keys can be found by logging into your Twitter developer account at https://apps.twitter.com/ and then clicking on your application. From there, click on the "API Keys" tab and you will see all of the information needed. The next line creates a Twython object called "twitter". This object contains your login information and establishes a connection to the Twitter site. The following line uses the search feature of the Twython object and searches for the phrase "big data" used in tweets in the English language within a 15km radius of latitude 36.77 and longitude –119.4. The lines below it open an output file (tweets.txt) for editing, and then go through the returned tweets and write the message content onto a new line in the file.

Code Sample 2: Python code to merge files collected from two separate servers into a single file for each day and city

```
import glob
import os
day=1
while day < 31:
    os.chdir("computer1")
    os.chdir("day"+str(day))
    for file in glob.glob("*.txt"):
            lines_computer1 = open(file,"rb").
            readlines()
            os.chdir("..")
            os.chdir("computer2")
            os.chdir("day"+str(day))
            lines_computer2 = open(file,"rb").
            readlines()
            unique_lines_total=set(lines_
            computer1+lines_computer2)
            os.chdir("..")
            os.makedirs("day"+str(day))
            open(str(file),"ab").
            writelines(unique_lines_total)
    day+=1
```

This script assumes that you have a text file for each city (i.e., 200 text files) saved in folders with the names "day1", "day2", . . ., "day30". It also assumes that those day folders for each computer are saved within another folder specifying the computer where the data originate (e.g., "computer1", "computer2"). For each day, the script goes into each computer's folder and extracts all of the text files for that day from every city's individual file. It then copies the information from a text file with the same name as that city's file and saves that file into a new folder with the same day name in the highest level directory (i.e., the one containing the two separate computer folders). Now you should have a set of folders in the directory where the above script was run equal to the number of days collected.

Code Sample 3: Python code to remove duplicate tweets from a text file

```
import glob
import os
day=1
while day < 31:
        os.chdir("day"+str(day))
        for file in glob.glob("*.txt"):
                uniquelines = open(file,"rb").
                readlines()
                unique_lines_total=set
                (uniquelines)
        os.chdir("..")
        os.makedirs("day_unique"+str
        (day))open(str(file),"ab").
        writelines(unique_lines_total)
        day+=1
```

This script assumes that you have 30 folders (one for each day) named in the following format: "day1", "day2", . . ., "day30". Within those folders are text files containing the tweets for each city (each tweet on a unique line). The script goes into each day's folder, and then for every city's text file, reads the lines, eliminates the duplicates, and makes a new folder to save a city file containing only the unique lines.

Code Sample 4: Python code to create a 200 [city] × 29 [day] data matrix containing each city's rate of "Love My Job" and "Hate My Job" dictionary matches for each day.

```
import re, os, numpy, glob
keywords = [line.strip() for line in
open("lovemyjobdic.txt","rb")]
keywords_re = re.compile(r'\b(' + r'|'.
join(keywords) + r')\b\s*', re.IGNORECASE)
```

```
adverbs = [line.strip() for line in open("adverbs.
txt","rb")]
adverb_re = re.compile(r'\b(' + r'|'.join(adverbs)
+ r')\b\s*', re.IGNORECASE)
data_matrix=[]
daynumber = 1
while daynumber < 30:
        os.chdir("day"+str(daynumber))for  city  in
        glob.glob("*.txt"):
        print city
        linecount=0
        phrasecount=0
        with open(str(city),"rb") as file:
                for line in file:
                        text=line.strip().lower()
                        text = re.sub(r'([^\s\w^\#]|_)+
                        ', ", text)
                        text = adverb_re.sub(", text)
                        if keywords_re.search(line):
                                phrasecount+=1
                                linecount+=1
                try:data_matrix.append(phrasecount/
                linecount)
                except:data_matrix.append(0)daynumber+=1
        os.chdir("..")
data_matrix=numpy.asmatrix(data_matrix).
reshape(200,30).T
np.savetxt("data_matrix.txt",data_matrix)
```

This script loads a file containing the target phrases or keywords (each phrase on a new line). All of the statements are saved into a regular expression object called "keywords" that will be used to match phrases in the tweet files. Next, the program opens a file containing a list of common adverbs. These adverbs are used to filter out unnecessary words and make it more likely that our dictionary will match. For example, a person saying "I really love my job" would have the adverb "really" removed, and so their phrase "I love my job" would be matched by the dictionary. After loading the dictionaries, the program opens the folder with the first day number (e.g., "day1"). In that folder, it finds all of the files with a. txt extension. Each of these text files should be named after the city whose tweets it contains. It then goes through each file and reads it one line at a time. Each line is searched for the relevant keywords. If it contains one of the keywords, a match is recorded for that city by incrementing the variable "phrasecount" by 1. After each line, the variable "linecount" is incremented by one. After the city's file is read, the program goes back to the original directory and writes that city's information (e.g., city name, day, number of lines, number of matches) to a text file.

Code Sample 5: Python code to collect unemployment data for each city using the Wolfram Alpha API

```
import wolframalpha
unemployment=[]
with open("city_list.txt", "rb") as cities:
for city in cities:
client = wolframalpha.Client("Wolfram ID Goes
here")
res = client.query('unemployment in '+city)
result = next(res.results).text
unemployment.append(result.split("%")[0])
with open("unemployment_rates.txt","ab") as f:
for rate in unemployment: f.write(str(rate)+"\n")
```

This script loads the Wolfram Alpha library for Python. It then creates an empty array to save the data (i.e., "unemployment"), and opens a text file containing all 200 city names (each on a new line). Next, for each city in the text file, it connects to the API using the user's login information and then submits a search to Wolfram Alpha for each city's unemployment rate. The information is then added to the unemployment array. Once the searches are complete, it saves the information in the unemployment array to a text file. We then can read that text file and merge its content into the job satisfaction data frame.

NOTE

1. Here are the sources where Twitter provides the technical information. They all originate from the same documentation manual (https://dev.twitter.com/docs), but the page has different chapters and sections specific to the points addressed above.

https://dev.twitter.com/docs/api/1.1/get/search/tweets
https://dev.twitter.com/docs/rate-limiting/1.1
https://dev.twitter.com/docs/api
https://dev.twitter.com/terms/geo-developer-guidelines

APPENDIX B

Machine Learning Approaches

For the current project, we chose to use a phrase-based dictionary approach for identifying tweets pertaining to job satisfaction and job dissatisfaction. However, an alternative method for identifying tweets relevant to a particular construct or category would be to use a *supervised machine learning algorithm*. Supervised machine learning is used to discover a black box function that predicts an outcome or category (e.g., "Love My Job" tweet) for the given input (e.g., a data matrix), by training a model (i.e., producing an optimal series of weights, rules, and functions on the features of the matrix; see Mohri, Rostamizadeh, & Talwalkar, 2012). The input is typically a matrix containing a set of observations (e.g., one row for each tweet) with values for a variety of features (e.g., one column for each particular word) and a column vector of predetermined outcomes or categories (e.g., "Love My Job" tweet, "Hate My Job" tweet, neutral tweet) associated with each observation. From these data, a model is trained to determine a function or functions that contain the best weighting of the features, which can then be used to predict the outcome or category of each tweet in a new dataset containing observations (tweets) and features (particular words). Some examples of this approach would be training a model to predict if a person has breast cancer (e.g., yes or no) based on the characteristics of the cells (e.g., smoothness, radius, area, symmetry; see Street, Wolberg, & Mangarasrian, 1994) or classifying a gray scale image into an alphabet letter (e.g., A, B, C, D, etc.) based on the statistical properties (e.g., mean, skewness, kurtosis) of the gray scale values in an image (Frey & Slate, 1991). By quantifying the data's characteristics, researchers can use machine learning to train a model based on the presence or absence of those characteristics to predict a category pertaining to the text (e.g., speaker, topic, readability). The following section describes the specific steps in applying machine learning to text.

TEXT CLASSIFICATION WITH MACHINE LEARNING

Machine learning algorithms allow researchers to take the features of a sample of text and predict an outcome or category related to that text. Given the unstructured nature of text data (i.e., the data have an open-ended format with varying lengths and characters), researchers have a variety of options for what features to use in the model. They could use sentence length, tense, part of speech, or dozens or other features. One of the most common choices is using the words themselves as the features to predict the category of a piece of text (Salton & MacGill, 1983). Specifically, researchers will represent their data as a two-dimensional document by term matrix, where each document or sample of text (e.g., a tweet) is a row in the matrix, and the column values for that row indicate how often a specific feature (e.g., word) associated with that column is present in the document (i.e., tweet). This vector-space representation of documents, where each document has a row vector of word counts disregarding word order, is also known as the bag-of-words model (Harris, 1954). In practice, to generate this matrix, a researcher starts with a vocabulary list of possible words (e.g., all words in the English language, all unique words in the corpus) and creates an empty matrix with as many columns are there are words in the vocabulary list and as many rows as there are documents. Then, for every document, a computer counts the number of instances of each word and increments the count in the column associated with that word. Once the researcher has a document by term matrix (e.g., a tweets by specific words matrix), and a predetermined coding of which category each row in the matrix has been assigned to (e.g., whether each tweet was assigned to the "Love My Job" category, the "Hate My Job" category, or the neutral category), then the machine learning algorithm attempts to find an optimal weighting for each feature (word) that can predict the category ("Love My job") using a specific function. For comparison, logistic regression is a simple example of such a function for which the function is linear and there are two outcome categories. A popular category or outcome to predict with text is sentiment or evaluation (e.g., whether an individual likes a movie; see Pang, Lee, & Vaithyanathan, 2002). That is, researchers can train a model to take a sample of text and predict whether it expresses a positive or negative sentiment or attitude. This classification task is similar to our current study where we are interested in one's sentiment toward her/his own job. Different algorithms exist for classifying sentiment based on text features such naïve Bayes, support vector machines, and maximum entropy; however, prior research on tweets suggests that these algorithms all perform similarly (accuracy rates within 2% of each other; see Go, Bhayani, & Huang, 2009). Given the similar performance between algorithms, to address the current question of how our job satisfaction and dissatisfaction phrase dictionary approach compares to tweet classification using a machine learning approach, we chose to use a naïve

Bayes classifier, which is one of the most commonly used choices for text classification (Manning & Schutze, 1999).

NAÏVE BAYES CLASSIFIERS AND TEXT

A naïve Bayes classifier uses the observed likelihood of an outcome occurring in the presence of a word (e.g., "love" is present in 2% of all job satisfaction tweets, but only 0.01% in all other job-related tweets), as well as the prior probability (i.e., base rate) of an outcome (e.g., only 8% of job-related tweets pertain to job satisfaction), to determine the posterior probability of category membership (i.e., if a tweet contains words "love", "my", and "job", what is the probability of this tweet belonging to the subjectively coded "job satisfaction" category?) It assumes that all features are independent from each other. In other words, each feature's weight is set without considering the weights of other features. Thus, a researcher must first specify all the words that could be encountered in a text as part of training the model. Training a naïve Bayes classifier is a two-step procedure where the text is first processed to generate a dictionary of all words, and then processed again to determine the likelihood of each word occurring for each outcome (e.g., the likelihood of the word "love" appearing in the "Love My Job" category of tweets). There are also advanced options a researcher can use to improve the performance of these classifiers. Because the simplest form of the naïve Bayes classifier uses a bag-of-words model, this model disregards the order of words. However, for some topics such as sentiment, the word order can be important for detecting the topic (e.g., "you love" versus "love you"). To address this limitation, bi-grams (i.e., two-word sequences) can also be treated as features in addition to the individual words, and every single two-word combination would also get a unique column in the tweets × word counts matrix. Additionally, because some words or bi-grams may only occur for one category in the entire training corpus, it would make the feature seem overly important at discriminating between categories. Thus researchers can also add counts to each category (known as Laplace/additive smoothing) so that all features occur at least once for each category. Similarly, researchers can choose to exclude features that do not occur a given number of times, to exclude stop words (e.g., "is", "the", "a", "as"), or to use word stems (e.g., "love", "loves", and "loved" all are considered as "love") because the difference between categories for those features is not theoretically meaningful. Another technique used to improve the performance of naïve Bayes classifiers is taking into account the part of speech for the word. That is, a word like "love" can be both a noun and a verb, each with differing abilities to predict an outcome (e.g., "love", the verb, predicts positive sentiment, but "love", the noun, does not). Therefore, by treating each word and associated part of speech as a separate feature, the researcher generates a much larger but nuanced feature list. Whereas a researcher can code her or his own naïve Bayes classifier with any programming or scripting language, a variety of software exist to simplify the process.

NAÏVE BAYES PERFORMANCE IN THE CURRENT PROJECT

We used the machine learning software WEKA (Waikato Environment for Knowledge Analysis; see Hall, Frank, Holmes, Pfahringer, Reutemann, & Witten, 2009) to construct the naïve Bayes classifier. This software automates the process of creating a word dictionary, extracting the likelihood of each word feature for the outcomes or categories and prior probabilities (e.g., the base rate for the "Love My Job" category of tweets among all job-related tweets).

The training data were the same set of job-related tweets described previously (i.e., that the first and third authors coded into Love My Job, Hate My Job, and neutral categories), which were used to construct the job satisfaction and dissatisfaction dictionaries. Specifically, the program provided a comma separated value (.csv) file with the categories in the first column (i.e., job satisfaction, job neutral, and job dissatisfaction) and the tweet text (with commas removed) in the second column. We specified a model with an exhaustive feature list with bi-grams, part-of-speech unigrams, and stemmed words then eliminated stop words and removed features that did not occur at least five times across all of the tweets. This model contains as many features as possible, and therefore the results will likely overestimate the performance of the model when cross-validated against another dataset (similar to validity shrinkage in a regression model). We used as many features as possible to provide an upper-bound estimate of the model's performance. The program then trained a model using the probabilities of the features and the prior probabilities of the categories. We then examined what the best-case performance of the trained model is by cross-validating against the same text used to train it. During this model validation, the program is given a selection of text and then assigns a probability to each topic using the probabilities from the trained model. The topic with the highest probability was recorded as the predicted topic, and these predicted values were then compared against the actual topics to assess the model's performance (see the confusion matrix in Table 4.B2 for full results).

To assess the performance of the model, we used five common benchmarks for classification tasks: accuracy, precision, specificity, negative predictive value, and sensitivity (Fawcett, 2006). Because these benchmarks are typically used for binary classifications, each outcome and category was examined separately. Each metric takes into account a combination of number of correct classifications (i.e., true positives), correct rejections (i.e., true negatives), incorrect classifications (i.e., false positives), and incorrect rejections (i.e., false negatives). These metrics are described in greater detail in Table 4.B1.

The accuracy levels for the tweet topics of job satisfaction, dissatisfaction, and neutral were all high (76.74%, 71.37%, and 73.28%, respectively). These values indicate that the model will usually make the correct choice of topic. Although the accuracy level is high, it does not necessarily mean that the model is suitable for identifying job satisfaction and dissatisfaction tweets. This metric does not take into account whether the model was better for correctly classifying versus correctly rejecting a given topic because the two are confounded in the equation. Even with high accuracy, the model may not be particularly informative or discriminating. For example, in the current dataset, the large majority of tweets mentioning the word "job" are unrelated to job satisfaction or dissatisfaction. By simply guessing that all tweets are not about job satisfaction, the model would have accuracy levels for the tweet topics of job satisfaction, dissatisfaction, and neutral of 98.15%, 95.03%, and 96.88%, respectively. Therefore, it is important to examine the four other metrics, which describe the model's performance for classifications and rejections of each topic.

Both precision and sensitivity relate to the model's performance at positive identification. The model showed high precision only for the neutral job tweets (99.09%), while job satisfaction (4.38%) and job dissatisfaction (9.94%) showed substantially lower performance. These values indicate that if the model were used to determine which tweets were related to job satisfaction, only 4.38% of the tweets identified would actually be related to job satisfaction, marginally better than what would be expected if the model uniformly guessed all tweets were neutral (0.00%, 95.026%, 0.00% for job satisfaction, neutral, and job dissatisfaction, respectively).

The sensitivity of the measure was high for the neutral tweets (72.55%), but lower for the job satisfaction (50.00%) and job dissatisfaction tweets (48.15%). Although these values are better than what would be expected by uniformly guessing neutral tweets (0.00%, 1.00%, 0.00%, respectively), the values indicate that if the model were provided with tweets actually expressing job satisfaction, only 50% of those tweets would be classified as relating to job satisfaction. Therefore, the precision and sensitivity both demonstrate that a machine learning approach to identifying job-related tweets would miss a large percentage of job satisfaction and dissatisfaction tweets and would also assign many construct irrelevant tweets to the job satisfaction and job dissatisfaction categories.

The other two metrics—negative predictive value and specificity—describe the model's performance at rejections. Both job satisfaction (98.83%) and dissatisfaction (98.21%) had a high negative predictive value relative to the neutral tweets (14.26%). These values are similar to and sometimes better than what would be expected by a baseline model uniformly guessing neutral tweets (98.14%, 0.00%, 96.88%, respectively), and they indicate that when the model says a tweet is not related to job satisfaction, it will be correct 98.83% of time. Thus, despite the model being poor at its positive classifications (i.e., predictions that a tweet is construct relevant), the model is good at making rejections (i.e., predicting that a tweet is irrelevant). The specificity levels for the job satisfaction, neutral, and dissatisfaction tweets were 79.43, 87.21%, and 91.94%, respectively. When a tweet is not related to job satisfaction, 79% of the time the model will classify that tweet as not relating to job satisfaction. Relative a baseline model whose specificity is 1.00%, 0.00%, and 1.00% for satisfaction, neutral, and dissatisfaction, respectively, the model seems to have much better specificity especially for the neutral tweets. The negative predictive value and the specificity both suggest the naïve Bayes model performs adequately at rejecting construct irrelevant tweets, but the precision and specificity indicate the model would not be a reliable method of classifying job satisfaction and job dissatisfaction. Most of the tweets classified as job satisfaction or dissatisfaction would have nothing to do with the intended construct, and may even capture the opposite construct.

Therefore, because we would a like a method of determining the average level of job satisfaction and dissatisfaction in a city, a machine learning approach does not seem like an ideal method for the current study. The phrase dictionary method we use in the chapter is more suited for areas where the machine learning method is lacking. That is, the phrase dictionaries were created to capture all tweets with a specific job satisfaction or dissatisfaction utterance. Thus, when it makes a classification, the classification should be correct. However, because we only generated phrases from a sample of 2,000 tweets, the phrases may not be exhaustive, and therefore the phrase-based model may make many rejections. This small sample size for the training data may also have limited the naïve Bayes classifier performance. For comparison, Go, Bhayani, and Huang (2009) used 1,600,000 tweets to train their sentiment classifier. We attempted to enhance reliability by aggregating job satisfaction and dissatisfaction counts for each city over time. However, aggregating across time would not improve the low precision and sensitivity of the classifier because aggregation would not separate the irrelevant tweets. Although the phrase dictionary method and machine learning classifier method both have their relative strengths, we chose to use the phrase counting method to minimize the number of construct irrelevant tweets in our sample for each city.

TABLE 4.B1

Classification metrics used to evaluate naïve Bayes classifier

Classification Metric	Definition	Equation
Accuracy	Proportion of all tweets that are correctly classified	$\dfrac{TP + TN}{TP + FP + TN + FN}$
Precision	Proportion of all tweets classified as a specific category that actually belong to that category	$\dfrac{TP}{TP + FP}$
Sensitivity	Proportion of all tweets that belong to given category that are classified as belonging to that category	$\dfrac{TP}{TP + FN}$
Specificity	Proportion of all tweets that do not belong to given category that are classified as not belonging to that category	$\dfrac{TN}{FP + TN}$
Negative Predictive value	Proportion of all tweets classified as not belonging to a category that do not actually belong to that category	$\dfrac{TN}{TN + FN}$

Note. In the equations, TP (true positives) is the total number of instances where a tweet actually belonged to a focal category (e.g., job satisfaction), and the model predicted that it belonged to that focal category. FP (false positives) is the total number of instances where a tweet did not belong to a focal category, but the model predicted that it belonged to that focal category. TN (true negatives) is the total number of instances where a tweet did not belong to a focal category, and the model predicted that it did not belong to that focal category. FN (false negatives) is the total number of instances where a tweet belonged to a focal category, and the model predicted that it did not belong to that focal category

TABLE 4.B2

Confusion matrix for classifying tweets as satisfaction, neutral, or dissatisfaction based upon naïve Bayes classifier (supervised machine learning)

		Classified as		
		Satisfaction	Neutral	Dissatisfaction
Confusion matrix	Actual satisfaction	16	0	16
	Actual neutral	332	1192	119
	Actual dissatisfaction	17	11	26
	Accuracy	76.74%	73.28%	71.37%
	Precision	4.38%	99.09%	9.94%
	Sensitivity	50.00%	72.55%	48.15%
Performance measures	Specificity	79.43%	87.21%	91.94%
	Negative Predictive value	98.83%	14.26%	98.21%

REFERENCES

Fawcett, T. (2006). An introduction to ROC analysis. *Pattern recognition letters, 27*, 861–874.

Frey, P. W., & Slate, D. J. (1991). Letter recognition using Holland-style adaptive classifiers. *Machine Learning, 6*, 161–182.

Go, A., Bhayani, R., & Huang, L. (2009). Twitter sentiment classification using distant supervision (pp. 1–12). *CS224N Project Report*, Stanford.

Hall, M., Frank, E., Holmes, G., Pfahringer, B., Reutemann, P., & Witten, I. H. (2009). The WEKA data mining software: an update. *ACM SIGKDD Explorations Newsletter, 11*, 10–18.

Harris, Z. S. (1954). Distribution structure. *Word, 10*, 146–162.

Manning, C. D. (1999). *Foundations of statistical natural language processing*. H. Schütze (Ed.). Cambridge, MA: MIT Press.

Mohri, M., Rostamizadeh, A., & Talwalkar, A. (2012). *Foundations of machine learning*. Cambridge, MA: MIT Press.

Newman, D. A. (2003). Longitudinal modeling with randomly and systematically missing data: A simulation of ad hoc, maximum likelihood, and multiple imputation techniques. *Organizational Research Methods, 6*, 328–362.

Pang, B., Lee, L., & Vaithyanathan, S. (2002). Thumbs up?: Sentiment classification using machine learning techniques. *Proceedings of the ACL-02 Conference on Empirical Methods in Natural Language Processing, 10*, 79–86. Philadelphia, PA: Association for Computational Linguistics.

Rubin, D. B. (1976). Inference and missing data. *Biometrika*, 63, 581–592.

Salton, G., & McGill, M. J. (1983). *Introduction to modern information retrieval*. New York, NY: McGraw-Hill.

United States Census Bureau. (2012). Population Estimates. Retrieved from http://www.census.gov/popest/data/cities/totals/2012/index.html

Wolberg, W. H., Street, W. N., & Mangasarian, O. L. (1994). Machine learning techniques to diagnose breast cancer from fine-needle aspirates. *Cancer Letters, 77*, 163–171.

Wolfram Alpha (2015). Wolfram|Alpha. Retrieved from http://www.wolframalpha.com

5

Data Visualization

Evan F. Sinar

In the era of big data, improvements in technology have made it easy for organizations to collect huge volumes of information of a vast variety of types and characteristics. From consumer shopping habits to real-time electricity usage, from internet connectivity to weather patterns, from social media data to employee accident and error rates, terabytes of data are constantly and meticulously collected, filed, sorted, and stored by automated and hand-entered systems. Big data provide the raw information needed to perform complex analysis and discern key patterns and trends to a degree that would have been impossible 20, or even five, years ago.

Despite the advancement in data tracking and accumulation, however, the human brain has not advanced at the same rate. It is simply not possible to readily make use of such a massive scope and scale of data in its raw form. This limitation is a key barrier to individuals and organizations seeking to leverage the power harnessed within newly accessible large-scale datasets. Even the most comprehensive and expansive databases are worthless without a way to understand and process their qualities and to translate these qualities into actionable insight. Although the potential of big data is substantial, methods for identifying and comprehending new aspects of knowledge hidden within these data are essential. Without approaches that enable this and that do so in a manner that increases accessibility of information to the broad array of those charged with extracting value from big data, this value will be underutilized at best, or ignored at worst. Data visualization brings accessibility and interpretability to big data.

In this chapter, I will review the topic of data visualization and its applications to big data in five major sections. First, I define data visualization and overview its emergence, function, and advantages in general, business, and big data contexts. Second, I briefly discuss the perceptual foundations for visualization. Third, I review several examples of specific data visualization types, applications for I-O psychologists, and publicly available tools to create them. Fourth, I expand on a discussion of research questions potentially well suited to visualization approaches and key design considerations in creating them. Finally, I discuss key issues and risk areas associated with data visualization and future opportunities for I-O psychologists to both advance the knowledge base and harness the advantages of data visualization within their own practice areas.

DATA VISUALIZATION: DEFINITION AND GOALS

In its simplest form, data visualization is a set of methods for graphically displaying information in a way that is understandable and straightforward, ideally while also incorporating aesthetic considerations to drive engagement and interest to in turn capture the attention of the intended audience. Data visualizations use distinctive techniques and design choices to guide users to easily absorb, understand, and make decisions based on information. How well this goal is accomplished is dependent not only on the qualities of the data themselves, but also on the skills of the researcher and visualization creator in choosing the right presentation method, and in guiding the user to observe key features in the data—while simultaneously considering the appropriateness of the format and guidance provided.

From an analytic perspective, visualization serves two primary functions—to explore data and to explain it (Iliinsky & Steele, 2011). The exploratory purpose of data visualization is to discover patterns, relationships, hierarchies, and differences that would be difficult or impossible to detect based solely on statistical procedures or by reviewing textual or tabular forms of data presentation. It is important to note that data visualization typically plays an inductive role in the analytic process, detecting observations and findings that themselves have a distinctive value, yet can also serve as centering points for further hypotheses and investigation using more traditional analytic techniques. That is, an exploration-focused use of data visualization can be an outcome in itself, or it can be a precursor to further analyses of high-level patterns detected.

A second function of visualization is to explain patterns, trends, or relationships involving variables of interest. Visualizations that originate not in a raw dataset, but rather in a research question or business objective, can graphically display alternative hypotheses, allowing the user to gauge which is most likely. The explanation function extends to communication of the findings themselves to reach a broader audience, to efficiently orient a user to a topic area, and to incite interpretation, inferences, and decisions to a degree that would not be possible using text- or numerically-based communication formats.

EMERGENCE OF VISUALIZATION FOR INFORMATION COMMUNICATION

Data visualization itself is not a new idea, nor is its ability to drive action novel—some of the most influential data visualizations emerged well over a century ago, such as John Snow's 1854 London cholera map, Florence Nightingale's 1858 war mortality graph, and Charles Minard's 1869 march on Moscow chart. Visualization has long played a role in communication of quantitative information through the foundational work of Tufte (1983, 1990, 1997), Cleveland (1993), and others decades before the term "big data" came into use. Making sense of complex information has always been necessary, and past a certain point, additional data beyond that available decades ago do not become meaningfully "bigger."

However, though visualization as a communication technique is not new, what has changed is the range of individuals charged with processing and making decisions based on data. Research by Manyika et al. (2011) projected a 2018 deficiency of 140,000 to 190,000 positions for data analytics experts, and more broadly a shortage of 1.5 million managers and analysts who—as a component of their job rather than their full-time employment—must make sense of and decisions based on large-scale datasets. Visualization is a critical component in this equation that enables broader information exchange and processing efficiency due to the advantages visualizations can provide.

The surge in public usage of graphical information presentation formats is also relatively recent. As one indicator of the growth of their prevalence as a data communication mechanism, interest in the term "infographics," as indexed by Google Trends, has increased five-fold in only three years, from 2011 to 2014. While infographics and data visualizations are considered somewhat distinct—infographics are usually designed for stylistic rather than analytic purposes and are less amenable to big data applications— the proliferation of infographics nonetheless has established a foundation for visualizations of all types. The acknowledgement by media companies of the value of graphical information formats for communicating complex concepts to a broad audience is also clearly evident from their rapid adoption of such approaches. Indeed, many of the leading practitioners of advanced data visualizations are based in large and influential media outlets such as the *New York Times* and the *Wall Street Journal*. Websites such as www.dadaviz.com have also emerged to compile visualizations of broad interest.

Visual analysis and production skills are integral to many projections of future work skills. For example, the Institute for the Future (Davies, Fidler, & Gorbis, 2011) defines a future need in response to the new media ecology—new communication tools requiring new media literacies beyond text for new media literacy. In their view, the next generation of workers, "will also need to be comfortable creating and presenting their own visual information. [...] As immersive and visually stimulating presentation of information becomes the norm, workers will need more sophisticated skills to use these tools to engage and persuade their audiences" (p. 13).

As more professionals and managers find themselves in the role of data analysts and presenters, it is likely that many forms of analysis will take a visual rather than purely quantitative form in order to reduce the gap between the relatively small number of quantitative specialists and the much larger employee base of those who can readily interpret, critically evaluate, and act upon information presented graphically.

ADVANTAGES OF VISUALIZED DATA

Increasingly, information presented in daily life and in business settings is presented visually. Visualization makes data approachable to a broad audience. It democratizes data access, interpretation, and analysis by drawing upon our substantial visual skills and by leveraging common visual referents. Through use of these cues, accessibility increases and training time to interpret the visuals is reduced to the degree that these cues are already inculcated in the audience. Visualization, regardless of the size of data to which it is applied, is also advantageous in comparison to textual or tabular forms of data presentation. They enable detection of relationships that would otherwise remain hidden, and do so efficiently. Visualizations facilitate integration of multiple data sources through the use of common visual referents that place different types and scales of data into a singular view. Through their influence on human cognition, visualizations produce benefits for decision-making, learning, and analytical reasoning (Parsons & Sedig, 2013). Although the number of studies into the persuasive impact of data visualizations is very limited at this time, early investigations have been promising: as one of the most recent examples, Pandey,

Manivannan, Nov, Satterthwaite, and Bertini (2014) found that information presented using graphs was more likely to persuade an audience, and to have a greater effect on their attitude change, than the same information presented using tables.

Visualization is increasingly being recognized across scientific domains as a valuable and effective approach for distributing information to populations with varying levels of information processing experience and literacy in the content domain. As one notable example from the health sciences, researchers developed a series of visualizations to display health status indicators (Arcia et al., 2013). This approach, to address communication gaps limiting the transfer of key quantitatively derived knowledge to target populations, is indicative of the broad value that data visualizations can generate.

VISUALIZATION AS A BIG DATA IMPERATIVE

Big data describe a class of information that is too large and complex to process using traditional database management techniques or conventional data refinement software—these challenges extend across functions including searching, capturing, sharing, storing, curating, transferring, and exploring, as well as visualizing (Russom, 2011). Visualization provides a method for introducing structure and a graphical representation to the data, and can include both static and interactive visualization approaches (Thomas & Cook, 2006). Visualization also provides access to data elements—and resulting discoveries—that would be difficult or impossible to connect using traditional methods (Lavalle, Lesser, Shockley, Hopkins, & Kruschwitz, 2011). In response to the rapidly growing level of data and aided by improvements in technology, visualizations counteract a state of data overload by enabling data processing at a more rapid rate, guiding decisions accordingly (Viégas & Wattenberg, 2007). Visually-based analytic methods combine the strengths of human cognition with new data tracking and storage technologies and increased availability of visualization toolsets to collectively produce valuable outcomes (Connolly & Wooledge, 2012).

Visualization provides specific advantages for each facet of big data: volume, velocity, and variety. In response to the volume parameter, big data generate sheer amounts of information that are too large to process without visual representations and interpretations. In response to velocity, it becomes inefficient and infeasible to have manual steps in the analysis process when data are arriving so rapidly. Visualizations provide a data structure that can be quickly updated and revised as more data become available, improving response time between data retrieval and decision guidance and reducing the need for users to re-acclimate themselves each time. Without the speed and synthesis advantages that visualizations provide, organizations will struggle to harness big data's potential for accelerating their growth and bolstering their competitive advantage. The velocity of big data also matches well with visualization's ability to show trending and time-series data. Visualization addresses the variety aspect of big data by visually aligning and integrating different data sources, providing a common visual structure for interpreting various forms of data. Visualization techniques can also incorporate unstructured as well as structured varieties of data, important as the former becomes increasingly prevalent and often can be more easily processed, categorized, and acted upon when visualization is a step in the analysis process. Some definitions of big data introduce a fourth "V," veracity, dealing with the quality of the data. Visualizations can serve a useful function for this component also, as they are ideal for identifying outlier and low-base rate occurrences within big data information sources to drive further investigation of the nature of these cases and, if appropriate, removal or reconciliation to produce a cleaner dataset for further analysis.

BUSINESS APPLICATIONS OF DATA VISUALIZATION

Alongside immense business pressures to generate and utilize big data, visualization is viewed as a key mechanism for unlocking the value of these data. Organizations accumulate an abundance of raw information, and their ability to produce smart enterprise decisions is in part based on their acumen and speed in examining and interpreting these data (Bonneau, Ertl, & Nielson, 2006). If critical data insights are present but not uncovered, it becomes increasingly likely that organizations will make weak business decisions as a result and will fall behind their competitors with higher proficiency in big data management. As organizations are charged with data-driven decision making, this also requires that a broader range of individuals becomes comfortable with, and sophisticated in, using data to guide decisions—and in this context, visualization's role to enable decisions becomes paramount. As big data are seen as an underleveraged source of business-critical insights, decision makers at all levels need to become much more adept at rapidly capturing, analyzing, and extracting value from the data they are accumulating.

As noted above, recent studies of the workforce impact of big data and analytics trends have noted the immense need for more individuals with analytical skills. Visualization is seen as one mechanism for reducing this gap—for allowing data-driven decision making without introducing a heavy reliance on quantitative skills. Within a business environment, visualization also drives collaboration among groups, providing a shared view for interpretation (Eppler & Bresciani, 2013). Visualization can also aid organizations in ensuring that their data are sufficiently clean and relevant to the business questions of interest, as it allows individuals who lack traditional quantitative analysis skills to nonetheless get close to the data and to identify issues for resolution. Further, visualizations serve an important function to combat data fatigue and skepticism: they provide a direct response to the "have to see it to believe it" viewpoint. Decision makers charged with making decisions at a higher pace and supported by a solid evidence foundation can more easily synthesize and communicate information when presented visually (Al-Kassab, Ouertani, Schiuma, & Neely, 2014; Parsons & Sedig, 2014). It is difficult to overstate the potential value of visualization for framing research findings in a manner that engages a non-technical audience, helping them interpret and internalize and simply making them want to share the information with others.

VISUAL PERCEPTION AS A FOUNDATION FOR DATA VISUALIZATION

The impact and advantages of data visualizations are based in their ability to leverage our extremely well-developed systems of perception, attention, and memory, enabling us to process visual information at a similar rate to that of an Ethernet connection (Koch, Mclean, Segev, Freed, Berry, & Balasubramanian, 2006). In particular, the speed advantages of visualizations begin with the initial stages of perception and the use of certain visual features, termed pre-attentive, that can be detected during a single glance lasting approximately 200 to 250 milliseconds (Healey & Enns, 2012). These features—such as position, length, density, and color—serve as the core elements of a visualization, drawing on our most deeply rooted perceptual skills. Though these pre-attentive features all provide an expedited path to perception, they can also be ordered in terms of the accuracy with which they can be interpreted (Cleveland & McGill, 1985). MacKinlay's (1986) research produced such an ordering of visual features—in this ranking, those higher on the list are generally better-suited for visual design features to enable interpretative accuracy due to their higher precision, and those lower on the list less-suited.

TABLE 5.1

	Categorical (Nominal)	Categorical (Ordinal)	Quantitative (All)
Most accurate	Position	Position	Position
	Color hue	Density	Length
	Texture	Color saturation	Angle
	Connection	Color hue	Slope
	Containment	Texture	Area
	Density	Connection	Volume
	Color saturation	Containment	Density
	Shape	Length	Color saturation
	Length	Angle	Color hue
	Angle	Slope	Texture
	Slope	Area	Connection
	Area	Volume	Containment
Least accurate	Volume	Shape	Shape

In addition to the processing speed benefits of visualizations that take advantage of pre-attentive perception, our memory for visuals in comparison to text-only information is also enhanced (Schnotz, 2002). This advantage is due to the use of two different cognitive subsystems applied to the processing of visual information—a concept referred to as dual coding theory (Clark & Paivio, 1991). In this theory, textual information is processed only within the verbal cognitive subsystem, yet visual information is encoded in the imagery subsystem as well.

Despite the extensive research base on perceptual and cognitive aspects of information processing, many unanswered questions remain for most facets of data visualization, particularly for newer types of visualizations (Johnson, 2004; Chen, 2005; Chen, 2010). Though early indications are positive about the ability of data visualizations to influence and create shared knowledge for a managerial audience (Al-Kassab, Ouertani, Schiuma, & Neely, 2014) and to exert more persuasive influence than purely numerical forms of information presentation (Pandey et al., 2014), much research remains to be conducted to validate these early signs of promise within applied settings.

DATA VISUALIZATION TYPES AND TOOLS

The field of available visualization methods is expanding rapidly—regardless of the type of data, there are an increasing number of approaches for communicating a message, and a growing number of tools available to facilitate visualization creation. Deciding on an appropriate type of visualization can involve a wide array of choices, but begins with two straightforward questions: what is the intended message and who is the intended audience. Only after making those considerations can the right visualization technique be chosen (Zhu, 2007). Choice of visualization method may also be enhanced by taking into consideration the input of end users (Fox & Hendler, 2011) or past examples of visualizations that have been more or less effective to increase the probability of a successful outcome. Due to their nature, visualizations are also extremely well-suited to "window shopping" examples drawn from other contexts, curated and compiled by visualization experts such as Stephen Few (2009), Alberto Cairo (2013), and Andy Kirk (2012); even a simple Google image search for any of the visualization types described in this chapter will typically produce thousands of examples.

Numerous taxonomies exist for classifying data visualization methods. I focus on the five-category structure proposed by Kirk (2012): comparing categories, assessing hierarchies and part-to-whole relationships, showing changes over time, plotting connections and relationships, and mapping geospatial data. I will highlight and briefly overview each of these categories, including a representative example (in most cases smaller-scale to allow legibility; in practice many visualizations would be displayed in a larger printed size or on a computer screen) of methods that are relatively common and that are well-suited to big data applications, corresponding to the focus of this volume. Of course, few, if any, of the techniques presented are exclusively associated with big data, but several derive greater value as a communication mechanism as the underlying datasets they represent grow larger. In addition, any of the visualization types shown can also be represented in interactive form, enhancing their utility for large-scale datasets. For more expansive lists and classification systems of graphical and visualization methods beyond those listed in the following sections, including those that are either less unique to big data visualizations or less frequently used, refer to Abela (2008), Few (2009), Heer, Bostok, and Ogievetsky (2010), and Kirk (2012).

COMPARING CATEGORIES

This data visualization category includes visualizations designed to compare groups based on their corresponding values. For I-O psychologists, this set of visualizations can be beneficial for exploring research questions comparing years, employee or organizational subgroups, and individual or organizational characteristics, for example. The sample visualizations below provide further illustrations of potential applications.

Slopegraph

A slopegraph compares various categories by visually connecting their values using a line. Common category examples are year (e.g., 2013 versus 2014) and level (e.g., front-line leader versus senior executive). By connecting the same category across representations, a slopegraph visually indicates rate of change between the representations, as well as each category's relative order compared to others to show how rank ordering

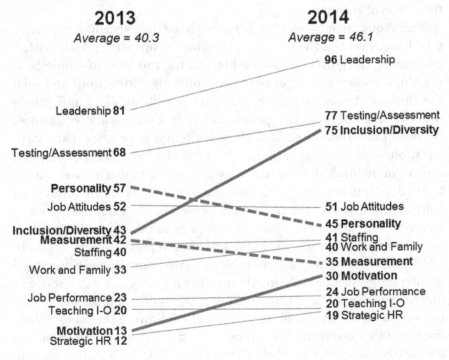

FIGURE 5.1
Slopegraph chart

varies. Slopegraphs can also benefit from the use of additional visual cues for the lines connecting categories—for example, coloring lines of upward slope green, downward slope red, and nominal slope gray or using bold or dashed lines to show noteworthy upward or downward trends. An example of a basic slopegraph is shown in Figure 5.1—this graph shows a subset of topic areas within the Society for Industrial and Organizational Psychology (SIOP) annual conference and compares the number of conference sessions on that topic between 2013 and 2014. Content areas with a high percentage increase are shown with a bold line, those with a high percentage decrease are shown with a dashed line.

Radial Chart

A radial chart uses a circular display format, with data categories ordered around the circle to show the standing of each category on a common numerical or ordinal scale ranging from the inside to the outside of the circle. In addition to distance from the center, radial charts can also incorporate color and shading variations to indicate other distinctions among categories, and their flexibility provides numerous advantages for large-scale data representation. Florence Nightingale's seminal 1858 chart of war mortality was a form of radial chart; a more modern radial chart using seven of the same SIOP Annual Conference content areas from the slopegraph example is shown in Figure 5.2.

Sankey (Alluvial) Diagram

A Sankey, also called alluvial, diagram shows how various categories flow together or apart across stages (indicative of their intercorrelations), with stages often representing, but not limited to, multiple time periods. Sankey diagrams can be thought of using a water analogy, where tributaries join to form larger streams or rivers split to form various branches. The width of the water flowing shows how categories change in size. Charles Minard's 1869 influential march on Moscow graphic, while it incorporates other visualization techniques as well, is a form of Sankey diagram, showing the joining and dividing of Napoleon's army during its attempted incursion into Russia. The example Sankey diagram (Figure 5.3) shows how a set of individuals experiencing job transitions moved between levels, displaying the number and proportions following each flow. This visualization type is particularly well suited to "to" and "from" research questions within I-O psychology, for example to illustrate employee flows between levels, countries, and companies.

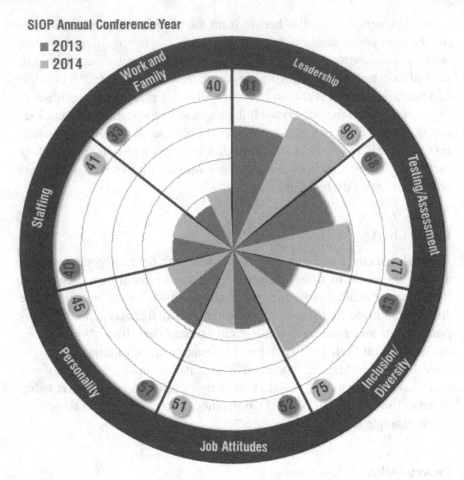

FIGURE 5.2
Radial chart

Small Multiples (Trellis) Chart

Small multiples charts, also referred to as trellis charts or sparklines, take advantage of humans' visual skill at detecting patterns to simultaneously depict—using various panels—several variables displayed individually but with common horizontal and vertical scales. Common examples of scales to enable accurate comparisons in a small multiples format are time along the horizontal axis (i.e., using a common start and end date), and percentage change for each variable along the vertical axis. Though the component graphs are typically line or area graphs, it is nonetheless useful to think of small multiples as a distinct visualization type due to the incremental visual impact and diagnostic potential of an integrated view

Role Transitioned
From

Role Transitioned
To

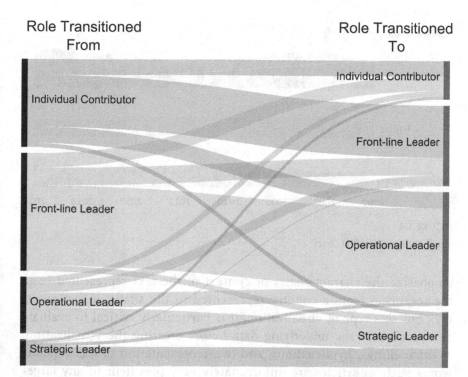

FIGURE 5.3
Sankey (alluvial) diagram

of the individual graphs. A small multiples example is shown Figure 5.4, again referencing a subset of content areas within the SIOP annual conference, but now extending that view across a wider range of years. For I-O psychologists, this visualization type can be useful for exploring virtually any type of longitudinal dataset. Alternatively, the X-axis can be used to represent ordered categories such as job level or continuous variables such as tenure.

Word (Tag) Cloud

A word cloud is a particularly distinct visualization type, as it is expressly designed for use with unstructured, textual data as an initial input and to display individual words and phrases based on their frequency and other characteristics that can be qualitatively extracted, such as word tone. The shape of the word cloud itself can also be modified to further

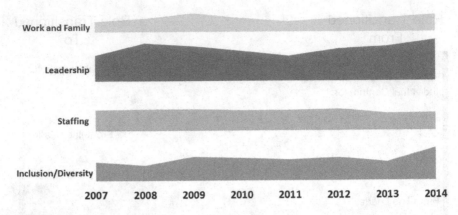

FIGURE 5.4
Small multiples (trellis) chart

emphasize the characteristics or context of the text represented (e.g., the responses from a country represented in the shape of that country). For this type of visualization, it is particularly critical to evaluate and preprocess the underlying data before creating the visualization, as misspellings, hyphenations, and overrepresentation of less valuable words such as articles are unfortunately very prevalent in any large-scale text database. More so than most visualization methods, the visual appeal of word clouds has driven very widespread use—a colleague of the author even reported that her 8-year old daughter created word clouds as a third grade class project. Thus, the potential for oversaturation of this approach should be recognized accordingly. However, an advantage of this method's uniqueness is that it has also driven more focused research and discussion (see Feinberg, 2009; Viégas, Wattenberg, & Feinberg, 2009). An example word cloud is shown in Figure 5.5, showing the most common responses among 13,000 leaders indicating the one word that best described their organization's leadership development program, with positive terms shaded in lighter gray and neutral or negative terms shaded in darker gray. Though this use, to display words or phrases sized based on frequency, is more common, I-O psychologists should also consider less traditional uses of word clouds. For instance, multiple word clouds can be generated to represent relative frequencies of competencies, countries, personality characteristics, or any other category with a large membership, with each limited to a particular subgroup (e.g., based on demographic characteristics, tenure, or turnover risk category) in order to facilitate visual exploration and comparison of their responses.

FIGURE 5.5
Word cloud

ASSESSING HIERARCHIES AND PART-TO-WHOLE RELATIONSHIPS

This data visualization category includes visualizations designed to depict how a particular category relates to a broader set as a component of this total or how a hierarchical structure extends through a dataset. This hierarchical structure, and the many layers of detail that can be present, also makes this category of data visualization ideal for interactive approaches such as those discussed in a later section. Visualization types within this section are useful for I-O psychology applications involving hierarchical data structures such as regions and countries, job levels, and business units, for example.

Circle Packing Diagram

Circle packing diagrams group circles into larger circles, with smaller circles representing subsets of the data, and larger circles representing supersets. Circles within a grouping are sized based on their amount or other quantitative characteristics. Circle packing methods are considered space-efficient for big data applications, yet are often unsuitable for trend and time investigations and cannot accommodate negative values used for sizing elements, making them less suited for certain variety and velocity

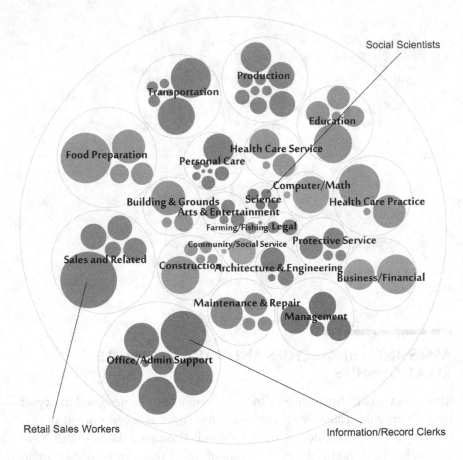

FIGURE 5.6

Circle packing diagram

aspects of big data (Gorodov & Gubarev, 2013). An example circle packing diagram is shown above (Figure 5.6), displaying two levels of structure and sizing of job categories within the United States based on 2013 employment levels, both sized to their relative proportions as well as highlighting three more specific job classifications.

Tree Map

Tree maps use a rectangular format to partition a dataset's components based on their size or other relative value (e.g., a larger component is displayed as a larger proportion of the overall rectangle). In addition to size, color can also be used to differentiate components—using more than one

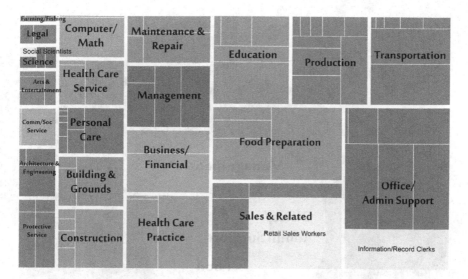

FIGURE 5.7
Tree map

distinguishing characteristic often becomes critical when multiple hierarchies are displayed within the same visualization. Regarding applicability to big data applications, tree maps are considered less space-efficient than circle packing and are subject to a similar set of disadvantages and some degree of insufficiency in response to big data variety and velocity (Gorodov & Gubarev, 2013). Tree maps are effective at showing hierarchical groupings and data outliers in the forms of particularly large and small groups relative to others. A well-known example of an interactive tree map is the website Newsmap (http://newsmap.jp/), which displays news grouped into categories such as sports, business, entertainment, and technology, with the size of a particular news story a function of its popularity. An example tree map is shown above (Figure 5.7) using the same data as above and with three more specific job classifications indicated.

Sunburst Diagram

Sunburst diagrams provide a concentric layout for a hierarchical structure, with subsets of data extending out from their supersets. Each new ring outward represents another layer in the hierarchy. This property, to efficiently display multiple levels of the structure, allows sunbursts to show data proportions as well as category depth since some categories

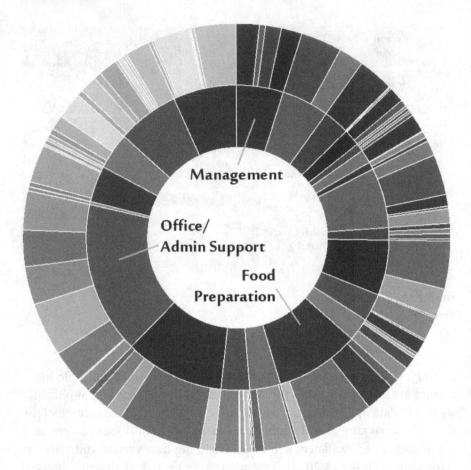

FIGURE 5.8
Sunburst diagram

will extend farther from the center than others. When viewed in the context of big data applicability, sunbursts share the same disadvantages as tree maps and circle packing for high-variety scenarios, yet do provide advantages for velocity due to the possibility of representing data through animation (Gorodov & Gubarev, 2013). An example sunburst diagram is shown above (Figure 5.8), displaying the same United States employment data as referenced earlier down to two levels of job categorization. Due to space limitations, only representative top-level categories are indicated. Sunburst diagrams have similar applications to circle packing and tree maps for displaying and guiding research exploration of hierarchical data structures within I-O psychology.

Cluster Dendogram

A cluster dendogram is a form of node-link diagram that presents a hierarchy in a circular format, with the deepest levels of the hierarchy placed uniformly along the outer ring and higher-order levels, or clusters, placed inward toward the center. These diagrams do not show the relative sizing of categories as do the prior types in this section but can accommodate a larger amount of text descriptors and show numbers of subcategories more efficiently than do the types above. An example cluster dendogram created based on three levels of structure within the United States employment dataset referenced above is presented in Figure 5.9. Though the text

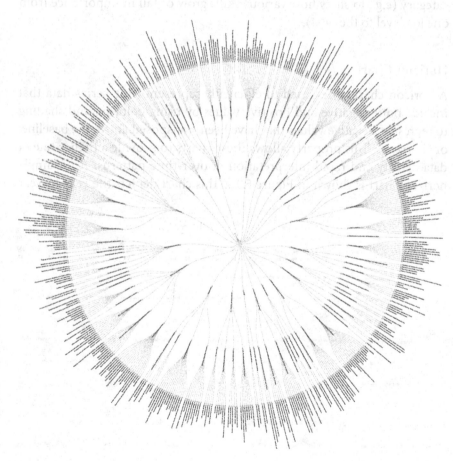

FIGURE 5.9
Circle dendogram

necessary to represent this complex structure is too small to be legible within the available page size, this example nonetheless shows the nature of this visualization type.

SHOWING CHANGES OVER TIME

This data visualization category includes visualizations designed to show variation across a time span. For I-O psychologists, these visualization types are useful for any form of longitudinal data where the focus is displaying change or absolute level of a set of values over time. These visualization types can also be adapted such that their X-axes are any ordered category (e.g., to show how various skills grow or fall in importance from one job level to the next).

Horizon Chart

A horizon chart is designed to efficiently represent time-series data that include both negative and positive values by using coloring and shading to represent negative values that have been transposed above the baseline, or "horizon." This property allows these charts to provide a higher rate of data density and rapid interpretation of over-time patterns. An example horizon chart is shown in Figure 5.10. This chart depicts the year-to-year

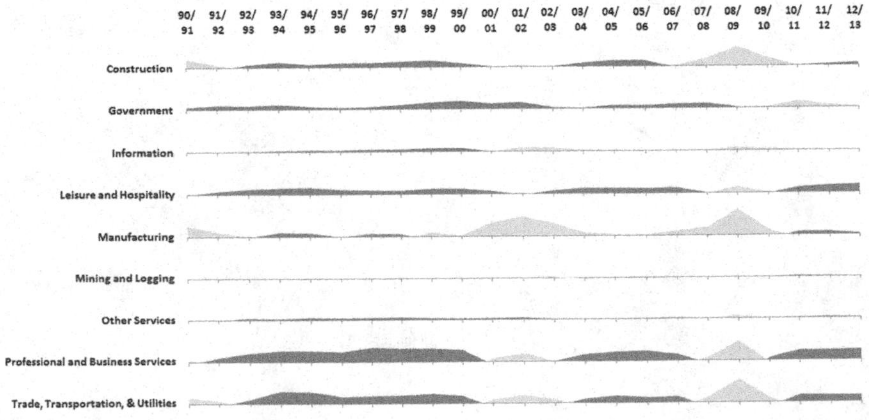

FIGURE 5.10
Horizon chart

United States employment change by industry from 1990 until 2013—darker-gray indicates a positive change from the prior year, lighter gray indicates a negative change, and in both cases height indicates the absolute number of jobs gained or loss within that industry. All industries use the same vertical scale to allow direct comparisons.

Stream Graph

A stream graph is a form of stacked area graph that displays how the relative proportions of data vary over time. While stream graphs do not support negative numbers and can obscure precise differences in some cases, they can facilitate identification of flow patterns, particularly when data are available over long periods of time and where a relatively small number of categories are present. Stream graphs are also well suited to interactivity, allowing exploration of individual segments of the dataset. An example stream graph is shown below displaying the same year-to-year United States employment change by industry from 1990 until 2013 data as above. In this case, however, the graph focuses on the absolute value of each industry's employment rather than the year-to-year change.

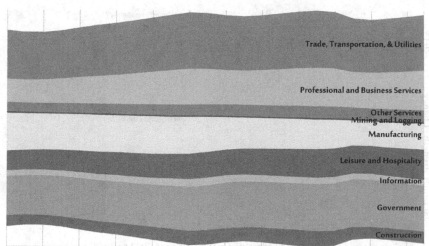

FIGURE 5.11
Stream graph

PLOTTING CONNECTIONS AND RELATIONSHIPS

This data visualization category includes visualizations designed to show how two or more variables relate to one another. As such, these visualizations can be useful for a wide range of research questions explored by I-O psychologists.

Bubble Plot

A bubble plot is a scatter plot—one dimension on the X-axis, one on the Y-axis, and data elements plotted in terms of their relative positions on these scales—but adds a third additional dimension of bubble size to indicate magnitude or another quantitative property. In some cases, a fourth dimension may be denoted by color. An example bubble plot is shown below, displaying several countries (intentionally left unlabeled for sample purposes, although the data are real) plotted in terms of changes in current leadership quality on the X-axis and leader "bench strength" (i.e., potential future leaders' projected abilities to fill key roles over the next three years) on the Y-axis between 2011 and 2014. Bubble size indicates the GDP growth rate for each country.

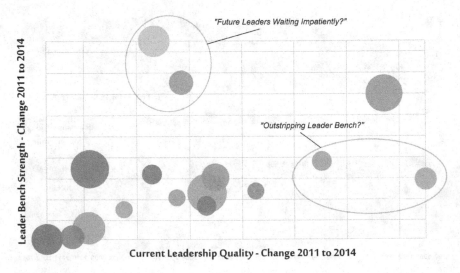

FIGURE 5.12
Bubble plot

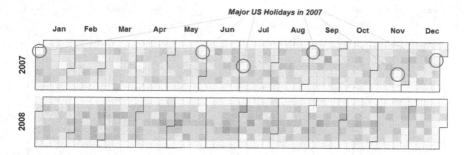

FIGURE 5.13
Heat map

Heat Map

A heat map displays the strength of relationship between any two variables in a matrix format using colors or shading to denote stronger connections. Because the level of detail represented within a heat map is relatively low (which also limits its precision for visual analytic purposes), this approach can make use of individuals' perceptual skills at detecting color and hue variation to display an extensive set of variables simultaneously, in some cases including hundreds of individual relationships. An example heat map—using a calendar view—is shown above (Figure 5.13). This example shows the candidate volumes for an organization's employment testing program over the course of two full years, 2007 and 2008 (the first row of each year represents Sundays, with further days of the week completing the other six rows).

Parallel Coordinates

Parallel coordinates are designed to visualize multivariate data by arraying a series of variables along an X-axis, showing the position of each data element on each axis using a point along the Y-axis, and then connecting these points with lines. The visual connections provided by these lines allow the user to rapidly view the profile of a particular case of data compared to others and when paired with interactive functionality, to identify a target profile and detect other cases with a similar profile. Parallel coordinates are viewed as a particularly versatile and powerful visualization method. In Gorodov and Gubarev's (2013) analysis of six common data visualization methods, parallel coordinates were the only method designated as well-suited for big data's velocity and variety characteristics, as well as its

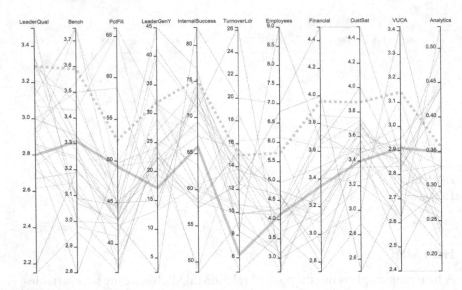

FIGURE 5.14
Parallel coordinates

volume. An example interactive parallel coordinates visualization displays data extracted from the USDA Nutrient Database: http://exposedata.com/parallel/. The example parallel coordinates visualization above (Figure 5.14) shows how 28 countries (intentionally unlabeled for this example) vary across average scores on 11 variables of organizations within each country.

Chord Diagram

Chord diagrams use a circular structure to display relationships between category members as lines connecting every pairing. Chord diagrams can incorporate dozens of individual category members and can also incorporate line color, shading, and thickness to show the strength and nature of interrelationships, as well as a category member's length along the circumference as a further indicator of its collective degree of interconnectivity. An example chord diagram is shown below. This chord diagram example, based on the co-occurrence of 10 leadership skills as a development focus within a large-scale organization sample, is best viewed in three parts: First, the outer ring—in this ring, skills extending across a greater portion of the circumference are more correlated, on average, with other skills (i.e., the skill most intercorrelated with the others is integrating culturally). Second, the lines extending from the right half of each skill's portion of the ring—the width of

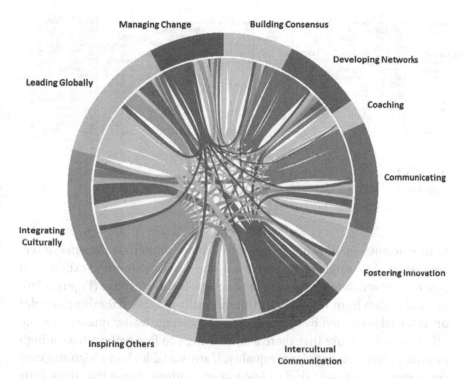

FIGURE 5.15
Chord diagram

these lines indicates the intercorrelation or co-occurrence of those skills (i.e., intercultural communication is most intercorrelated with integrating culturally). Third, the lines extending from the left half of each skill's portion of the ring—the width of these lines indicates the corresponding intercorrelation of each other skill (i.e., intercultural communication has a low co-occurrence with managing change).

Table Lens

A table lens is designed to enable rapid detection of intercorrelated variables by showing numerous variables simultaneously. After choosing and sorting a single column's values highest to lowest, all other columns inherit that sort order accordingly, allowing the user to see which other columns are positively (with a similar pattern of long to short horizontal bars) or negatively (with the opposite pattern of short to long bars) correlated. Due

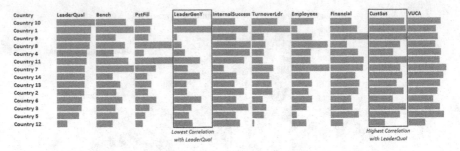

FIGURE 5.16
Table lens

to its efficiency in allowing the user to explore numerous potential inter-correlations in a single view, a table lens can serve as an initial exploration step for a new dataset. An example table lens is shown above (Figure 5.16), displaying data from 12 countries (intentionally unlabeled for this example) on 11 variables sorted by the first variable (average leader quality). Of the other variables, those that share a similar high to low pattern have a high positive correlation with leader quality. If any variables had a high negative correlation, they would show a low to high pattern. Those that show little correspondence have a nominal correlation.

MAPPING GEOSPATIAL DATA

Choropleth and Dot Plot Maps

A choropleth map uses a similar concept as a heat map but applies the color and shade variations to a map rather than a matrix. This can be done at the lowest-level visual, where mutually-exclusive borders can be established and displayed—depending on the size of the map, this could be counties, states, countries, continents, or other existing groupings. A minor variation is a dot plot map, which represents distinct geographic entities as dots rather than by their actual shapes (an example dot plot map showing the spread of the Code Red computer virus over a single day in 2001 can be viewed at http://www.caida.org/research/security/code-red/newframes-small-log.gif). An example choropleth map is shown below—this chart displays the proportion of SIOP annual conference attendees from each

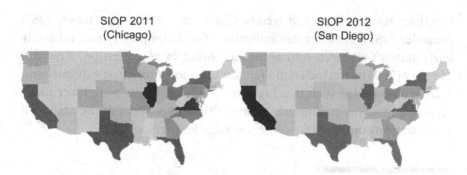

SIOP 2011
(Chicago)

SIOP 2012
(San Diego)

FIGURE 5.17
Choropleth

state in the continental US for 2011, when the conference was held in Chicago, Illinois, and for 2012, when the conference was held in San Diego, California.

ANIMATED DATA VISUALIZATIONS

Animated visualizations are a distinct form of data presentation. The most notable example of an animated visualization—noteworthy both because of the heavy influence it exerted across a broad audience and because of its compelling topical focus—is that designed by Hans Rosling and made available in various forms, including a TED talk drawing over eight million views (http://www.ted.com/talks/hans_rosling_shows_the_best_stats_you_ve_ever_seen) and an extensive website, Gapminder, drawing on an expanded set of data and accompanying videos displaying various visualizations in animated form (www.gapminder.org). The popularity of this particular graphics-focused presentation speaks positively to the potential benefits of animation to enhance visualization communication.

While the available research on static visualizations is limited, studies on animation are even more so (Shah & Hoeffner, 2002). Some studies have shown that applying animation to visual displays can facilitate detection of three-dimensional aspects of the data such as clustering and interrelationships among three variables concurrently (Becker, Cleveland, & Wilks, 1988; Marchark & Marchark, 1991). However, other studies have raised questions about an audience's ability to appropriately interpret relationships and trends when animated (e.g., Huber, 1987; Stuetzle, 1987). As a further indicator of the complexity and relatively early state of research into animated forms of visualization, Kriz and Hegarty (2007) detected an interaction between animation exposure and learner knowledge such that high-knowledge learners were more likely to revise their mental models after multiple exposures to the animated visualization compared to low-knowledge learners.

INTERACTIVE DATA VISUALIZATIONS

Though static forms of visualization are sufficient for many big data applications, interactive data visualizations are often critical for deep exploration of large-scale datasets. Interactive visualizations move beyond the representation of data to allow users to dynamically change and focus their view of the information. Importantly, many forms of visual analytics, such as the parallel coordinates example above, are limited or impossible with static visualizations alone—interactivity enables a form of "self-service" analytics that can greatly expand the impact and utility of visualization approaches.

Whereas static visualizations are created for a predefined purpose and application, interactive visualizations allow—often through controlled access to the full underlying dataset—the audience to define the message and insight of greatest interest to a particular context and business question. In many cases, the data views derived from an interactive approach can be saved for repeated use. Because the users of interactive visualization methods bring new content knowledge and expertise, they may detect findings that the original researcher had not. For this reason, interactive visualizations are particularly valuable when information is being shared with an audience with deeper or differing perspectives. Well-designed interactive approaches also provide a feedback loop to the original researcher to help progressively define new research questions.

Interactivity in the context of big data visualization can be classified on a number of dimensions—Soo Yi, Kang, Stasko, and Jacko (2007) proposed a seven-category taxonomy for interaction techniques based on their review and synthesis of existing frameworks, emphasizing the interplay between the user's goal in seeking a particular form of interaction and the specific mechanisms used to accomplish these objectives. This taxonomy also covers the majority of interaction techniques available in commercial data visualization products.

Soo Yi et al.'s (2007) first interaction technique is to select, or to assign a marker to, a particular data element for revising and further investigation. Importantly, once a selection is made, it is retained through further manipulations of the data view to facilitate tracking of, and the ability to easily return to, a particular case or set of cases throughout. In many software packages, selecting is accomplished simply by clicking on the case or set of interest.

A second interaction technique from this taxonomy is to explore a different portion of the dataset, typically a parallel partition (e.g., shifting between countries). In visualization software packages, exploring often involves panning the view to the new target or clicking on a segment, which in turn reorients the visual display to place the new target at the center. Exploration functionality is often essential for big data visualizations since the scope of data precludes full visibility in any one on-screen viewpoint.

A third interaction technique is to reconfigure the user's perspective on the data. Common reconfigurations include sorting, changing axis ranges, establishing a new baseline, rotating a 3D view of the data to improve the visibility of certain cases, and reordering data elements such as columns to better align with a more intuitive ordering. A particularly unique form of reconfiguring deployed in visualization software—useful when many data points overlap, thus making their density invisible—is a "jitter" technique, which shifts the position of each case very slightly and randomly.

A fourth interaction technique from Soo Yi et al.'s (2007) framework is to visually encode properties of data elements such as their size, color, and shape. While such encoding choices can seem relatively minor, they can have a substantial influence on the interpretability of a data visualization. For example, poorly chosen colors or shapes can slow the pre-attentive velocity that provides key advantages for visualizations above other data presentation methods, as discussed above. Whereas software packages will produce a default encoding, the researcher may alter this based on the objectives of the visualization.

A fifth interaction technique—and one particularly relevant to big data applications—is to abstract/elaborate, to orient the view to a lower level of the data structure (e.g., individual business units versus the organization as a whole) or back to a higher-order structure. In some cases, this may allow examination at the level of individual cases. Certain visualization types, such tree maps and sunbursts, utilize abstract and elaboration approaches extensively. For other visualization types, such as scatterplots, elaboration through a zooming function is essential to spread out and detect the details of individual positions within a tightly clustered set of data points.

A sixth interaction technique within this taxonomy is to filter, to reduce the number of data elements displayed in the visualization based on pre-defined parameters. When a filter is applied, data elements not meeting the specified condition are removed from or de-emphasized within the view. Filtering is a major feature set within visualization software packages, in many cases driven dynamically using slider bars placing parameters on a high to low scale or by using checkboxes or radio buttons to set categories. In many business applications of big data, compiled datasets serve a wide variety of functions, and for any one visualization objective, a sizeable portion of the dataset may be irrelevant. Filtering techniques ensure that extraneous data can be excluded and do not cloud messaging and interpretation.

Soo Yi et al.'s (2007) final interaction technique is connect, to show related items across or within visualizations. If multiple visualizations are presented for the same dataset, connect interactivity allows the researcher to simultaneously view the appearance of a single data point in each view. Parallel coordinates also rely heavily on this interaction technique, as one of that visualization type's primary advantages is its ability to guide identification of other data elements possessing a similar profile across the variables displayed.

Few big data visualizations reach their full illustrative and diagnostic potential without interactivity. While interactive visualizations undoubtedly provide major advantages over static forms, these advantages are accompanied by three important consequences for when and how they are deployed by psychologists. First, some—though not all—of the interactive techniques require the availability of and the researcher's proficiency in commercial visualization software. This dependence, paired with a situation where only one such toolset may be available, makes interactive capabilities a key decision criterion when evaluating visualization software for purchase and adoption. Second, it creates a potential disconnect between the full potential of data visualizations (i.e., incorporating their interactive components and presentation/publication avenues for the work). While less an issue when interactive visualizations are being shared internally to an organization, it does mean that visualizations published in static formats such as print will be relatively limited in their ability to inform and influence new audiences. Third, interactive visualizations rely on deep data access and availability that may not always be feasible and appropriate, particularly when sharing these interactive views outside of the core research team.

ONLINE VISUALIZATION TOOLS

Due to the vast range of data visualization software packages available, this chapter will not be reviewing specific options due to their number and commercial nature. However, numerous online—and free in basic form—tools now exist to enable a wide range of visualizations, encompassing many of those described above and others. Four specific such tools are briefly discussed here: Wordle, Infogr.am, Raw, and D3.js. Despite its commercial nature, due to its widespread availability, I also include a brief description of visualization capabilities available using Microsoft Excel and its extensions.

Wordle (http://www.wordle.net) is an online tool for creating word and tag clouds, using raw data, or (in its advanced form) word frequencies as input. Wordle (used to generate the word cloud earlier in this chapter) provides a range of text generation options including the ability to color words distinctly based on their properties as entered into the site.

Infogr.am (http://infogr.am), which offers a free as well as a paid version, is a toolset for producing static and interactive infographics. As part of its functionality, Infogr.am allows users to generate a range of visualization types including radial charts, bubble charts, word and tag clouds, and tree maps.

Raw (http://app.raw.densitydesign.org/) allows users to enter their own data and to generate Sankey (alluvial) diagrams, circle packing, cluster dendograms, parallel coordinates, tree maps, and stream maps, among other data visualization types. When paired with a vector graphics editor such as Inkscape (http://www.inkscape.org/en/), Raw can rapidly produce free, high-quality visualizations.

D3.js (http://d3js.org/) involves a heavier requirement for programming knowledge, yet is perhaps the most expansive of the tools mentioned, providing JavaScript functionality to generate chord diagrams, circle packing, stream graphs, sunbursts, parallel coordinates, scatterplot matrices, tree maps, choropleths, Sankey (alluvial) diagrams, word clouds, and others (it is also the toolset underlying Raw).

Finally, Microsoft Excel, though relatively limited in its native visualization capabilities, can be configured to produce many of the visualization types listed above; a large and often-updated compilation of such templates is available at https://sites.google.com/site/e90e50charts/. The 2013 version of Excel also enables numerous visualization types through add-on apps designed for this purpose (Knies, 2013). Specialized software is not needed to generate data visualizations; all examples presented above were generated with real data using either Raw or Excel 2010.

VISUALIZATION APPLICATIONS AND RESEARCH QUESTIONS

Though the versatility of visualizations is substantial, certain research questions are better matched to visualization techniques than others due to characteristics of the available data—not only volume, variety, and velocity considerations, which extend across all forms of big data, but also other properties as well. Paired with the visualization types described above and their associated examples, I have attempted to overview various representative examples. More generally, longitudinal and time-series data are often very well-suited to visualized display. Many visualization types, such as those described above, are specifically designed to illustrate time-based trends and patterns. Data with a complex hierarchical structure, too, can draw on an entire class of visualizations to represent this structure in static and interactive formats. Geographical, map-based data are common source material for visualizations produced by the media, and as such, familiarity with associated visualization types has been instilled in many potential users. More generally, multivariate datasets in which categories can be distinguished on many dimensions, especially when each dimension uses a different scale, have visualization types specifically designed for exploring these data efficiently and insightfully. Unstructured text data are also associated with visualization types to guide initial review and interpretation of this information.

In the context of data commonly available to I-O psychologists, research and content domains that may be fruitful for further application of visualization techniques include cultural differences (which can draw on visual techniques for linking category members as well as displaying geographic data), teams (where intact groups can be readily compared on key properties), customer service (due to the vast amounts of data being tracked), standardized testing (for educational and large-scale employment purposes), technology-captured data (e.g., social networking; wearable sensors), diversity-related topics (which involve comparison of different groups, and often produce compelling interpretations that can be represented accordingly through visualizations), historical/over-time datasets for score trends, and more generally, interventions targeting large segments of the employee population, such as hourly and entry-level employees.

KEY CONSIDERATIONS WHEN CREATING BIG DATA VISUALIZATIONS

Objectives

Any visualization design process must begin not with the data, but rather with a careful inventory of the objectives of the resulting output. This step is a critical precursor to choosing among the various visualization types and techniques, and to mitigate risk of a visualization with aesthetic properties that far exceed its desired impact and influence on the intended audience. Common objectives of data visualizations include decision initiation or modification (i.e., what will the user do for the first time, or do differently than they do currently, as a result of the visualization), enhancing understanding (i.e., what will the user know after viewing and interpreting the visualization that they did not previously), and communication expansion (i.e., will the visualization allow you to reach a new audience with an existing message).

Source Data

Stephen Few (2009) proposes several "traits of meaningful data," many of which intersect with big data applications and are notable when considering how to identify, structure, and clean data prior to initiating the visualization design process. First, meaningful data well suited for visualization is high volume—visualizations will be less advantageous over numerical or tabular forms of information presentation when the volume of data is relatively low. Second, historical—as noted above, many advanced visualization methods are specifically designed to illustrate trends in over-time data. A third set of traits is data consistency, clarity, and cleanliness—data veracity of these forms is a common challenge for large-scale datasets, and so a key focus for data qualification and cleaning efforts occurring before visualization must be generated. Fourth, multivariate—similar to volume, visualizations become exponentially more useful as an exploration technique when more variables are present. Fifth, richly segmented—if visualizations can draw on data that have been presegmented into meaningful groups, this pre-established logic for categorization helps to ensure that resulting interpretations of the data have an inherent and interpretable meaning. By selecting data that innately fulfill most or all of these criteria, or that can be made so prior to beginning the visualization creation process, resulting outputs will be more likely to produce interpretable, prescriptive guidance for the user.

Information Transfer to the Audience

When designing visualizations, it is critical to consider the process by which the information gets transferred to the viewer. A data visualization applies an interpretive framework to the data toward the goal of communicating new information to the user. In this model, the designer of the visualization encodes information to in turn drive an intended form of decoding and to produce insight and understanding for the user's benefit (Cairo, 2013). Ensuring that this transfer occurs requires careful consideration of the audience for the visualization—the researcher may make very different design choices for an audience comprising senior executives compared to one of fellow researchers or students, as these audiences have different levels of experience with visualized information formats and different orientations to the depth of attention and time that they are willing to give to the interpretive process.

Though visual forms of information have become increasingly common, variation in sophistication levels for processing visualizations remain. Shah and Hoeffner (2002) discuss mechanisms for teaching students this form of "graphical literacy" and these recommendations—including using multiple representations of data when possible, focusing on the meaning associated with different visual features, and guiding users to consider visualization a critical evaluation and interpretation opportunity—extend to non-student audiences as well. As I-O psychologists have opportunities to foster these skills in our roles interacting with students and professionals, our orientation toward these factors, particularly the "meta-cognition" (Shah & Hoeffner, 2002) associated with the act of visualization reading itself, will produce benefits for future as well as current instances of visualized information transfer.

Design

Design plays an essential role in the success of data visualizations in achieving their goals, with practical benefits that far outweigh the increased demands placed on the visualization's creator (Vande Moere & Purchase,

2011). An initial set of design considerations relates to the use of visual features that combine the benefits of pre-attentive processing with accuracy of interpretation for the types of data represented within the visualization as summarized above. A second early step in the design process is to choose a particular class of visualization—for example, to show connections and relationships or to display trends in data over time—to match the research question and intended use. Within a visualization class, a designer may choose to select and test multiple options for specific types, taking into account the visual metaphor that best blends the message, the need to prioritize depiction of either patterns or details, and the aesthetic qualities of the output (Kirk, 2012). Once a narrow range of options has been selected, pretesting with individuals representative of the target audience can help in confirming a final option.

Kelleher and Wagener (2011) propose a set of useful guidelines for effectively visualizing data in scientific publications. These guidelines are applicable across levels of sophistication from the basic to the advanced, and a subset of recommendations from this discussion that relate particularly well to big data visualization applications is summarized here. A first consideration is simplicity—to create the simplest graph that still depicts the intended message (Tufte, 1983). While many of the examples displayed above are far from simple, they also are designed for use with extremely complex and multifaceted datasets, so they may still be the most efficient way to present information of big data's typical scope and scale. A second consideration highly relevant to such datasets is how to address density of data points in a way that can render them still visible. Options for dealing with this condition include making data points transparent or as unfilled circles or reducing the size of the points to allow more to be visible simultaneously. A final design consideration is color choice—to select an appropriate color scheme based on the qualities of the data (which can also include key distinctions such as significance or non-significance, with the latter indicated by a distinct coloring) and the message the visualization should convey. Color can either detract from the brain's ability to process a graphic or enable it, and the temptation to overuse color (an unfortunate default characteristic of many visualization tools) should be avoided— Cairo's (2013) guidance accordingly is that:

> The best way to disorient your readers is to fill your graphic with objects colored in pure accent tones. Pure colors are uncommon in nature, so limit them to highlight whatever is important in your graphics, and use subdued hues—grays, light blues, and greens—for everything else. (p. 105)

Two related sets of color considerations are for printing and color-blindness. Various websites provide self-evaluation tools to gauge and avoid potential issues in these areas.

GRAPHICAL OVERLAYS AND ANNOTATIONS

A special class of design considerations is graphical overlays and annotations—for certain forms of big data visualizations, these are very useful design features to illustrate trends not directly observable from the graphic itself. These features can serve a valuable function to guide the reader to a level of clarity and form of interpretation not otherwise assured. Although graphical overlays and annotations play a critical role in transferring the intended visual message to the user, they are not automatically generated by data visualization tools in most cases; rather, they must be added by the researcher and visualization creator. Although adding graphical overlays and annotations requires additional design steps, their potential value should not go unrecognized, as they have been shown to improve memorability of visually-presented information (Borgo et al., 2012) and reduce working memory demands placed on a user, a common risk area for large-scale visualization (Shah & Hoeffner, 2002). Borgo et al. (2012) also found that the use of graphical overlays can negatively impact visual search, so these advantages can come at a cost.

Kong and Agrawala (2012) define five types of graphical overlays applicable to data visualizations. While these are also relevant to more traditional visualizations such as bar, line, and pie charts, they are worth noting for big data visualizations due to their ability to reduce working memory demands (Shah & Hoeffner, 2002).

Reference Structures

Overlays can serve as reference structures to clarify the linkage between the underlying data and its visual representation. Reference structures can include gridlines at standard intervals, such as might be generated by default from a software package. The placement of these lines can also be placed in accordance with the desired interpretation, for example to denote the high and low value range for a particular group. An example reference structure is shown above in Figure 5.12 (the gridlines within the bubble plot).

Highlights

Highlights use color and shading to emphasize particular key components of the data or conversely, to de-emphasize others. This form of annotation can be useful to show the scores for one particular country's growth over time among all other countries displayed, for example. Highlights can also be added and removed sequentially to progress through an interpretive view of the data. Certain big data visualization methods, such as parallel coordinates, make frequent use of highlights to add prominence to selected elements within the visual field, without which trend and pattern detection would be difficult or impossible. Examples of highlighting are shown above in Figure 5.7 (highlighting certain specific job classifications in a distinct color) and in Figure 5.14 (thicker and dotted lines to emphasize particular countries' patterns).

Redundant Encodings

Redundant encodings can be simply data labels to indicate values within a visualization. These can be applied either across the full set of data or selectively to indicate key points of note. Redundant encodings can also include supplementary indications of trends within the data that do not appear within the standard visualization (e.g., an additional line connecting two specific data points). Redundant encoding is also shown above in Figures 5.6 and 5.7 (the labeling of certain specific job classifications).

Summary Statistics

Summary statistics can be very useful as annotations to display a common reference point within the visualization based on an average, maximum, or minimum value. This supplementary visual information can aid the user in putting individual data points in context. Slopegraphs make frequent use of summary statistics to display an average set of values. An example of summary statistics is shown above in Figure 5.1 (average values for 2013 and 2014).

Annotations

Annotations are textual notes or comments added directly to the visualization as a mechanism for communicating directly with the user about aspects of or information within the data that he or she may not otherwise detect or that warrant special emphasis. The use of annotations is more appropriate for data visualizations with a focus on explanation, and less so for those where the user should be allowed to explore the dataset independently. However, when used responsibly, annotations can substantially reduce the risk of mis- or underinterpretation of the visualization. Many visualizations presented in news media use annotations—as well as other graphical overlays—to bridge the gap between the expertise level of the researcher and the user in order to allow the latter to benefit from the context and experience of the former. Examples of annotations are shown above in Figure 5.12 (labels applied to certain clusters of countries), Figure 5.13 (indicating US holidays), and Figure 5.16 (indicating the variables most and least correlated with leader quality).

KEY ISSUES AND RISKS

As the expectations for data visualization are growing, so too does the risk of unfulfilled hopes for their ultimate value. These risks are particularly salient for poorly designed and presented visualizations. In this section, we focus on several risks and disadvantages that are unique to or exacerbated by big data applications. For an expanded list, Bresciani and Eppler (2009) provide a thorough representation of key risks associated with data visualizations of all types.

Imprecision and Inaccuracy

A primary disadvantage of visualizations is that they display information at a lower level of precision and accuracy than numerical or tabular formats. Though the human eye can, based on a well-designed visualization, easily spot patterns and variations in the pre-attentive variables described above, we are much less proficient at detecting minute differences between individual data points unless guided to do so by a graphical annotation or other indicator. Certain relationships are also frequently overstated in visual as compared to numerical formats—for example, correlation magnitude is often over-estimated with high-density scatterplots (Cleveland, Diaconis, & McGill, 1982; Lauer & Poster, 1989).

"Optical Significance"

A critical limitation of data visualizations is their treatment of and, in some cases, inability to incorporate statistical and practical significance concepts. If a user of a specific visualization detects a pattern he or she feels is meaningful and that warrants corresponding action, this reaction is often driven by an idiosyncratic interpretation of the finding as it is visually depicted. Beyond practical and statistical significance indices, visualizations are susceptible to a third form of significance, which we are terming "optical significance," such that the viewer will interpret a difference or pattern as meaningful based on his or her perception, often without corresponding quantitative evidence to support this interpretation. This issue is further clouded by design choices made when constructing the visualization. Most data visualization software packages provide no easy way to denote significance—however, the designer can add annotation or shading variation to a visualization to help reduce the risk of the audience either over-interpreting an effect that appears large but does not meet traditional thresholds for either practical or statistical significance, or under-interpreting an effect that is noteworthy despite its trivial appearance.

When significance concepts are incorporated alongside data visualizations, this occurs in one of three ways: First, the visualization designer may have only included patterns within the visualization that met a minimum threshold for statistical or practical significance. Second, as noted above, significance can be indicated by distinctive coloring and shading or graphical overlays such as annotations to denote findings that meet these criteria. Third, visualizations can serve a screening function to detect preliminary findings that can subsequently be subjected to further significance testing.

Visualization Oversaturation

Overuse and excessive prominence of data visualization is the downside of the increasing popularity of these approaches, impacting those who wish to make use of these methods in two ways. First, while the proliferation of data visualizations has led to a vastly increased number of high-quality examples, it has also led to a dramatic increase—possibly even a steeper one—in deficient and flawed visualizations. Blogs such as JunkCharts (http://junkcharts.typepad.com/) are dedicated to visualizations appearing in widely read sources yet lacking, at least in the view of the website's author, key elements of quality. The lack of high-quality, peer-reviewed research on many aspects of visualization also means that less evidence is available to provide solid guidance to creators.

Second, the state of overuse itself can engender skepticism and cynicism about such methods—as with big data as an overarching topic (see, for example, the diagnosis by LeHong, Fenn, and Leeb-du Toit for research firm Gartner in 2014 of big data passing the peak of inflated expectations and sliding into the trough of disillusionment). This risk area can be mitigated by setting careful expectations for one's own as well as others' visualizations, and as a researcher, by solid design choices when creating these graphics as outlined above.

FUTURE DIRECTIONS FOR I-O PSYCHOLOGISTS AND DATA VISUALIZATION

Advanced forms of data visualization are proliferating within the commercial software market and in popular media, yet remain understudied not just as applied to big data and I-O psychology, but more generally as well. As new research studies are conducted, I-O psychologists must extend beyond their natural research domains and information sources to remain current about new developments. We must also push for greater use of visualizations, for appropriate purposes, in our practice and publication efforts—to do otherwise risks missing an opportunity to convey our ideas and extend our influence to audiences who would otherwise fail to connect with our messaging. The use of visualizations within scientific publications is itself a challenging issue, as many forms of visualization are poorly-suited for traditional paper forms of information presentation such as professional journals—as more journals offer online access to their articles, and in interactive formats to draw on the full scope of visualization options outlined above, this will extend the possibilities of these methods to gain a stronger hold within scientific discourse. Researchers who can make their datasets accessible to others in raw format can also benefit from doing so if it allows others to explore the dataset to find otherwise unseen patterns, and conversely, those who are themselves proficient in data visualizations can leverage existing datasets to detect and display new findings not visible through traditional methods. Finally, data visualization can be seen as a form of narrative storytelling (Segel & Heer, 2010) to enhance our ability to convert the inherent but largely unleashed potential of big data into influence and impact. I-O psychologists are extremely well-positioned to be the conduit between data and insight for our constituents within the scientific, practice, and general public communities—our awareness and mastery of data visualization techniques and applications will be an increasingly critical enabler of our success in this role.

REFERENCES

Abela, A. (2008). *Advanced presentations by design: Creating communication that drives action.* San Francisco, CA: Pfeiffer.

Al-Kassab, J., Ouertani, Z.M., Schiuma, G., & Neely, A. (2014). Information visualization to support management decisions. *International Journal of Information Technology & Decision Making, 13,* 407.

Arcia, A., Bales, M.E., Brown, W., Co., M. C., Gilmore, M., Lee, Y. J., . . . & Bakken, S. (2013). Method for the development of data visualizations for community members with varying levels of health literacy. *Proceedings from AMIA Annual Symposium 2013,* 51–60.

Becker, R.A., Cleveland, W.S., & Wilks, A.R. (1988). Dynamic graphics for data analysis. In W.S. Cleveland & M.E. McGill (Eds.), *Dynamic graphics for statistics* (pp. 1–50). Pacific Grove, CA: Brooks/Cole.

Bonneau, G. P., Ertl, T., & Nielson, G.M. (2006). *Scientific visualization: The visual extraction of knowledge from data.* New York, NY: Springer.

Borgo, R., Abdul-Rahman, A., Mohamed, F., Grant, P.W., Reppa, I., Floridi, L., & Chen, M. (2012). An empirical study on using visual embellishments in visualization. *IEEE Transactions on Visualization and Computer Graphics, 18*(12), 2759–2768.

Bresciani, S., & Eppler, M.J. (2009). The risks of visualization: A classification of disadvantages associated with graphic representations of information. In P. J. Schulz, U. Hartung & S. Keller (Eds.), *Identität und Vielfalt der Kommunikationswissenschaft* (pp. 165–178). Konstanz, Germany: UVK Verlagsgesellschaft mbH.

Cairo, A. (2013). *The functional art: An introduction to information graphics and visualization.* Berkeley, CA: New Riders.

Chen, C. (2005). Top 10 unsolved information visualization problems. *IEEE Computer Graphics and Applications, 25*(4), 12–16.

Chen, C. (2010). Information visualization. *Computational Statistics, 2*(4), 387–403.

Clark, J.M., & Paivio, A. (1991). Dual coding theory and education. *Educational Psychology Review, 3,* 149–210.

Cleveland, W.S. (1993). *Visualizing data.* Murray Hill, NJ: AT&T Bell Laboratories.

Cleveland, W.S., Diaconis, P., & McGill, R. (1982). Variables on scatterplots look more highly correlated when the scales are increased. *Science, 216,* 1138–1141.

Cleveland, W.S., & McGill, R. (1985). Graphical perception and graphical methods for analyzing scientific data. *Science, 229*(4716), 828–833.

Connolly, S., & Wooledge, S. (2012). *Harnessing the value of big data analytics.* Retrieved from https://site.teradata.com/Microsite/wc-0217-harnessing-value-bigdata/landing/.ashx

Davies, A., Fidler, D., & Gorbis, M. (2011). Future work skills 2020. University of Phoenix. Retrieved from http://asmarterplanet.com/studentsfor/files/2012/10/future_work_skills_2020_full_research_report_final_1.pdf

Eppler, M.J., & Bresciani, S. (2013). Visualization in management: From communication to collaboration. *Journal of Visual Languages & Computing, 24*(2), 146–149.

Feinberg, J. (2009). Wordle. In J. Steele & J. Illinsky (Eds.), *Beautiful visualizations* (pp. 37–58). Sebastopol, CA: O'Reilly Media, Inc.

Few, S. (2009). Now you see it: Simple visualization techniques for quantitative analysis. Oakland, CA: Analytics Press.

Fox, P., & Hendler, J. (2011). Changing the equation on scientific data visualization. *Science, 331*, 705–708.

Gorodov, E. Y., & Gubarev, V. V. (2013). Analytical review of data visualization methods in application to big data. *Journal of Electrical and Computer Engineering, 2013*, 1–7.

Healey, C., & Enns, J. (2012). Attention and visual memory in visualization and computer graphics. *IEEE Transactions on Visualization and Computer Graphics, 18*, 1170.

Heer, J., Bostock, M., & Ogievetsky, V. (2010). A tour through the visualization zoo. *Communications of the ACM, 53*(6), 59–67.

Huber, P. J. (1987). Experiences with three-dimensional scatterplots. *Journal of the American Statistical Association, 82*, 448–453.

Iliinsky, N., & Steele, J. (2011). *Designing data visualizations.* Sebastopol, CA: O'Reilly.

Johnson, C. (2004). Top scientific visualization research problems. *IEEE Computer Graphics and Applications, 24*(4), 13–17.

Kelleher, C., & Wagener, T. (2011). Ten guidelines for effective data visualization in scientific publications. *Environmental Modelling & Software, 26*(6), 822–827.

Kirk, A. (2012). Data visualization: A successful design process. Birmingham, UK: Packt Publishers.

Knies, R. (2013, May 23). New ways to visualize your data. Retrieved from http://blogs.technet.com/b/inside_microsoft_research/archive/2013/05/23/new-ways-to-visualize-your-data.aspx

Koch, K., Mclean, J., Segev, R., Freed, M. A., Berry, M. J., Balasubramanian, V., . . .& Sterling, P. (2006). How much the eye tells the brain. *Current Biology, 16*(14), 1428–1434.

Kong, N., & Agrawala, M. (2012). Graphical overlays: Using layered elements to aid chart reading. *IEEE Transactions on Visualization and Computer Graphics, 18*, 2631–2638.

Kriz, S., & Hegarty, M. (2007). Top-down and bottom-up influences on learning from animations. *International Journal of Human-Computer Studies, 65*(11), 911–930.

Lauer, T. W., & Post, G. V. (1989). Density in scatterplots and the estimation of correlation. *Behaviour and Information Technology, 8*, 135–244.

Lavalle, S., Lesser, E., Shockley, R., Hopkins, M. S., & Kruschwitz, N. (2011). Big data, analytics and the path from insights to value. *MIT Sloan Management Review, 52*, 21–32.

LeHong, H., Fenn, J., & Leeb-du Toit, R. (2014). *Hype cycle for emerging technologies, 2014.* Retrieved from https://www.gartner.com/doc/2809728

Mackinlay, J. (1986). Automating the design of graphical presentations of relational information. *ACM Transactions on Graphics, 5*(2), 110–141.

Manyika, J., Chui, M., Brown, B., Bughin, J., Dobbs, R., Roxburgh, C., & Byers, A. H. (2011). *Big data: The next frontier for innovation, competition, and productivity.* Retrieved from http://www.mckinsey.com/insights/business_technology/big_data_the_next_frontier_for_innovation

Marchak, F. M., & Marchak, L. C. (1991). Interactive versus passive dynamics and the exploratory analysis of multivariate data. *Behavioral Research Methods, Instruments, & Computers, 23*, 296–300.

Pandey, A. V., Manivannan, A., Nov, O., Satterthwaite, M. L., & Bertini, E. (2014). The persuasive power of data visualization. *New York University Public Law and Legal Theory Working Papers, Paper 474.*

Parsons, P., & Sedig, K. (2013). Common visualizations: Their cognitive utility. In W. Huang (Ed.), *Handbook of human centric visualization* (pp. 671–691). New York, NY: Springer.

Parsons, P. & Sedig, K. (2014). Adjustable properties of visual representations: Improving the quality of human-information interaction. *Journal of the American Society for Information Science & Technology, 65*(3), 455–482.

Russom, P. (2011). *Big data analytics.* Retrieved from http://tdwi.org/research/2011/09/~/ media/TDWI/TDWI/Research/BPR/2011/TDWI_BPReport_Q411_Big_Data_ Analytics_Web/TDWI_BPReport_Q411_Big%20Data_ExecSummary.ashx

Schnotz, W. (2002). Towards an integrated view of learning from text and visual displays. *Educational Psychology Review, 14,* 101–119.

Segel, E., & Heer, J. (2010). Narrative visualization: Telling stories with data. *IEEE Transactions on Visualization and Computer Graphics, 16*(6), 1139–1148.

Shah, P., & Hoeffner, J. (2002). Review of graph comprehension research: Implications for instruction. *Educational Psychology Review, 14*(1), 47–69.

Soo Yi, J., Kang, Y., Stasko, J. Y., & Jacko, J. A. (2007). Toward a deeper understanding of the role of interaction in information visualization. *IEEE Transactions on Visualization and Computer Graphics, 13*(6), 1224–1231.

Stuetzle, W. (1987). Plot windows. *Journal of the American Statistical Association, 82,* 466–475.

Thomas, J. J., & Cook, K. A. (2006). A visual analytics agenda. *IEEE Computer Graphics and Applications, 26,* 10–13.

Tufte, E. R. (1983). *The visual display of quantitative information.* Cheshire, CT: Graphics Press.

Tufte, E. R. (1990). *Envisioning information.* Cheshire, CT: Graphics Press.

Tufte, E. R. (1997). *Visual explanations: Images and quantities, evidence and narrative.* Cheshire, CT: Graphics Press.

Vande Moere, A., & Purchase, H. (2011). On the role of design in information visualization. *Information Visualization, 10*(4), 356–371.

Viégas, F. B., & Wattenberg, M. (2007). Artistic data visualization: Beyond visual analytics. *Online Communities and Social Computing, 4564,* 182–191.

Viégas, F. B., Wattenberg, M., & Feinberg, J. (2009). Participatory visualization with Wordle. *IEEE Transactions on Visualization and Computer Graphics, 15*(6), 1137–1144.

Zhu, Y. (2007). Measuring effective data visualization. *Advances in Visual Computing, 4842,* 652–661.

6

Sensing Big Data

Multimodal Information Interfaces for Exploration of Large Data Sets

Jeffrey Stanton

There really is nothing quite as convenient as the humble bar graph. On a single sheet of paper, one can represent a comparison between several groups or show the movement of a variable over a period of time. The paper on which the bar graph is printed is easily portable, can be viewed under a wide variety of conditions, and can be filed in a very small space for short-term or long-term storage. Almost every educated person can understand the results presented on a bar graph because many people begin practicing the interpretation of bar graphs and related visual displays of data as early as first grade.

Yet the bar graph also has its limitations. Adding more data points eventually begins to obscure any finer patterns of variation that may exist in the data. In cases where the data represent dynamic processes that unfold over time, the static nature of the printed bar graph may limit one's ability to recognize temporal patterns at different scales that may exist in the data. When the complexity and meaning of a data set lies in the connections between more than two or three variables, the bar graph is useless. We may solve this problem by moving to a scattergram with a regression line, but our sheet of paper can still only support a few hundred points before the patterns are again obscure. We can sometimes fake a decent 3D diagram, but it is challenging to represent more than three variables on a 2D surface. In short, beyond a certain level of size and/or complexity, our traditional and comfortable tools for data visualization begin to lose their utility.

For most of the history of the scientific endeavor, it was so expensive to collect data that most data sets were relatively small (Carr-Hill, 1987). In psychology, for example, a review of almost any peer reviewed research journal shows that data sets in the range of a few hundred observations were the norm through most of the twentieth century. With data sets of that size, bar graphs, histograms, boxplots, and scattergrams sufficed. When applied to the early stages of data cleaning, screening, and exploration, histograms and other simple data displays provided enough insight to diagnose most of the typical problems one might encounter in a data set. Thinking more generally, visualization techniques that were developed in the age of print publications were especially well suited for working with the modest amounts of data that scientists could typically collect.

In the present day, not only are data sets larger on average, but there are also a vastly larger number of data sets available for public use (Manovich, 2012). For example, the U.S. federal government publishes more than 87,000 data sets on a web site called data.gov. More closely allied with psychology and the social sciences, the Inter-university Consortium for Political and Social Research, located at the University of Michigan, publishes more than 3,000 data sets ranging from very small to very large. These two examples represent the tip of the iceberg, as thousands and thousands of other data sources covering a broad range of interesting human phenomena are widely available to contemporary researchers (Gurin, 2014).

Given the research potential of these varied data sources, the research community arguably needs innovative tools for making sense of large, complex data sets (Manovich, 2012; Moody & Healy, 2014; Newman et al., 2012). Fortunately, for several decades researchers have been exploring new techniques for perceiving and interpreting data. These include examples such as heads up displays that overlay data on a visual scene, sonification of data for interpretation by the ear, and haptic displays that present information to the body through touch and motion. Taken together, these innovations represent the promise of immersive information interfaces that facilitate the perception and understanding of data using multiple senses. In this chapter, a review of this research—with a detailed exploration of sonification and haptics as complements to visualization—leads to considerations for the future design of immersive information interfaces.

BACKGROUND

The Big Data Challenge

The trade press is rife with descriptions of the vast amount of data currently available for analysis (Lynch, 2008; McAfee & Brynjolfsson, 2012).

Thanks to Moore's law, the cost of sensor devices has declined precipitously. Moore's law, coined by Gordon Moore of Intel corporation, posited that processing power per unit cost would double every 18 months indefinitely into the future (Schaller, 1997). While we first noticed the action of Moore's law on the power and prices of personal computers, the same forces have worked on electronics of all types. Gadgets such as bar code readers, RFID systems, video surveillance cameras, and myriad other devices and systems constantly collect data on the ebb and flow of contemporary life. As a result, massive amounts of data exist in virtually every area of human endeavor and across all sectors including government, education, science, and industry. Much of this data has relevance to the behavioral sciences, as it represents traces of the choices and actions that people take in a range of everyday environments.

There is an analog to Moore's law in the area of data storage, called Kryder's law, that also predicts exponential increases in the density of data storage over time. Specifically, Mark Kryder, formerly of Seagate Corporation (a hard disk drive manufacturer) suggested that the density of data storage on magnetic hard disk drives was increasing at a rate that exceeded Moore's law (Walter, 2005). Given recent advances in solid state data storage (e.g., SD cards, thumb drives, SSD drives in Mac computers, etc.) the medium of storage is probably less important than the idea that there have been and probably will continue to be radical decreases in the cost of data storage. These decreases have meant that IT professionals who run our servers, cloud storage, and backup systems spend much less time worrying about the amount of data they have to store on our behalf and much less effort getting us to delete it to make room for new data. The end result of this desuetude of deletion is that massive amounts of data beyond what any analyst could hope to tackle continue to accrete in the archives of organizations everywhere.

The proliferation of data in every corner of every sector represents both an opportunity and a problem. The opportunity lies in using large amounts of data to find novel patterns, research insights, operational efficiencies, and evidence to support improved decision-making. Many of these insights can be obtained in areas of immense interest to behavioral scientists, such as the workplace, consumer behavior, and health behavior (Stanton, 2013). The challenge is that the tools and techniques that have served us well during the period of small data are not up to the task of supporting us in the time of big data. Every task in the lifecycle of data, including acquisition, cleaning, exploration, analysis, visualization, and archiving, is inhibited by having a large number of variables with limited or absent data dictionaries, by having data with unknown provenance, by having missing data, by the complexity of the relationships among the many variables in the data, and by the massive number of observations to be considered in making sense of the data.

Each of these problems demands better tools so that the social scientist can make sense of large data sets more efficiently. Consider the steps you may have used the most recent time that you undertook an analysis of a new or unfamiliar data set. It is likely that you spent time on each variable—creating histograms and scatterplots, screening for missing data and outliers, etc.—before undertaking any substantive analysis. You might have even flagged a few individual observations for close examination because they seemed anomalous. In a dataset with thousands of variables and millions of observations, this kind of handiwork is not longer feasible. In the same vein, it is not simply the increased size of the data but the increased complexity—e.g., in cross-linked tables, network data, and unstructured data—that makes these exploration processes more challenging. We need better tools with more automation to facilitate the exploration of these complex configurations. Although visualization—the use of bar graphs, histograms, scattergrams, box plots, and myriad other data displays—has long been a mainstay in the analyst's toolkit, a set of emerging techniques that engage the other senses has the promise of improving the process of making sense of data.

Traditional Data Visualization and Computer-based Visualization

As visualization techniques are substantially covered in Chapter 5 in this volume, only a few key points about the historical trajectory of data visualization need elucidation here. In the 1300s, philosopher Nicole Oresme created some of the earliest data charts known to appear in print (Clagget, 1968). These charts—some of which are analogous to modern bar charts—detail the path of a moving object by documenting observations of the height of the object at successive time intervals (Oresme was also notable for publishing the first known printed critique of astrology). Visualization expert Edward R. Tufte has documented many of the remarkable and creative approaches to data visualization that have appeared in the intervening 700 years since Oresme's first printed bar chart (Tufte, 1991). Tufte's examples demonstrate a dizzying variety of techniques that artists have harnessed to make data visually accessible and comprehensible to readers of books and reports. Fundamentally, however, all artists and analysts working in the pre-computer era faced an essential limitation that ink on a flat piece of paper was a limited medium for representing more than a few variables and/or a few hundred observations at a time.

The emergence of the electronic computer in the 1950s opened the window for transcending these limitations (Molnar, 1997). Computer screens, starting with basic cathode ray tube technology, made possible displays with movement as well as the use of dynamic shading and perspective to provide a more convincing illusion of three-dimensionality. As display density improved, particularly with the introduction of the liquid crystal display in the 1980s, the opportunities to represent the movement of multiple variables over time became enhanced, although these flat screen displays still limited the data representations to a two-dimensional matrix of pixels. In subsequent developments, researchers began to experiment with heads up displays, head mounted displays, and augmented reality applications in the 1990s (Azuma, 1997). These displays had the capability of providing a more realistic sense of three-dimensionality and also opened the possibility of overlaying data representations on top of naturally occurring visual scenes. Recently, these efforts have culminated in the development of a product known as Oculus Rift—a display device primarily intended for gaming but with a range of industrial and medical applications already imagined (Byagowi, Lambeta, Aldaba, & Moussavi, 2014). Oculus Rift goggles fit over the head, block out one's vision of the outside world, and provide an independent image to each eye as well as motion detection, so that as the head moves, the three-dimensional scene changes accordingly.

The progression of visual displays undoubtedly has more stages left in its evolution, as holographic three-dimensional systems become more cost effective and user friendly (Blanche et al., 2010). Ultimately, though, the amount of data that the user can perceive from any display has an intrinsic limit that lies in the characteristics of the human visual system and the brain. Although human vision excels in stereoscopic perception of dynamic and colorful scenes, the other senses have complementary capabilities that researchers have begun to explore and system designers have begun to exploit. In the next section, an overview of some of this research provides insights into how, for example, vision and hearing might be used together to explore large datasets. After this initial orientation to the state of the art, the conclusion of the paper attempts to develop a compelling use case for behavioral and social scientists to begin working with multimodal displays.

Beyond Visualization

Despite the standard notion that humans possess five senses, physiologists commonly recognize proprioception (joint position), vestibular balance, and sensory feedback from muscle tension as additional modes of perception (Chang, 2013). Nonetheless, among these eight senses, hearing and touch are the most commonly exploited (other than vision) for displays. Taste and olfaction have obvious limitations with respect to provision of usable interfaces, whereas proprioception, balance, and muscle strain have only occasionally been examined as a basis for displays. In contrast, researchers have made considerable progress in understanding how people make sense of audible and tactile inputs, and designers have created displays that use these senses effectively (Walker, 2002; 2007). Two commonplace historical examples illustrating this point are Geiger counters—which translate radioactive particle decay into an audible signal—and the stall warning system on aircraft that causes the control stick to shake when the plane is in imminent danger of stalling. The latter system in particular has been the subject of many studies in the area of human factors.

Researchers who conduct work on audible data displays frequently refer to this area of research as sonification (Bonebright et al., 1997). A 1992 conference in Santa Fe, New Mexico, the first International Conference on Auditory Display, marked the beginning of an era of intensive research interest in sonification (Kramer, 1994). Early developments in this area focused on understanding how the essential characteristics of human hearing would affect the interpretation of data presented via sound. Humans can hear sounds in the range between 20 Hertz and 20,000 Hertz (although age-related hearing loss makes most of the population deaf to sounds above 15,000 Hertz). Hertz is a measurement of vibration frequency that is also known as cycles per second. By way of comparison, an 88-key grand piano has as its lowest key an A (four octaves below A-440 or 27.5 Hertz) and as it's highest key a C (four octaves above middle C or 4186.01 Hertz). Each octave represents a doubling of the frequencies from the octave below, so the piano leaves roughly two audible octaves on the high end to make room for the violin, flute, cymbals, and other high-pitched instruments and sounds. Western listeners who are not trained musicians can usually hear the pitch difference between any two neighboring keys on the piano, suggesting that many people can easily differentiate about 100 unique pitches in the full range of human hearing. Note that this idea pertains to the perception of relative rather than absolute pitch. Many listeners can say whether one note is higher than another note, but they cannot identify whether one of the notes is middle C.

In addition to pitch, individuals with normal hearing can detect the timbre of a sound (e.g., the difference between the bray of a trumpet and the twang of a guitar), the loudness of a sound, the position of a sound in horizontal space (i.e., panning), and the apparent distance of a sound in a reverberant field. Each of these dimensions can map to data parameters for display purposes. For example, to display a histogram using audio, one might map the height of each bar to the pitch of a corresponding note and then pan the notes in a left-to-right field according to the position of each bar on the range of the variable represented by the histogram. Hermann and Ritter (1999) refer to this strategy as *parameter-based sonification*: direct translation of the scaled value of a data point into one or more of the sonic parameters described above. A variety of modest successes, particularly in the area of sonification of scientific data, have demonstrated that the parameter-based approach can work for certain auditory display applications. For example, researchers at CERN have translated the outputs of particle detectors into sound as a way of understanding the energy levels and path angles of particles emitted during a nuclear collision (Vogt et al., 2010). A wide range of parameter-based data sonification examples exists on the music and sound hosting site SoundCloud.com (soundcloud. com/tags/sonification). Notably, the great majority of sonification examples stored on this site pertain to physical science data sets (e.g., from the large hadron collider), where scientists have wrestled with very large data sets for decades.

Where the ear really excels, however, is in the detection of rhythm. Gfeller, Woodworth, Robin, Witt, and Knutson (1997), Ashmead, Leroy, and Odom (1990), Tervaniemi and Brattico (2004), and many other researchers have explored the limits and capabilities of rhythmic sound perception. For very brief sounds, such as the click of a finger snapping, the human ear can separate two sonic events that are as little as five milliseconds apart. More complex sounds than a click require more time to recognize and more separation between events for them to seem distinctive. Even at intervals longer than five milliseconds, however, there is sufficient room for more than 100 simple sonic events to fit into the space of a single second. This far exceeds the capability of the eye: the eye fuses together events spaced any closer than 35–40 milliseconds (hence the successful illusion of continuous motion in movies projected at 30 frames per second). One possible implication of this capability is that sound might be usable in the review of time series data that is presented to the analyst at a higher rate than what the eye can comfortably perceive.

The ear is also acutely sensitive to changes in the regularity of occurrence of sonic events, so any disturbances in rhythm are immediately noticeable by the ear. Relatedly, there is ample evidence—manifested, for example, in the cocktail party effect—that it is possible to independently and simultaneously monitor audible and visible events with a high degree of acuity (Janata & Childs, 2004; Roginska, Childs, & Johnson, 2006). This point hints at one possible application of a multimodal interface: sound can potentially represent an independent dimension of data for the user to monitor while simultaneously considering visual data—potentially a method of discovering data anomalies. For example, Janata and Childs (2004) showed how user accuracy in a review of time-series financial data could improve by using an audio warning when an outlier was detected.

In a parallel set of developments, researchers have explored the use of so-called haptic interfaces since the 1960s (Steelman, 1968). The word haptic derives from a Greek word meaning to touch or grasp; when used in reference to interfaces and displays, it refers to any system that provides tactile (including touch, temperature, texture, vibration, and pressure) or kinesthetic feedback to the individual who is interacting with the system. Imagine, for example, putting your hand into a grocery bag containing some bottles of soda, and based on what you can touch, feel, and lift, being able to infer the sizes of the bottles, the bottle material, how full the bottles are, and the temperature of the soda they contain. Now imagine hardware and software that allows you to accomplish the same task "robotically" when the environment under exploration is too small, too large, or too distant to be directly explored with the body. Such an interface would engage the sense of touch, but would also incorporate proprioception and the sensing of muscle tension. Thus, the hand can sense data—either directly or through an interface—to the extent that the data can be presented as objects with properties such as texture, weight, and/or motion resistance. In statistical analysis, and especially in visualization tasks, it is reasonably common to represent raw data or results in the form of shapes or surfaces, so the potential for haptic exploration as a component of data exploration seems evident.

One of the earliest practical projects where a haptic display complemented a visualization task had the interesting name Project GROPE, and was used for scientific visualization of complex molecular structures. Brooks Jr., Ouh-Young, Batter, and Kilpatrick (1990) described how the combination of force feedback together with visualization improved users' accurate comprehension of the molecular structures under exploration. The interface on this project provided a controller arm with which the user could "feel" the surface of a molecular structure. Although exploring a molecule differs from typical data analysis tasks, the fact that user performance improved based on the combination of visual and tactile inputs suggests the possibility that such interfaces could benefit other types of complex sensing activities. Consider analytical approaches such as response surface methodology (see Edwards, 2002), where effective use of the technique depends upon interpretation of contour plots. While the typical two-dimensional contour plots provided by a traditional statistical program do support the analyst's work, a system that supported effective three-dimensional exploration of responses could enhance effective use of this technique.

Some of the contemporary impetus for the development of haptic displays has come from research on medical devices. Endoscopic and arthroscopic surgery using camera-guided instruments provide some of the most advanced applications of combined haptic-visual displays, particularly for training and simulation (Perez-Guttierez, Martinez, & Rojas, 2010; Tsujita et al. 2012). A second area where haptic displays have received considerable research attention lies in the area of providing technological accommodations for the blind and deaf (Eberhardt, Bernstein, Coulter, & Hunckler, 1993; Rastogi & Pawluk, 2013).

Sigcrist, Rauter, Riener, and Wolf (2013) have provided a comprehensive review of the state of haptic and multimodal interfaces with respect to their influence on motor learning. Their review shows that, while much is still poorly understood about optimal design principles for haptic and multimodal interfaces, existing research seems to fully support the idea that multi-modal interfaces are more effective than single mode interfaces at promoting learning. This not only parallels some of the findings in sonification research, it also makes intuitive sense: humans excel at the performance of certain tasks that engage multiple senses simultaneously. Consider how sports such as basketball or soccer, or alternatively more primal activities such as hunting and wayfinding, incorporate visual, sonic, and tactile cues in the service of effective performance. Evolution has molded the body and the brain to make effective use of multimodal input for a variety of complex sensing tasks.

Multimodal Sensing Environments

Forward-looking designers have taken this notion to heart, particularly during the era of the computer, to design and/or build multimodal environments for a variety of tasks. One of the earliest examples comes from Ivan Sutherland (1965), who proposed what he called the "ultimate display." Sutherland was a 1960s student at MIT, a professor at Harvard, and one of the first directors of the Information Processing Techniques Office of the U.S. Federal Government's Advanced Research Projects Agency. His proposal for the ultimate display was for a system that combined visual and haptic feedback to support tasks such as exploration of microscopic objects. Sutherland even imagined a system that foreshadowed today's augmented reality systems. Not coincidentally, later in his career Sutherland won the Turing Award from the Association for Computing Machinery based on a design for a head-mounted virtual reality display that was the predecessor to today's Oculus Rift immersive virtual reality goggles.

More contemporary instances of immersive environments include a wide range of variations on the theme of CAVEs (computer assisted virtual environments) that typically comprise room-sized installations integrating multiple displays, audio, and gestural controls. For example, DeFanti et al. (2009) described StarCAVE as a "third generation virtual reality portal." The authors custom-built StarCAVE as an empty, cubical room with a width, depth, and height of approximately 8 feet, high-resolution displays on every surface (including the floor, by means of a ceiling mounted projector) and a surround-sound audio system with subwoofers. A wireless optical tracking system followed the head and hand motions of the user standing in StarCAVE and used these inputs to shift the visualizations and modify the audio output. Figures in DeFanti et al.'s article depicted the user exploring the surface of an RNA molecule. Indeed, most of the applications of StarCAVE imagined by the authors pertained to the multimodal display and interactive exploration of large scientific data sources.

As the StarCAVE example suggests, multimodal interfaces have already proven their value in the area of scientific data exploration. Alexander et al. (2011) described a 13-year project to make sense out of data downloaded from the Advanced Composition Explorer satellite. This satellite has provided hundreds of large data sets with information about the solar wind, cosmic rays, and solar energetic particles. Alexander et al. (2011) noted that the interpretation of these data was problematic until research began to include a sonification channel in their work to review the data. With the introduction of the audio component to the data displays, new revelations emerged about different varieties of solar wind.

Based on these insights, the authors asserted their belief that multimodal interfaces would have substantial ongoing benefits in their area of research. Up until recently, however, the technology had not matured to the point where sonified or haptic-enabled displays were widely feasible for researcher use. With appropriate funding and a speculative mindset, research teams that had the right mix of hardware and software skills could cobble together a demonstration unit as a proof of concept, but simple, inexpensive tools for mashing together visualization, sonification, and haptic display were unavailable. Because of the emerging popularity of open source software tools and the cost effectiveness of adaptable hardware platforms, however, those barriers have substantially diminished (see Kato, 2010).

EXISTING TOOLS FOR CREATING MULTIMODAL DISPLAYS AND INTERFACES

By far the most popular tool for contemporary statistical analysis is the open source R platform (Culpepper & Aguinis, 2011). While academic researchers in the U.S. appear to continue to prefer commercial packages such as SPSS and SAS (Dembe, Partridge, & Geist, 2011), in the larger worldwide community of statistical analysts, R is becoming the standard language for statistical programming (Kapenga, McKean, & Gustafson, 2014). One of the reasons for R's popularity and its continuing relevance in the analyst community is the system of packages that permits integration of a wide range of analytical software contributions from members of the community (German, Adams, & Hassan, 2013). The R package system boasts a high level of success: 5,457 user contributed packages at the time of this writing. These packages span an incredibly wide array of analytical applications. With respect to multimodal display, R offers dozens of packages for graphics and visualization as well as a handful of possibilities for sonification. Packages supporting sonification include Audio, Cscound, PlayItByR, SeeWave, and Tuner. Using the sonification packages, it is possible with a few lines of code to create sonic displays of data that complement traditional graphs. Brown and Bearman (2012) described a range of sonified data display applications that have provided unique data insights. For example, they highlighted a climate change mapping application that overlaid predicted temperatures on a map of a land surface using color-coding. The designers of the map interface were at a loss as to how to represent uncertainty in the predictions until they hit on the idea of representing the width of confidence intervals with a synthesized tone. Users of the interactive map reported that the sonified version was helpful in making sense of the climate change data. Likewise, McIntosh, Mittelhammer, and Middleton (2013) described an application of PlayItByR to the sonification of econometrics data. One particularly satisfying aspect of their paper was the finding that sonification could be used effectively to diagnose the error terms in a complex statistical model. To illustrate this possibility, they constructed and compared two econometric models:

a complete model with random errors centered on zero and an omitted variable model. After translating the residuals to a stream of tones, they illustrated how users could hear a characteristic pattern in the residuals of the omitted variable model that could allow an analyst to diagnose the problem with the model. An exhaustive search of R packages did not reveal any packages pertaining to haptic or touch-based data exploration.

A second software platform relevant to the creation of multimodal displays is the graphics programming language known as Processing (Reas & Fry, 2003). Unlike R, Processing is optimized for the creation of interactive graphics displays (as opposed to command line or "batch" mode that is the most common way of interacting with R). Like R, Processing has a system of packages (known as libraries) that permit the addition of new features and capabilities to the core of the platform. For example, the Minim library provides access to a wide range of audio playback and audio synthesis functions that analysts can use to transform data into both light and sound. The visual power of Processing has proved appealing to artists such as Hannes Jung, who created a tactile interface he calls. fluid using an Arduino board (Arduino is an inexpensive, do-it-yourself computer circuit board that was developed to give schoolchildren the opportunity to build and program interactive systems like robots and drones), a viscous fluid (corn starch and water), an ordinary speaker cone, and Processing (Serrano, 2013). Jung used a multi-touch interface to provide input to an algorithm that used the speaker to create a standing wave in the fluid medium. In turn, the user could touch and interact with the fluid medium as it displayed different textures and patterns.

While such projects demonstrate a great deal of ingenuity, more structured solutions for adding haptic features to an interface also exist. One of the simplest and least expensive (under $100 USD) force feedback devices available is the Logitech Wingman mouse. Using a special mouse pad, the device adds resistance and vibration both to gaming tasks and everyday computer activities such as web browsing. Yu and Brewster (2002) reviewed the use of the Wingman mouse for research applications and found that the software development kit was easy to use for creating haptically enabled displays. The primary limitation of this device is that it only works in two dimensions.

The most mature solution for three-dimensional haptics comprises a proprietary hardware device and an open source software development kit offered by a firm called Geomagic (http://www.geomagic.com). Their Geomagic Touch product looks like a stylus attached to a small robotic arm. The user can move the stylus with six degrees of freedom and the device can provide force feedback on three of those dimensions (pitch, roll, and yaw). The software toolkit, known as OpenHaptics Toolkit, provides developers with high-level tools for creating interactions with the device. The firm boasts that a basic display that combines tactile and visual aspects can be constructed with as little as six lines of code. As noted earlier in the chapter, the essential task of constructing a haptic display lies in creating virtual objects that have texture, weight, resistance, and other properties that the user can feel with the device. The OpenHaptics Toolkit facilitates the straightforward and rapid creation of these virtual objects.

The OpenHaptics toolkit became available in 2005, and researchers have used it for a variety of explorations. Theoktisto, Fairén, Navazo, and Monclús (2005) tackled a critical problem in haptic interfaces—the capability of efficiently and accurately representing the surfaces in a virtual model that provides the user with force feedback. Leino et al. (2009) examined whether a combined visual and haptic interface could enhance the process of designing industrial machinery by planning more effective maintenance tasks at the design stage. They found that about half of the engineers who evaluated their system believed that the haptic-enabled interface could improve the maintenance readiness of the industrial designs. Finally, Gao, Li, Su, and Li (2011) described an application of the OpenHaptics system to training of surgeons on robotic surgery systems. Because of the high cost of robotic surgery systems and the many barriers preventing training on live patients (or cadavers, for that matter), much of the training that surgeons complete by necessity occurs on a simulator. Surgical simulators provide highly realistic visual displays of the (virtual) site of the operation. By using a force-feedback haptic device as a controller, the designers of these simulators can also provide the surgeon with a controller that closely emulates the feel of the instrument that the surgeon will use during a live operation. As with other haptic applications, the force feedback system described in their paper provides the hand and the arm with a realistic sense of texture and resistance as the interface traverses the virtual biological objects represented in the display.

FUTURE DESIGN OF IMMERSIVE INFORMATION INTERFACES

The research reviewed above shows a great deal of experimental activity occurring both in the areas of sonification and haptics. Given the state of the research, however, it is challenging to figure out how these new technologies might be harnessed in service of big data exploration. Parameterized sound appears to give the promise of simultaneous review of additional dimensions of data in conjunction with visualization. Likewise, haptics seem to facilitate the exploration of virtual objects and environments in ways that transcend standard 2D or 3D graphs. What is less clear and obvious is how a visualization system with force feedback and sound could provide substantial benefits for big data analytics tasks over and above standard visualization techniques.

Fortunately, Panëels and her colleagues have spent a lot of time thinking about this question and devising studies to explore it (Panëels & Roberts, 2010; Panëels, Roberts, & Rodgers, 2009; Panëels, Ritsos, Rodgers, & Roberts, 2013; Roberts & Panëels, 2007). To illustrate the work that is underway, we can return to the beginning of the paper and the introduction of that workhorse of visualizations: the bar graph. Panëels and Roberts (2010) described haptically- and sonically-enabled bar graphs that transcended the traditional printed bar graph. With a few embellishments gleaned from related work by other authors, here is a scenario that illustrates some of the possibilities.

In the new multimodal version of the bar graph, the user drags display variables and grouping variables from a tray and drops them on a textured display surface. The bars representing those variables then appear on the display. Each bar is "engraved" onto the display so that the force-feedback stylus, when moving up and down along a bar, stays in the groove in order to facilitate exploration of the data encapsulated in that bar. A musical pitch mapped to the z-score of each data point facilitates comparisons between different bars of data points at similar points in the distribution. The border lines painted on each engraved bar are so-called tactons—they feel sticky to the touch when the stylus moves over them, and pressing on them activates a new function or aspect of the display. For example, pressing on the top border of any bar lights up any univariate outliers that may exist in the distribution of points represented by that bar. Pressing on the side border of a cluster of bars facilitates manipulation of the grouping variable: creating finer or coarser subdivisions of the grouping variable reveals hidden patterns or anomalies in the data.

Additional interactions with the force feedback stylus can also enable statistical exploration of the data. Lassoing a number of bars together runs and reports an ANOVA on the selected groups; a piece of string connecting any two individual bars conducts a post hoc test. The size of the eta-squared, Cohen's D, or other effect size measure is represented audibly by a chord containing varying levels of sonic noise. Drag another variable from the tray to serve as a control variable in the ANOVA. Chain several additional variables together to form a unit weighted composite for further analysis. Composites with heavier weights when manipulated by the force feedback device have higher reliability than lighter-weight composites.

Panëels and her collaborators refer to scenarios like these as "haptic data visualization," and much of what was described above already exists, albeit in prototype form. Note that by focusing on the simple example of a haptically- and sonically-enabled bar chart, we have barely scratched the surface of what might be possible with a fully rendered haptic data visualization. Multimodal interfaces for other graphical types such as scattergrams, network diagrams, and choropleth maps have hardly been explored at all, even in experimental prototypes. In more complex areas of analysis such as clustering, supervised machine learning, latent growth curve models, hierarchical linear analysis, ARIMA time series analysis, and structural equation modeling, there could be a host of multimodal display applications for model building and diagnosis.

One fruitful direction for further development would be to add immersive three-dimensional viewing to a multimodal display either using virtual reality goggles (e.g., Oculus Rift) or a 3D enabled conventional LCD display. The use of a haptic controller device in the three-dimensional environment would facilitate the exploration of more complex data sets by allowing the user to model the interconnections between three variables simultaneously. The integration of parameter-mapped audio into such an environment could potentially add one or more additional variable dimensions to the display. Likewise, with separate sound sources for each ear, it would be possible to reinforce the position of a data object in three-dimensional virtual space by having its sonic position and its visual position match (a common technique in immersive gaming environments).

In the short term, while we wait for software and hardware developers to catch up with this wide range of possibilities, there are a few ways to get started with sonified and haptically-enabled displays at low cost and with only a minimal initial learning curve. The first exploration is to examine the research and try out the tools at the Georgia Institute of Technology's Sonification Lab in the School of Psychology (sonify.psych.gatech.edu). Bruce Walker and the other researchers at the Sonification Lab offer a Java application called the Sonification Sandbox that can be downloaded and used by researchers at no cost. The application runs on most types of computers and will produce parameterized audio displays and corresponding visualizations for use in research studies.

For those seeking greater control over audio parameters, the PlayItByR package for the R statistical computing platform has a more substantial learning curve but is also free and open source. The author of the package, Ethan Brown, maintains a website (playitbyr.org) that contains many code examples and sound samples illustrating the use of the package. One key feature of PlayItByR that differentiates it from the Sonification Sandbox is that the former can play multiple audio events simultaneously (what musicians call *polyphonic*): this facilitates the creation of more complex data displays that represent two (or more) different variables within the same sound stream.

Finally, there are at least two options to get started at low cost in experimentation with haptic displays. One option, as noted in the earlier discussion above, is the Logitech Wingman force feedback mouse. Logitech provides a software development kit that allows users to develop their own customized uses of the device. The second option in this area is the Arduino approach. Firms like Precision Microdrives (www.precisionmicrodrives.com) offer Arduino-enabled devices that contain force feedback features.

APPLICATIONS TO ORGANIZATIONAL RESEARCH

As the foregoing review suggests, the exploration of large, complex datasets has the potential to benefit from innovative approaches to the tools that analysts can use to exploit their data more fully. While point-and-click statistical packages are usually sufficient to the job of working with smaller datasets, the basic 2D and 3D graphs they produce are rooted in the history of printed figures in books and journals. While many of the historical insights of the field of industrial and organizational psychology have been recorded in this form, these graphs have intrinsic limitations in the number of variables that can be represented as well as the density of the data. As data complexity and size continues to grow, these limitations may prove problematic for effective data analysis.

As organizational researchers, many of us got our methods and statistics training on well-tempered and modestly-sized data sets containing employment records, survey results, or test outcomes. Of course, survey, test, and demographic data will continue to be valuable for the indefinite future, but their importance and centrality to our research may be dwarfed by the availability of other types of information and other sources of data. Consider as just one example the availability of data from social media platforms. We can learn a lot about organizational behavior from people's interactions and uses of social media applications: the literature has become quickly populated with such research. Yet data streams, from sources such as the Twitter application programming interface, contain a complex mixture of text, geocoded, timing, and numeric data amounting to millions of records *per hour*. There may be gold in there, in terms of insights into critical organizational problems, but mining that gold cannot be accomplished using the traditional analytical tools that have served us so well over recent decades. To take advantage of voluminous new sources of data that are relevant to contemporary organizational problems, we need better tools for screening, diagnosing, and organizing our data.

Newer technologies, enabled by open source software and low-cost hardware, enable the construction of multimodal displays that engage more senses than just vision. As discussed in this paper, two promising additional modalities for displays are sound and touch. Most computers have audio built-in, and software solutions for sonification already exist. Hardware solutions for touch interfaces with force feedback, so-called haptic devices, are not as common as audio capabilities and not as easy to program, but the costs of these devices are declining, and it seems likely that their integration into mainstream software products will improve. What remains is for developers to put prototype multimodal displays into the hands of data analysts to assess the opportunities and benefits of innovative display features. Armed with better tools for exploring new forms of organizational big data, we may learn new strategies for improving the workplace and enhancing the effectiveness of organizations.

REFERENCES

Alexander, R.L., Gilbert, J., Landi, E., Simoni, M., Zurbuchen, T.H. and Roberts, D. (2011). Audification as a diagnostic tool for exploratory heliospheric data analysis. Proceedings of the 17th International Conference on Auditory Display (ICAD2011), Budapest, Hungary. 20–23 June, 2011. International Community for Auditory Display, 2011.

Ashmead, D.H., Leroy, D., & Odom, R.D. (1990). Perception of the relative distances of nearby sound sources. *Perception & Psychophysics, 47*(4), 326–331.

Azuma, R.T. (1997). A survey of augmented reality. *Presence, 6*(4), 355–385.

Blanche, P.A., Bablumian, A., Voorakaranam, R., Christenson, C., Lin, W., Gu, T., & Peyghambarian, N. (2010). Holographic three-dimensional telepresence using large-area photorefractive polymer. *Nature, 468* (7320), 80–83.

Bonebright, T., Cook, P., Flowers, J., Miner, N., Neuhoff, J., Bargar, R., . . . & Tipei, S. (1997). Sonification report: Status of the field and research agenda. *Report prepared for the National Science Foundation by members of the International Community for Auditory Display.* Retrieved from: http://icad.org/websiteV2.0/References/nsf.html

Brooks Jr., F. P., Ouh-Young, M., Batter, J. J., & Kilpatrick, P. J. (1990). Project GROPE: Haptic displays for scientific visualization. *ACM SIGGraph Computer Graphics, 24*(4), 177–185.

Brown, E., & Bearman, N. (2012). Listening to uncertainty: Information that sings. *Significance, 9*(5), 14–17.

Byagowi, A., Singhal, S., Lambeta, M., Aldaba, C., & Moussavi, Z. (2014). Design of a naturalistic navigational virtual reality using Oculus Rift. *Journal of Medical Devices, 8(3)*, 030946-030946-2. doi:10.1115/1.4027114

Carr-Hill, R. A. (1987). When is a data set complete? A squirrel with a vacuum cleaner. *Social Science & Medicine, 25*(6), 753–764.

Chang, W. H. (2013). Common disorders causing balance problems. *Brain & Neurorehabilitation, 6*(2), 54–57.

Clagett, M. (1968). *Nicole Oresme and the medieval geometry of qualities and motions.* Madison, WI: University of Wisconsin Press.

Culpepper, S. A., & Aguinis, H. (2011). R is for revolution: A cutting-edge, free, open source statistical package. *Organizational research methods, 14*(4), 735–740.

DeFanti, T. A., Dawe, G., Sandin, D. J., Schulze, J. P., Otto, P., Girado, J., & Rao, R. (2009). The StarCAVE, a third-generation CAVE and virtual reality OptIPortal. *Future Generation Computer Systems, 25*(2), 169–178.

Dembe, A. E., Partridge, J. S., & Geist, L. C. (2011). Statistical software applications used in health services research: Analysis of published studies in the US. *BMC Health Services Research, 11*(1), 252.

Eberhardt, S. P., Bernstein, L., Coulter, D. C., & Hunckler, L. A. (1993). OMAR: A haptic display for speech perception by deaf and deaf-blind individuals. *Proceedings of the IEEE Virtual Reality Annual International Symposium* (195–201). Seattle, WA. doi:10.1109/VRAIS.1993.380778

Edwards, J. R. (2002). Alternatives to difference scores: Polynomial regression analysis and response surface methodology. In F. Drasgow & N. W. Schmitt (Eds.), *Advances in measurement and data analysis* (pp. 350–400). San Francisco, CA: Jossey-Bass.

Gao, Y., Li, J., Su, H., & Li, J. (2011). Development of a teleoperation system based on virtual environment. *Proceedings of the 2011 IEEE International Conference on Robotics and Biomimetics*, 766–771. Karon Beach, Phuket. doi:10.1109/ROBIO.2011.6181379

German, D. M., Adams, B., & Hassan, A. E. (2013). The evolution of the R software ecosystem. *Proceedings of the 2013 17th European Conference on Software Maintenance and Reengineering*, 243–252. doi:10.1109/CSMR.2013.33

Gfeller, K., Woodworth, G., Robin, D. A., Witt, S., & Knutson, J. F. (1997). Perception of rhythmic and sequential pitch patterns by normally hearing adults and adult cochlear implant users. *Ear and Hearing, 18*(3), 252–260.

Gurin, J. (2014). *Open data now: The secret to hot startups, smart investing, savvy marketing, and fast innovation.* New York, NY: McGraw Hill Professional.

Hermann, T., & Ritter, H. (1999). Listen to your data: Model-based sonification for data analysis. *Advances in Intelligent Computing and Multimedia Systems, 8*, 189–194.

Janata, P., & Childs, E. (2004). Marketbuzz: Sonification of real-time financial data. *Proceedings of the Tenth Meeting of the International Conference on Auditory Display.* Retrieved from: http://www.icad.org/websiteV2.0/Conferences/ICAD2004/papers/janata_childs.pdf

Kapenga, J. A., McKean, J. W., & Gustafson, P. A. (2014). R: An open source system for statistics and data exploration. *Proceedings of the 55th AIAA/ASME/ASCE/AHS/SC Structures, Structural Dynamics, and Materials Conference*, 1–11. National Harbor, MD. doi:10.2514/6.2014-0349

Kato, Y. (2010). Splish: A visual programming environment for Arduino to accelerate physical computing experiences. *Proceedings of the 2010 Eighth International Conference on Creating, Connecting, and Collaborating through Computing*, 3–10. La Jolla, CA. doi:10.1109/C5.2010.20

Kramer, G. (1994). *Auditory display: Sonification, audification, and auditory interfaces.* Reading, MA: Addison-Wesley.

Leino, S. P., Lind, S., Poyade, M., Kiviranta, S., Multanen, P., Reyes-Lecuona, A., & Muhammad, A. (2009). Enhanced industrial maintenance work task planning by using virtual engineering tools and haptic user interfaces. In *Virtual and Mixed Reality* (pp. 346–354). Berlin: Springer.

Lynch, C. (2008). Big data: How do your data grow? *Nature, 455*(7209), 28–29.

Manovich, L. (2012). Trending: The promises and the challenges of big social data. In M. K. Gold (Ed.), *Debates in the digital humanities* (pp. 460–475). Minneapolis, MN: University of Minnesota Press.

McAfee, A., & Brynjolfsson, E. (2012). Big data: The management revolution. *Harvard Business Review, 90*(10), 60–68.

McIntosh, C. S., Mittelhammer, R. C., & Middleton, J. N. (2013). Listen to your data: Econometric model specification through sonification. *Proceedings of the 2013 Agricultural and Applied Economics Association Annual Meeting.* Washington, DC: Agricultural and Applied Economics Association.

Molnar, A. (1997). Computers in education: A brief history. *The Journal, 24*(11), 63–68.

Moody, J. W., & Healy, K. (2014). Data visualization in sociology. *Annual Review of Sociology, 40* (1), 105–128.

Newman, G., Wiggins, A., Crall, A., Graham, E., Newman, S., & Crowston, K. (2012). The future of citizen science: Emerging technologies and shifting paradigms. *Frontiers in Ecology and the Environment, 10*(6), 298–304.

Panëels, S. A., Ritsos, P. D., Rodgers, P. J., & Roberts, J. C. (2013). Prototyping 3D haptic data visualizations. *Computers & Graphics, 37*(3), 179–192.

Paneels, S., & Roberts, J. C. (2010). Review of designs for haptic data visualization. *IEEE Transactions on Haptics, 3*(2), 119–137.

Panëels, S. A., Roberts, J. C., & Rodgers, P. J. (2009). Haptic interaction techniques for exploring chart data. In M. Ercan Altinsoy, U. Jekosch & S. Brewster (Eds.), *Haptic and audio interaction design* (pp. 31–40). Berlin: Springer.

Perez-Gutierrez, B., Martinez, D. M., & Rojas, O. E. (2010). Endoscopic endonasal haptic surgery simulator prototype: A rigid endoscope model. *Proceedings of the 2010 IEEE Virtual Reality Conference*, 297–298. Waltham, MA. doi:10.1109/VR.2010.5444756

Rastogi, R., & Pawluk, D. T. (2013). Toward an improved haptic zooming algorithm for graphical information accessed by individuals who are blind and visually impaired. *Assistive Technology, 25*(1), 9–15.

Reas, C., & Fry, B. (2003). Processing: A learning environment for creating interactive web graphics. *ACM SIGGRAPH 2003 Web Graphics*, 1–1. doi:10.1145/965333.965356

Roberts, J. C., & Paneels, S. (2007). Where are we with haptic visualization? *Second Joint EuroHaptics Conference, 2007 and Symposium on Haptic Interfaces for Virtual Environment and Teleoperator Systems*, 316–323. doi:10.1109/WHC.2007.126

Roginska, A., Childs, E., & Johnson, M. K. (2006). Monitoring real-time data: A sonification approach. *Proceedings of the 12th International Conference on Auditory Display*, 176–181. Queen Mary, UK.

Schaller, R. R. (1997). Moore's law: Past, present and future. *Spectrum, 34*(6), 52–59.

Serrano, A. (2013, March 7). Fluid by Hannes Jung experiments with touch and texture. *TrendHunter Tech*. Retrieved from: http://www.trendhunter.com/trends/fluid-by-hannes-jung

Sigrist, R., Rauter, G., Riener, R., & Wolf, P. (2013). Augmented visual, auditory, haptic, and multimodal feedback in motor learning: A review. *Psychonomic Bulletin & Review, 20*(1), 21–53.

Stanton, J. M. (2013). Data mining: A Practical introduction for organizational researchers. In J. M. Cortina & R. S. Landis (Eds.), *Modern research methods for the study of behavior in organizations* (pp. 199–232). New York, NY: Routledge Academic.

Steelman, H. S. (1968). The GROPE-I system: An analysis of friction and backlash problems (Unpublished master's thesis). Computer Science Department, University of North Carolina, Chapel Hill.

Sutherland, I. E. (1965). The ultimate display. *Proceedings of IFIP 65* (506–508, 582–583).

Tervaniemi, M., & Brattico, E. (2004). From sounds to music towards understanding the neurocognition of musical sound perception. *Journal of Consciousness Studies, 11*, 9–27.

Theoktisto, V., Fairén, M., Navazo, I., & Monclús, E. (2005). Rendering detailed haptic textures. *Second Workshop in Virtual Reality Interactions and Physical Simulations*, 16–23.

Tsujita, T., Ohara, M., Sase, K., Konno, A., Nakayama, M., Abe, K., & Uchiyama, M. (2012). Development of a haptic interface using mr fluid for displaying cutting forces of soft tissues. *Proceedings of the 2012 IEEE International Conference on Robotics and Automation*, 1044–1049. Saint Paul, MN. doi:10.1109/IRCA.2012.6225109

Tufte, E. R. (1991). Envisioning information. *Optometry & Vision Science, 68* (4), 322–324.

Vogt, K., Höldrich, R., Pirro, D., Rumori, M., Rossegger, S., Riegler, W., & Tadel, M. (2010). A sonic time projection chamber: Sonified particle detection at CERN. *Proceedings of the International Conference on Auditory Display, Washington, DC*. Retrieved from: https://www.qcd-audio.at/publications/icad10_tpc_cameraready.pdf

Walker, B. N. (2002). Magnitude estimation of conceptual data dimensions for use in sonification. *Journal of Experimental Psychology: Applied, 8*(4), 211–221.

Walker, B. N. (2007). Consistency of magnitude estimations with conceptual data dimensions used for sonification. *Applied Cognitive Psychology, 21*(5), 579–599.

Walter, C. (2005). Kryder's law. *Scientific American, 293*(2), 32–33.

Yu, W., & Brewster, S. A. (2002). Comparing two haptic interfaces for multimodal graph rendering. *10th Symposium on Haptic Interfaces for Virtual Environment and Teleoperator Systems*, 3–9. Orlando, FL. doi: 10.1109/HAPTIC.2002.998934

Part II

Big Ideas for Big Data in Organization

7

Implications of the Big Data Movement for the Advancement of I-O Science and Practice

Dan J. Putka and Frederick L. Oswald

The recent interest in the big data movement among the industrial-organizational (I-O) psychology community has been quite intriguing in that big data—as traditionally defined in terms of volume, velocity, and variety—has been discussed for more than a decade (Laney, 2001), yet it remains a rare experience for most I-O science practitioners and academicians.[1] However, that does not mean the zeitgeist behind the big data movement has failed to have impact on I-O related practice in organizations. Specifically, the big data movement has been manifesting itself on a smaller scale within the context of *human capital analytics* or *talent analytics* functions that are cropping up within many large organizations and giving rise to a new breed of analytics-centric service firms (Bersin, 2013; Biga, 2014; Kemp, 2014; Roberts, 2014).

Of course, the use of data to understand organizational phenomena and help improve human capital decision making and processes is nothing new for organizations or I-O psychology (Putka, 2013). What is new is the broadening and continual growth of technology and analytic resources available and, perhaps equally as important, the renewed attention and support from corporate executives looking to leverage their data to improve their human capital programs (think *Moneyball*). With these newfound resources come both promises and perils for the I-O field. On the one hand, we see clear potential in the big data movement for advancing I-O science and creating new opportunities for I-O work to shine within organizations and improve the quality of individuals' work lives. However, we also see a real risk of this movement making I-O science as it manifests itself today less relevant in the eyes of key organizational stakeholders, adding yet another wrinkle to the lamented science-practice gap (Cascio & Aguinis, 2008; Silzer & Cober, 2010).

To focus on the positive side, we see the big data movement facilitating accelerated development of the science of I-O psychology and improving its relevance and benefit to organizational practice. Historically, much scientific development in the I-O field has occurred in ways that lag behind what is now possible in light of the big data movement: relatively small sample sizes (e.g., $N = 200$ is often considered a large data set), fairly limited types of data (e.g., limited individual-, team-, and organization-level characteristics), specification of psychology-specific theories, variables, and models, and relatively narrow sets of approaches to analyzing data on phenomena of interest (e.g., parametric statistical models, such as general linear models and structural equation models fitted to cross-sectional data; Aguinis, Pierce, Bosco, & Muslin, 2009; Austin, Scherbaum, & Mahlman, 2002; Shen, Kiger, Davies, Rasch, Simon, & Ones, 2011). That is, the development and evaluation of I-O theories and scientific literature regarding organizational phenomena has largely been bounded by the data, measures, research designs, and analytic tools that have been propagated within the I-O academic and professional communities over the past century.

Of course this is to be expected, as some of the bounds referenced above are practical, just like the phenomenon of big data was not possible before the advent of advances in computing and communication technologies. Other bounds are conceptual and statistical, such as the confluence of multilevel thinking and multilevel modeling emerging only in the past 15 years. Regardless, the point here is that the new technology, methods, and ideas underlying the big data movement provide the means to observe, summarize, understand, and forecast reality in ways that break the current paradigms for advancing I-O psychology. From a theory and science building perspective, big data offer a non-trivial set of new resources for the discovery of important *stylized facts* regarding human capital processes that have historically been of concern to I-O science and practice, but which the I-O field may currently not yet be well equipped to leverage (Helfat, 2007). So what are these new resources that the big data movement provides?

For starters, over the last several years, large organizations have been positioning themselves to continuously accrue data that can help one understand and improve numerous human capital processes of interest to I-O psychologists and management scholars (e.g., the recruitment, selection, development, management, and retention of a skilled workforce) and are far more relevant to their local situation than the I-O field has typically been able to provide in any single published study or meta-analysis. The emergence and implementation of data systems underlying the processes above—including applicant tracking and hiring management systems (ATS/HMS), learning management and performance management systems (LMS/PMS), human resources management or information systems (HRMS/HRIS), and overarching integrated talent management systems (TMS)—coupled with longitudinal employee survey databases bring us closer to this reality. Moreover, over the past few decades, technology has emerged that has afforded organizations the capacity to accrue large amounts of external and internal data in a quick and cost-effective manner for the purposes of measure development, validation, model testing, and benchmarking for competitive advantage (e.g., Amazon's MTurk web service, online survey and data collection technology, proprietary online user networks).

The developments above set the stage for a time when large organizations, consulting firms, and vendors of HR technology systems will not only have access to *more* data on a particular phenomenon than has been traditionally afforded by the I-O or management literatures, but also more *relevant* data that is not hamstrung by the need to increment existing literature or provide a critical expansion or test of a theory (Hambrick, 2007). These developments create the possibility for organizations and well-positioned HR service and IT firms to develop and refine practically meaningful and stable models of key outcomes more quickly, and in turn inform effective interventions for improving human capital processes faster than current scholarly publication cycles allow.

Although the quick accrual of large stores of data is a critical element of the big data and analytics movement that offers new resources to the I-O field, it is only one element. Also in play from the big data movement is the emergence of alternative perspectives and new methods for learning from data, some of which represents a clear departure from advancing I-O science as we traditionally have known it. Perhaps the clearest statement about these broad alternative perspectives comes from the late Leo Breiman in a 2001 article he wrote for *Statistical Science*, where he describes two cultures within statistical modeling—the *data modeling culture* and the *algorithmic modeling culture* (Breiman, 2001b).

Historically, the development of I-O science and evaluation of theory has largely fallen within what Breiman described as the data modeling culture, which emphasizes the theoretical specification and evaluation of statistical models and parameter estimation (e.g., parameters in general linear models and structural equation models). Indeed, this culture aligns with traditional inferential statistics, which form a core part of the curriculum in graduate I-O programs and psychology departments in general (Aiken, West, & Millsap, 2008; Society for Industrial and Organizational Psychology, 1999). Breiman contrasts the data modeling culture with what he calls the *algorithmic modeling culture*, which puts emphasis on finding a function or algorithm that maximizes accuracy of prediction upon cross-validation. This culture was not largely borne out of statistics, but rather sub-disciplines of computer science—specifically, machine learning and data mining (Hastie, Tibshirani, & Friedman, 2009; cf. Chapter 3 by Oswald & Putka in this volume).

It is worthwhile to place these two perspectives in the context of our typical training and expertise as I-O psychologists. Much of our formal training and philosophy about drawing inferences based on data is clearly grounded in traditional statistical models—most I-O psychologists have not been trained to see the algorithmic methods as something that could have value for advancing I-O science. Indeed, Breiman makes the case that across many applied scientific disciplines, there is a tendency to adopt a purely data modeling perspective given its grounding in traditional statistics. However, as we illustrate by example later, a pure data modeling perspective can suffer from some key limitations, including decrementing the overall quality of prediction of outcomes we care about, failing to identify key drivers of those outcomes that are surprising because they don't neatly fit within prevailing theories (e.g., independent variables, mediators, moderators), and limited flexibility for addressing various elements a modeling problem (e.g., nonlinearities, interactions, managing the tradeoff between model complexity/parsimony, and model uncertainty). In the past, these three limitations were actually important strategic assets because the small sample sizes that I-O psychologists tended to encounter required strong theories and deductive rationale to avoid a confound between small sample sizes with small-yet-meaningful prediction, surprising relationships, nonlinearities, and so on. Larger sample sizes provided by big data allow for these latter factors to be unconfounded and explored, and thus the big data movement and associated algorithmic methods provide a new and important approach to incrementing our foundations of scientific and practical knowledge.

As we will discuss later in this chapter, modern algorithmic methods can be used alongside traditional data modeling approaches in a reciprocally informative manner to identify deficiencies in theoretically-driven models and to discover systematic, recurring factors that are predictive of our outcomes of interest yet fall outside of current theory (i.e., key stylized facts that beg for future scientific inquiry; Berk, 2006; Gibby, McCloy, &

Putka, 2013). This gives us the potential not only to improve existing theory in a data-driven manner but also to develop and refine it in a way that makes it more practically meaningful and relevant.

Despite the advances described above, little information on conducting applied research within a dynamic, diverse, data rich environment that leverages both data and algorithmic modeling traditions appears to be making its way into I-O graduate school curricula. Although SIOP has a big data task force that is carefully considering how to incorporate algorithmic modeling approaches into I-O graduate school curricula, this is a work in progress. This state of affairs, along with the gains the data science field is making into traditional I-O related work (e.g., Lohr, 2013; Overby, 2013), raises the question: How can I-O graduates capitalize on this emerging reality, whether they are going into practice or academe?

Unfortunately, several recent commentaries suggest the I-O field as whole is trending in the opposite direction of this reality. Most notably, recent literature has observed: an overarching emphasis on theory testing and new theory creation in top-tier management journals and historically practice-sensitive journals (Hambrick, 2007; Silzer & Parson, 2012),[2] migration of I-O faculty to business schools that do not train graduate students for applied practice and place extreme value on publishing in theory-centric management journals (Aguinis, Bradley, & Brodersen, 2014; Shapiro, Kirkman, & Courtney, 2007), decreased emphasis on traditional I-side topics that have direct corollaries to the key HR processes often of concern in human capital analytics efforts because they tend to be viewed as less theory-driven and thus receive less attention in management journals (Aguinis et al., 2014), and continued limitations in the teaching of graduate-level statistics and measurement methods (Aiken et al., 2008; Borsboom, 2006; Merenda, 2007). Collectively, these trends point towards the possibility that new I-O graduates may be increasingly at a disadvantage to capitalize on some of the substantial opportunities the big data movement affords the I-O field, whether they are going into academe or practice.

From the perspective of I-O psychology as a science, the observations above point to what we see as one of the prime risks and, at the same time, opportunities of the big data movement. We present this risk as a quote—one that we do not fully believe, but one that is offered to provoke thought and help frame the reminder of the chapter:

Why, as a data and business savvy practitioner who runs a well-funded and staffed, multidisciplinary human capital analytics function, should I be concerned with what is being published about outcome Y in scientific I-O or management journals? My team not only has more data, but more data that captures the nuances of my local operating environment (e.g., business unit, regional, seasonal differences). Not only that, but my analytics team can capitalize on a far broader range of analytic methods than is currently reflected in the I-O psychology literature. My analytics team can use theory and big data methods together, thus achieving better prediction and understanding of outcome *Y* within my organization than any theory-based structural model from small and irrelevant samples found in the past two decades of published work. My analytics team can continually revisit and refine predictions over time as necessary, given my extensive and integrated data flow. So what value does what is currently being published in scholarly journals add in terms of understanding and predicting outcomes of concern to my organization and how those vary across time and different elements of my operational environment? Let the small organizations who don't have big data or the resources to invest in it hobble along on old academic findings.

The above quote is an amalgamation of sentiments expressed in conversations we've had (or popular press pieces we've read) over that past several years in which we've effectively been put in a position to defend the science of I-O in light of myriad data and analytic advances now upon us. Unfortunately, there are several elements of this quote that present real challenges—but incredible opportunities—for the I-O field. Simply dismissing them as faddish or just the latest manifestation of dustbowl empiricism fails to see that there are real, observable differences now with regard to data and analytic resources relative to where we were 20 to 30 years ago that could serve to benefit I-O science and practice. It also fails to see where research and practice in business, economics, education, and the natural sciences is headed, a world in which we as I-O psychologists presumably seek to be a vital part.

THE CURRENT CHAPTER

One purpose we hope to fulfill with the current chapter is to provide a call to action for our field to begin to reshape the training of I-O psychologists in a way that positions us to take advantage of the evolution in data and analytic technology that has, in part, already raced right by us. We will begin by offering an overview of the data and analytics picture that is starting to take shape within the modern, data-savvy organization. Though this section largely focuses on the situation unfolding in practice, it provides critical context for subsequent discussion of the implications of the big data and analytics movement for I-O science. We follow our description of the modern, data-savvy organization with a discussion of some opportunities this picture creates for advancing science (and practice) by highlighting examples pertaining to validation, assessment refinement, and model development and evaluation. After that, we juxtapose these examples against current limiters on the rate of I-O scientific advancement to further illustrate the promise and peril that the big data movement holds for I-O science. Lastly, we will close with some thoughts on constructive directions that the I-O field can take to be better positioned to capitalize on the advantage of the big data opportunities before it.

THE MODERN, DATA-SAVVY ORGANIZATION

A critical function of the human capital management (HCM) enterprise is to develop and administer programs and processes that help ensure an organization sources, selects, develops, manages, and retains a satisfied, engaged, high performing workforce. From an analytics perspective, one helpful way to conceive of HCM is from the perspective of the employment lifecycle, which typically begins with recruitment and continues to

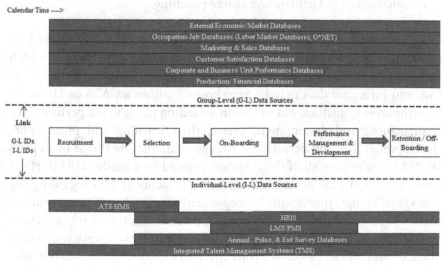

FIGURE 7.1

selection, on-boarding, performance management and development, and retention and off-boarding. Underlying each phase of the employment lifecycle, we can also conceive of an underlying *human capital data lifecycle*, where the organization accrues data about employees as they progress through their careers, the groups or contexts in which they work, and various individual- and group-level outcomes of interest to the organization. Figure 7.1 provides a juxtaposition of phases of the traditional employment lifecycle against the data sources that many organizations aspire to establish to understand and optimize their HCM programs and processes.

The middle layer of Figure 7.1 is a typical depiction of an individual's linear progress through an organization expressed in terms of phase of the employment lifecycle. Organizations are striving to gain efficiencies and improvements to these phases by:

- continuously capturing various types of data over time;
- warehousing those data in various types of data systems;
- establishing key metrics based on those data to report on and track how HCM programs and processes are functioning over time;
- building statistical models with those data to help them understand key predictors (drivers) of their valued outcomes of interest (e.g., engagement, job performance, retention, customer satisfaction, business unit financial success) and inform process improvements; and
- building statistical models with those data to forecast future human capital needs to facilitate workforce planning.

With regard to the different data stores underlying the employment lifecycle, they can be broken down into some basic types, the labels of which seem to be constantly evolving. Recruiting, application, employment testing, and interview data may be warehoused within an ATS or HMS. As the employee transitions out of the on-boarding phase to the performance management and development phase, their learning and professional development data and performance review data may be stored in an LMS or PMS. Underlying all of these systems would be a master HRMS/HRIS that captures critical demographics and transactional data regarding the individual's employment with the organization (e.g., date of hire, compensation, absenteeism, disciplinary actions, promotions, transfers), and eventual exit from the organization. The data stores above create a dynamic trace of an employee's career from entry to exit that, in the ideal world, would be seamlessly linked. As we'll note below, however, the majority of organizations are still far from realizing this vision. But as these integrated data warehousing technologies continue to mature and become even easier to operate and afford, they will show greater penetration in organizations large and small.

Complementing the individual-level data stores and accrual of data for individual employees, group-level data stores are pertinent to the ongoing evaluation and improvement of the HCM programs and processes underlying the employment lifecycle (top half of Figure 7.1). In this case, we are using the term group-level quite generically; for example, it may include job-level, team-level, department-level, region-level, business-unit level, organization-level, or even industry-level data. As the examples in Figure 7.1 illustrate, these data may be externally or internally maintained in macro-economic, financial, production, consumer satisfaction, and job analytic databases, just to name a few. Collectively, they represent potential sources of group-level data that might serve as predictors, moderators, mediators, or outcomes in models of individual-level (or group-level) outcomes of interest when modeling potential improvements to various HCM programs and processes or forecasting future needs.

Although organizations are trending towards integrated HCM data systems that support large-scale analytics programs, most organizations still appear to be far from fully capitalizing on such systems. For example, in a recent worldwide survey of 1,406 HR professionals from organizations around the world, Kantrowitz (2014) found that only 25% of respondents were satisfied with the ability of their organization's HR systems to manage talent data. Furthermore, Bersin (2013) conducted survey research among 435 U.S. and Canadian organizations, reporting that although more than 60% of organizations use big data analytic tools to improve their HR functions, these organizations varied widely in terms of the maturity of human capital analytics programs, with the vast majority them (86%) limiting their analytics to simple reporting and dashboards rather than predictive models. Thus, although organizations are putting themselves in a position to understand how they are performing in various human capital areas, most do not yet appear to be leveraging their data to statistically understand factors that are driving outcomes they care about in order to take evidence-based steps to improve them.

Our experiences working in this area over the past decade are largely consistent with the survey research above. Specifically, early on in the build-up of a human capital analytics function, a good deal of time is spent taking stock of potential data sources and dealing with data integrity issues. Simply getting the data in place to support a well-oiled human capital analytics function within a large organization is fraught with technical and political challenges that can literally take years to hammer out, if they get hammered out at all. For example, some of these challenges include:

- identifying and achieving buy-in and data sharing agreements from owners of relevant data sources throughout the organization;
- achieving sufficient clarity with regard to rules governing the use of data from various sources (e.g., data privacy agreements, specified purpose and timeline of data use, sensitivity to international differences in laws regarding data use in the case of multinationals);
- ensuring one has a sufficient set of uniform identifiers for linking across various sets of data from different sources, levels, and time periods (we have suffered the slings and arrows of not having the necessary IDs);
- achieving sufficient clarity with regard to business rules that data owners and users employ when they capture data and populate data sources; also, understanding if and how those business rules have changed over time (e.g., coding changes, data definition changes, emergence and retirement of data fields over time);
- achieving sufficient clarity with regard to timing of when data were captured and consistency of that timing across individuals and groups of interest;
- assessing data owners' level of confidence in the quality of various data elements, particularly those deemed core or of interest to the analytics effort—this can provide extremely useful information about the data which the data themselves will not confess; and
- establishing the software and data structures that handle numerous types of nesting and cross-classification of individuals and groups, as well as changes in those classifications across time.

There are a few things we want to point out regarding the list above that have implications for members of the I-O field. First, solving all of them has a clear human element—these are not issues that suddenly disappear with the purchase of even the most sophisticated data warehousing and analytics technology. I-O psychologists offer core expertise when it comes to evaluating the quality of measures of individual differences, providing a value-added contribution over other members of an analytics team (e.g., econometricians, labor economists, database managers, computer scientists, professional HR staff). Second, addressing these issues often requires buy-in from several different elements of the organization outside of HR, who have access to key data (e.g., financials) but may have competing priorities and resources. Thus, finding and establishing a pipeline for continuous access to data that exist even in-house can be a challenge. Third, addressing these issues often requires multidisciplinary expertise. For example, just as I-O psychologists may be in the best position to evaluate the quality of individual differences data, econometricians and those with formal training in finance are likely in the best position to evaluate the quality of corporate financial data.

The importance of leveraging the expertise from multiple disciplines also arises on model development and evaluation front. For example, many of the outcomes an organization may wish to impact through its HCM programs and processes may be financial or consumer-related in nature, and may be best modeled and understood not only as a function of individual differences of interest to I-O psychologists, but also as factors identified in labor economics, financial, and consumer behavior theories, into which I-O psychologists will have limited visibility. These latter points are critical because they suggest how a multidisciplinary team drawing on theory and methods from their fields' literatures has the potential to offer a far more well-rounded perspective on an outcome of interest than any single theory produced within a single discipline (e.g., I-O science, economics, marketing). As noted in the opening address of the 2014 Society for Industrial and Organizational Psychology conference, I-O psychology as a discipline tends to be very insular based on our citation patterns (Allen, 2014)—and in a big data environment, this limitation becomes screamingly obvious.

The previous discussion provided a snapshot of where we see large-scale human capital analytics programs headed, and some of the challenges they face as they mature. In our view, this is the front line in terms of where the zeitgeist behind the big data movement is interfacing with I-O psychology. It is clearly an area where I-O psychologists have the potential to play a key role given our training; however, at the same time it is important to realize that the issues at hand are not something germane to the study of I-O psychology, and that they can benefit from the input and perspectives of a multidisciplinary team of experts from other fields as well. Despite this early stage of development, it is not hard to imagine the benefits that can be realized with a mature human capital analytics function in place for both practice and I-O science. To provide a more concrete illustration of the possible benefits, the section below offers three examples grounded in topics of historical importance to the advancement of I-O psychology, namely: validation, assessment, and model development and evaluation. Perhaps not surprisingly, these represent topic areas where substantive content, method, and data and statistical considerations intersect.

OPPORTUNITIES FOR ADVANCEMENT

As alluded to above, the data technology and analytic advances that have emerged over the past few decades create the foundation for some new ways to think about and advance I-O science. In this section, we highlight three examples that are core to the scientific endeavor—validation, assessment, model development, and model evaluation—but as we'll see below, also have clear practical value to the aims of most human capital analytics functions, namely the improvement of human capital programs and processes.

Validation: Breaking out of the Single Study and Meta-analytic Mindset

To date, most pedagogical treatments of validity of measurement in I-O psychology have framed the concept of validity in static terms (see Binning & Barrett, 1989; Guion, 1998; Ployhart, Schneider, & Schmitt, 2006). That is, the traditional focus is on establishing *summative* evidence of the validity of assessment scores for a given purpose, documenting it, and using that documentation to justify or defend the use of those scores. Sometimes, this evidence comes in the form of a single study; other times, it might be cumulated across multiple studies or samples via meta-analysis. Given the technology advances described above, particularly with regard to online data collection and large-scale tracking and warehousing of data across time, it is now possible to conceive of validity in terms that are more dynamic than ever before. Specifically, it is possible to frame validity as a malleable characteristic of scores that offers a diagnostic, *formative* metric for refining measurement content over time, and for empirically understanding when situations upon which assessment use is premised appear to have changed. This dynamic notion of validity can capitalize on the value the of big data movement (data capture and analytics), with the potential to yield greater dividends than even the most ambitious longitudinal validity study in the research literature.

For example, consider the case where an organization sets up an online, nationwide selection testing system for its applicants. As part of that selection process, the organization administers a variety of measures traditionally of interest to I-O researchers (e.g., situational judgment tests, personality measures, interviews) to an annual pool of 100,000 applicants. All of these data are captured via the organization's HMS, and data from roughly 2,000 new applicants are added to the HMS each week. Of course, some percentage of these applicants subsequently get hired, and after fixed periods of time (e.g., daily, quarterly, yearly after entry), data on the behavior of hired applicants (e.g., turnover, absenteeism, disciplinary actions, promotion rates, awards, job performance) are captured and recorded in the organization's PMS or HRIS. Given the fairly continuous stream of applicants, hires, and regularity in post-hire data capture, the organization has at its disposal a database of predictor-criterion data that is not only continuously growing but also sensitive to the nuances of that organization and its systems and operating environment. Such a continuous stream of data could be used in several ways to benefit both the hiring organization and the science of I-O psychology that are beyond the reach of any single validation study, longitudinal study, or meta-analytic summary of single studies.

First, with such a continuous stream of data, the organization would have a mechanism for monitoring and strategically tweaking the composition of assessment content over time based on item-level statistics that are updated on a continuous basis (e.g., item-level criterion-related validities). Though it may be tempting to dismiss such an approach as an empirical fishing expedition, tracking and differentiating between content that functions effectively and ineffectively (and capitalizing on such information) would be based on large quantities of item-level data that could be revisited for stability continuously by using strategically selected sub-samples of the data for purposes of independent cross-validation. In other words, such a framework could provide a replicable empirical basis for inductive theory building regarding the functioning of various item and content types (e.g., in terms of constructs targeted, item structure, item type, response formats; Lievens, De Corte, & Westerveld, 2015; Mael, 1991) in ways that are not readily achievable through our current methods of research (Locke, 2007), and that are also sensitive to temporal drift in item parameters over time (DeMars, 2004).

Another example that arises from the continual stream of predictor-criterion validation data is leveraging those data to help diagnose changes in job requirements over time and when job analysis data or assessment batteries might need to be updated (Bobko, Roth, & Buster, 2005). Unfortunately, the I-O scientific literature offers little guidance or past research with regard to how often organizations should check the accuracy of the job analysis data on which many key HCM programs and processes should be based (e.g., recruiting, selection, performance management and development). With a continuous stream of predictor-criterion data across multiple job families, an organization could set up analysis programs to calculate and track changes in the criterion-related validity of predictor content designed to measure a given competency or construct, and establish thresholds or triggers for determining when there is a need to revisit that content based on increases or drops in criterion-related validity or model prediction. For example, such changes could indicate that the importance of various competencies to successful job performance had shifted since the original job analysis and might trigger a follow-up discussion with job subject matter experts. To the extent such efforts are conducted by organizations, the field of I-O psychology could come to a greater understanding of not only how quickly job requirements may change over time for various types of jobs, but also how they change and the implications for the weighting of variables and the validity of common assessment methods. Again, this would seem to be of both practical and scientific value.

Improving Assessment

As we noted in the introduction, the use of data to inform decision making is nothing new for organizations or for I-O psychology. One common type of assessment for which I-O psychologists have typically leveraged data to inform the creation of assessment scores is biodata measures. Biodata measures have a long history in personnel selection research (see Mumford & Owens, 1987; Owens, 1976). In constructing biodata measures, the focus is often on questions about one's past behavior or experiences believed to relate to psychological constructs most pertinent to prediction of one or more criteria (e.g., job performance, retention). Although identification and measurement of relevant constructs help guide measure development, the quality of prediction achievable with biodata is often more than just a function of identifying relevant content. For example, a key topic in the biodata research literature has been the evaluation of empirical approaches to keying (scoring) biodata measures designed to maximize validity (see Brown, 1994; Cucina, Caputo, Thibodeaux, & MacLane, 2012; Hogan, 1994).

Although current approaches to empirically keying biodata have proven valuable from a predictive standpoint, it is important to note that they were largely developed long before the advent of modern computer technology, and certainly before the big data movement. Indeed, most commonly used approaches to empirical keying reflect statistical methods developed in the early to middle 20th century (for reviews, see Cucina et al., 2012 and Hogan, 1994). Indeed, none of the currently espoused and researched methods for keying biodata measures take advantage of the significant advances in modern statistical learning methods and concepts that have emerged from the computer science, machine learning, and statistics literatures over the past two decades (e.g., bagging, boosting, ensembles, Hastie et al., 2009; cf. Chapter 3 by Oswald & Putka in this volume).

There are several benefits to recasting biodata keying efforts in terms of a general, modern modeling problem that not only can benefit I-O practice, but also I-O science. First, the methods discussed in the existing biodata literature represent a very narrow range of strategies for combining item data (or more generally, variables) for the purposes of prediction. Modern statistical learning methods not only offer a more diverse set of analytic strategies to consider, but also, more importantly, the methods reduce or even eliminate many of the methodological and practical limitations of traditional empirical keying approaches.[3]

For example, several statistical learning methods offer mechanisms for simultaneously detecting and modeling item interactions and non-linear relations between items and criteria while also accounting for relations (covariance) among items. In contrast, traditional option-level keying approaches (e.g., mean criterion, correlational, vertical percent, and horizontal percent; Hogan, 1994) account for non-linear relations between items and criterion but ignore the multivariate nature of the prediction problem by keying each item in isolation without consideration of its relationship with other items.

Second, approaches to implementing statistical learning methods have become quite sophisticated in using model meta-parameters (i.e., model tuning parameters; Hastie et al., 2009) that serve to balance the problem of a model over-fitting the data (using a key or model that is so complex that it will not generalize to a new sample) versus a model under-fitting the data (using a key or model that is so simplistic that it doesn't take full advantage of the data at hand). Essentially, model meta-parameters are additional model features that help researchers scale the complexity of the model in light of the data available (e.g., the ratio of the development sample size to the number of items [predictors] on a biodata measure) and put constraints on model parameter estimates that reduce the degree to which they are sensitive to features of the local data. To give an example based on traditional methods: In the ridge regression form of linear regression, there is a meta-parameter (lambda) that penalizes (shrinks) large coefficients so that they are not as sensitive to the data, which is especially important when predictors are highly correlated (multicollinear). Ridge regression creates bias but is guaranteed to reduce mean-squared error in a given sample, and it can provide similar benefits on cross-validation. Related to this latter point, meta-parameters are difficult to choose rationally, so in big data approaches, they are often chosen empirically via cross-validation (e.g., 10-fold cross-validation; Hastie et al., 2009). In contrast, traditional option-level keying methods do not involve model fitting or use of meta-parameters, and thus offer no means for managing the complexity-parsimony tradeoff in model fitting, except via ad-hoc decision rules regarding option-level scoring (e.g., dichotomizing keyed scores based on some arbitrary level of statistical significance) or via item inclusion (e.g., dropping items that do not satisfy some arbitrary level of statistical significance or minimum effect size; Mumford & Owens, 1987).

Third, several modern statistical learning methods offer mechanisms for dealing with model uncertainty through model averaging (Breiman, 1996, 2001a; Burnham & Anderson, 2002; Chatfield, 1995; Hoeting, Madigan, Raferty, & Volinksy, 1999). Model uncertainty reflects the notion that there are often several models that may fit the data well, and in choosing and assuming that any single one of them as best, one is not only losing information valuable to prediction of the criterion of interest but also underestimating the standard errors of parameter estimates. As a means to deal with such uncertainty, researchers in multiple domains have introduced the concept of model ensembles, or model averaging, which involves aggregating predictions made by multiple models to yield a more stable set of predictions. In contrast to traditional empirical and rational keying approaches that base overall biodata scores on a single key, several statistical learning methods incorporate model averaging concepts that make it possible to efficiently base overall scores on an ensemble of empirically viable keys that may provide different, complementary perspectives on the prediction problem.

Beyond helping to maximize the generalizability and accuracy of prediction across samples, modern statistical learning methods can be viewed as providing a new way to build theory inductively with respect to the evaluation and functioning of each biodata item. For example, many modern statistical learning methods can index the contribution of each biodata item to prediction, and this can be coupled with relative importance methodologies familiar to I-O researchers that serve a similar goal (see Johnson & LeBreton, 2004; Scherbaum, Putka, Naidoo, & Youssefina, 2010). Given that no single scoring model in isolation can provide an adequate picture of the contribution of biodata items to prediction in light of model uncertainty, one can leverage the modern notion of model ensembles to identify construct-item characteristic combinations that tend to be most predictive regardless of model considered. Such information can provide a robust basis for inductively building theories of biodata functioning (Mael, 1991) and more practically, leveraging that theory to build measures that focus more strategically on the most critical combinations of constructs and item characteristics. Such a perspective stands in rather stark contrast with traditional approaches to empirical keying, which have rarely been viewed as beneficial for advancing theory or bringing clarity to the basis of a measure's prediction.

Model Development and Evaluation

The examples above illustrated how advances with regard to large-scale warehousing and accrual of HCM data, as well as advances in statistical learning methods, can impact validation and assessment, respectively, which are two areas central to I-O science. In this section, we offer an example that illustrates how theory-based models can inform and be informed by recent developments in data warehousing and statistical learning methods. Specifically, we illustrate how traditional theory-based approaches to model evaluation can effectively be used in combination with the algorithmic methods described earlier. Unlike the previous examples, we frame this example in terms of a hypothetical story.

Imagine that the large organization we discussed in our first example was concerned with understanding key drivers of turnover among its employees, and the organization subsequently sought to invest in interventions that act on those key drivers to reduce turnover. As part of that effort, the organization wants to leverage its substantial stores of human capital data, as well as prevailing I-O theories and research regarding employee turnover (see Griffeth & Hom, 2001; Griffith, Hom, & Gaertner, 2001). For purposes of the current analysis cycle, let's say the organization culls data on hires from the past four fiscal years, as well as subsequent employee survey, performance, demographic, and economic data that it has available in this timeframe. The organization's leaders want the human capital analytics team to build and evaluate models to help them understand why people are leaving. So what are some options the team may pursue to inform the creation of these models? Here are some options the team considers:

- review prevailing scientific theory and academic literature
- review past internal company and industry-specific research

- review qualitative data from exit surveys and interviews
- review potential models and their critical components with business unit leaders
- based on the best models and data available, apply modern statistical learning algorithms to discover potential drivers

In this case, let's say the analytics team lead is an I-O psychologist whose first instinct is to look internally to see what research the organization has conducted in the past with regard to turnover. As it turns out, the organization doesn't have much of a history of conducting turnover-related work, so there is not much to go on there. Furthermore, let's say the organization resides in an industry where little is known about drivers of turnover, beyond the general theoretical perspectives and models provided in the I-O literature.

Being empty handed up to this point, the lead reviews the I-O literature for theories and models of turnover. Upon review of the prevailing theories and models and comparing their substantive content to the survey and HRIS data available in-house, the team finds that they have the ability to develop and test several theoretically-informed structural models of turnover. However, the team realizes that measures of some variables within the models will be limited because the organization's annual employee surveys were designed for broader purposes than evaluating pre-existing models of turnover.

Upon specifying several turnover models based on prevailing I-O turnover theory and research, the I-O team lead shares the models with a labor economist and econometrician affiliated with the analytics team. They provide additional insights into variations in economic and market conditions present throughout the past four years that research from their respective fields' literatures suggest would also predict stay-level decisions, and they highlight data from group-level databases that could be leveraged. Based on this work, the team now has multiple sets of structural models, some based purely on I-O theories and research, and others reflecting a blend of research from I-O and labor economics.

After completing the steps above, the team conducts a content analysis of available open-ended responses from the past several years of employee exit survey data. Upon analyzing these data, the team discovers several themes that suggest there are occupation-level, supervisor-level, and region-level differences in the reasons why individuals are leaving. These reasons are inductive surprises in that they fall outside the scope of both the working models the team has developed based on multidisciplinary theories and research on turnover. With these qualitative themes identified, the team searches its data sources for data fields that might account for such differences, gives thought to how those variables would fit into the existing structural models, and specifies yet another set of structural models that incorporate these factors as adequately as possible. It is important to note that at this point in the process, no models have actually been fit to the data—at this point the team is simply focused on formulating multiple alternative structural models for subsequent evaluation.

To summarize, the team has already identified predictors of turnover that have been informed by theories and research in I-O and labor economics, and has effectively mined its qualitative exit survey data and identified potential occupation-level, supervisor-level, and region-level differences to be further examined. Next, the team decides to take stock of what it can learn from the substantial quantitative data to which it has access. Prior to taking the next step with its quantitative data, the team creates multiple random three-part partitions of their data:

- An *exploration set* where they will employ a variety of algorithmic statistical learning methods to identify what predictors consistently come up as important in the prediction of turnover regardless of the algorithm examined. These may be variables not previously specified in the structural models under consideration but that are available in the broader survey and HRIS data.
- A *calibration set* where they will compare and contrast various alternative structural models of turnover, including models that are augmented with variables identified via the exploration set, after they are informed by input from team members and business unit leaders (discussed below).
- An *evaluation set* where they will examine the cross-validity of their best-bet single structural models and model ensembles whose parameters were estimated in the calibration set.

Within the exploration set, the team turns to its resident computer scientist and statistician to leverage a range of modern statistical learning methods for the effective prediction of binary criteria such as turnover (e.g., random forests, stochastic gradient boosted trees, support vector machines; Hastie et al., 2009). The team then formulates a matrix of variable importance metrics by predictor and modeling method, and identifies those predictors that consistently come up as important across methods as determined via k-fold cross-validation within the exploration data set.

Through this process, the team identifies several predictors and interactions that show consistent and stable relationships with turnover, yet these relationships have slipped through the cracks of their theoretical, rationally-derived models formulated during previous steps in the model development process.

Now the I-O team lead fully realizes that the modern statistical learning techniques used to discover potential predictors for consideration do little to inform if and how such predictors causally relate to turnover. As such, the team takes stock of the most important predictors identified through the statistical learning methods and gives thought to how and where they should fit into the theoretical, rationally-derived structural models formulated during previous steps. Realizing that they may not fully be able to explain the role certain predictors may play, they also consult business unit leaders who may be able to offer insight into the predictors in question and use their feedback and consensus from the team to formulate yet another new set of structural models augmented with the newly discovered predictors.

Upon completing the steps above, the team has a wide variety of alternate structural models of turnover to fit within its calibration set. Remember that this calibration set is an independent set of data, so any results from this data set do not capitalize on chance factors that might have influenced model development in the earlier stages. Thus, the team then formally fits the models to the calibration set, records their fit statistics, and also records information that allows them to index each model's uncertainty. Past experience has taught the team that when dealing with multiple models of a common outcome, the probability of any one model clearly being the best model given the data at hand is very small, and that by relying on a single model to draw inferences, they would be losing information and robustness that are potentially valuable for durable prediction and understanding of the outcome of interest.

With the models estimated, the team then applies the model parameters estimated in the calibration sample to the evaluation set to evaluate whether fit statistics hold up and to examine the cross-validity of model-predicted values for predicting turnover. In addition to applying model parameters for each model individually, the team also forms ensembles of the best fitting models from the calibration sample (where each model "votes" on the outcome by way of its prediction) and evaluates the cross-validity of their predictions in the evaluation set.

In reviewing the results, the team finds that several models offer good levels of fit to the data and prediction of turnover, but that the models are substantively different and imply different causal mechanisms under-lying turnover (i.e., a case of model uncertainty). In fact, the team finds that ensembles substantially outperform their single-model counterparts in terms of prediction in the evaluation set. Thus, instead of simply going with one "best" model, the team boils down results to best bets for inter-vention based on the set of information across the best fitting models; then in concluding the project, the team briefs their organizational leadership on the findings and interventions most likely to impact the key drivers of turnover.

Upon completion of this effort, the analytics team lead feels compelled to publish the findings in a journal designed by and for I-O psychologists. Having experience with the publication process, there is a distinct concern by the team that reviewers will be concerned with the psychometrically non-ideal measures for some of the core components of the theory-driven models, which are a function of the data that were available in the applied setting. At the same time, the lead knows that his organizations found very strong prediction relative to past research in the turnover literature based on stable empirical findings regarding several new predictors and func-tional forms of turnover. Moreover, these new findings have reasonable substantive interpretations that can pave the way for future research based on improved measures and models. On the balance, the team is confident in the work and submits the work for publication.

Alas, the paper gets rejected on several grounds laid out by the editor and reviewers: the study did not adequately test existing theory, could not test the statistical and practical increments in validity or value in predic-tion for the new models over the more traditional models specified purely by theory (which the team did not have full data to test), did not theoreti-cally justify some of the structural models proposed (despite the fact that theory drove parts of the model, and a principled approach was taken to extend theory in areas where the variables were promising but related the-ory could not be found), and failed to reach an unambiguous decision with regard to a single best model (although model ensembles clearly provided valuable, more stable prediction for the organization beyond traditional models).

On the flip side of this picture, a few more years pass, and the models developed and evaluated in the previous round of research have since been used to inform development of interventions designed to reduce turnover within the organization. After the interventions were implemented, follow-up evaluation revealed that they have helped dramatically reduce turnover in various areas of the organization, helping save the organization millions of dollars. As a result of this effort, the organization has gained knowledge and understanding of turnover that is clearly beneficial and potentially generalizable to other organizations, yet it remains largely invisible to the outside world and academic community because theory-centric editorial policies hampered the dissemination of research motivated by a broader combination and process of theory, induction, multidisciplinary insight, and discovery.

ADDRESSING CURRENT LIMITERS ON THE ADVANCEMENT OF I-O SCIENCE

The previous section illustrated how the big data and analytics movement currently underway in organizations offers the potential to advance both I-O science and practice. Admittedly, many of the examples above were borne out of practical applications; however, the concepts examined—validation, assessment, model development, and model evaluation—happen to be critical in both science and practice. To better appreciate the implications of the emerging state of affairs for I-O science, it is interesting to juxtapose the discussion above with current limiters on the advancement of I-O science.

First, with regular flow of data and recurring analytic cycles, one conclusion is that large organizations will increasingly be in a position to allow rapid development of knowledge far faster than current publication and peer review cycles allow. This may or may not lead to analytic results providing proprietary and competitive advantage to the organizations, but to the extent that it does, this can be looked at as a partial threat to the continued relevance of I-O science to organizations. Nevertheless, we'd like to put a more positive spin on this—given these early years of the evolution of big data in organizations, we look at it as a renewed impetus to find new ways to develop and disseminate relevant organizational knowledge at an accelerated rate, something critical for I-O science.

Second, the scope of data being accrued, along with the big data movement, allows organizations to investigate the ways in which their specific context supports and/or qualifies theoretical relationships. By contrast, traditional attempts to generalize to specific organizations from the findings of published studies, or even replications and meta-analyses, require a leap of inference that the previous sorts of investigations might start removing. For example, one concern that arises in practice is whether general, theory-driven models generalize across different facets of the organization's operating environment (e.g., geographic regions, business units, departments, and teams). To be more concrete, let's say we're dealing with a large multinational company that has data to inform whether models of turnover and engagement generalize across global regions or countries. The scope of data available in a large multinational corporation with a mature HCM function allows one to evaluate the applicability and generalizability of those models, over time and across the aforementioned facets of the organization, in a way that hasn't really been feasible in traditional I-O research given historical data access issues and previous limitations on data collection technology. The degree to which information on generalizability of findings is lacking limits advancement in both science and practice. More specifically, it limits the rate at which I-O psychology can accrue useful knowledge about our theory-driven models—how durable particular findings are, where findings might be context-dependent, and where theories might need some fundamental revision as refined by the data. Note how this issue goes far beyond whether bivariate correlations generalize, as has been the historical focus of validity generalization studies (Schmidt & Hunter, 1977).

The scope of HCM data also lends itself to very rich, multilevel, longitudinal research. Historically, research in I-O science has largely been cross-sectional as opposed to longitudinal in nature (Austin et al., 2002), but as revealed in Figure 7.1, from both a calendar time and individual (tenure) perspective, time is a central component in the HCM data lifecycle. Modern longitudinal methods are available to accommodate the influx of large numbers of variables for many people and units across numerous time points (see Ployhart & Vandenberg, 2010; Walls & Schafer, 2006). Similarly, research in I-O science has predominantly been performed at the individual-level, yet as Figure 7.1 reveals, modern HCM analytic efforts are becoming increasingly concerned with folding in group-level data of various types as both predictors and outcomes (see Gibby et al., 2013; Wiley, 1996). These characteristics put organizations in a better position to build and evaluate rich, multidisciplinary, longitudinal models of outcomes than the academic community has typically been in as a result of data access issues. They also allow one to assess the value of our more "micro" human capital (reserve of employee skills) and interventions (selection, training) on more "macro" outcomes (profit and profit growth; Kim & Ployhart, 2014).

Lastly, the natural variation that occurs in the operation of an organization across separate departments, business, and units creates the potential for natural experiments—something occasionally seen in the I-O psychology academic literature, but an increase of which would be extremely helpful for advancing science and practice. The mix of centralized and decentralized HR processes that exists within many large organizations can allow for ongoing cycles of natural experimentation with factors hypothesized to affect the impact of various HR processes, programs, and interventions. Quasi-experiments of this nature have always been possible within large organizations, but big data systems allow for geographically dispersed units to be more readily visible, given the feeds into HCM data and reporting systems described earlier.

THE ROAD AHEAD

To set up the remainder our discussion, we'd like to start by offering an excerpt from an interview Leo Breiman conducted late in his career (Olshen, 2001). The subject matter involves the study of statistics, but there is an analogy that can be drawn to I-O psychology. The interviewer asked Breiman what advice he would offer a new student seeking to study statistics. Here is a snippet of Breiman's response:

> My feeling is, to some extent, that academic statistics may have lost its way. When I came, after consulting, back to the Berkeley Department, I felt like I was almost entering *Alice in Wonderland*. That is, I knew what was going on out in industry and government in terms of uses of statistics, but what was going on in academic research seemed light years away. It was proceeding as though it were some branch of abstract mathematics. One of our senior faculty members said a while back, "We have to keep alive the spirit of Wald." But before the good old days of Wald and the divorce of statistics from data, there were the good old days of Fisher, who believed that statistics existed for the purposes of prediction and explanation and working with data. (pp. 195–196)

The reason we include this quotation is that we see a very similar phenomenon happening within our own field. Many have commented on over exuberance in organizational research with regard to theory creation and testing at the expense of evaluating empirical support for phenomena that organizations care about and wish to impact through their human capital processes and programs (Hambrick, 2007; Silzer & Parson, 2012). In the days of old within the I-O field, there was arguably a much clearer tie between what was being published in our journals and what was actually happening in organizations, as evidenced by greater percentages of published authors practicing and a greater percentage of practitioners on editorial boards (Aguinis et al., 2014). Taking a look across the historical foundations of selection, training, performance appraisal, and other areas of I-O psychology, you will find scores of publications that are firmly grounded in and highly relevant to organizational practice (Koppes, 2007). These publications are almost refreshing in their emphasis on real-world impact, as opposed to theory without a cause.

In our view, achieving a robust applied science requires striking a balance between induction from observation and exploration of *persistent* human capital issues faced in organizations, and deduction driven from organizational theories receiving past empirical support. Where induction leans more towards being open to local phenomena in organization, deduction leans towards support for more general and generalizable findings. Over the course of decades of organizational research, there has been an imbalance in the direction of theory and deduction and away from practical insights regarding persistent organizational needs, with practice being dismissed as too atheoretical (yet clearly important and potentially theory-relevant). Unfortunately, with the advent of the big data and analytics era, the imbalance is perhaps even more problematic. Specifically, I-O psychologists working with big data, in organizations with access to the HCM data systems described earlier, are now substantially better positioned than in the past to generate substantial and potentially generalizable scientific knowledge about organizational processes and outcomes through deductive processes. Nevertheless, with many practitioners considering their work of a proprietary nature and with few practitioners having the time or incentive to publish or serve on editorial boards of major I-O and management journals, we see the current situation as a clear detriment to the advancement of our field, as much of that potentially valuable knowledge available through practice may likely remain largely invisible in academic outlets.

In light of the issues raised above and throughout this chapter, the remainder of our discussion focuses on laying out ideas that may help I-O graduate students, I-O psychologists, and I-O psychology as a field in general capitalize on opportunities the big data and analytics movement now afford us. We have grouped these ideas into two broad categories: one focused on areas for individual development and the other focused on more macro-level shifts in our perspectives on research and practice that help strengthen the I-O field within the new data-rich environment.

Areas for Individual Development

The history of I-O psychology reveals that our field has become incredibly diverse over time in terms of substantive topic areas and the researchers and practitioners contributing to them (Koppes, 2007). Because instruction time in graduate school has not grown accordingly, some types of training have had to be compromised. For I-O and psychology graduate training, that generally has meant statistics, research methods, and measurement (Aiken et al., 2008; Merenda, 2007). When one couples this observation with the big data movement and substantial advances in statistics and measurement in recent decades, it is not an understatement to declare that we face a situation where the statistics and methods training of new academicians and practitioners in I-O psychology can be outdated prior to leaving grad school, thus limiting the progress, value, and multidisciplinary potential of I-O psychology as a science.

So with these observations in mind, here are some areas we see as helpful for current and future I-O psychologists interested in capitalizing on the big data movement to have at least a basic understanding of:

- common data stores in organizations and how they relate to researching and evaluating different elements of the employment lifecycle
- different disciplines that "play" in the HR-related big data space and how their contributions complement those of I-O psychology
- archival data preparation, cleaning, and data reduction
- analysis methods and research designs for longitudinal, multilevel data
- modern algorithmic modeling methods and the value they can have for large-scale HC analytic efforts and the evaluation and refinement of theory
- how modern algorithmic modeling methods and cross-validation strategies compare and add value to models and methods traditionally used in I-O psychology
- emerging "tools of the trade" (e.g., R, SQL, Python, data visualization tools) and the roles they play in a large-scale HC analytics program and HR-related big data initiatives
- strategies and stories that effectively convey complex modeling results to corporate executives, lay audiences, and even other I-O psychologists, all of whom may not have the depth of expertise with regard to modeling.

Again, in most cases, gaining awareness and a basic understanding of a topic area and its relevance to one's work would arguably suffice in that it would provide a general educational foundation that helps to facilitate conversations with others involved with big data. The acquisition of deeper expertise and specialization will grow more naturally in that it often will depend on one's emerging practical needs and research interests. Many of the topics above would arguably require a substantial amount of time to become truly expert in, which is part of the reason why teams of individuals are often critical to big data efforts. Indeed, most big data efforts we have seen, and indeed in the examples provided earlier, are accomplished with diverse teams of individuals who have complementary areas of expertise.

Big Data Should Shift How We View Research and Value Practice

Taking advantage of the big data and analytics movement to advance I-O science and practice arguably requires going beyond just brushing up on new statistics, methods, and informational resources. Another key element we see as critical to I-O psychology's successful adaptation to the big data environment involves expanding our perspectives beyond our traditional research training and fundamentally reconsidering the value of practice for advancing science.

Regarding the first point, we have arguably been trained as I-O psychologists to think largely of research in terms of the dissertations, research projects, and applied work that reflect static, single-shot studies reflecting a narrow data collection effort that is focused on variables of interest within the theoretical framework in which we work. Often we lack formal training beyond tried and true concurrent research designs (lab or field), meta-analyses, or longitudinal research designs as they have traditionally been framed. More specifically, we have not been conceptually or analytically trained to deal with continuous streams of diverse sets of data and how such data can be creatively leveraged to improve theory and practice. Thus, one fundamental shift we see being required is breaking out of the mindset of thinking of research and theory testing solely in terms of traditional types of single-shot studies and data collections. Once we have a big data mindset—in terms of the possibilities that having access to large, dynamic, continuous, diverse streams of data create for advancing I-O science and practice—it becomes easier to appreciate that the standard methodological toolkit of I-O psychologists needs to expand.

Regarding the second point—an increased appreciation for the growing amount of potentially scientifically valuable knowledge that resides in practice—we noted that I-O psychologists working in organizations with access to HCM data systems are currently better positioned to generate significant scientific knowledge about organizational processes and outcomes. However, given that many organizations might view such findings as proprietary and do not necessarily reward practitioners for publishing, we cannot expect to see any sudden uptick in first-author journal submissions by practitioners—no matter how much friendlier journals become towards inductive research and practitioner findings. What this means is that the academic-practitioner gaps and misalignments in our knowledge may increase even further, unless academics can serve as a conduit for practitioners who wish to publish their knowledge and convince journals that inductive research findings from big data will meaningfully advance our science.

We see it as imperative for our field to find ways that tangibly reinforce academic I-O psychologists for leading research partnerships with practitioners as well as those researchers and practitioners in other fields that "play" in the big data space. To our knowledge, reinforcement for such partnerships is neither reflected in the editorial policies of top-tier journals in our field nor the tenure and reward criteria for faculty in typical I-O graduate programs. Though it is beyond our scope to detail how this state of affairs might be improved, we felt compelled to raise this issue because we view such partnerships as increasingly critical to maintaining the relevance of I-O psychology to the world of work. Simply put, the practice side of our field continues to accrue substantial data and technological resources of relevance to I-O science, and other fields are gaining more prominence working in what has traditionally been considered I-O psychology's domain (e.g., labor economists, computer scientists, applied statisticians). This creates the potential for widening gaps in the I-O scientific knowledge base and steps should be taken to address it.

CLOSING THOUGHTS

A final point we want to make in closing regards our choice of focus for this chapter. In past discussions of big data with various I-O colleagues, one of the first perils that have always come up was the danger of blind empiricism. Though not mentioned in this chapter, we certainly recognize some obvious facts, namely: blind empiricism can lead to false conclusions and flawed interventions, correlation is not causation, and research design and psychological measurement are critical and have implications for drawing causal inferences—these do not magically disappear in a big data environment. As I-O psychologists, we already hold the substantive, psychometric, and research training and expertise to help organizations avoid this peril of the big data movement, so long as we are proactive and bring ourselves into the fold. What we are generally not trained to see is the peril—and promise—to our field as a whole that the big data and analytics movement presents, and therein lies our choice to focus this chapter as we have.

One of the major goals of this chapter was to serve as a call to action for the I-O field. We see a wonderful opportunity before us. Never before has our field been presented with as much diversity of data, information, and technology as we have before us now. At this point, we are only limited by our creativity (and computing power!) for leveraging it, and the speed at which we can become aware of new techniques and resources for taking advantage of it. We hope this chapter helps to persuade readers that I-O psychologists should expand upon their traditional perspectives on analytic methods and approaches to research because although they have served us well over the years, the movement into big data research and analysis paradigms provides substantial value and vitality to our research and practice.

NOTES

1. This observation is based on a sampling of content from multiple big data symposia and panel discussions held at the 2014 Society for Industrial and Organizational Psychology (SIOP) conference. Also of note here, recent discussions of big data have sometimes included a fourth "V"—veracity—however, we tend to agree with the original conceptualization of big data in that all data, whether big or small, are ideally accurate. In our view, adding the veracity term does nothing to differentiate big data from other data.
2. In recognition of this trend, there have been recent visible attempts to provide alternative types of outlets for both academicians and practitioners that put more of an emphasis on exploratory research and highlighting important organizational phenomena. Examples include the Academy of Management's *Discoveries* journal, as well as the International Personnel Assessment Council's *Personnel Assessment and Decisions*.
3. Though the present example uses biodata items as predictors, our final example in this chapter illustrates how the beneficial characteristics of modern statistical learning methods can generalize to other modeling situations I-O psychologists may face (e.g., predicting turnover, engagement, or other outcomes of interest to science and practice).

REFERENCES

Aguinis, H., Bradley, K. J., & Brodersen, A. (2014). Industrial-organizational psychologists in business schools: Brain drain or eye opener? *Industrial and Organizational Psychology: Perspectives on Science and Practice, 7*, 284–303.

Aguinis, H., Pierce, C. A., Bosco, F. A., & Muslin, I. S. (2009). First decade of Organizational Research Methods: Trends in design, measurement, and data-analysis topics. *Organizational Research Methods, 12*, 69–112

Aiken, L. S., West, S. G., & Millsap (2008). Graduate training in statistics, measurement, and methodology in psychology: Replication and extension of Aiken, West, Sechrest, and Reno's (1990) survey of PhD programs in North America. *American Psychologist, 63*, 32–50.

Allen, T. A. (2014). Opening presidential address. Presented at the 29th Annual Society for Industrial and Organizational Psychology Conference, Honolulu, HI.

Austin, J. T., Scherbaum, C. A., & Mahlman, R. A. (2002). History of research methods in industrial and organizational psychology: Measurement, design, analysis. In S. G. Rogelberg (Ed.), *Handbook of research methods in industrial and organizational psychology* (pp. 3–33). Malden, MA: Blackwell Publishing.

Berk, R. A. (2006). An introduction to ensemble methods for data analysis. *Sociological Methods & Research, 34*, 263–295.

Bersin, J. (2013, October 7). Big data in human resources: A world of haves and have-nots. *Forbes*. Retrieved from: http://www.forbes.com/sites/joshbersin/2013/10/07/big-data-in-human-resources-a-world-of-haves-and-have-nots/

Biga, A. (2014). Using big and small data to make better people decisions. Presented to the Personnel Testing Council of Metropolitan Washington, Washington, DC.

Binning, J. F., & Barrett, G. V. (1989). Validity of personnel decisions: A conceptual analysis of the inferential and evidential bases. *Journal of Applied Psychology, 74*, 478–494.

Bobko, P., Roth, P. L., & Buster, M. A. (2005). A systematic approach for assessing the recency of job-analytic information. Presented at the 29th Annual International Public Management Association Assessment Council Conference, Orlando, FL.

Borsboom, D. (2006). The attack of the psychometricians. *Psychometrika, 71*, 425–440.

Breiman, L. (1996). Bagging predictors. *Machine Learning, 26*, 123–140.

Breiman, L. (2001a). Random forests. *Machine Learning, 45*, 5–32.

Breiman, L. (2001b). Statistical modeling: The two cultures. *Statistical Science, 16*, 199–231.

Brown, S. H. (1994). Validating biodata. In G. S. Stokes, M. D. Mumford & W. A. Owens (Eds.), *Biodata handbook: Theory, research, and use of biographical information in selection and performance prediction* (pp. 199–236). Palo Alto, CA: Consulting Psychological Press.

Burnham, K. P., & Anderson, D. R. (2002). *Model selection and multimodel inference: A practical information-theoretic approach* (2nd ed.). New York, NY: Springer.

Cascio, W. F., & Aguinis, H. (2008). Research in industrial and organizational psychology from 1963 to 2007: Changes, choices, and trends. *Journal of Applied Psychology, 93*, 1062–1081.

Chatfield, C. (1995). Model uncertainty, data mining, and statistical inference. *Journal of the Royal Statistical Society A, 158*, 419–466.

Cucina, J. M., Caputo, P. M., Thibodeaux, H. F., & MacLane, C. N. (2012). Unlocking the key to biodata scoring: A comparison of empirical, rational, and hybrid approaches at different sample sizes. *Personnel Psychology, 65*, 385–428.

DeMars, C. (2004). Detection of item parameter drift over multiple test administrations. *Applied Measurement in Education, 17*, 265–300.

Gibby, R. E., McCloy, R., & Putka, D. J. (2013). *Viewing linkage research through the lenses of current practice and cutting edge advances*. Presented at the 28th Annual Society for Industrial and Organizational Psychology Conference, Houston, TX.

Griffeth, R. W., & Hom, P. W. (2001). *Retaining valued employees*. Thousand Oaks, CA: Sage Publications.

Griffith, R. W., Hom, P. W., & Gaertner, S. (2001). A meta-analysis of antecedents and correlates of employee turnover: Update, moderator tests, and research implications for the next millennium. *Journal of Management, 26*, 463–488

Guion, R. M. (1998). *Assessment, measurement, and prediction for personnel decisions.* Mahwah, NJ: Lawrence Erlbaum.

Hambrick, D. C. (2007). The field of management's devotion to theory: Too much of a good thing? *Academy of Management Journal, 50*, 1346–1352.

Hastie, T., Tibshirani, R., & Friedman, J. (2009). *The elements of statistical learning: Data mining, inference, and prediction* (2nd ed.). New York, NY: Springer.

Helfat, C. E. (2007). Stylized facts, empirical research and theory development in organizations. *Strategic Organization, 5*, 185–192.

Hoeting, J. A., Madigan, D., Raferty, A. E., & Volinksy, C. T. (1999). Bayesian model averaging: A tutorial. *Statistical Science, 14*, 382–417.

Hogan, J. B. (1994). Empirical keying of background data measures. In G. S. Stokes, M. D. Mumford & W. A. Owens (Eds.), *Biodata handbook: Theory, research, and use of biographical information in selection and performance prediction* (pp. 69–107). Palo Alto, CA: Consulting Psychological Press.

Johnson, J. W., & LeBreton, J. M. (2004). History and use of relative importance indices in organizational research. *Organizational Research Methods, 7*, 238–257.

Kantrowitz, T. M. (2014). *2014 global assessment trends report.* Alpharetta, GA: SHL.

Kemp, M. (2014). *Starting the analytics engine: Practical approaches and lessons learned.* Presented at the 29th Annual Society for Industrial and Organizational Psychology Conference, Honolulu, HI.

Kim, Y., & Ployhart, R. E. (2014). The effects of staffing and training on firm productivity and profit growth before, during, and after the Great Recession. *Journal of Applied Psychology, 99*, 361–389.

Koppes, L. L. (Ed.) (2007). *Historical perspectives in industrial-organizational psychology.* Mahwah, NJ: Lawrence Erlbaum Associates.

Laney, D. (2001). 3D data management: Controlling data volume, velocity, and variety. *Application Delivery Strategies.* Stamford, CT: Meta Group, Inc. Retrieved from http://blogs.gartner.com/doug-laney/files/2012/01/ad949-3D-Data-Management-Controlling-Data-Volume-Velocity-and-Variety.pdf

Lievens, F., De Corte, W., & Westerveld, L. (2015). Understanding the building blocks of selection procedures: Effects of response fidelity on performance and validity. *Journal of Management, 41*, 1604–1627.

Locke, E. A. (2007). The case for inductive theory building. *Journal of Management, 33*, 867–890.

Lohr, S. (2013, April 20). Big data, trying to build better workers. *New York Times.* Retrieved from: http://www.nytimes.com/2013/04/21/technology/big-data-trying-to-build-better-workers.html?pagewanted=all

Mael, F. A. (1991). A conceptual rationale for the domain and attributes of biodata items. *Personnel Psychology, 44*, 763–792.

Merenda, P. F. (2007). Psychometrics and psychometricians in the 20th and 21st centuries: How it was in the 20th century and how it is now. *Perceptual and Motor Skills, 104*, 3–20.

Mumford, M. D., & Owens, W. A. (1987). Methodology review: Principles, procedures, and findings in the application of background data measures. *Applied Psychological Measurement, 11*, 1–31.

Olshen, R. (2001). A conversation with Leo Breiman. *Statistical Science, 16*, 184–198.

Overby, S. (2013, August 27). HR departments invaded by data scientists. *CIO.com.* Retrieved from: http://www.cio.com/article/2383195/business-intelligence/hr-departments-invaded-by-data-scientists.html

Owens, W. A. (1976). Background data. In M. D. Dunnette (Ed.), *Handbook of industrial and organizational psychology* (pp. 609–644). Chicago, IL: Rand-McNally.

Ployhart, R. E., Schneider, B., & Schmitt, N. (2006). *Staffing organizations: Contemporary practice and theory* (3rd ed.). Mahwah, NJ: Lawrence Erlbaum Associates.

Ployhart, R. E., & Vandenberg, R. J. (2010). Longitudinal research: The theory, design, and analysis of change. *Journal of Management, 36*, 94–120.

Putka, D. J. (2013). HEY! We've been doing this for 100 years! *Personnel Testing Council of Metropolitan Washington Quarterly Newsletter, 9*, 2–9.

Roberts, S. (2014). *Pivot tables to p-values: Creating an internal HR analytics function*. Presented at the 29th Annual Society for Industrial and Organizational Psychology Conference, Honolulu, HI.

Scherbaum, C., Putka, D. J., Naidoo, L., & Youssefina, D. (2010). Key driver analyses: Current trends, problems, and alternative approaches. In S. Albrecht (Ed.), *Handbook of employee engagement: Models, measures, and practice* (pp. 182–196). Cheltenham, UK: Edward-Elgar Publishing House.

Schmidt, F. L., & Hunter, J. E. (1977). Development of a general solution to the problem of validity generalization. *Journal of Applied Psychology, 62*, 529–540.

Shapiro, D. L., Kirkman, B. L., & Courtney, H. G. (2007). Perceived causes and solutions of the translation problem in management research. *Academy of Management Journal, 50*, 249–266

Shen, W., Kiger, T. B., Davies, S. E., Rasch, R. L., Simon, K. M., & Ones, D. S. (2011). Samples in applied psychology: Over a decade of research in review. *Journal of Applied Psychology, 96*, 1055–1064.

Silzer, R., & Cober, R. (2010). The science-practice gap in I-O psychology: A fish bowl exercise. *The Industrial-Organizational Psychologist, 48*, 95–103. Retrieved from: http://www.siop.org/tip/july10/14silzer.aspx

Silzer, R., & Parson, C. (2012). Industrial-organizational psychology journals and the science-practice gap. *The Industrial-Organizational Psychologist, 49*, 97–117. Retrieved from: http://www.siop.org/tip/apr12/15silzer.aspx

Society for Industrial and Organizational Psychology. (1999). *Guidelines for education and training at the doctoral level in industrial/organizational psychology*. Bowling Green, OH: Society for Industrial and Organizational Psychology. Retrieved from: http://www.siop.org/PhDGuidelines98.aspx

Walls, T. A., & Schafer, J. L. (Eds.) (2006). *Models for intensive longitudinal data*. New York, NY: Oxford University Press.

Wiley, J. W. (1996). Linking survey data to the bottom line. In A. I. Kraut (Ed.), *Organizational surveys: Tools for assessment and change* (pp. 330–350). San Francisco, CA: Jossey-Bass.

8

Big Data in Talent Selection and Assessment

A. James Illingworth, Michael Lippstreu, and Anne-Sophie Deprez-Sims

This chapter provides a discussion of the role of big data in talent selection and assessment. It begins by defining big data and highlighting how it overlaps with the principles and goals of staffing practice. This is followed by a review of how big data are used and vary across the different components of an organization's selection and assessment processes, with an emphasis on the similarities and differences between big data in talent management and other disciplines. The chapter then presents three business case studies to illustrate the types of big data encountered in applied settings and the related challenges and benefits. Finally, future applications of big data in selection and assessment are discussed, followed by several practical considerations associated with the collection, analysis, and interpretation of big data in talent management. For the purposes of this chapter, talent selection and assessment is defined narrowly to include organizational processes for attracting, selecting, developing, and retaining human capital (Society for Human Resource Management, 2015).

DEFINING BIG DATA IN SELECTION AND ASSESSMENT

Big data is a term used to describe large and complex forms of data that have arisen due to advancements in technology. It can be characterized by various dimensions of data complexity, with the literature commonly defining big data in terms of the three Vs—volume, velocity, and variety (McAfee & Brynjolfsson, 2012; Laney, 2001). That is, data are likely to be considered big if the amount of data being gathered is large in terms of file size or the number of observations and variables (volume), the capture and processing of data occurs rapidly (velocity), and the types of data being collected and analyzed are diverse (variety). More recently, other dimensions have been added to include two additional Vs: veracity and value (Prokopeak, 2014). These refer to the accuracy and integrity of the data being collected and analyzed, and the meaningfulness of the data to the research or business question.

These dimensions have also been widely used to conceptualize big data in the talent management domain (Church & Dutta, 2013; Gale, 2014b; Maurath, 2014; Prokopeak, 2014). This chapter will similarly rely upon the five-V framework to link these concepts to selection and assessment practices. In addition, this chapter adopts the premise that a major objective of working with big data is to predict relationships that have important organizational implications. In taking this approach, we propose that the concept of big data fits well with the existing principles of selection and assessment practices. However, it is also important to note that big data is a relative term and that different domains can have different standards for what are considered big data. Thus, we will examine the similarities and differences of key big data concepts as they relate to different contexts in relation to selection and assessment. This will include differences between the usage of big data in selection and assessment work compared to other disciplines, as well as the different applications of big data across the various aspects of the selection and assessment process.

Overlap of Big Data Concepts with Selection and Assessment Principles

An often-promoted benefit of working with big data is that it allows for decisions to be based on evidence rather than intuition by linking and analyzing data from different sources. A review of the popular press and even some talent management literature would incorrectly suggest that this concept is new and revolutionary to selection and assessment practices (Bersin, 2013b; Galagan, 2014; Gardner, McGranahan, & Wolf, 2011; Harvard Business Review Analytic Services, 2013; Prokopeak, 2014; Walker, 2012). For example, the current state of employee selection practices (e.g., hiring) has been described as being based on hunches and intuition rather than data. These big data articles describe supposedly groundbreaking studies that strive to address such questions as what are the best predictors of an employee's success on the job and what assessment tools can be used to more accurately predict productivity. A number of practitioners and researchers who specialize in selection and assessment work have commented on these inappropriate and misleading assumptions about the state of the field, noting that the fundamental analytics behind big data have already been practiced for 100 years in selection and assessment work (Doverspike, 2013; Poeppelman, Blacksmith, & Yongwei, 2013; Putka, 2013).

There are good reasons for rejecting the idea that the foundations of big data are new to selection and assessment work. Big data at its core is applied in orientation and seeks to address a business problem. It is based on predictive analytics that attempt to link a predictor or set of predictors to outcome variables (Harvard Business Review Analytic Services, 2013; Prokopeak, 2014; Roberts, 2013). Rather than simple analyses of a descriptive nature, relationships between variables are examined using correlation and regression analyses. These methods are similar to standard practices in selection and assessment research. For example, a common approach to validating an assessment involves demonstrating the relationship between the assessment and important criteria, such as job performance or organizational outcomes, using similar statistical procedures. Other data-driven techniques, such as job analysis, competency modeling, and content validation methods, are used to build and support the job relevance of the selection instrument. Although these selection and assessment methods can be applied to various forms of data and are not necessarily limited to the context of big data, the analytical foundations of selection and assessment principles and big data are aligned.

Differences in Big Data Characteristics with Other Disciplines

There are also important distinctions between big data as typically described in the general literature in comparison to big data as they normally exist today in the selection and assessment domain. Table 8.1 provides a summary description of the big data characteristics and considerations in selection and assessment relative to the prototypical big data example in the literature as it is used for other applications. These characteristics are described in terms of the five Vs: volume, velocity, variety, veracity, and value. It is important to note that these comparisons are intended to illustrate the current state of big data in selection and assessment relative to those of other disciplines. The nature of big data in selection and assessment is expected to evolve over time, and as such, the differences in big data characteristics across disciplines could begin to converge. Examples of these future big data opportunities and their associated challenges will be discussed in later sections.

TABLE 8.1

Summary comparison of big data characteristics

Big Data Character-istics	Description	Prototypical Big Data Characteristics and Considerations	Selection and Assessment Big Data Characteristics and Considerations
Volume	The magnitude or size of data and the associated computational requirements	• Terabytes or petabytes of data • Observations based on processes or discrete components of systems	• Gigabytes of data • Observations based on number of people and associated variables
Velocity	The speed at which data arrive and reach obsolescence	• Real time data capture • Real time data analysis (e.g., algorithms, machine learning)	• Real time data capture • Archival data capture • Data management prior to analysis
Variety	The different types of data being collected in terms of form, technique, or source	• Unstructured data (e.g., video, text, images) • Integration of structured (e.g., spreadsheet format) and unstructured data from multiple sources	• Structured data (e.g., spreadsheet format) • Unstandardized data across multiple datasets
Veracity	The integrity, quality, and accuracy of the data	• Accuracy in data capture, processing, and export	• Accuracy in data capture, processing, and export • Reliability of assessment measures • Validity of assessment measures
Value	The meaningfulness of the data to the research or business question	• Based on exploratory research and analyses (e.g., data mining) • Financial or operational impact of data on business	• Based on hypotheses and theory • Utility of selection or assessment process • Bias

It can be seen from Table 8.1 that big data are generally not as large or complex in the typical selection and assessment situation as it is in other applications such as retail and financial services. In particular, the *volume* of data in the typical selection and assessment situation are on a smaller scale. This is largely due to the nature of the data being collected. For example, in selection and assessment work, observations are limited by the number of job candidates or employees in the organization, so the resulting data size is likely to be smaller. This is true even after accounting for the other aspects of volume in the context of selection and assessment that could contribute to the challenge of handling data, such as the potentially high number of variables associated with the predictor and outcome variables and multiple observations made over time within each employee. In contrast, an online retailer that tracks every mouse click by each customer to customize product offerings is likely to have a far greater amount of data collected. It is no surprise, then, that the size of the data in selection and assessment is unlikely to reach the terabyte or petabyte level of some of the big data situations in other disciplines (Davenport, 2014; Doverspike, 2013; McAfee & Brynjolfsson, 2012).

Furthermore, selection and assessment data are unlikely to be processed at the same *velocity* as in other disciplines. Continuing with the online retailer example, the endless flow of customer data and immediate feedback to the customer would necessitate data to be captured in real time and analyzed in real time through the use of algorithms or other automation. In selection and assessment, technology has allowed for real time capture of incoming data through computerized testing, but the predictive analytics involved in examining the data will usually first require some data management prior to investigating a complex research question. The data management process could also involve performing cleaning activities that are specific to a research study, as well as restructuring activities to link the assessment data with other databases. Thus, the nature of selection and assessment data when conducting complex research studies is different from other applications and does not typically provide the same opportunities for collecting data at extremely high velocity.

The other dimensions of variety, veracity, and value have greater focus and relevance in describing big data in a selection and assessment setting. In terms of *variety*, data from selection and assessment settings as well as data from other disciplines are likely to contend with different types of variables and the interrelationships among them. The collection of variables can include different tests or assessments administered throughout an overall selection process or at different points along an employee's progression within the organization. The variables can also be smaller units of data within each of these tests or assessments, such as test items, dimensions, or individual behaviors reflecting standards of performance. These same tests or assessments may even be administered multiple times to the same individual across time, such as in retesting situations or at scheduled periodic performance evaluations. The variety of data expands further when considering similar opportunities for variation across the universe of outcome variables and how they can be linked to one or more of the predictors. As part of the challenge in dealing with a variety of data, selection and assessment analyses usually contend with multiple data sources and the need to integrate these different sources of data (Davenport, 2013; Roberts, 2013).

The sources of data can be unstandardized, making the cleaning and linking of the data difficult across datasets. Examples of unstandardized data across datasets include inconsistent formatting of the merging variable (e.g., names or other identifiers), record keeping differences in data capture and retention (e.g., archival paper records versus electronic data), dataset design idiosyncrasies (e.g., storing item-level test data and overall test scores in separate databases, storing all item-level data in a single column spanning multiple rows within a person), and working with variables that cut across different levels of analysis (e.g., applicant variables versus organizational variables). Overcoming obstacles related to the linking of unstandardized data sources is often a necessary requirement to establish a relationship between the assessment variables (e.g., cognitive ability and personality) and the outcomes of interest (e.g., employee productivity and organizational performance). The data for the predictor variables are typically stored in a different format from the data for the outcome variables, and even individual predictors and outcomes can be stored in separate databases. These sources of data can also be maintained by different functions or business units in the same organization or across organizations that use their own unique protocol for data management, which creates challenges in aligning data across these sources.

Although selection and assessment work can involve collecting and analyzing a variety of data, there are also important differences in the level of data variety in selection and assessment work compared to big data situations found in other disciplines. In the selection and assessment context, these data are generally arranged in a structured format (i.e., having rows and columns of data), or the data may originate from an unstructured format (e.g., behavioral observations or free responses) and become coded in such a way to retain the most critical information within a structured format. In other disciplines, the data are more likely to be unstructured, but the unstructured data are of greater complexity and are captured, analyzed, and applied continuously in real time, which may include data in the form of videos, text, images, and web clicks (Davenport, 2014). Thus, there is an additional layer of unstructured complexity that frequently contributes to big data challenges in other disciplines. Although the more complex unstructured data has not yet become prevalent in selection and assessment work, new types of assessments that come along with advancements in technology could introduce these issues in the future.

The big data characteristic of *veracity* has significant relevance in the context of selection and assessment. There are well-supported methodologies, principles, and guidelines set forth by professional and government organizations that prescribe the processes for developing and validating selection and assessment instruments (American Educational Research

Association, American Psychological Association, & National Council on Measurement in Education. (2014); Equal Employment Opportunity Commission, Civil Service Commission, Department of Labor & Department of Justice, 1978; Society for Industrial & Organizational Psychology, 2003). These standards always require the collection of accurate and meaningful data. In this sense, veracity holds special meaning for selection and assessment because it describes the nature of big data that is necessary and represents a defining characteristic of the field. Other disciplines also place an emphasis on ensuring the integrity, quality, and accuracy of their data, but it is not as integrated into their identity and there can be a higher tolerance for less veracity depending on the context.

Finally, with regards to the *value* of big data, selection and assessment are not unlike other disciplines in that big data can be used to answer a number of important questions. However, selection and assessment does differ from other disciplines in how it derives value from big data. Many disciplines frequently rely on exploratory research without any basis in established standards or requirements. This practice often involves data mining, where the data sources already exist and research ideas are generated after the fact. All possible relationships between variables may be explored without regard to how they conceptually or theoretically relate to each other. If this approach were followed in selection and assessment, it could be problematic if it produced spurious relationships or relationships that were difficult to explain (Barton & Court, 2012; Maurath, 2014; Poeppelman et al., 2013). Without a clear linkage to the job, the results would be difficult to interpret and could potentially lead to bias and legal challenges.

In contrast, selection and assessment derives value from big data with hypothesis-testing and theory-testing that aim to empirically link selection and assessment practices to specific job or organizational standards (Cascio & Fogli, 2010; Doverspike, 2013; Morris & Lobsenz, 2003). The focus is on demonstrating the reliability and validity of selection instruments using established methods and guidelines. Reliability pertains to the consistency in measurement. Validity concerns can include issues such as whether the assessment is measuring what it is intended to measure (construct validity), whether it reflects the content of the job and is related to the job (content validity), and whether it can be linked to effective job performance (criterion-related validity). The concepts of reliability and validity are well-established in the field, and strict methodologies are followed to demonstrate these properties according to professional standards and legal guidelines (American Educational Research Association, American Psychological Association, & National Council on Measurement in Education, 2014; Equal Employment Opportunity Commission, Civil Service Commission, Department of

Labor, & Department of Justice, 1978; Society for Industrial & Organizational Psychology, 2003). In addition, a typical selection project would include a job analysis to further establish the job relatedness of the assessment. Thus, the value of data-based inferences and conclusions is of high concern during a validation study where these assessment properties are examined and the objective is to ensure value is maintained once the test is implemented.

With a validated assessment, the value of the assessment can also be observed after implementation. As more test data are collected during the implementation of the test, the test data can be linked to such utility outcomes as cost savings per employee. Other outcomes of interest to be linked to the test data could include training data, job performance data, and organizational performance. The bias of the test can also be monitored periodically as more test data is generated to further evaluate the meaningfulness and value of the test. These practices are common in selection and assessment work and, taken together, suggest that the value of data are already well-covered in relation to big data opportunities in other disciplines.

Big Data Characteristics across Selection and Assessment Processes

Big data characteristics can also be differentiated across the various selection and assessment events within the talent management life cycle. Figure 8.1 summarizes the selection and assessment practices that are relevant to the pre-hire phase and post-hire phase of the talent acquisition and management process and how the big data characteristics differ across these functions. This includes the recruiting, screening, and assessing stages of the pre-hire phase, as well as the internal talent assessment process (i.e., performance management or training) and the internal talent selection process (i.e., promotions) of the post-hire phase.

The five Vs of big data are differentially associated with the pre- and post-hire processes, as some of the Vs are more descriptive of the data than others at any given stage of the process. The relevance of the five Vs is indicated by the degree of shading shown in each bar. The darker shading indicates that the particular big data attribute is highly descriptive of the data for that particular stage of the process, whereas the lighter shading indicates that the big data attribute is less descriptive of the data. The figure also shows that the various selection and assessment practices can be linked to important business outcomes, such as

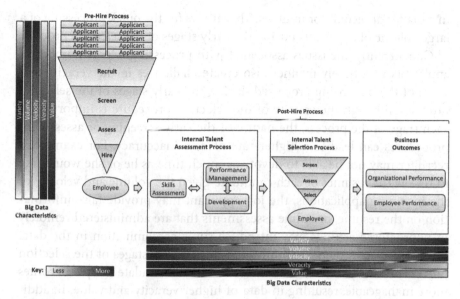

FIGURE 8.1

Relevance of big data to selection and assessment processes

employee and organizational performance, which is consistent with the evaluative goals of selection and assessment research as well as big data principles.

During the pre-hire phase, the selection process involves attracting a potentially large number of job applicants and subsequently evaluating those applicants against a series of screening and assessment standards that are relevant to the job. The volume of data is expected to be larger during the early stages of the selection process and smaller during subsequent stages of the process, as additional screening and assessment criteria are applied until the pool of candidates becomes reduced to a more competitive sample. The velocity of the data is also likely to be higher during earlier stages of the process. The large number of applicants (e.g., hundreds or thousands per day) requires timely processing through screening methods that are cost and resource effective. Advancements in and the accessibility of technology have allowed organizations to make timely decisions on the fit of the candidate for the organization in these cases. For example, resumes submitted online by job applicants and logged in the applicant tracking system are evaluated against the requirements of the job, and decisions can be made on the basic qualifications of the applicant in a matter of seconds or minutes. This allows for the quick processing of a large volume of applicants during the early stages of the selection process.

Concurrently, the issues associated with processing a large number of applicants in a timely manner also create challenges in the veracity and value of the data being processed during the early stages of the selection process. Although the validity of the selection procedure is important at each stage of the process, the nature of the early screening or assessment procedures can lead to a higher rate of data inaccuracy. For example, a recruiter may not be able to devote as much time as he or she would like to review the resumes of each candidate given the volume and velocity of the incoming applications, the job applicant may provide false information on the resume, or online assessments that are administered remotely in unproctored settings may introduce some contamination in the data. In contrast, assessments administered during later stages of the selection process are likely to be more controlled as the candidate sample becomes more manageable, resulting in data of higher veracity and value. In addition, as the candidate moves through the selection process, there are larger data points (variety) to consider in this situation that could strengthen the overall meaningfulness and value of the data. The results from individual tests and assessments may be combined or serve as independent hurdles to jointly paint a more accurate picture of the candidate's abilities. Thus, the data collected during the later stages are expected to be more accurate and of higher value in predicting organizational outcomes after taking into account the overall selection process. Assuming that reliable and valid screening and assessment procedures are used at every step of the selection process during the pre-hire phase, greater opportunities for improving the veracity and value of data may exist closer to the beginning stages of the process.

For the post-hire phase, some of the big data characteristics differ slightly within the individual processes, but are more stable. During the internal talent assessment process, the amount of data in terms of volume, velocity, and variety are expected to be high due to the frequent and broad range of assessment opportunities that can occur over time (e.g., skills assessment, performance management, training), whereas the amount of data from the internal talent selection process may be lower in comparison due to restrictions in candidate eligibility and potentially long intervals between assessments for any given employee. In contrast, data veracity and value remain high for both the internal talent assessment process and the internal talent selection process. The assessment of knowledge, skills, or abilities for the purpose of informing training needs or promotion decisions is based on procedures that are job-relevant and administered in a standardized environment, which helps ensure the quality and meaningfulness of the data. Similarly, organizations are now able to collect a more continuous flow of data throughout an employee's career, including periodic performance management data, training data, and other internal assessments as they occur, and all of this data further enhances the data's veracity and value to the post-hire phase.

In summary, the big data characteristics comprising the five-V framework vary in their relevance across the selection and assessment events within the talent management life cycle. During the pre-hire phase, volume and velocity decrease over time as organizations narrow the applicant pool and exert increasing control over the decision-making process and methods of data collection, which leads to an increase in the variety, veracity, and value of the data relative to information received at the beginning of the hiring process. The post-hire phase is primarily defined by data veracity and value due to the ongoing collection of employee data in a controlled environment for very specific reasons. Data of greater volume, velocity, and variety is collected during the internal talent assessment process because that process occurs with greater frequency during an employee's career and includes more components (i.e., performance management, training, skills assessment) than the talent selection process.

CASE STUDIES IN BIG DATA

This section presents several case studies to illustrate the role of big data in talent selection and assessment. Based on our experience working with organizations to develop, validate, implement, and evaluate talent selection and assessment processes, these case studies highlight the types of big data that may be encountered in applied settings, profile the challenges associated with compiling, managing, and analyzing big data, and describe the benefits of using big data to answer questions about various aspects of the talent selection and assessment process. Specifically, the case studies involve the role of big data in the implementation of a large-scale selection process on mobile devices, the evaluation of coaching effectiveness on employee outcomes, and the analysis of the relationship between selection processes and employee and organizational outcomes. Table 8.2 presents a summary of each case study.

TABLE 8.2

Summary comparison of big data case study examples

Case Study Focus	Relevant Big Data Characteristics	Big Data Challenges
Talent selection	• Volume—Individuals, variables, computational • Variety—Structured • Velocity—Continuous, real time	• Coordinating with cross-functional teams to obtain data • Problematic data collection and aggregation • Lack of data standardization • Lack of data availability • Problematic results interpretation
Talent assessment	• Volume—Individuals, variables • Variety—Structured • Velocity—None, archival	• Data collection and aggregation • Identification of data location
Talent selection and assessment	• Volume—Individuals, variables, computational • Variety—Structured, individual outcomes, organizational outcomes • Velocity—Sporadic, archival	• Coordinating with cross-functional teams to obtain data • Problematic data collection and aggregation • Lack of data standardization • Problematic results interpretation

Implementation of Selection Process on Mobile Devices

Business Problem

With the recent growth in information technology and the Internet, organizations now have the ability to deliver talent assessments on-demand to job applicants in any location throughout the world (Reynolds & Rupp, 2010; Scott & Mead, 2011; Tippins, 2011). This has not only expanded and diversified the potential talent pool from which future employees can be drawn, but also dramatically reduced the costs associated with talent selection processes while simultaneously standardizing the administration, scoring, and security of talent assessments (Tippins, 2011). In response to this trend and its potential benefits, one of our clients, a large global retailer with domestic and international outlets, asked for assistance to update its pre-employment selection process for all hourly positions in 11 job families at its United States-based stores. A job analysis was conducted for all of the positions to identify the critical competencies required for success (e.g., conscientiousness and teamwork), and this information served as the basis for developing separate non-cognitive, text-based assessments for each job family. The assessments were designed and piloted to be administered over the Internet in an unproctored environment, and the results of a concurrent criterion-related validation study indicated the assessments were psychometrically sound and predicted job performance. Following the validation study, the assessments were integrated into the organization's web portal and made available online as part of the application process.

After approximately a year, the assessments had been completed by over two million applicants, and during a routine check of the qualification rates, something very interesting was noticed. As would be expected, most applicants were using a non-mobile device such as a personal computer (PC) to complete the assessments, but surprisingly, there was a small group of applicants who completed the assessments with a mobile device, such as a tablet computer (e.g., iPad) or mobile phone (e.g., Android phone). This finding raised several questions. First, to what extent were applicants using mobile devices to complete the assessments? Second, when the assessments were completed on mobile devices, did they have the same construct validity, psychometric properties, and predictive validity as when they were completed on non-mobile devices? Finally, did applicants using one type of device perform better than those using other types of devices? All of these questions speak to the larger issue of whether or not it was appropriate to allow applicants to complete the assessments with mobile devices, and this could only be determined by collecting and analyzing multiple types of big data from several different sources.

Types of Big Data

Several types of big data were available to determine if it was appropriate for applicants to use mobile devices to complete the assessments. Since the assessments were at the beginning of the organization's talent selection process, there was a large *volume* of individuals who completed the assessments. Across the 11 job families, approximately two million assessments were completed in the first year, or 167,000 assessments per month. There was also a large volume of information available about each individual who completed the assessment. For each assessment completed, data was collected for approximately 125 variables that included identifying information about the applicant (e.g., login ID and password, applicant unique ID, and demographics), assessment session information (e.g., time started, time completed, time remaining, time to complete, form completed, language option chosen, and audio option chosen), assessment results (e.g., item-level responses, item-level scores, overall score, and qualification decision), and information about the device used to complete the assessment (e.g., device type, device brand, device browser, and device operating system). The volume of data for each individual applicant was also multiplied significantly as a result of the data analyses. Whenever the original data were recoded into new variables or manipulated to conduct an analysis, additional variables were created for each applicant that increased the number of variables beyond the original 125 collected about the applicant from the assessment.

As noted earlier, the amount of data collected for each applicant also contained a wide *variety* of information. Every aspect of the assessment experience was identified and captured by the assessment administration platform, from the time spent completing the assessment to what device was used. However, although there was a great deal of variety in the types of information collected from each applicant, this data was standardized in a well-defined, structured format and did not involve unstructured data formats, such as audio, video, text, or mouse clicks and movements, which have come to be the defining characteristics of big data in other fields and the popular media.

Finally, the *velocity* of the data received from the assessment process remained relatively constant over time, with thousands of applicants completing the assessments each hour. Only some slight fluctuations occurred throughout the year that appeared to correspond to hiring announcements, seasonal needs, and national and global economic trends (e.g., industry growth or dilation, unemployment). The organization had little control over the velocity of applications and completed assessments during the initial stages of the talent selection process, but after the first assessment, the velocity of data collection was entirely determined by the organization as it made decisions about which candidates would move to the next stages of the process. Within the assessment itself, the data velocity remained constant and was dictated by the 75-minute time limit for completing the assessment. However, since applicants could choose to exit and return to the assessment multiple times, there was some variability in data velocity, although very few applicants did not complete the assessment once they started it.

Big Data Challenges

There were a number of challenges associated with the use of big data for this project. The main challenge was compiling the applicant and assessment data into a single database. The client organization used a human resources information system (HRIS) and applicant tracking system (ATS) to collect identifying information about each applicant and track their progress through the talent selection process, whereas the data related to the completion of the assessments were housed in the database of a third-party vendor. Because none of these systems were integrated to share information and it was never anticipated that the data from these systems would be combined to answer these types of questions, it was necessary to obtain data files from all three systems and merge them into a single data file. This involved relying on multiple cross-functional teams in the client organization to obtain the necessary data. The teams responsible for providing the data from each system were involved to varying degrees in the day-to-day operations of the organization, and this responsibility always superseded any other requests that were not directly related to the organization's immediate mission and needs. Consequently, there were some inevitable, but not unexpected, delays in collecting the data.

Once all of the required data were available, the second challenge involved the standardization of the data across the different system formats. Each system was designed to store and code data differently. As a result, once the data were merged into a single file, it took several iterations to match and align the data for each applicant and then ensure the proper interpretation and recoding of the data for analysis. This also required the assistance of several cross-functional teams in the client organization, which were again limited in their responsiveness by the ongoing needs of the organization.

A third challenge involved the availability of data to answer the research questions. Although most of the questions could be answered with data available from the three systems of record, there were some data that were not captured in any of the systems. For example, one of the questions involved the criterion-related validity of the assessments when completed on mobile devices. To answer this question would require on-the-job performance information about applicants who completed the assessments on a mobile device and were subsequently hired. However, this information was not available, and the client organization did not have the resources to collect research-based performance information on these employees. Thus, although the answer to this question was critical and could impact the decision to allow applicants to continue using certain devices to complete the assessments, it remained unanswered.

The final challenge was interpreting the results of statistical analyses based on large n-sizes. Many of the analyses required to answer the research questions involved comparing groups of mobile and non-mobile device users with samples in the thousands and hundreds of thousands. Groups of this size require awareness and careful consideration of the assumptions underlying statistical analyses, use of appropriate alternative statistics when those assumptions are not met, and reliance on multiple indicators to judge the practical significance of the results. For this work, trivially small differences between groups of device users were significant and required additional evaluation to determine if they were practically significant and meaningful. As an example, there were significant mean differences in total assessment scores for mobile and non-mobile device users, but the effect sizes (η_p^2) were zero and the observed scores were all within one-third of a point of each other. It was also necessary to account for unequal cell sizes according to prescribed methods in the literature when conducting factorial ANOVAs. All of these analysis considerations highlight the need to couple mechanical analysis with subjective judgment to determine the meaningfulness and value of results based on big data.

Big Data Benefits

The primary benefit of big data for this project was their availability to answer the questions of interest. With the exception of information about the devices being used to complete the assessments, the applicant and assessment data were the same types of information that have been collected since testing first migrated to computer-based formats. But these data have never been collected in such quantities and been so readily available for analysis. The sheer volume of data also allowed greater certainty in the final results. In the recent past, the volume of data available to answer these types of questions was much smaller, and the resulting conclusions were more tenuous until further research was conducted. With datasets of this magnitude, approaching population-level sample sizes, there is less potential error in the results, despite the quasi-experimental nature of the research. The results need to be replicated and should be replicated in other job families, organizations, and business sectors, but the findings and conclusions, as they apply to this particular organization, appear to be fairly robust given the sample sizes involved. The combination of the volume and velocity of big data being captured by the organization was also a benefit. As hundreds of thousands of new applicants complete the assessment each month, the organization can continuously monitor the usage of various devices, evaluate the construct validity and psychometric properties of the assessments on different devices, and determine if there are any significant performance differences for applicants using one type of device over another. Additionally, as these data accumulate over time, the organization can conduct more specific analyses by device brand, and even by the types of browsers and operating systems available on the different devices, which could also impact performance on the assessments. Finally, the use of big data for this project provided significant business value to the organization. Unexpectedly, the capture of big data by the organization's assessment platform identified a new testing medium that had been previously acknowledged by the field of personnel selection, but had yet to be researched. Without a research base to guide its decision-making, the organization was able to use big data to determine if it was appropriate to allow applicants to complete its assessments on mobile devices. As a result of its findings, the organization has now been able to capitalize on this new medium to significantly expand its applicant pool in a way that is valid and legally defensible.

Evaluation of Coaching Effectiveness

Business Problem

Once employees enter an organization, a number of different resources are often made available to them, including onboarding, training and continuous learning, career management, and coaching. Of all of these resources, coaching that emphasizes direct and immediate feedback in an environment tailored to facilitate employee growth and development can have a significant impact on an organization's talent management processes (Boyatzis, Smith, & Van Oosten, 2011; Peterson, 2009). However, like other components of an organization's talent assessment process, coaching must also be evaluated to determine its impact on the organization and those participating in the coaching program (Peterson & Kraiger, 2003). As part of its efforts to continuously enhance its coaching programs, a multinational pharmaceutical company initiated a research program with its sales force to identify the time spent coaching, quality of coaching, and coaching proficiency levels, determine if coaching proficiency was related to employee engagement and attainment of sales goals, and develop a coach training program that focused on the methods and practices of the most effective coaches. In support of this initiative, we worked with this organization to analyze several sources of big data and determine the effectiveness of its coaching program.

Types of Big Data

The focus of this project involved data collected as part of the organization's talent development process, focusing on the impact of front-line managers (e.g., coaches) within the sales force. As noted earlier, the attributes of big data in this process are somewhat more stable and predictable than in the talent selection process. The *volume* of data was relatively small in terms of the number of people participating in the research, which involved approximately 2,900 sales personnel from the North American affiliate of a larger organization containing approximately 40,000 employees. Among the sales force, a considerable volume of information was collected for the coaches as part of identifying the organization's baseline coaching effectiveness. For each coach, a 14-item survey was administered as part of a 360-degree assessment process to collect perceptions of coaching effectiveness from direct reports, the coaches themselves, and their managers. During the 360-degree assessment process, the respondents also estimated the desired and actual time devoted to coaching. Data were also collected for the participants in the coaching program, including their direct reports' responses to the organization's annual engagement survey and both their individual progress and their teams' progress toward established sales goals. When combined with identifying information, such as employee numbers and demographics, the number of data variables for coaches and participants only ranged from 80–120. With regards to the data volume associated with computations and analyses, there was a minimal increase in the number of data points for the coaches and participants.

Aside from the volume of the data, none of the other big data attributes were as relevant to the project. The *variety* of the data was fairly limited, consisting of standardized employee data, survey response data, and several well-defined and frequently recorded organizational outcomes related to individual sales performance. All of the data were stored in traditional formats associated with common database programs and organized in well-defined ways using rows and columns. Data *velocity* was also not a factor since the results of the 360-degree assessment process and employee engagement surveys had already been computed, were part of the organization's archival datasets, and were not being updated regularly with new data. Finally, the *veracity* or quality of the data was readily checked to confirm it was complete, reliable, and valid, while the *value* of the data was demonstrated by its relevance to the questions being asked about the impact of the coaches and the hypothesized relationships between coaching effectiveness and employee outcomes.

The types of big data associated with this project highlight several important points. First, as was discussed earlier, the characteristics of big data can vary significantly as a function of the different components of the talent management process. Within an organization, there is much more control of most big data characteristics, with the exception of *volume*, which now involves fewer people but an exponential collection of data points per person over time. Second, although this conceptualization of big data is quite different from how it is described in the popular media or even within the field of industrial-organizational psychology, it is a very realistic representation of the types of big data collected and analyzed by organizations to answer these types of questions. Third, in practice, this is the type of big data commonly encountered by industrial-organizational psychologists in their work with organizations. Finally, to identify the data required to answer these types of questions, it is first necessary to sift through the big data available and determine what information is most relevant.

Big Data Challenges

For this project, the big data did not represent any challenges for the client organization. As a metrics-based organization, it has a long history of collecting multiple types of data to evaluate the impact, effectiveness, and functioning of every aspect of its business and workforce. This means the organization has well-developed and highly integrated infrastructure for capturing, managing, and analyzing data from its talent selection and assessment processes, as well as supplemental processes involving external vendors. The ability to obtain data across functions within the organization, which is often one of the greatest obstacles when working on big data projects, was also facilitated by the influence of the talent management group and its recognized value among the organization's leadership. From an analytical perspective, the computational and analytical demands were equivalent to traditional client engagements based on small data and did not involve very many variables. Additionally, the sample sizes were well within the small-sample requirements and expectations underlying the inferential statistics (t-tests, ANOVAs, and correlations) used to evaluate the impact of the coaching program.

Big Data Benefits

The big data in this project produced several benefits. First, it provided the foundation for being able to ask much broader questions about the effectiveness of the coaching program. What may have once been limited to questions about individual sales behaviors that could only be answered using holistic judgments could now be expanded to questions involving objective indicators of employee performance that are directly tied to their behavior. This produced the second benefit of the big data, which was the demonstration of the business value of the coaching program, not just to the balance sheet, but in the engagement of employees within the organization as well. The results of the research indicated there was a continuum of coaching proficiency and effectiveness, and this continuum was predictive of employee engagement levels and the attainment of sales goals. When employees were paired with top coaches (top 25th percentile), they tended to be more engaged with the company and ultimately more likely to reach or exceed their sales goals. That coaches indirectly fostered greater employee engagement was an unexpected finding, one that would not have been identified without the use of big data.

Impact of Selection Processes on Employee and Organizational Outcomes

Business Problem

The goal of developing, validating, and implementing a talent selection process is to increase the chances of hiring workers with the knowledge, skills, and abilities to be successful (Morris & Lobsenz, 2003; Ployhard, Schneider, & Schmitt, 2006). In recent years, as organizations have realized the importance and value of their human capital and the impact they have on the organization's bottom-line, human resources (HR) departments are being asked not just to determine the return on investment associated with the talent selection process, but to expand the scope and also demonstrate the business impact of the process on both employee outcomes (e.g., turnover) and organizational outcomes (e.g., customer satisfaction, profitability) (Cascio & Fogli, 2010; Steinhaus & Witt, 2003). The desire to identify these types of relationships has become more pronounced as organizations find themselves operating in economic environments that are becoming increasingly competitive and driving a focus on internal cost containment and business value.

This was the situation one of our clients faced after updating its talent selection process. As a global hospitality company, it spent several million dollars to develop, validate, and implement web-based assessments for managerial and front-line positions at all of its properties. After the assessments were operational for approximately four years, the organization's leadership asked for an evaluation of the return on investment (ROI) in the selection process. Specifically, the leadership wanted to know if the process was producing a more qualified workforce, whether or not that workforce was more likely to remain with the organization, the extent to which this workforce was impacting key metrics used to evaluate the performance of the properties where they worked (e.g., labor costs, customer satisfaction, profit margins), and if the overall selection process resulted in any overall cost savings to the organization. We collaborated with this organization to capitalize on the availability of big data to answer these questions.

Types of Big Data

The attributes of big data are different for the talent selection process, talent management process, and organizational and employee outcomes. For this project, the big data originated from the talent management process and organizational and employee outcomes. In terms of *volume*, the total number of applicants hired at the conclusion of the updated hiring process was approximately 50,000, which is relatively small when compared to the almost 2.3 million people who originally applied for positions with the organization. For these 50,000 new hires, the organization maintained records of their performance on the assessments, collected additional data regarding their job performance, and documented their organizational tenure and turnover status. All of these data were represented with multiple variables and various levels of detail (e.g., item responses from the assessments and ratings of job performance on multiple questions). This additional data multiplied the total volume of information for each employee well beyond the volume of data when just the total of number of employees is considered. Additionally, for each of its properties, the organization collected information related to labor costs, customer evaluations, and financial performance. This property-level data was linked to the employees at each property, which also further expanded the total volume of information available for each individual employee. This indicates that while the number of individual data points represented by a single employee may be small, the total number of data points for each individual employee can be quite large and continue to grow throughout an employee's career life-cycle with the organization. Finally, the volume of data involved with the project was also multiplied as a result of the data cleaning and analyses. Since different pieces of data for each employee were located in multiple datasets, and these datasets often used different spellings of employee names, a "fuzzy matching" process was used to match employee data across datasets by name. This process required the iterative evaluation of billions of case combinations to identify matched and unmatched records according to several different algorithms that varied in their level of precision (e.g., match on different number of letters in the first and last name, match on the sounds of words). At the end of the process, there were a large number of additional variables for each employee that reflected their predicted likelihood of matching thousands of other cases in the data files.

The data collected for each employee and property also represented a wide *variety* of information. It included identifying information about the employees, such as their unique employee number, country identifier, property identifier, demographic information, performance on the selection assessments, and job performance. For each of the properties, there was specific information about the labor costs associated with business operations and the assessment process, results from customer satisfaction surveys, and financial information that was used to calculate profitability. The structure of these data was well defined and consistent with traditional data types and formats collected to answer these types of research questions.

The *velocity* of the data was relatively low and completely controlled by the organization because it represented archival data that was not being actively collected or received. When this research was initiated, all of the employee talent selection results and job performance information had been previously collected. Similarly, the property data was also collected and analyzed according to predetermined organizational schedules, so this information was also readily available from company, regional, property, and vendor databases. Thus, the velocity of data did not pose any issues to the completion of the project.

Big Data Challenges

The big data required to evaluate the ROI of this organization's talent selection process resulted in several significant challenges. As indicated in the previous case studies, the most critical challenge was obtaining the data needed to answer the research questions. For this organization, even though there were extensive archival records at the employee and property level, this information was spread across multiple systems and databases, including a human resources information system (HRIS), applicant tracking system (ATS), and third-party assessment vendor. Additionally, some of the data were maintained at the property level in a wide range of data files and database systems. To obtain all of the necessary data from each property for each employee, extensive coordination and communication with a variety of cross-functional teams within the organization was required to ensure a common understanding of the data needed and fill in any data gaps as they were compiled.

As the data were received from the organization, it became apparent that there was a lack of standardization in how the data were captured, stored, coded, and reported across the facilities. Although the level of standardization was higher for common data systems such as the HRIS and ATS, when the various regions and properties were solely responsible for managing the data collection and reporting, there tended to be a mix of software packages, programs, and databases used to manage the data. As a result, there were a number of issues related to the conversion and merging of data files that were in different formats and file types. This issue of standardization also extended to what information was being captured, with some properties missing information critical to the study, such as turnover, labor costs, and in some instances, assessment results from the talent selection process.

Another challenge was the nature of some of the employee and organizational outcome data. For example, the turnover data and labor costs were based on self-report data from the properties, and these data were reported sporadically depending on the location. The issues associated with these data raised a number of questions about validity and reliability, as well as utility as an outcome measure for assessing the effectiveness of the talent selection process. However, because there were no other objective measures available for these variables and the time to evaluate the ROI of the talent selection process was limited, the decision was made to move forward with the data and analyses while simultaneously acknowledging some of their limitations.

Finally, it is important to note that this research attempted to identify relationships between the results of the talent selection process and very distal business outcomes, such as labor costs and profitability. The use of big data to assess these relationships does not change the fact that there are many other intervening factors, the ubiquitous third variable problem, that could also explain any positive results. Despite the volume and variety of the data, the basis of the analysis is still correlational in nature and does not provide any insight into the cause of the organization's financial success. Unfortunately, the term big data has also become synonymous with omniscient and conclusive decision-making, which in this context would ignore the fact that there may well be other factors that could explain any relationships that were identified and be completely unrelated to the talent selection process or the qualities associated with those members of the organization's workforce who were hired as a result of it. This highlights again the need to combine the raw mechanical analysis with expert, subjective judgment to ensure the correct interpretation and communication of results based on big data.

Big Data Benefits

There were a number of benefits associated with using big data to evaluate the effectiveness of the organization's talent selection process. First, the availability of big data expanded the number and type of employee and organizational metrics that could be used to evaluate the effectiveness of the talent selection process. In the past, these types of studies were limited to using employee job performance as the primary outcome variable. But now with so much additional information being captured about employee and organizational performance on a continuous basis, the number of metrics has increased exponentially and, assuming they can be matched conceptually to the predictor variables, allows for more calibrated prediction of possible relationships.

Second, the type of outcome data available for organizations is becoming more objective. This type of data helps to alleviate concerns regarding the subjectivity and bias inherent in self-report or other ratings of employee performance. The ability to collect data for individual employees that is directly linked to, for example, customer experience perceptions, is a significant improvement over the information contained in standard performance management systems that is often several steps removed from actual employee behaviors and outcomes.

Finally, the use of big data helped to demonstrate the business value of the talent selection process. By using data of different types from various sources, it was possible to show that those hired with the updated process tended to perform better, remain with the organization longer, produce lower labor costs and increased customer satisfaction, and were associated with greater organizational profitability. Without the availability of big data, the ability to arrive at this conclusion may have been somewhat limited, inconclusive, or still unknown.

FUTURE APPLICATIONS

The nature of big data will continue to evolve based on advancements in and the accessibility of technology. Compared to other big data environments, current big data in the selection and assessment context are smaller in scale in terms of volume, velocity, and variety. Moreover, the volume and velocity of data in current selection and assessment practice have been less of a concern up to this point relative to the data's variety, veracity, and value due to the limitations of technology in talent management. As technology improves and becomes more readily available, the characteristics of big data in talent management are expected to approach those currently found in other disciplines. In this section, we discuss emerging trends and potential future applications of big data in selection and assessment practices.

Online Recruitment

Online recruiting methods have created new opportunities for identifying and attracting job candidates. The use of internal career platforms, external job boards, and social networks for recruiting purposes has opened up new talent pipelines that attract candidates with different skillsets and at remote locations. The volume of applications received has also increased, where at some companies the hundreds of applications that were previously being processed have turned into thousands.

The large amount of incoming data has led to opportunities to examine and analyze new relationships to help improve recruiting efforts, including questions pertaining to the source of recruiting that has produced the best candidates and the best method to identify the candidates with a particular set of skills. The new types of analyses have even crossed into more complex data. For example, some HR organizations are analyzing unstructured data from career-oriented social networking sites for purposes of recruiting and learning and development (Harvard Business Review Analytic

Services, 2013). Other external resources have become more widely available to recruiters, and these tools have allowed the focus to shift toward targeted recruitment. Companies specializing in recruiting are mining social and public data to identify who the candidates are, where they are, and when they will seek a position change (Bersin, 2013a). Solution providers such as LinkedIn now offer advertising to help find people with specific characteristics. In sum, the technological changes in the recruiting space have allowed companies to take advantage of opportunities to identify better talent from new talent sources in a timely manner. The timeliness and increased quality of the talent pool are in turn benefitting the organizations through decreased delays in hiring and reduced costs.

There may be additional future opportunities to capitalize on technology for targeted recruitment and identifying better matches between the candidate and organization. The real time capture and analysis of data could provide immediate feedback about the candidate's fit for a job. For example, algorithms can be developed to provide recommendations about job fit to the recruiter as well as the candidate. The recruiter could get real time information on recommended jobs that is based on an alignment between the candidate's skills profile and the job requirements. Candidates could receive similar feedback to help identify additional jobs of interest for which they could apply. Suggestions could also be made to the recruiter in terms of similarities in skillsets between candidates in the database to identify additional candidates who meet a certain level of standard. All of these examples would occur in real time, which would bring greater focus back to the volume and velocity of big data in a selection and assessment setting.

Assessment and Measurement

The same technology that is driving the big data movement can also be incorporated into the assessments organizations use as part of their talent selection processes. With the application of computer-based testing and other innovative technologies to selection assessments (see Reynolds & Rupp, 2010), it will be possible to collect a continuous stream of candidate performance data, and the information contained in this data will provide a much more granular and nuanced understanding of a candidate's knowledge, skills, and abilities than is possible with current assessment technology. Consequently, the information available about candidates will become more accurate, and the assessment process itself will become more precise in its measurement of job-related behaviors and the prediction of future success on the job.

Work samples or simulations are one assessment method where the combination of big data and technology will have a significant impact. For example, consider the hiring process for a maintenance position at a manufacturing facility that requires candidates to complete a hands-on exercise designed to assess basic electrical, mechanical, or electronic skills. As part of the exercise, candidates are placed in a simulated, high-fidelity production environment and asked to troubleshoot, diagnose, and repair some aspect of the manufacturing process. Using computers and sensors embedded in the environment, it would be possible to track a candidate's exact movements, determine the steps followed to troubleshoot the issue, identify which tools or pieces of equipment were selected and used to perform the repairs, record the resources (e.g., manuals) relied upon to assist with the problem, recognize and draw attention to potential safety violations, and collect information about responses to stressors or other demands that are introduced into the testing environment. Similar volumes and variety of data could also be obtained from technology-based simulations designed to assess the competencies required for a customer service or sales role. In this type of simulation, candidates would be required to interact with customers represented by digital avatars who are programmed to engage candidates in a variety of customer service scenarios and alter their behavior in response to the candidates. During the simulation, several streams of data could be collected about candidates, including recordings of their conversation, body language and movement, voice tones and inflections, and facial expressions, which could all be analyzed to assess performance relative to the requirements of the position. In both of these examples, the use of technology to deliver, monitor, and record the assessment provides multiple paths for collecting performance data that were previously unavailable or unobservable.

The increased integration of technology into assessments and the resulting deluge of available performance data will provide a number of benefits and opportunities for talent selection. Performance behaviors that were once difficult to observe and constructs that were not easily assessed can now be operationalized, measured, and quantified using multiple indicators available from these types of assessments. This has the effect of significantly expanding the predictor space to include more precise measurement of candidate capabilities in real-time situations that closely mimic on-the-job conditions. As assessments become more automated in their recording of performance behavior, there will be less of a reliance on human raters who are susceptible to fatigue, rater drift, perceptual errors, and rating biases. This reduces the short- and long-term costs of the assessment because rater training and maintenance is eliminated, and increases the business value of the assessment through greater predictive utility as a result of more precise measurement. The ability to capture and process performance data in real time also allows for the design of work simulations that dynamically change and adapt in response to candidate behavior. Similar to computer adaptive testing (CAT) (see McCloy & Gibby, 2011), the simulation could alter the presentation of information, level of difficulty, or types of interactions in response to strengths or weaknesses detected while the simulation is in progress, and probe as necessary the extent of any gaps in knowledge, skill, or ability. This type of assessment would greatly enhance measurement efficiency by increasing reliability and reducing administration costs.

Performance Management

Technology and big data also have the potential to change the practice of performance management in organizations (see Krauss & Snyder, 2009). In a typical performance management process, employees receive feedback about their performance annually or bi-annually relative to expectations described in an organization's competency model, but this information about employee performance tends to be unreliable, based on a single source with limited opportunities to observe on-the-job performance, and restricted to outcomes as opposed to behaviors (Lepsinger & Lucia, 2001; Murphy & Cleveland, 1995). Additionally, although it is recommended that performance feedback be provided consistently and repeatedly over time, it is often not received until well after the occurrence of positive or negative job behaviors and their related outcomes. Finally, employees often have no knowledge of how they are performing relative to organizational or individual goals.

The incorporation of technology into the monitoring and tracking of employee behavior has the potential to change every aspect of how performance management is practiced in organizations (Tippins & Coverdale, 2009). Objective, reliable data can be obtained, processed, and summarized in real time, and then communicated immediately to supervisors or managers who can quickly provide positive feedback or coaching to address developmental needs related to both behaviors and outcomes (see Pulakos & O'Leary, 2010). This information can also be fed back directly to employees so they can monitor their own behavior, evaluate progress toward performance goals, identify opportunities for improvement, and receive recommendations regarding additional training that is available to target specific performance deficiencies. As these types of data capture systems become more sophisticated and are augmented with machine learning, it may also be possible to provide computer-generated coaching and feedback in response to live employee work behaviors. For metrics-rich environments like call centers, some aspects of this technology and the data it produces already exist. Call center workers are evaluated on average hold times, average handling times, number of transfers, number of customer escalations, and even the impact of their behavior on customer actions (e.g., sales, up-sales, cancellations). This continuous stream of data can be leveraged to flag potentially troublesome calls and optimize the assignment of customers to specific call center representatives.

Integration of Selection and Post-hire Assessment

The integration of data across multiple sources is critical to understanding the bigger picture in which the data operate. There are two types of integration opportunities that are of particular interest in the selection and assessment context. The first integration opportunity pertains to the linkage of assessment data with business data. The second opportunity involves the integration of selection and assessment data with the larger talent management function.

Linkage research includes the analysis of the relationship between assessment data and important business outcomes. Examples of business outcomes include cost of salary, shareholder value, sales revenue, return on investment, cost of turnover, time to hire costs, and increase in performance as a function of investment on training (Asselman, 2012; Roberts, 2013). The purpose of the linkage is to demonstrate the value of selection and assessment practices. Although organizations see the integration of talent management with financial data as a critical application of big data, one commonly reported obstacle needs to be overcome to make this a reality for most organizations: the talent management data and business data often reside in distinct and compartmentalized silos, and it can be difficult to gain access to data across different functions and business units (Harvard Business Review Analytic Services, 2013; Roberts, 2013). This can be attributed to several things, such as lack of technical support to retrieve and integrate the data, the mentality that the data are unrelated, and privacy and confidentiality concerns. Organizations interested in leveraging linkage research to understand the value of their selection and assessment practices must begin the process of creating an environment that facilitates the sharing of data across business units.

In addition to linking selection and assessment data with business outcomes, an equally important application of big data involves the integration of various HR processes within talent management. This includes developing applications that integrate data across an employee's career (including relevant selection and post-hire assessment data) in order to facilitate selection, classification, and promotion decisions. The integration of data across the entire tenure of the employee suggests that data will be collected continuously within the electronic human resource systems and new ways of integrating the different data points will need to be explored. For example, employee selection and assessment data can be integrated with data related to training, performance management, feedback and goal setting, and developmental activities. Within each of these components are smaller subcomponents that can be captured and analyzed, such as examining a training program in terms of its content, methods, resources, participants, and outcomes to improve the training and assessment process. The employee observations and characteristics can also be compared to job data that define job requirements to identify gaps in skills and readiness for promotion. The resulting data can then generate profiles of successful employees that can inform recruitment and assessment for future employees, including additional potential assessment procedures that predict job performance.

The rate of data capture in this scenario is much more rapid compared to the typical big data situation in selection and assessment practices and will likely require changes in technology and a near overhaul in the way an organization thinks about their various HR data. Some of this burden in the future will be alleviated by vendors of talent management software that are starting to create integration tools (Bersin, 2013a; Gale, 2014a). Indeed, there is ample opportunity to pursue these integration efforts, as only 14% of companies have integrated their talent analytics (Bersin, 2013b). The integrative software and other supportive infrastructure (e.g., computer networks, cloud computing) can be leveraged to help transition into the world of big data.

PRACTICAL CONSIDERATIONS

The role of big data in talent selection and assessment will continue to grow as organizations build the infrastructure required to capture and manage it and industrial-organizational psychologists identify new and innovative ways to utilize it as part of the talent management process. However, regardless of the nature of the data being used to inform human capital decisions, there are boundary conditions related to its use that impact its application, interpretation, and appropriateness. In this section, we present several practical considerations related to the use of big data in talent selection and assessment.

Big Data in a Theory-Based Science

In the popular media, the role of big data in talent selection and assessment tends to focus on data mining and the role of extrinsic predictors (see Doverspike, 2013; Peck, 2013), which is in stark contrast to the theory-based science that underlies industrial-organizational psychology. The field of industrial-organizational psychology has a rich theoretical and applied history related to the examination of work, the identification of capabilities required to be successful at work, and the development and validation of assessments to determine if applicants and job candidates have the knowledge, skills, abilities, and other characteristics (KSAOs) needed to perform work effectively. This extensive history is the basis of legal guidelines (Equal Employment Opportunity Commission, Civil Service Commission, Department of Labor, & Department of Justice, 1978) and professional standards (American Educational Research Association, American Psychological Association, & National Council on Measurement in Education, 2014; Society for Industrial & Organizational Psychology, 2003) that govern the development and validation of any tool or process used by organizations based in the United States to make employment decisions related to hiring, promotion, or termination. The primary theme running throughout this history is job-relatedness. Whether assessing a job candidate's technical knowledge, an employee's annual performance using traditional data sources, or the more diverse data streams associated with big data, it must be based on intrinsic characteristics that have a demonstrated relationship to the work performed in the job. This is a prerequisite for making valid and legally defensible employment decisions. The use of big data does not remove these requirements and, in fact, makes them even more necessary as the variety of data collected by organizations expands exponentially and industrial-organizational psychologists must determine its relevance to known job and worker characteristics.

Analysis and Interpretation of Big Data

The analysis and interpretation of big data is complicated by the large sample sizes available. Many of the analyses conducted in talent selection and assessment are based on inferential statistics (e.g., t-tests, ANOVA, regression, correlation, chi-square) that were designed to be used with small to moderately sized samples. As the datasets associated with big data exceed these sample size limitations, all statistical tests will be significant, even those involving trivial differences and relationships. In these situations, a strict reliance on mechanically-derived analyses would produce an inaccurate and misleading interpretation of the results. Therefore, when dealing with such large datasets, careful consideration must be given to the assumptions underlying statistical analyses, the use of appropriate alternative statistics when those assumptions are not met, and the reliance on multiple indicators of significance, such as effect-size measures and business impact calculations to judge the practical significance. There must also be a consideration of the conceptual relationships associated with findings of significance, especially in statistical tests of bivariate or multivariate relationships. One benefit of big data is the availability of large numbers of variables. However, as the volume of analyses conducted on these variables increases, significant results will occur by chance alone. In combination, all of these analysis considerations highlight the need to combine analytic techniques with subjective judgment to determine the meaningfulness and value of results based on big data.

Reactions to Big Data

Although it is widely known that organizations use a variety of methods in their hiring processes, only recently with the rise of big data in talent selection and assessment has the general public and business community been able to learn how some of these methods are developed. As organizations increase their use of big data in the selection and assessment process, they must be aware of how applicants and employees may respond to this knowledge and factor it into the decision-making process when implementing talent management processes based on big data. A great deal of research has found that applicants and employees do respond to the processes used to make hiring decisions, and these reactions can have an impact on perceptions of the hiring process, intentions to pursue employment with an organization, and potentially the desire to take legal action (see Anderson, 2011; Anderson, Salgado, & Hülsheger, 2010; Ford, Truxillo, & Bauer, 2009; Hausknecht, Day, & Thomas, 2004; McCarthy, Hrabluik, & Jelley, 2009; Ryan & Ployhart, 2000). Reactions to the use of big data in talent management may be very similar. As a result, organizations should carefully weigh the costs and benefits of incorporating big data and its related technology into the talent management process. While big data may reveal predictive relationships of very high utility to organizations, if applicants do not perceive it to be job-related and respond negatively, then organizations should evaluate the true value of the information. Similarly, organizations should be aware of and manage reactions to the collection and use of big data involving employee performance and outcomes. Employees may perceive the data collection and aggregation as invasive and unnecessary, which could negatively impact their work performance, job satisfaction, and desire to remain with the organization. Thus, organizations and industrial-organizational psychologists should carefully consider applicant and employee reactions when developing and implementing talent selection and assessment processes based on big data.

Big Data Protection, Security, and Privacy

The use of big data in selection and assessment comes with great responsibility related to the protection and security of the data, as well as the need to maintain the privacy of applicants, candidates, and employees who participate in an organization's talent management processes. This becomes even more important as organizations begin collecting a wide variety of big data from non-traditional Internet sources (e.g., social media) and cross-functional employee databases containing sensitive data. In the United States, the protection and security of this type of data is largely unregulated with the exception of laws protecting the privacy of health (Health Insurance Portability and Accountability Act of 1996) and financial information (Financial Services Modernization Act of 1999). In recent years, the United States has collaborated with the European Union to create the US-EU Safe Harbor program (U.S. Department of Commerce, 2000), which is a set of guidelines for organizations regarding the handling of personal and sensitive consumer data, but this program is completely voluntary, and organizations are not required to follow its seven principles for the collection, analysis, or sharing of data. Despite this lack of regulation, industrial-organizational psychologists are ethically bound to ensure the security, protection, and privacy of data obtained in the course of their work (American Psychological Association, 2010). As a result, when working with personal or sensitive data or consulting with organizations regarding the collection, analysis, and management of this type of data, they must be aware of these issues and implement appropriate data handling protocols as necessary.

CONCLUSION

The big data movement continues its expansion to the farthest reaches of almost every industry and field of study. On a daily basis, the popular media describes exciting big data discoveries and applications. The impact of big data will only continue to grow as more data becomes available from a wider array of sources and is integrated, analyzed, and interpreted in new and unexpected ways. However, from descriptions of big data in the popular press, it would be easy to presume that the revolutionary nature of big data is an inherent characteristic of all data, regardless of its origin, but this would be misleading because the true value of big data is only derived from its application in very specific contexts. The definition, analysis, applications, limitations, and value of big data can vary dramatically depending on the context.

The intent of this chapter was to provide the context for understanding big data in talent selection and assessment. Although talent management scientists and practitioners have been dealing with big data for quite some time, they have not traditionally conceptualized it in the ways that characterize the current big data movement. To this end, we clarified the definition of big data as it is currently understood in terms of the five-V framework (volume, velocity, variety, veracity, value), demonstrated how each characteristic within this framework was applicable to talent selection and assessment, and then highlighted how big data in selection and assessment differed from other disciplines. We then mapped the five-V framework onto the pre- and post-hire processes that comprise selection and assessment to illustrate the dynamic nature of big data throughout the talent management life cycle. Several real-world examples involving big data at different points in the pre- and post-hire processes were presented to illustrate some of the more common benefits and challenges associated with big data in applied practice. Finally, we described some potential future applications of big data, as well as several considerations specific to the field of talent management that impact the use of big data in selection and assessment.

We believe our attempt to contextualize big data in talent selection and assessment from the perspective of applied practitioners comes at an important time. While the current conversation among scientists and practitioners in this area has been helpful, it tends to focus more heavily on the collection, management, and analysis of big data. We believe it is also important to supplement this deep knowledge of data management and analysis techniques with a thorough conceptual understanding of big data and its applications. This will help to broaden the continuing discussion about big data within talent management, and also provide a framework for organizing the discussion and directing future inquiries as the field continues to evolve in its relationship with big data.

REFERENCES

American Educational Research Association, American Psychological Association, & National Council on Measurement in Education (2014). *Standards for educational and psychological testing.* Washington, DC: American Educational Research Association.

American Psychological Association (2010). *Ethical principles of psychologists and code of conduct.* Washington, DC: American Psychological Association.

Anderson, N. (2011). Perceived job discrimination: Toward a model of applicant propensity to case initiation in selection. *International Journal of Selection and Assessment, 19,* 229–244.

Anderson, N., Salgado, J. F., & Hülsheger, U. R. (2010). Applicant reactions in selection: Comprehensive meta-analysis into reaction generalization versus situational specificity. *International Journal of Selection and Assessment, 18,* 291–304.

Asselman, S. (2012, June). Screen grabbers. *People Management,* 43–46.

Barton, D., & Court, D. (2012, October). Making advanced analytics work for you. *Harvard Business Review,* 78–83.

Bersin, J. (2013a). Predictions for 2014: Building a strong talent pipeline for the global economic recovery. *Bersin by Deloitte.* Retrieved from http://marketing.bersin.com/predictions-for-2014.html

Bersin, J. (2013b, February 17). Big data in human resources: Talent analytics comes of age. *Forbes.* Retrieved from http://www.forbes.com/sites/joshbersin/2013/02/17/bigdata-in-human-resources-talent-analytics-comes-of-age/

Boyatzis, R. E., Smith, M. L., & Van Oosten, E. B. (2011). Coaching for sustained, desired change: Building relationships and talent. In L.A. Berger & D.R. Berger (Eds.), *The talent management handbook* (pp. 217–226). New York, NY: McGraw-Hill.

Cascio, W. F., & Fogli, L. (2010). The business value of employee selection. In J.L. Farr & N.T. Tippins (Eds.), *Handbook of employee selection* (pp. 235–254). New York, NY: Rutledge.

Church, A. H., & Dutta, S. (2013). The promise of big data for OD: Old wine in new bottles or the next generation of data-driven methods for change? *OD Practitioner, 45*(4), 23–31.

Davenport, T. (2013, December). Analytics 3.0. *Harvard Business Review,* 64–72.

Davenport, T. (2014). *Big data at work: Dispelling the myths, uncovering the opportunities.* Boston, MA: Harvard Business School Publishing.

Doverspike, D. (2013). A small, quick commentary on big data and predictive analytics. *Assessment Council News, 1,* 11–12.

Equal Employment Opportunity Commission, Civil Service Commission, United States Department of Labor, & Department of Justice (1978). Uniform guidelines on employee selection procedures. *Federal Register, 43*(166), 38290–38315.

Financial Services Modernization Act of 1999, Pub. L. 106–102, 113 Stat. 1338.

Ford, D., Truxillo, D. M., & Bauer, T. N. (2009). Rejected but still there: Shifting the focus to the promotional context. *International Journal of Selection and Assessment, 17,* 402–416.

Galagan, P. (2014). HR gets analytical. *T + D, 68*(3), 22–25.

Gale, S. F. (2014a). Beneath the hood of twin trends. *Talent Management Magazine, 10*(1), 33–35.

Gale, S. F. (2014b). Taking the long view. *Talent Management Magazine, 10*(1), 42–43.

Gardner, N., McGranahan, D., & Wolf, W. (2011, March). Question for your HR chief: Are we using our 'people data' to create value? *McKinsey Quarterly.* Retrieved from http://www.mckinsey.com/insights/organization/question_for_your_hr_chief_are_we_using_our_people_data_to_create_value

Harvard Business Review Analytic Services (2013). The big data opportunity for HR and finance. *Harvard Business Review.* Retrieved from https://hbr.org/hbr-analytic-services

Hausknecht, J. P., Day, D. V., & Thomas, S. C. (2004). Candidate reactions to selection procedures: An updated model and meta-analysis. *Personnel Psychology, 57,* 639–683.

Health Insurance Portability and Accountability Act of 1996, Pub. L. 104–191, 110 Stat. 1936.

Krauss, A. D., & Snyder, L. A. (2009). Technology and performance management: What role does technology play in performance management? In J. W. Smither & M. London (Eds.), *Performance management: Putting research into action* (pp. 445–490). San Francisco, CA: John Wiley & Sons.

Laney, D. (2001). 3D data management: Controlling data volume, velocity, and variety. *META Group.* Retrieved from http://blogs.gartner.com/doug-laney/files/2012/01/ad949-3D-Data-Management-Controlling-Data-Volume-Velocity-and-Variety.pdf

Lepsinger, R., & Lucia, A. D. (2001). Performance management and decision making. In D. W. Bracken, C. W. Timmreck, & A. H. Church (Eds.), *The handbook of multisource feedback* (pp. 318–334). San Francisco, CA: Jossey-Bass.

Maurath, D. (2014). A critical incident for big data. *The Industrial-Organizational Psychologist, 51*(3), 16–25.

McAfee, A., & Brynjolfsson, E. (2012, October). Big data: The management revolution. *Harvard Business Review,* 60–68.

McCarthy, J. M., Hrabluik, C., & Jelley, R. B. (2009). Progression through the ranks: Assessing employee reactions to high-stakes employment testing. *Personnel Psychology, 62,* 793–832.

McCloy, R. A., & Gibby, R. E. (2011). Computerized adaptive testing. In N. T. Tippins & S. Adler (Eds.), *Technology-enhanced assessment of talent* (pp. 153–189). San Francisco, CA: John Wiley & Sons.

Morris, S. B., & Lobsenz, R. (2003). Evaluating personnel selection systems. In J. Edwards, J. C. Scott, & N. S. Raju (Eds.), *The human resources program-evaluation handbook* (pp. 109–129). Thousand Oaks, CA: Sage Publications.

Murphy, K. R., & Cleveland, J. N. (1995). *Understanding performance appraisal: Social, organizational, and goal-based perspectives.* Thousand Oaks, CA: Sage Publications.

Peck, D. (2013). The future of work: How big data is transforming hiring, firing, and your chances of getting ahead. *The Atlantic, 312*(5), 72–84.

Peterson, D. B. (2009). Coaching and performance management: How can organizations get the greatest value? In J. W. Smither & M. London (Eds.), *Performance management: Putting research into action* (pp. 115–156). San Francisco, CA: John Wiley & Sons.

Peterson, D. B., & Kraiger, K. (2003). A practical guide to evaluating coaching: Translating state-of-the-art techniques to the real world. In J. Edwards, J. C. Scott, & N. S. Raju (Eds.), *The human resources program-evaluation handbook* (pp. 262–282). Thousand Oaks, CA: Sage Publications.

Ployhart, R. E., Schneider, B., & Schmitt, N. (2006). *Staffing organizations: Contemporary practice and theory* (3rd ed.). Mahwah, NJ: Lawrence Erlbaum Associates.

Poeppelman, T., Blacksmith, N., & Yongwei, Y. (2013). "Big data" technologies: Problem or solution? *The Industrial-Organizational Psychologist, 51*(2), 119–126.

Prokopeak, M. (2014). L&D's big data moment. *Talent Management Magazine, 10*(1), 16–19.

Pulakos, E. D., & O'Leary, R. S. (2010). Defining and measuring results in workplace behavior. In J. L. Farr & N. T. Tippins (Eds.), *Handbook of employee selection* (pp. 513–530). New York, NY: Rutledge.

Putka, D. (2013). HEY! We've been doing this for 100 years! *Quarterly: A Publication of the Personnel Testing Council of Metropolitan Washington, 9*(2), 2–9.

Reynolds, D. H., & Rupp, D. E. (2010). Advances in technology-facilitated assessment. In J. Scott & D. Reynolds (Eds.), *Handbook of workplace assessment: Evidence-based practices for selecting and developing organizational talent* (pp. 609–642). San Francisco, CA: Jossey-Bass.

Roberts, B. (2013). The benefits of big data. *HR Magazine, 58*(10), 21–30.

Ryan, A. M., & Ployhart, R. E. (2000). Applicants' perceptions of selection procedures and decisions: A critical review and agenda for the future. *Journal of Management, 26*, 565–606.

Scott, J. C., & Mead, A. D. (2011). Foundations for measurement. In N. Tippins & S. Adler (Eds.), *Technology-enhanced assessment of talent* (pp. 21–65). San Francisco, CA: John Wiley & Sons.

Society for Human Resource Management (2015). *Glossary*. Retrieved from http://www.shrm.org/TemplatesTools/Glossaries/HRTerms/Pages/t.aspx

Society for Industrial and Organizational Psychology (2003). *Principles for the validation and use of personnel selection procedures* (4th ed.). College Park, MD: Society for Industrial and Organizational Psychology.

Steinhaus, S. D., & Witt, L. A. (2003). Criteria for human resources program evaluation. In J. Edwards, J. C. Scott, & N. S. Raju (Eds.), *The human resources program-evaluation handbook* (pp. 49–68). Thousand Oaks, CA: Sage Publications.

Tippins, N. T. (2011). Overview of technology-enhanced assessments. In N. Tippins & S. Adler (Eds.), *Technology-enhanced assessment of talent* (pp. 1–18). San Francisco, CA: John Wiley & Sons.

Tippins, N. T., & Coverdale, S. H. (2009). Performance management of the future. In J. W. Smither & M. London (Eds.), *Performance management: Putting research into action* (pp. 555–584). San Francisco, CA: John Wiley & Sons.

U.S. Department of Commerce (2010). US-EU Safe Harbor program.

Walker, J. (2012, September 20). Meet the new boss: Big data companies trade in hunch-based hiring for computer modeling. *The Wall Street Journal*. Retrieved from http://online.wsj.com/news/articles/SB10000872396390443890304578006252019616768

9

Big Data in Turnover and Retention

John P. Hausknecht and Huisi (Jessica) Li

Managing talent inflows and outflows remains a top organizational priority. Given the substantial costs and consequences associated with talent loss and the difficulties in fully explaining the phenomenon, employee turnover has maintained a central position in HR, OB, and I-O research and practice for many decades. Yet, for most of its history, turnover research has been guided, directed—and at the same time, constrained—by the data available to researchers, organizations, and their joint efforts in research collaboration. However, this is changing. Advances in technology, heightened company interest, and the proliferation of new and varied sources of information are giving rise to numerous interesting and provocative ways to understand employee movement and its effects on organizational functioning and performance. This chapter explores the potential applications of big data within the domain of employee turnover and retention, examining current practices and how they could evolve as researchers and organizations leverage big data in the coming years.

OVERVIEW

In this chapter, we examine how turnover research and practice can benefit from advances in big data by first describing characteristics of recent turnover research. Such an analysis provides a starting point for understanding the extent to which researchers already leverage big data in their design, measurement, and analysis. We then move to a discussion of prominent turnover theories at the individual and group levels as a guide to thinking about how big data could inform, change, and extend these perspectives. Finally, we develop four key means by which big data could strengthen understanding and management of employee turnover from theoretical, methodological, and practical standpoints.

DEFINITIONS

Defined simply, turnover involves people leaving organizations (Mobley, 1982). More formally, turnover represents "the degree of individual movement across the membership boundary of a social system" (Price, 1977, p. 4). Recognizing that not all departures are the same, leavers have been further differentiated into voluntary (employee-initiated) and involuntary (organization-initiated) types, and research has shown that the causes and consequences of each are conceptually and empirically distinct (see Shaw, Delery, Jenkins, & Gupta, 1998). Other terms for voluntary turnover include quits and resignations, whereas involuntary turnover is sometimes described in terms of dismissals or terminations. Other dimensions of turnover include the extent to which turnover is avoidable and/or functional. Avoidability hinges upon whether the organization *could have* done something (within reason) to prevent a departure (Abelson, 1987), whereas functionality denotes the extent to which the organization *would have* done something to prevent the departure (Dalton, Todor, & Krackhardt, 1982), which is presumably based on leaver performance, replaceability, and/or willingness to rehire.

A great deal of turnover research focuses on predicting individual departures, which can be seen in the near-exclusive focus of turnover theory and research at the individual level from the 1950s forward. More recently, researchers have supplemented this understanding by studying causes and consequences of collective turnover, or employee turnover at higher levels such as the group, work unit, or firm (Hausknecht & Trevor, 2011). This work appears under various labels—unit-level turnover, organizational turnover, collective turnover—but all are focused on understanding that factors drive turnover rates and, in turn, how aggregate departures influence various group and firm-level consequences (e.g., productivity, customer outcomes, and financial performance). As we will discuss, this two-class distinction (i.e., individual and group/unit/firm) becomes important as we consider implications of big data for research design, measurement, and analysis.

TYPICAL APPROACHES TO STUDYING TURNOVER AND RETENTION, 2009–2014

To begin, and to provide context for understanding what could (or should) change within turnover research in the realm of big data, we summarize typical characteristics of recent turnover and retention research. As the basis for this effort, we searched online databases for studies published between 2009 and 2014 with the word "turnover" or "retention" appearing in the title or as a keyword. For the sake of manageability, we restricted our search to six journals that are often viewed as top outlets for publishing turnover research: *Academy of Management Journal, Journal of Applied Psychology, Journal of Management, Organization Science, Organizational Behavior and Human Decision Processes*, and *Personnel Psychology*. We reviewed abstracts and the method sections of these papers to ensure that the study included an actual measure of employee turnover. A total of 31 studies met our inclusion criteria. We then coded the following characteristics for each study: (1) sample size, (2) sample type (entry-level, managerial, or executive), (3) level of analysis (individual, group, or firm), (4) turnover type (voluntary, involuntary, or total), (5) role of turnover (independent variable, dependent variable, or moderator), (6) data sources (self, manager, HR record, or public data), and (7) analytic methods (e.g., OLS, survival analysis, random coefficient modeling, and latent growth modeling).

Table 9.1 lists coding results for the 31 studies. In terms of sample sizes, these studies ranged from 112 to 114,198 employees (mean = 6,649, s.d. = 21,717) in 45 to 1,255 teams (mean = 375, s.d. = 415) and in 1 to 718 organizations (mean = 130.47, s.d. = 235). Across the set of studies, 30 (97%) included entry-level employees in their samples, 7 (23%) included managers, and only 1 (3%) included executives (percentages exceed 100 because some studies included multiple job levels). Of the total, 23 studies (74%) examined individual-level of variables, while 13 (42%) and 3 (10%) respectively examined group- and firm-level variables. Further, 15 (48%) studies focused on voluntary turnover, 3 (10%) included involuntary turnover, and 13 (42%) considered undifferentiated or total turnover.

In most cases—26 of 31 studies (84%)—researchers studied turnover as a dependent variable, with 5 (16%) modeling turnover as an independent variable (e.g., predictor of firm performance), and 1 (3%) as a moderator. Across studies, 23 (74%) collected data from the employees themselves, 7 (23%) from managers, 1 (3%) from customers, 18 (58%) from company HR records, and 7 (23%) from publicly available sources (e.g., Bureau of Labor Statistics, National Longitudinal Survey of Youth, and industry blue books). Various analytic methods were used in these studies, ranging from t-tests, MANOVA, and OLS regression to survival analysis, random coefficient modeling, and latent growth modeling.

TABLE 9.1

Key elements of turnover and retention research, 2009–2014

Authors	Year	Journal	Sample Size and Type	Level of Analysis	Turnover Type	Role of Turnover	Data Sources	Analytic Methods
Ballinger, Lehman, & Schoorman	2010	OBHDP	807 employees in 45 firms	Individual	Total	DV	Self, HR record	OLS, survival analysis
Becker, Connolly, & Slaughter	2010	PP	3,012 employees in 1 firm	Individual	Total	DV	Manager, HR record	Logistic regression, t-test
Becker & Cropanzano	2011	JAP	1,755 employees	Individual	Voluntary	DV	HR record	Cox proportional hazard regression
Bidwell & Briscoe	2010	OS	2,823 employees	Individual	Total	DV	Self	Cox proportional hazard regression
Burris, Detert, & Romney	2012	OS	7,578 employees in 335 groups of 1 firm	Individual, group	Involuntary	DV	Self, manager, HR record	HLM, multilevel logit regression
Carnahan & Somaya	2013	AMJ	163 employees in 232 groups	Individual, group	Total	IV	HR record	Dyadic fixed-effects Poisson estimates
Felps, Mitchell, Hekman, Lee, Holtom, & Harman	2009	AMJ	8,663 employees in 1,037 groups	Individual, group	Voluntary	DV	Self	OLS, HLM
Fugate, Prussia, & Kinicki	2012	JOM	153 employees in 1 firm	Individual	Voluntary	DV	Self	SEM

(Continued)

TABLE 9.1 (Continued)

Authors	Year	Journal	Sample Size and Type	Level of Analysis	Turnover Type	Role of Turnover	Data Sources	Analytic Methods
Gardner, Wright, & Moynihan	2011	PP	1,748 employees in 93 groups	Individual	Voluntary	DV	Self, manager, HR record	OLS, MANOVA
Godart, Shipilov, & Claes	2013	OS	349 employees in 356 firms	Firm	Total	IV	Public data	Cross-sectional time-series panel regressions
Hauskneckt, Trevor, & Howard	2009	JAP	5,631 employees in 75 groups of 19 firms	Individual, group	Voluntary, involuntary, total	IV	Self, customer, HR record, public data	HLM
Hom & Xiao	2011	OBHDP	417 employees in 4 firms	Individual	Voluntary	DV	Self	HLM
Kraimer, Seibert, Wayne, Liden, & Bravo	2011	JAP	264 employees	Individual	Voluntary, involuntary	DV	Self, manager	OLS
Kraimer, Shaffer, Harrison, & Ren	2012	AMJ	112 employees	Individual	Voluntary	DV	Self	OLS, logistic regression
Liu, Zhang, Wang, & Lee	2011	JAP	817 employees in 115 groups	Individual, group	Total	DV	Self, HR record	HLM, Mediated moderation
Mackenzie, Podsakoff, & Podsakoff	2011	PP	150 groups	Group	Total	DV	Self, manager, HR record	SEM
Maltarich, Nyberg, & Reilly	2010	JAP	5,310 employees	Individual	Voluntary	DV	Self, public data	Survival analysis, mediation

Author	Year	Journal	Sample	Level	Type	IV/DV	Data source	Analysis
McClean, Burris, & Detert	2013	AMJ	5,200 employees in 136 groups of 1 firm	Group	Total	DV	Self, manager, HR record	HLM
Messersmith, Guthrie, Ji, & Lee	2011	JAP	2,570 employees in 528 firms	Firm	Total	DV	Public data	HLM
Nishii	2013	AMJ	1,324 employees in 100 groups	Group	Voluntary	DV	Self	SEM
Nyberg	2010	JAP	12,545 employees in 884 groups	Individual	Voluntary	DV	Self, HR record, public data	Survival analysis, mediation
Owens, Johnson, & Mitchell	2013	OS	704 employees in 218 groups	Individual, group	Voluntary	DV	Self, HR record	HLM
Ployhart, Weekley, & Ramsey	2009	AMJ	114,198 employees in 1,255 groups	Individual, group	Total	IV	Self, HR record	Random coefficient growth model
Rafferty & Restubog	2010	JOM	115 employees in 1 firm	Individual	Voluntary	DV	Self, HR record	SEM
Ramesh & Gelfand	2010	JAP	797 employees	Individual	Voluntary	DV	Self, HR record	Logistic regression
Russell & Sell	2012	OBHDP	525 employees	Individual	Voluntary	DV	Self	Logistic regression
Shaw, Dineen, Fang, & Vellella	2009	AMJ	209 firms	Firm	Involuntary, total	DV	HR record, public data	OLS
Shin, Taylor, & Seo	2012	AMJ	242 employees in 45 groups in 1 firm	Individual, group	Voluntary	DV	Self, manager	HLM

(Continued)

TABLE 9.1 (Continued)

Authors	Year	Journal	Sample Size and Type	Level of Analysis	Turnover Type	Role of Turnover	Data Sources	Analytic Methods
Siebert & Zubanov	2009	AMJ	1,625 employees in 325 groups in 1 firm	Group	Total	IV, moderator	HR record	OLS
Swider, Boswell, & Zimmerman	2011	JAP	895 employees in 1 firm	Individual	Voluntary	DV	Self, public data	Logistic regression
Van Iddekinge, Ferris, Perrewé, Perryman, Blass, & Heetderks	2009	JAP	861 groups in 1 firm	Group	Total	DV	HR record	Latent growth model, cross-lagged panel analyses

Note: Search limited to six journals (see text for full list of inclusion criteria); AMJ=*Academy of Management Journal*, JAP=*Journal of Applied Psychology*, JOM=*Journal of Management*, OS=*Organization Science*, OBHDP=*Organizational Behavior and Human Decision Processes*, and PP=*Personnel Psychology*.

Looking across the pattern of results, we offer several observations regarding the extent to which big data already influence turnover research. First, it is fairly clear that in almost no case did we find a study that truly fits emerging big data definitions. According to Davenport (2014), the hallmarks of big data typically include one or more of the following characteristics: (1) massive size (e.g., file is too large to fit on a single server), (2) unstructured formats (e.g., not the typical row-and-column structure), (3) flowing or streaming data (e.g., continuous rather than static measurements), (4) diverse sources (e.g., social media, HR records, and external sources), and (5) new data collection methods (e.g., sensors, video). We consider each of these in turn relative to the literature and then discuss how big data could enhance future work in this domain.

Regarding size, we would characterize nearly all of the studies as fairly small data when considered against the backdrop of truly big data sets mentioned elsewhere (e.g., Wal-Mart's collection of 2.6 *billion* megabytes of customer transaction data *per hour*; McAfee & Brynjolfsson, 2012). Most of the studies included fewer than 1,000 employees. This said, sample sizes were often adequate from sampling and statistical power standpoints, many were fairly large relative to others found in the literature, and some included very large sample sizes (e.g., 114,198 employees in Ployhart, Weekley, & Ramsey, 2009; further, although published prior to our inclusion window, Hom, Roberson, & Ellis, 2008 studied quit patterns among 475,458 professionals across 20 firms). Others include multiple observation periods, thus multiplying the size of the data sets considered. However, the majority of studies include data sets that are quite manageable in size (e.g., the data set for Hausknecht, Trevor, & Howard, 2009 was less than one megabyte).

Looking at format, all of the studies included would fit the more traditional row-and-column format that typifies structured data rather than big data's usual foray into unstructured information (e.g., qualitative data, video data, and images). Quantitative survey data, demographic information, and publicly available sources were commonly represented, all of which fit a standard structure.

Concerning the dimension of continuous versus static measurement, about three-fourths of the studies gathered measures at a single time point. Several others adopted three-wave or longer data collection periods (such as Ployhart et al., 2009; Van Iddekinge, Ferris, Perrewe, Perryman, Blass, & Heetderks, 2009), but in no case did researchers report continuous flow or streaming data that has been discussed elsewhere as a common big data ingredient (see Davenport, 2014; George, Haas, & Pentland, 2014).

On the dimension of data source diversity, many of the studies did in fact incorporate data from multiple sources. Most commonly this involved merging internal sources (e.g., HRIS records and attitude survey data) with those external to the organization (e.g., Bureau of Labor Statistics unemployment rate data, customer satisfaction data, and benchmark data from industry reports). Looking across the 31 studies, the average number of predictor variables included in researchers' models was around 12 (including control variables). Most ranged between 7 and 15 and included data from multiple sources. It is on this dimension that existing research already seems to capitalize on the purported benefits of big data variety.

Finally, in terms of data collection methods, most of the studies gathered information using more traditional means such as online or paper surveys or company records. In no case did researchers report newer data collection methods stemming from sources such as social media, sensors, or video.

Looking across the five characteristics, it is clear that turnover research to date fits often more traditional definitions of data size, structure, measurements, sources, and methods. This leaves open numerous opportunities to supplement existing knowledge with new studies that take advantage of the features common to big data. Before considering these possibilities, it is useful to consider dominant theoretical perspectives in this domain (particularly since turnover theory is not necessarily constrained by data availability). In the following section, we briefly review extant turnover theory to understand how big data could be used to test, change, or extend current thinking in this domain. Despite the appeal of big data, it is our belief that theory-driven approaches should dominate future efforts to understand and predict employee turnover. Otherwise, there is the risk of identifying empirical patterns that do not replicate, cannot be explained, and therefore add little to science and practice. On the other hand, it is also useful to consider how access to big data could allow for inductive approaches to theory generation, a point we revisit in our conclusion.

TURNOVER THEORY AT INDIVIDUAL AND ORGANIZATIONAL LEVELS

Our approach to reviewing theoretical perspectives is meant to provide a brief rather than comprehensive overview of the dominant perspectives in the area. The interested reader is encouraged to review the original sources and other detailed reviews for more information (see Holtom, Mitchell,

Lee, & Eberly, 2008; Hom & Griffeth, 1995; Hom, 2011; Maertz & Campion, 1998).

Individual-level Turnover Theory

March and Simon's (1958) model of organizational equilibrium advanced the notion that turnover is jointly determined by employees' *ease of movement* (i.e., alternative employment prospects) and *desirability of movement* (i.e., job satisfaction). It represented one of the earliest efforts at formalizing a model of employee turnover and remains consequential in guiding researchers' thinking today. Notably, March and Simon are credited for recognizing the fact that quit decisions are constrained by market alternatives and for laying the foundation for thinking about the major determinants of ease and desirability of movement.

Following and building upon March and Simon (1958), a number of influential articles and books appeared that included refined frameworks of the turnover process (Mobley, 1977; Porter & Steers, 1973; Price, 1977). In one form or another, Hom (2011) suggested that these models aim to capture *how* (i.e., via specification of mediating mechanisms between cognitions and withdrawal; Mobley, 1977) or *why* employees to quit (i.e., specifying organizational and environmental determinants; Price, 1977). Subsequent to this work, further modifications, empirical tests, and literature reviews followed, all of which have served to develop a strong foundation for understanding likely drivers of individual employee turnover (see Hom, Griffeth, & Sellaro, 1984; Price & Mueller, 1981; Steers & Mowday, 1981). Despite their promise, and as several critics have noted, the predictive power of these frameworks has been underwhelming, rarely explaining more than 25% of the variance in turnover (Hom, 2011; Maertz & Campion, 1998). Such findings led researchers to propose alternative conceptual perspectives that better explained how, when, and why people leave or stay.

Lee and Mitchell's (1994) unfolding model of employee turnover represents one such endeavor, representing a major shift in thinking about the employee turnover process. Noting limitations of the traditional attitudes and alternatives view of March and Simon (1958) and later descendants, these authors proposed a series of alternative decision paths that employees might take prior to departure. They formalized the notion that employees sometimes leave abruptly without an alternative in hand (and with or without experiencing dissatisfaction) after experiencing shocks that prompt thoughts of quitting (e.g., unsolicited job offers, changes in personal situation). A growing number of empirical studies provide support for the key contributions made by the unfolding model beyond traditional views (Lee, Gerhart, Weller, & Trevor, 2008; Lee, Mitchell, Holtom, McDaniel, & Hill, 1999; Lee, Mitchell, Wise, & Fireman, 1996).

Researchers have also supplemented traditional thinking about why employees leave by thinking more deeply about why they *stay*. Emerging research on job embeddedness—i.e., the extent to which employees have links to other people and activities, fit with the organization and community, and the degree of sacrifice associated with leaving—reveals incremental value in predicting turnover (and other job outcomes) beyond traditional determinants found in earlier theories (Jiang, Liu, McKay, Lee, & Mitchell, 2012; Lee, Mitchell, Sablynski, Burton, & Holtom, 2004; Mitchell, Holtom, Lee, Sablynski, & Erez, 2001; Swider, Boswell, & Zimmerman, 2011).

Group and Organizational-level Turnover Theory

Although not absent from early (i.e., pre-1990s) discussions, much less attention has been paid to developing theoretical models of the causes and consequences of employee turnover at the group, work unit, and firm levels. One notable exception was Staw's (1980) framework that outlined the likely positive and negative organizational consequences of turnover (as well as moderating conditions). In terms of positive outcomes, Staw reasoned that turnover could increase innovation, reduce conflict, and increase internal mobility. The range of hypothesized negative outcomes included increased selection and training costs, operational disruption, and demoralization of membership. Aside from a handful of empirical papers (e.g., Mueller & Price, 1989; Terborg & Lee, 1984), much of the early period in turnover research was dominated by individual-level research.

By the late 1990s and early 2000s, however, researchers began to take a more formal look at how aggregate levels of employee turnover influence social capital and organization performance (see Dess & Shaw, 2000) and, in turn, theorized and investigated possible determinants of voluntary and involuntary turnover rates (Shaw et al., 1998). A series of studies by Shaw and colleagues (e.g., Shaw et al., 2005a, 2005b, 2009) as well as others (such as Batt, 2002) paved the way for later work aimed at understanding turnover antecedents and outcomes at group and firm levels. In 2011, Hausknecht and Trevor summarized extant research to date on turnover at the collective level (i.e., group, unit, or firm) and developed a conceptual framework that included a range of determinants (e.g., HR practices, collective attitudes, and other collective characteristics) and consequences (e.g., productivity, firm performance, and customer outcomes). More recently, researchers have taken a closer look at the composition (and thus meaning) of collective turnover rates (Hausknecht & Holwerda, 2013) and have offered richer theoretical accounts that specify the emergent nature of collective turnover in explaining how human capital leads to firm performance (Nyberg & Ployhart, 2013). Meta-analyses at the collective or organizational level have also emerged, highlighting known findings while pointing out how much remains to be learned (Hancock, Allen, Bosco, McDaniel, & Pierce, 2013; Heavey, Holwerda, & Hausknecht, 2013; Park & Shaw, 2013).

TURNOVER THEORY, METHODS, AND BIG DATA

When considered alongside one another, we see many opportunities to leverage big data for theory testing at both individual and group levels. In this section, we highlight several such possibilities. As background, we quote a recent review of employee turnover by Hom, Mitchell, Lee, and Griffeth (2012), who summarized the traditional turnover research design as follows: "measure antecedents (e.g., job satisfaction) with surveys or personnel records; track employees for 6 months to 2 years; identify stayers and voluntary leavers from records; and then statistically estimate predictor-quit relationships" (p. 833). In addition, Allen and colleagues conducted a major review of the common approaches or "analytical mind-sets" that underlie the design and execution of turnover research (Allen, Hancock, Vardaman, & McKee, 2014). We highlight selected findings from their analysis throughout the chapter, but note here their conclusion that "the bulk of turnover research is quantitative, conducted in field settings, at the individual level of analysis, utilizing correlational designs, with a heavy reliance on survey measures and regression-based methods" (Allen et al., 2014, pp. S76–S78). Given these typical design choices, we offer several directions for turnover research that may better fit with the big data elements described above.

Studying Dynamic Processes

At the individual level, turnover scholars have long advocated for better understanding of the temporal dynamics underlying quit decisions (Mobley, 1982; Steel, 2002). Indeed, advances in analytical methods have allowed researchers to capitalize on the collection of repeated measurements of key antecedents (see Kammeyer-Mueller, Wanberg, Glomb, & Ahlburg, 2005; Sturman & Trevor, 2001). Given the heavy focus in turnover theory on understanding process, leveraging big data methodology (e.g., the notion of continuous and streaming data collection from new and inventive sources such as mobile, social media, and/or sensor networks) may reveal more reliable insights about the patterning and processes underlying decisions to quit. Longitudinal and time-series studies could become more the norm rather than the exception going forward, as they are often regarded as a substantial improvement over static or one-shot measurement approaches (see Steel, 2002). For example, within the unfolding model paradigm, organization-initiated shocks could be modeled more carefully in terms of effects on attitudes and subsequent departures (see Ballinger, Lehman, & Schoorman, 2010).

The types of data needed to track turnover processes dynamically involve collecting repeated measures of key antecedents over a theoretically-appropriate time period. A common rule of thumb is to collect at least three, and preferably more, observations per individual over the period of interest (see Ployhart & Vandenberg, 2010). Historically, it is relatively atypical for a study to measure turnover predictors such as job satisfaction or perceived alternatives more than once. In fact, among the studies reviewed here (see Table 9.1), the modal number of times that predictors were measured was one. The strength of empirical tests of theories that involve temporally-ordered mediational chains (see Lee et al., 1996; Steel, 2002) will remain limited if researchers continue to rely on single-shot measures of turnover antecedents.

The benefits of collecting antecedents on multiple occasions are starting to be seen in turnover research. As one example, Chen and colleagues departed from the traditional research design by collecting multiple measures of job satisfaction and turnover intentions from multiple samples over time (Chen, Ployhart, Anderson, Thomas, & Bliese, 2011). Drawing upon multiple theoretical accounts (e.g., within-person spirals: that people act on not just levels of attitudes such as satisfaction but also trajectories that develop over time), they hypothesized and found support for the incremental prediction offered by job satisfaction *change* in explaining turnover intentions beyond static job satisfaction levels. Such insight only becomes accessible via repeated-measures designs so that one can treat the *variability* in work attitudes or related constructs as an important determinant in its own right. Of course, stable characteristics need not be collected on multiple occasions (e.g., demographics), but it seems safe to say that the vast majority of turnover antecedents are indeed likely to be dynamic in nature. It is here where big data—specifically, the increased granularity afforded by repeated measurements (George et al., 2014)—have significant potential to enhance research and practice.

As one possible means of increasing measurement frequency, researchers might partner with organizations to implement data collection methods that are less obtrusive. For example, periodically presenting a brief survey to employees on their mobile device or as they log in to a company portal could provide the necessary data without the encumbrances of a more formal standalone survey. Employees may be more willing to complete multiple measures over time if the data collection medium allows for simple and efficient responses.

Evaluating Context

Classic and emerging work shows that quit decisions are influenced by factors that extend beyond the quality of one's immediate work environment. A host of non-work, social, and economic contextual factors have been identified as likely either directly affecting turnover or moderating relationships between known antecedents and quit decisions. Researchers have called for better understanding of context within turnover research for many decades (see Schwab, 1991), but it is apparent that much remains to be understood about the conditions under which various antecedent-turnover relationships are strengthened or weakened. For instance, Allen et al. (2014) reported that the majority of turnover studies (54%) focused on direct effects only, whereas just 30% addressed moderation.

Consistent with the themes of big data, addressing context involves supplementing internal (often survey-based and self-reported) predictor data with measures that reflect the broader social and economic environment within which employees reside. For example, Trevor (2001) supplemented repeated-measures job satisfaction data with a composite measure of unemployment that included both local and occupation-specific information. Such data, available freely from the Bureau of Labor Statistics, offer a tangible means of addressing context, and incorporating such data is consistent with the big data theme of integrating diverse sources. As another example of addressing context, researchers have begun to explore the social dynamics that influence turnover. One study reports that coworkers' embeddedness and job searches influence individual quit decisions beyond other individual and group-level antecedents—i.e., that turnover is contagious (see Felps, Mitchell, Hekman, Lee, Holtom, & Harman, 2009).

In a similar vein, researchers have documented that turnover occurs in clusters based on employee communication networks (Krackhardt & Porter, 1985, 1986). Further network-based studies of turnover are needed that build upon and extend these initial findings.

There are several possible means by which researchers could continue to address context via multisource data. For example, with the rise of big data, social network data should become much easier to access, which would likely benefit both individual and collective-level understanding of turnover (see Dess & Shaw, 2001). Researchers could measure connections to individuals inside the firm (more internal connections might promote embeddedness and increase retention), as well as those externally (where more connections may increase exposure to alternatives and increase turnover). Further, building a richer and more connected data set (e.g., life cycle surveys) about employees could facilitate understanding of contextual factors surrounding the pre-entry influences most strongly associated with employee turnover. Such information, when connected with post-exit data (from surveys or third-party sources such as LinkedIn) could facilitate understanding of post-exit destinations (Hom et al., 2012). Such connected data sets, with pre-hire through post-exit information, are virtually unheard of in the turnover literature but could become a reality as part of big data efforts. It is our sense that many of these data points exist in various pockets of organizations, but are fragmented and not easily integrated.

Enhancing Causal Inference Through Experiments

Big data also perhaps open up greater opportunities for experimentation, an approach not often associated with turnover research. Allen et al. (2014) reported that only 12% of turnover studies have used quasi-experimental or true experimental designs (86% were correlational). They also note that the use of quasi-experiments has actually declined over time. This is unfortunate given that both researchers and practitioners often care most about determining turnover causes rather than correlates. In many ways, the advent of big data has the promise to revive interest in, and facilitate the use of, experimental approaches. With more companies investing in their internal analytics capabilities (e.g., better systems, more analysts), practitioner-generated interest in carefully designed evaluation studies that help document the impact of various interventions on employee retention should rise. As one rare example at the collective level, Peterson and Luthans (2006) manipulated characteristics of incentive practices across different business units and tracked the effects on turnover rates both across time (multiple measures pre- and post-intervention) and relative to a control group. Similar studies that track the effects of changes in HR policies or practices on turnover (see Trevor & Nyberg, 2008) could be conducted to understand short- and long-term organizational consequences.

Building Global Understanding of Employee Turnover

Anecdotally, we have heard of numerous U.S. companies that are more or less content with turnover levels domestically, but struggle to attract and retain talent in emerging markets. The challenge is that nearly all of the employee turnover literature is U.S.-based, raising questions about its usefulness in studying turnover dynamics abroad. As Hom (2011) summarized, "Unfortunately, prevailing theory and research on turnover offer little guidance to U.S. multinationals on ways to retain host-country nationals" (p. 345). As companies invest in big data technology, researchers may begin to gain access to larger, more reliable, multinational company data sets that could be leveraged to conduct large-scale studies of turnover antecedents and consequences across regions. To date, such multi-country (or multi-culture) comparative work has been sparse to non-existent (see Ramesh & Gelfand, 2010, for an exception).

One obvious place to launch such investigations is within large, multinational corporations that have sizable employee populations in regions beyond the U.S. As one example, IBM employed over 430,000 employees in more than 170 different countries in 2012. Qualitative fieldwork is needed to establish the relevance of traditional turnover theories in emerging and established markets outside of the U.S. given variations in labor supply and demand as well as cultural values. Another possibility, successfully employed in other literatures, is to form research teams from multiple universities across the globe to assemble large-scale data sets that offer the opportunity to conduct comparative model tests across regions and cultures.

SUMMARY: ENVISIONING POSSIBILITIES FOR TURNOVER RESEARCH

In Table 9.2, we recap our views on the potential of big data to influence turnover research and practice. Drawing from our review of recent turnover research, as well as the comprehensive analysis by Allen et al. (2014), the dominant or traditional paradigm for studying employee turnover involves individual-level, survey-based studies, where predictors are measured at a single point and from one or a few sources to forecast voluntary exit from the firm. Without question, this literature has been vast and informative in clarifying relevant influences on decisions to quit. However, opportunities lie ahead to supplement this understanding with more ambitious investigations that capitalize on the hallmarks of big data. In particular, we expect to see researchers' broadening the focus to include pre-entry as well as post-exit destinations, using more innovative approaches to data collection (e.g., social, mobile) from a variety of sources (e.g., peers, external sources), with multiple waves of measurements, and across multiple levels of analysis. From a theoretical standpoint, we suggest that researchers begin by providing more appropriate tests of existing theories, many of which involve reasoning that calls for exactly these types of dynamic, multisource, and multilevel investigations. This said, we encourage the development of novel, inductively-developed theories as researchers' discover

TABLE 9.2

Big data's potential influence on turnover research

	Traditional Approach	Influence of Big Data
Period of interest	Entry to exit	Pre-entry, entry, exit, and post-exit
Level of analysis	Individual	Individual, collective, and multilevel
Research design	Static cohort or cross-sectional	Longitudinal and repeated-measures; experimental
Measurement strategies	Traditional (e.g., formal opinion surveys, HR records)	Innovative (embedded surveys; use of mobile devices, sensor networks, social media)
Frequency of predictor measurement	Static (single-wave)	Dynamic (three or more waves)
Source of predictor data	Mostly single-source self-reports	Multi-source to include self-reports, coworker, community, and "ambient" data
Data analysis techniques	OLS, logistic regression, survival analysis	Survival analysis, repeated-measures/longitudinal/time series analyses; network analysis, HLM

patterns and profiles that explain employee turnover but that do not neatly fit within existing frameworks.

To conclude, research on employee turnover has a long and rich history. Substantial progress has been made in outlining and testing prominent conceptual frameworks, but many opportunities for further evaluation remain. As we have found, the characteristics typically associated with big data have generally been slow to arrive in the turnover domain (and in HR more generally), but offer promise in helping explain how and why employees choose to leave organizations, as well as how these aggregate decisions impact organizations more broadly.

REFERENCES

An asterisk (*) denotes articles that are provided in Table 9.1.

Abelson, M. A. (1987). Examination of avoidable and unavoidable turnover. *Journal of Applied Psychology, 72*(3), 382–386.

Allen, D. G., Hancock, J. I., Vardaman, J. M., & McKee, D. N. (2014). Analytical mindsets in turnover research. *Journal of Organizational Behavior, 35*, S61-S86.

*Ballinger, G. A., Lehman, D. W., & Schoorman, F. D. (2010). Leader-member exchange and turnover before and after succession events. *Organizational Behavior and Human Decision Processes, 113*(1), 25–36.

Batt, R. (2002). Managing customer services: Human resource practices, quit rates, and sales growth. *Academy of Management Journal, 45*(3), 587–597.

*Becker, W. J., Connolly, T., & Slaughter, J. E. (2010). The effect of job offer timing on offer acceptance, performance, and turnover. *Personnel Psychology, 63*(1), 223–241.

*Becker, W. J., & Cropanzano, R. (2011). Dynamic aspects of voluntary turnover: An integrated approach to curvilinearity in the performance-turnover relationship. *Journal of Applied Psychology, 96*(2), 233–246.

*Bidwell, M., & Briscoe, F. (2010). The dynamics of interorganizational careers. *Organization Science, 21*(5), 1034–1053.

*Burris, E. R., Detert, J. R., & Romney, A. C. (2012). Speaking up vs. being heard: The disagreement around and outcomes of employee voice. *Organization Science, 24*(1), 22–38.

*Carnahan, S., & Somaya, D. (2013). Alumni effects and relational advantage: The impact on outsourcing when a buyer hires employees from a supplier's competitors. *Academy of Management Journal, 56*(6), 1578–1600.

Chen, G., Ployhart, R. E., Thomas, H. C., Anderson, N., & Bliese, P. D. (2011). The power of momentum: A new model of dynamic relationships between job satisfaction change and turnover intentions. *Academy of Management Journal, 54*, 159–181.

Dalton, D. R., Todor, W. D., & Krackhardt, D. M. (1982). Turnover overstated: The functional taxonomy. *Academy of Management Review, 7*(1), 117–123.

Davenport, T. (2014). *Big data at work: Dispelling the myths, uncovering the opportunities.* Boston, MA: Harvard Business School Publishing.

Dess, G. G., & Shaw, J. D. (2001). Voluntary turnover, social capital, and organizational performance. *Academy of Management Review, 26*(3), 446–456.

*Felps, W., Mitchell, T. R., Hekman, D. R., Lee, T. W., Holtom, B. C., & Harman, W. S. (2009). Turnover contagion: How coworkers' job embeddedness and job search behaviors influence quitting. *Academy of Management Journal, 52*(3), 545–561.

*Fugate, M., Prussia, G. E., & Kinicki, A. J. (2012). Managing employee withdrawal during organizational change: The role of threat appraisal. *Journal of Management, 38*(3), 890–914.

*Gardner, T. M., Wright, P. M., & Moynihan, L. M. (2011). The impact of motivation, empowerment, and skill-enhancing practices on aggregate voluntary turnover: The mediating effect of collective affective commitment. *Personnel Psychology, 64*(2), 315–350.

George, G., Haas, M. R., & Pentland, A. (2014). From the editors: Big data and management. *Academy of Management Review, 57*, 321–326.

*Godart, F. C., Shipilov, A. V., & Claes, K. (2013). Making the most of the revolving door: The impact of outward personnel mobility networks on organizational creativity. *Organization Science, 25*(2), 377–400.

Hancock, J. I., Allen, D. G., Bosco, F. A., McDaniel, K. R., & Pierce, C. A. (2013). Meta-analytic review of employee turnover as a predictor of firm performance. *Journal of Management, 39*(3), 573–603.

Hausknecht, J. P., & Holwerda, J. A. (2013). When does employee turnover matter? Dynamic member configurations, productive capacity, and collective performance. *Organization Science, 24*(1), 210–225.

Hausknecht, J. P., & Trevor, C. O. (2011). Collective turnover at the group, unit, and organizational levels: Evidence, issues, and implications. *Journal of Management, 37*(1), 352–388.

*Hausknecht, J. P., Trevor, C. O., & Howard, M. J. (2009). Unit-level voluntary turnover rates and customer service quality: Implications of group cohesiveness, newcomer concentration, and size. *Journal of Applied Psychology, 94*(4), 1068–1075.

Heavey, A. L., Holwerda, J. A., & Hausknecht, J. P. (2013). Causes and consequences of collective turnover: A meta-analytic review. *Journal of Applied Psychology, 98*(3), 412–453.

Holtom, B. C., Mitchell, T. R., Lee, T. W., & Eberly, M. B. (2008). Turnover and retention research: A glance at the past, a closer review of the present, and a venture into the future. *The Academy of Management Annals, 2*(1), 231–274.

Hom, P. W. (2011). Organizational exit. In S. Zedeck (Ed.), *APA handbook of industrial and organizational psychology* (Vol. 3): *Selecting and developing members for the organization* (pp. 325–375). Washington, DC: American Psychological Association.

Hom, P. W., & Griffeth, R. W. (1995). *Employee turnover.* Cincinnati, OH: South-Western College Publishing.

Hom, P. W., Griffeth, R. W., & Sellaro, C. L. (1984). The validity of Mobley's (1977) model of employee turnover. *Organizational Behavior and Human Performance, 34*(2), 141–174.

Hom, P. W., Mitchell, T. R., Lee, T. W., & Griffeth, R. W. (2012). Reviewing employee turnover: Focusing on proximal withdrawal states and an expanded criterion. *Psychological Bulletin, 138*(5), 831–858.

Hom, P. W., Roberson, L., & Ellis, A. D. (2008). Challenging conventional wisdom about who quits: Revelations from corporate America. *Journal of Applied Psychology, 93*(1), 1–34.

*Hom, P. W., & Xiao, Z. (2011). Embedding social networks: How guanxi ties reinforce Chinese employees' retention. *Organizational Behavior and Human Decision Processes, 116*(2), 188–202.

Jiang, K., Liu, D., McKay, P. F., Lee, T. W., & Mitchell, T. R. (2012). When and how is job embeddedness predictive of turnover? A meta-analytic investigation. *Journal of Applied Psychology, 97*(5), 1077–1096.

Kammeyer-Mueller, J. D., Wanberg, C. R., Glomb, T. M., & Ahlburg, D. (2005). The role of temporal shifts in turnover processes: It's about time. *Journal of Applied Psychology, 90*(4), 644–658.

Krackhardt, D., & Porter, L. W. (1985). When friends leave: A structural analysis of the relationship between turnover and stayers' attitudes. *Administrative Science Quarterly, 30*(2), 242–261.

Krackhardt, D., & Porter, L. W. (1986). The snowball effect: Turnover embedded in communication networks. *Journal of Applied Psychology, 71*(1), 50–55.

*Kraimer, M. L., Seibert, S. E., Wayne, S. J., Liden, R. C., & Bravo, J. (2011). Antecedents and outcomes of organizational support for development: The critical role of career opportunities. *Journal of Applied Psychology, 96*(3), 485–500.

*Kraimer, M. L., Shaffer, M. A., Harrison, D. A., & Ren, H. (2012). No place like home? An identity strain perspective on repatriate turnover. *Academy of Management Journal, 55*(2), 399–420.

Lee, T. H., Gerhart, B., Weller, I., & Trevor, C. O. (2008). Understanding voluntary turnover: Path-specific job satisfaction effects and the importance of unsolicited job offers. *Academy of Management Journal, 51*(4), 651–671.

Lee, T. W., & Mitchell, T. R. (1994). An alternative approach: The unfolding model of voluntary employee turnover. *Academy of Management Review, 19*(1), 51–89.

Lee, T. W., Mitchell, T. R., Holtom, B. C., McDaniel, L. S., & Hill, J. W. (1999). The unfolding model of voluntary turnover: A replication and extension. *Academy of Management Journal, 42*(4), 450–462.

Lee, T. W., Mitchell, T. R., Sablynski, C. J., Burton, J. P., & Holtom, B. C. (2004). The effects of job embeddedness on organizational citizenship, job performance, volitional absences, and voluntary turnover. *Academy of Management Journal, 47*(5), 711–722.

Lee, T. W., Mitchell, T. R., Wise, L., & Fireman, S. (1996). An unfolding model of voluntary employee turnover. *Academy of Management Journal, 39*(1), 5–36.

*Liu, D., Zhang, S., Wang, L., & Lee, T. W. (2011). The effects of autonomy and empowerment on employee turnover: Test of a multilevel model in teams. *Journal of Applied Psychology, 96*(6), 1305–1316.

*Mackenzie, S. B., Podsakoff, P. M., & Podsakoff, N. P. (2011). Challenge-oriented organizational citizenship behaviors and organizational effectiveness: Do challenge-oriented behaviors really have an impact on the organization's bottom line? *Personnel Psychology, 64*(3), 559–592.

Maertz, C. P., & Campion, M. A. (1998). 25 years of voluntary turnover research: A review and critique. *International Review of Industrial and Organizational Psychology, 13*, 49–82.

*Maltarich, M. A., Nyberg, A. J., & Reilly, G. (2010). A conceptual and empirical analysis of the cognitive ability-voluntary turnover relationship. *Journal of Applied Psychology, 95*(6), 1058–1070.

March, J. G., & Simon, H. A. (1958). *Organizations*. New York, NY: John Wiley.

McAfee, A., & Brynjolfsson, E. (2012). Big data: The management revolution. *Harvard Business Review, 90*(10), 60–68.

*McClean, E. J., Burris, E. R., & Detert, J. R. (2013). When does voice lead to exit? It depends on leadership. *Academy of Management Journal, 56*(2), 525–548.

*Messersmith, J. G., Guthrie, J. P., Ji, Y. -Y., & Lee, J. -Y. (2011). Executive turnover: The influence of dispersion and other pay system characteristics. *Journal of Applied Psychology, 96*(3), 457–469.

Mitchell, T. R., Holtom, B. C., Lee, T. W., Sablynski, C. J., & Erez, M. (2001). Why people stay: Using job embeddedness to predict voluntary turnover. *Academy of Management Journal, 44*(6), 1102–1121.

Mobley, W. H. (1977). Intermediate linkages in the relationship between job satisfaction and employee turnover. *Journal of Applied Psychology, 62*(2), 237–240.

Mobley, W. H. (1982). *Employee turnover: Causes, consequences, and control.* Reading, MT: Addison-Wesley.

Mueller, C. W., & Price, J. L. (1989). Some consequences of turnover: A work unit analysis. *Human Relations, 42*(5), 389–402.

*Nishii, L. H. (2013). The benefits of climate for inclusion for gender-diverse groups. *Academy of Management Journal, 56*(6), 1754–1774.

*Nyberg, A. (2010). Retaining your high performers: Moderators of the performance-job satisfaction-voluntary turnover relationship. *Journal of Applied Psychology, 95*(3), 440–453.

Nyberg, A. J., & Ployhart, R. E. (2013). Context-emergent turnover (CET) theory: A theory of collective turnover. *Academy of Management Review, 38*(1), 109–131.

*Owens, B. P., Johnson, M. D., & Mitchell, T. R. (2013). Expressed humility in organizations: Implications for performance, teams, and leadership. *Organization Science, 24*(5), 1517–1538.

Park, T., & Shaw, J. D. (2013). Turnover rates and organizational performance: A meta-analysis. *Journal of Applied Psychology, 98*(2), 268–309.

Peterson, S. J., & Luthans, F. (2006). The impact of financial and nonfinancial incentives on business-unit outcomes over time. *Journal of Applied Psychology, 91*(1), 156–165.

Ployhart, R. E., & Vandenberg, R. J. (2010). Longitudinal research: The theory, design, and analysis of change. *Journal of Management, 36*, 94–120.

*Ployhart, R. E., Weekley, J. A., & Ramsey, J. (2009). The consequences of human resource stocks and flows: A longitudinal examination of unit service orientation and unit effectiveness. *Academy of Management Journal, 52*(5), 996–1015.

Porter, L. W., & Steers, R. M. (1973). Organizational, work, and personal factors in employee turnover and absenteeism. *Psychological Bulletin, 80*(2), 151–176.

Price, J. L. (1977). *The study of turnover.* Ames, IA: Iowa State University Press.

Price, J. L., & Mueller, C. W. (1981). A causal model of turnover for nurses. *Academy of Management Journal, 24*(3), 543–565.

*Rafferty, A. E., & Restubog, S. L. D. (2010). The impact of change process and context on change reactions and turnover during a merger. *Journal of Management, 36*(5), 1309–1338.

*Ramesh, A., & Gelfand, M. J. (2010). Will they stay or will they go? The role of job embeddedness in predicting turnover in individualistic and collectivistic cultures. *Journal of Applied Psychology, 95*(5), 807–823.

*Russell, C. J., & Sell, M. V. (2012). A closer look at decisions to quit. *Organizational Behavior and Human Decision Processes, 117*(1), 125–137.

Schwab, D. (1991). Contextual variables in employee performance-turnover relationships. *Academy of Management Journal, 34*, 966–975.

Shaw, J. D., Delery, J. E., Jenkins, G. D., & Gupta, N. (1998). An organization-level analysis of voluntary and involuntary turnover. *Academy of Management Journal, 41*(5), 511–525.

*Shaw, J. D., Dineen, B. R., Fang, R., & Vellella, R. F. (2009). Employee-organization exchange relationships, HRM practices, and quit rates of good and poor performers. *Academy of Management Journal, 52*(5), 1016–1033.

Shaw, J. D., Duffy, M. K., Johnson, J. L., & Lockhart, D. E. (2005a). Turnover, social capital losses, and performance. *Academy of Management Journal, 48*(4), 594–606.

Shaw, J. D., Gupta, N., & Delery, J. E. (2005b). Alternative conceptualizations of the relationship between voluntary turnover and organizational performance. *Academy of Management Journal, 48*(1), 50–68.

*Shin, J., Taylor, M. S., & Seo, M. -G. (2012). Resources for change: The relationships of organizational inducements and psychological resilience to employees' attitudes and behaviors toward organizational change. *Academy of Management Journal, 55*(3), 727–748.

*Siebert, W. S., & Zubanov, N. (2009). Searching for the optimal level of employee turnover: A study of a large U.K. retail organization. *Academy of Management Journal, 52*(2), 294–313.

Staw, B. M. (1980). The consequences of turnover. *Journal of Occupational Behavior, 1,* 253–273.

Steel, R. P. (2002). Turnover theory at the empirical interface: Problems of fit and function. *Academy of Management Review, 27*(3), 346–360.

Steers, R. M., & Mowday, R. T. (1981). Employee turnover and post-decision justification. In L.L. Cummings & B.M. Staw (Eds.), *Research in organizational behavior* (Vol. 3, pp. 235–282). Greenwich, CT: JAI Press.

Sturman, M. C., & Trevor, C. O. (2001). The implications of linking the dynamic performance and turnover literatures. *Journal of Applied Psychology, 86*(4), 684–696.

*Swider, B. W., Boswell, W. R., & Zimmerman, R. D. (2011). Examining the job search–turnover relationship: The role of embeddedness, job satisfaction, and available alternatives. *Journal of Applied Psychology, 96*(2), 432–441.

Terborg, J. R., & Lee, T. W. (1984). A predictive study of organizational turnover rates. *Academy of Management Journal, 27*(4), 793–810.

Trevor, C. O. (2001). Interactions among actual ease of movement determinants and job satisfaction in the prediction of voluntary turnover. *Academy of Management Journal, 44,* 621–638.

Trevor, C. O., & Nyberg, A. J. (2008). Keeping your headcount when all about you are losing theirs: Downsizing, voluntary turnover rates, and the moderating role of HR practices. *Academy of Management Journal, 51,* 259–276.

*Van Iddekinge, C. H., Ferris, G. R., Perrewé, P. L., Perryman, A. A., Blass, F. R., & Heetderks, T. D. (2009). Effects of selection and training on unit-level performance over time: A latent growth modeling approach. *Journal of Applied Psychology, 94*(4), 829–843.

10

Using Big Data to Advance the Science of Team Effectiveness

Steve W. J. Kozlowski, Georgia T. Chao, Chu-Hsiang (Daisy) Chang, and Rosemarie Fernandez

Many influences have shaped the nature of organizational science during the transition from the 20th to the 21st century, but arguably two influences have been significantly transformative (Kozlowski, 2012). First, groups and teams research migrated from their long time home in social psychology to settle into their new location in organizational psychology and behavior (OPB). Indeed, Levine and Moreland (1990, p. 620) concluded famously that, "Groups are alive and well, but living elsewhere . . . The torch has been passed to (or, more accurately, picked up by) colleagues in other disciplines, particularly organizational psychology." Team research in OPB exploded during the 1990s and 2000s (Kozlowski & Bell, 2013). Second, the heightened interest focused on team effectiveness coincided serendipitously with the migration of multilevel theory from the fringes of organizational science to become a core focus of mainstream OPB research. These two influences have revolutionized the field with respect to theory (incorporating multiple levels), research methods (resolving construct measurement and data alignment across levels), and analytics (capturing the interplay of effects across levels). But the revolution has also been substantially limited by the absence of one critical focus. That focus goes by many names, but it is in essence attention to processes, their dynamics over time, and their emergence as higher-level phenomena (Cronin, Weingart, & Todorova, 2011; Kozlowski & Chao, 2012). The next frontier for the science of team effectiveness, and OPB more generally, is to incorporate process dynamics at the core of our theories and research (Kozlowski, in press). This will necessitate another revolutionary advance . . . and this one will be energized by the advent of big data.

As other chapters in this book described and scholars have opined, big data in the form of digital traces (e.g., email, web surfing, blogging, social media networks, financial transactions, location services, etc.), video surveillance (e.g., while shopping, working, traveling, etc.), and other data traces that people generate during the interactions that comprise daily life in the modern world offer the promise of a *computational social science* (Lazar et al., 2009). The ability to pull together large pools of disparate data that capture human interactions and exchanges, identify meaningful patterns, and use them to predict important outcomes has the potential to radically transform the way we live our lives . . . and how we conduct science.

The potential capabilities and benefits are substantial, so there is a vigorous push to advance computational techniques to collect, integrate, and archive big data and develop statistical methods to explore, analyze, and extract meaning from it.[1] These efforts bring big challenges too. To draw meaningful inductive inferences, the data have to be representative and as complete as possible. Techniques for cleaning, integrating, and aligning such data sets are in their infancy, so the effort is laborious and fraught with problems.[2] Our research is more focused. Rather than striving to collect "everything about everybody all of the time" (e.g., Google, the National Security Agency [NSA]), we have a middle-range focus on particular contexts (i.e., medicine, military, spaceflight), levels (i.e., individual, team, team networks), and time frames (i.e., minutes, months, years). These constraints or boundaries that we place around the phenomena of interest targets a middle range that allows us to capture "everything about somebody some of the time," thereby harnessing the promise of big data, but in a targeted way.

We study the dynamics of team processes and how team-level phenomena emerge over time from the interactions and exchanges among team members. We examine behavioral processes for emergency medical teams by video recording and coding team processes in high-fidelity patient simulation. We examine the dynamics of team learning and knowledge emergence in teams with distributed expertise that emulate a wide range of decision tasks used by the military and organizations. This research couples computational modeling (i.e., agent-based simulation) with a human team simulation. Finally, we study the dynamics of team cohesion and collaboration in a range of spaceflight analog environments that include teams in the Antarctic (i.e., summer and winter-over deployments) and teams working in a range of National Aeronautic and Space Administration (NASA) mission simulations (e.g., transit, surface exploration). To provide some perspective, the data generated by these projects range—on the smaller end—from approximately 10 to 20 thousand data points per study for medical teams to—on the higher end—20 to 500 million data points per study for the computational modeling and human team simulation, respectively, and to 250 to 750 million data points per team for one study for the NASA research. The teams are small, but the data generated are quite big! There are useful lessons to be learned across the projects that are useful for other investigators contemplating big data that we think merit sharing.

The chapter is organized as follows. First, we will discuss the longstanding treatment of team processes as static constructs rather than as dynamic processes per se. They are clearly treated as dynamic theoretically, but the treatment in research is overwhelmingly static. We suggest that this static treatment is largely due to limitations inherent in research design preferences and practices (i.e., limited view of dynamics, over-reliance on retrospective self-reports, and use of cross-sectional designs). Second, we will highlight research design issues that need to be considered in any effort to directly observe, assess, and capture teamwork process dynamics. The promise of big data is on the use of induction in a discovery mode, but we see important roles for coupling deduction and induction. Big data techniques are predicated on the use of classification and pattern recognition analytics to draw inductive inferences from an incomprehensible mass of linked data, but the quality of inference is ultimately determined by the quality of the data. One still has to know what data one needs to collect, why they will be useful, and how to examine them—so it is useful to have a strategy to guide research design. Third, we will explain how researchers can directly assess and capture team process dynamics using illustrations from three ongoing projects. Here we will discuss the research design considerations by grounding them in the research illustrations, focusing on targeting the research design and aligning measurement and data analytics. Finally, we will offer some concluding thoughts about the role of big data in advancing the scientific frontier with respect to dynamic phenomena.

TEAM PROCESSES: EMERGENT AND DYNAMIC PHENOMENA OR STATIC CONSTRUCTS?

Overview

It is interesting to note that early interest in social psychology that centered on group or team[3] interaction processes was very much focused on the dynamic aspects of interpersonal communication and exchange processes.

This interest is readily apparent, for example, in Lewin's field theory (Lewin, 1951) and Bales' interaction process analysis (Bales, 1950). Indeed, the later development of the system for the multiple level observation of groups (SYMLOG; Bales & Cohen, 1979) incorporated a method for recording individual behavioral acts in sequence as they occurred during group interactions. McGrath (1964), of course, is also well known for his interest in the temporal aspects of team interactions as evidenced in his work on group interaction and performance (1984) and, later, time, interaction, and performance (1991). Even with the shift in the locus of team research from social psychology to OPB, theorists are in near universal agreement that team processes are dynamic phenomena (e.g., Ilgen, Hollenbeck, Johnson, & Jundt, 2005; Kozlowski, Gully, McHugh, Salas, & Cannon-Bowers, 1996; Kozlowski, Gully, Nason, & Smith, 1999; Kozlowski & Ilgen, 2006; Marks, Mathieu, & Zaccaro, 2001; Mathieu, Maynard, Rapp, & Gilson, 2008; McGrath, Arrow, & Berdahl, 2000; Salas, Stagl, & Burke, 2004) that are shaped by team inputs and influence team performance. Team performance, in turn, has reciprocal, cyclical influences back to inputs and/or processes. Team processes are viewed overwhelmingly as dynamic, at least on the theory side.

Unfortunately, they are not generally researched that way once investigators have to translate theory about dynamics into data. A review by Cronin et al. (2011) noted that the evident theoretical interest in team dynamics, rise of multilevel theory and methods, and advent of statistical tools for modeling time dependence and recursion should have "... invigorated the study of group dynamics; but did they? Regrettably, they did not ... dynamics are still largely missing from the study of groups" (pp. 572–573). Why? There are many potential influences (Cronin et al., 2011; Kozlowski, in press), but three in particular stand out. One is the apparent preference for "chain-like unidirectional cause-effect relationships" (McGrath et al., 2000, p. 97) that characterizes much team effectiveness research. A consideration of process dynamics necessitates a much more complex conceptualization of team phenomena. A second is the practice of treating dynamic processes as static constructs. In their review of the team effectiveness literature, Kozlowski and Bell (2003) observed that the static nature of team process research "... is due in large part to the assumed causal linkage inherent in the IPO heuristic, and the way that process is represented—by a box" (p. 346). This limitation is largely attributed to the way most team processes are assessed using dominant research practices (Kozlowski, in press; Kozlowski & Chao, 2012): as retrospective self-reports to a series of items tapping emergent constructs or what Marks et al. (2001) characterize as "emergent states." A third is the dominance of cross-sectional research designs in OPB:

Although cross-sectional designs are clearly more efficient, they by necessity can only treat temporally relevant phenomena like "team processes" as a box—a static representation of the essence by which teams create collective products. Longitudinal designs, though less efficient, will be far more revealing of the team phenomenon under investigation. (Kozlowski & Bell, 2003, p. 364)

RESEARCH DESIGN PRINCIPLES AND CHALLENGES

Develop a Targeted Research Design

One key promise of big data is the potential to use it as a fundamental tool for scientific discovery, particularly with respect to understanding complex, adaptive systems: "Fueled by cheap sensors and high throughput technologies, the data explosion that we witness today, from social media to cell biology, is offering unparalleled opportunities to document the inner workings of many complex systems" (Barabási, 2012, pp. 14–15). Drawing meaningful inductive inferences requires complete, inclusive, and expansive data. That's a challenge. And, although that is a challenge worthy of pursuit, we have deliberately focused our efforts on team process dynamics in particular organizational and work environments. Thus, we deliberately constrain context, level, and temporal focus.

Our team process focus is carefully targeted. We focus on observational indicators, core process mechanisms, and emergent constructs that are well supported by substantive evidence. This ensures that our research examines primary team processes, rather than those that may be novel or intriguing but are superfluous. For process dynamics, we examine core interaction events and associated behavioral, physiological, and/or psychological indicators. For emergence, we examine core micro-process mechanisms that drive interaction patterns and ultimately yield the manifestation of team phenomena. For example, our research on medical teams is targeted on team process behaviors consistent with the Marks et al. (2001) typology (Grand, Pearce, Rench, Fernandez, Chao, & Kozlowski, 2013). Research on teams operating in isolated, confined, and extreme (ICE) environments for NASA examines emergent constructs and team process dynamics based on Kozlowski and Ilgen (2006), who were guided by findings from meta-analyses and promising research results. And research on knowledge emergence focuses on core learning and sharing process mechanisms

(Kozlowski, Chao, Grand, Braun, & Kuljanin, 2013, in press) that underlie team knowledge building. Parsimony is a useful principle to apply so that the data are directly germane to the substantive issue of interest. Our data are big, but less sifting is required.

Consider the Interplay of Deduction and Induction

Our operative approach is primarily deductive, but there is also an important role for inductive exploration to play. For example, our projects are all theory-driven, and thus deductive in orientation. However, the team process data are distinctly different across the research settings. Considered broadly, the diverse data will begin to provide a basic descriptive foundation for describing and documenting team process dynamics under different contextual constraints and across different timeframes (hours to days to months to years). Indeed, for one project, that descriptive aspect is essential so the research can document to what extent team processes vary and how much they do so. Big data will be important for establishing normative profiles of team evolution and long-term functioning that will be used as benchmarks to assess new teams. Such data will also have a role to play in inductive exploration. Extant theory provides some notions about how individual and team process interactions may have lagged and cyclical influences on team performance, but it is fair to say that theory on team dynamics is substantially underdeveloped. Thus, big data will also be valuable for exploratory research to identify synchronous (i.e., conflict today relates to lower cohesion today), time-lagged (i.e., lower cohesion today relates to lower performance tomorrow), and reciprocal (i.e., lower performance relates to future cohesion and subsequent performance) relationships that can be used to aid theory building. As we will discuss, some of the tools, namely computational modeling and agent-based simulation, are explicitly designed to enable virtual experimentation in just such an exploratory role. Inductive inference and theory building then helps to fine-tune research design, measurement, and analysis, so there is the potential for a very useful interplay between pure deduction and pure induction. Our projects are sensitive to this interplay between both modes of knowledge development.

Align Research Design with the Process Dynamics of Interest

At a fundamental level, a research focus on process dynamics means that the data collection design must go beyond the routine use of cross-sectional, self-reported survey designs. Obviously, the cross-sectional aspect of many studies precludes any potential of capturing team process dynamics, so that is out. On the other hand, it is often the case that self-reports are a primary, and sometimes perhaps the only way (i.e., reporting internal psychological states), to assess certain phenomena. So, there is a role for self-reported data, but it is desirable to supplement them with multi-source reports, other types of observations, and/or objective data. Moreover, as we discuss below, other considerations such as the desired resolution for capturing process dynamics (i.e., how frequently the phenomenon is assessed) will quickly constrain the utility of self-reported survey methods as the degree of desired resolution increases.

A well-aligned middle-range research design will have a clearly defined, bounded context and an overall time-frame that enables the observation of theoretically meaningful periods of teamwork interaction processes relevant to team effectiveness. Within that overall research time-frame, the design needs to incorporate assessments of core team processes at a frequency commensurate with the relevant rates of change needed to capture the micro-mechanisms of emergence, the emergence of team constructs, and/or their fluctuation over time and influences on other team phenomena (Kozlowski, in press). This means that some tuning is required with respect to the nature of measurement (i.e., by what modality team processes are assessed) and the frequency of measurement (i.e., how often the phenomenon is sampled).

As with most research design decisions, tradeoffs and challenges have to be balanced. That is the primary reason why we discuss three different projects. Each one illustrates different tradeoffs; across the projects, there is an overall balance. For example, one project uses video and audio recording, so (in theory) it has a very high (i.e., essentially continuous) recording rate. However, such raw observational data by necessity have to be coded, and the methodology of the codes sets the sampling frequency and the degree of resolution for capturing team process dynamics. Another project uses experience sampling methods (ESM) to capture relatively short sets of perceptual responses. We noted previously that one of the contributing factors to the treatment of processes as statics is the heavy reliance on the use of retrospective self-reports to assess team processes. ESM overcomes that limitation because the perceptions are sampled closer in time to actual experience and at rates much higher than one-shot surveys (Beal, 2015). However, there are limits to how much you can ask, how often you can ask it, and for how long you can maintain compliance, so there are tradeoffs. We also use a novel technology—a wearable sensor package—that captures multiple data streams at very high sampling frequencies (i.e., essentially continuous) in real time. Here the challenge is fusing the copious multimodal data into a meaningful inference about the individual, dyadic, and team interaction quality; again, there are tradeoffs. The guiding principle is to sample at the highest frequency possible with the least degree of obtrusiveness, given what your resources and technology will enable (Kozlowski, in press).

RESEARCH ILLUSTRATIONS: CAPTURING THE DYNAMICS OF TEAM PROCESSES

Overview

The purpose of this section is to provide a series of illustrations using our ongoing research projects as grounded exemplars to demonstrate how targeted individual and team process dynamics can be successfully investigated using rigorous quantitative methods and sophisticated analyses. The projects we discuss include research on:

- emergency medical teams in which the focus is on shaping team behavioral processes and linking them to team effectiveness;
- teams in isolated, confined, and extreme (ICE) environments that serve as analogs for space flight crews, in which the focus is on the dynamics of cohesion and collaboration and how those dynamics influence the psycho-social health of the team; and
- decision-making teams in which the focus is on the process dynamics of team knowledge emergence (i.e., how team members acquire problem-relevant knowledge and share it such that it manifests as a collective property) that can be applied to problem solving.

Each project is focused on a different type of team context, substantive focus, and targeted type of process dynamics. Thus, although not exhaustive, as a set they provide a good range of exemplars to illustrate how the theoretical foci regarding process dynamics can be instantiated in a research design that addresses the issues discussed previously: (a) targeting design to guide the collection of big data, (b) balancing deduction and induction, and (c) achieving alignment among the dynamic process of interest, sampling frequency, and analysis.

Team Behavioral Processes

Research focus and context. Emergency medical teams are at the "pointy end of the stick" in hospital emergency departments. When a person suffers a catastrophic injury, they are whisked away as quickly as possible (under ideal conditions) to the nearest emergency department. During the journey, emergency medical technicians compile whatever information is available regarding the circumstances of the injury and the patient's vital signs. Upon arrival, the appropriate medical team is quickly assembled (whoever is on call) and presented with the available information on the status of the patient. Their task is to stabilize the deteriorating condition of the patient as quickly as possible so that the patient can be passed off to the intensive care unit or appropriate interventional unit (e.g., operating room). The capabilities of such teams to quickly assess the situation, diagnose a course of action, and coordinate their expertise are key precursors of the clinical outcomes for the patient. These capabilities constitute the team behavioral processes of interest.

Targeted design. Studying emergency medical teams *in situ* is not impossible (e.g., Klein, Ziegert, Knight, & Xiao, 2007), but it is very difficult. Because the project is focused on training intervention design and assessment, it is necessary to craft a research platform that is standardized and replicable. Hence, this research uses high-fidelity simulation to create synthetic experiences. It is conducted using a medical suite equipped with a high-fidelity programmable manikin that is capable of emulating a range of human disease states and associated physiological responses (see Figure 10.1).

High fidelity patient simulators are in widespread use throughout the United States for medical education. Often, however, they are used to deliver an experience rather than training per se. That is, participants are presented with a realistic resuscitation scenario, the team performs, and their performance is video and audio recorded. Then, the instructor leads an after action review using the video to highlight aspects of good and poor performance, offering process feedback, and providing lessons learned for the students. The experience is no doubt instructive, but the knowledge and skills acquired are not systematic, so it is not training. Moreover, the knowledge and skills are rarely assessed, so what is acquired is essentially unknown.

Our use of this problem context and research setting necessitated the creation of a methodological infrastructure in the form of scenario design, measurement development, and validation so the simulator could be harnessed for systematic investigation of team processes. As noted previously,

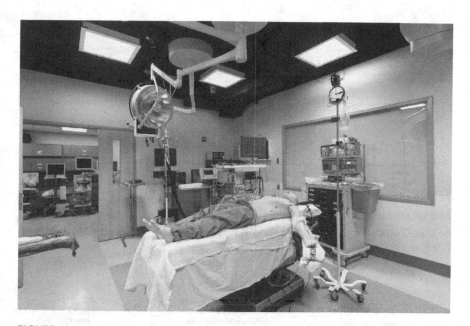

FIGURE 10.1
Medical team simulation suite

the capabilities of emergency medical teams to quickly assess the patient, diagnose a course of action, and coordinate expertise influence patient outcomes. Conceptually, these capabilities conform to a planning-action-reflection phase structure, with specific team process behaviors relevant in each phase (see Figures 10.2a and 10.2b). This conceptual structure represents an integration of the team regulation cycle (Kozlowski, Gully, McHugh, Salas, & Cannon-Bowers, 1996; Kozlowski, Gully, Nason, & Smith, 1999) and team task episode (Marks, Mathieu, & Zaccaro, 2001) models (Fernandez, Kozlowski, Shapiro, & Salas, 2008). Team process behaviors and their dynamics across phase shifts are the focus of our research.

The development of this infrastructure is discussed in detail elsewhere (Grand, Pearce, Rench, Chao, Fernandez, & Kozlowski, 2013). Here we highlight the key steps in brief. First, we developed representative, realistic patient resuscitation scenarios—content validated by subject matter experts (SMEs)—that were designed to provide a backdrop within which targeted team process behaviors could be exhibited. As shown in Figure 10.2a, a scenario comprises a series of events that drive a planning-action-reflection phase structure (Fernandez et al., 2008). Resuscitation

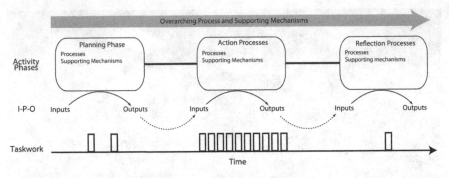

FIGURE 10.2a

Medical team dynamic process model

Reprinted with permission from Fernandez, R., Kozlowski, S. W. J., Shapiro, M., & Salas, E. (2008, p. 1106).

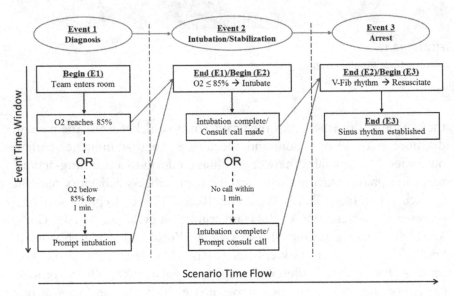

FIGURE 10.2b

Event time windows and scenario timeflow

scenarios generally fall within a 20 to 30 minute overall time window, with specific events (e.g., intubation, cardiac arrest) taking approximately five to 10 minutes each. Second, using the Marks et al. (2001) behavioral process taxonomy, we mapped specific behavioral indicators for relevant team process dimensions—content validated by SMEs—onto the event structure of the scenarios. Third, a similar process was followed to develop behavioral (observed) and objective (manikin) metrics of clinical care quality that were also validated by SMEs. Finally, the overall system was empirically validated (Fernandez et al., 2013).

This research provides a lot of targeted data, on the order of 10 to 20 thousand data points per study. The video and audio are recorded in high definition (HD), so the raw data in absolute file size are substantial. Coding of the video, which uses independent coders for the team processes and performance outcomes, comprises hundreds of behavioral indicators of team processes and team performance for a given team across a scenario. Add multiple teams and multiple scenarios, and you have an extensive data set for capturing and exploring team process dynamics that are precisely focused.

Deduction—induction. This research is heavily oriented toward deduction. As shown in Figures 10.2a and 10.2b, research design is driven by contemporary team effectiveness theory that conceptualizes team processes as dynamic across a phased structure encompassing a series of IPO "cycles" (Fernandez et al., 2008; Kozlowski et al., 1996) or "episodes" (Marks et al., 2001). Team process measurement is consistent with the Marks et al. (2001) taxonomy. The research is focused on developing targeted interventions that shape the quality of team behavioral processes. For example, we have developed and evaluated a short computer-based training intervention designed to improve team processes (Fernandez et al., 2013). Current research is developing a team leader training intervention that also targets team process improvement. A primary focus of our work is on science translation; that is, applying theory and research findings from OPB to the medical team context, so the primary emphasis on deduction is appropriate.

Nonetheless, the research platform can be used as a very rich source of information for inductive research. For example, one investigator is researching team leadership behaviors. This work necessitates an interplay between induction to develop appropriate dimensions and codes to capture leadership indicators and deduction to evaluate a model examining the influence of leadership behaviors on team process behaviors and team effectiveness. Video and audio are very rich sources of big, flexible data. In this case, the big data are obtained within a targeted context with an explicit theory and measurement structure to guide what to examine.

Alignment and analytics. High definition video is a continuous stream of behavioral action data coupled with synchronous audio so that communication can also be extracted. Such data are very rich and highly flexible within their targeted time window and contextual constraints. However, in the absence of a targeted measurement system, aligned sampling frequency, and appropriate analytics, the data are just movies. Many novice investigators have recorded interesting team interactions, but then their big problem is: Now what? The research design has to be aligned.

A research focus on process dynamics necessitates careful consideration of temporal alignment. Thus, a key measurement principle is that one has to develop a targeted sampling of the data stream to populate the theory-driven team process dimensions. In our approach, this alignment is guided by the episodic event structure that is designed into the scenarios. For example, Figure 10.2b illustrates the event structure (diagnosis, intubation, and arrest) and time windows for a scenario. Each event has an associated time window within which an event begins to unfold (e.g., initial indication of cardiac arrest—arrhythmia) that should trigger planning behaviors (e.g., goal specification—resuscitation), action behaviors (e.g., coordination to execute the advanced cardiovascular life support algorithm of drug administration and defibrillation), and then reflection behaviors (e.g., sinus rhythm is restored; feedback—"good job" or "we should have accomplished that more quickly"), at which point the event time window has closed and the team shifts back to stabilizing the patient or another event begins to unfold. Specific behaviors are mapped to the event structure to index the team process dimensions. Depending on the research focus, behaviors can be aligned to the temporal structure of the unfolding event (within event), aggregated to the event level (within scenario), or aggregated to the scenario level (across scenario and/or between team).

An event structure allows precision in temporal alignment because the events set the tempo for the unfolding of team process behaviors. The key lesson is that the sampling frequency of the phenomena has to be commensurate with the rate of change (i.e., the dynamic frequency) that one is trying to capture. If the sampling rate is misaligned (i.e., too slow), then meaningful micro-dynamics in the phenomena of interest will not be captured and cannot be recovered. On the other hand, sampling at high frequency has costs (e.g., many more surveys, more specific coding, etc.) As a general rule-of-thumb, we advocate sampling at the highest frequency possible given resource constraints and participant engagement. High frequency data can always be sampled or aggregated, but missed observations are simply lost.

As noted previously, recorded video and audio provide highly flexible raw data. Codes extracted from the raw data can be very precisely time-aligned or aggregated upwards to capture meaningful team process clusters. Behaviors can be sampled at the team level, or the coding can be linked to individual team members to track process linkages as a dynamic network of actions. It can be resampled and recoded to supplement existing codes or to focus on entirely different process phenomena (within the context). Thus, researchers can increase or decrease the behavioral units under observation and the time frequency to hone in on exactly what they want to assess. Unfortunately, this approach is labor intensive. One has to have a rigorous measurement framework, or you will not be able to extract reliable and meaningful codes (Grand et al., 2013).

Analytics, of course, need to fit the research question. The research we are conducting—as translational science—is examining the effect of interventions on team processes and effectiveness. From an intervention evaluation perspective, we are simply interested in the effects of an intervention on enhancing team processes and team performance (see Fernandez et al., 2013). However, such a focus does not get at process dynamics per se.

The data could also be examined with a more sophisticated approach using structural equation modeling (SEM) that would better capture the temporal structure. For example, consider a design that incorporates a scenario, assessment of emergent process states (e.g., team mental model, efficacy, and cohesion), another scenario, and an assessment of effectiveness perceptions (e.g., viability, satisfaction). One could examine the influence of input factors (e.g., team experience, training) on team behavioral processes and performance, the effects of inputs, processes, and performance on subsequent emergent states, and the effects of the emergent states (incorporating the process and performance lags) on subsequent processes, performance, and viability outcomes. This is merely one possible model, as SEM is quite flexible (e.g., one could endeavor to unpack the event structure as well). This approach gets us closer to dynamics.

Alternatively, we might be interested in identifying the patterns of team processes that were most effective. Such an analysis could be applied at the scenario or event level. For example, Grand, Pearce, and Kozlowski (2013) used a regression-based pattern recognition analysis (Davison & Davenport, 2002) to identify profile patterns of team processes that covaried with the performance of effective teams across scenario events. The findings indicated that the pattern of team processes explained significant and substantial variance beyond that accounted for by the average level of team processes. Thus, beyond the amount of team process behavior exhibited, the particular configuration of processes was predictive of team effectiveness. This approach begins to capitalize on the promise of big data to unpack team processes.

Dynamics of Team Cohesion and Collaboration

Research focus and context. Someday in the not too distant future, a team of astronauts will depart near-Earth orbit to embark on a journey to explore our solar system including an inter-planetary expedition to Mars. What will such a mission be like? The composition of the crew and mission specifics have yet to be finalized, but ongoing planning allows some parameters to be reasonably estimated. For example, the Orion Multi-Purpose Crew Vehicle[4] will likely be the crew module (i.e., takeoff, abort, reentry) for deep space missions. The first test flight for Orion in December 2014 was successful. Launch was provided by a new space launch system, and Orion was mated with a new service module for exploration that will serve as the habitat for the crew. For a mission to Mars, the crew compliment is likely to be six astronauts. The habitable volume in the Orion and service module configuration will be quite tight. There will be high propinquity and very little privacy, creating some degree of interpersonal stress. The crew will be together for a very long time. Beyond the years of training, mission duration is likely to be 32 months at a minimum. Transit is estimated at 8.5 months each for outbound and return. Time for surface exploration is dictated by a planetary alignment that is needed for the return flight, so the exploration aspect of the mission cannot be shorter and any increase means a much longer overall mission. Communications with mission control (and family and friends) will be difficult (e.g., roughly 40 minutes—20 minutes each way—to have a two-way exchange at maximum distance with Mars). Thus, one can anticipate an astronaut team being subjected to a mission characterized by isolation, confinement, and extreme conditions for a very lengthy time. It is a very immersive experience. What can be done to help the team maintain its effectiveness under these challenging conditions?

Several lines of systematic research, large scale literature reviews, and meta-analytic summaries have firmly established that team processes, as key indicators of psycho-social team health, are critical contributors to team effectiveness (Ilgen et al., 2005; Kozlowski & Bell, 2003, 2013; Kozlowski & Ilgen, 2006; Mathieu et al., 2008). Disruptions to teamwork, due to conflict, low cohesion, or poor collaboration, have the potential to threaten team functioning under the ICE conditions that can be anticipated for long duration space missions. These difficult operating environments are further exacerbated by high team autonomy given time-lagged communications with mission control. For high reliability teams, a disruption in good teamwork, especially when team coordination is critical, can have disastrous consequences (Weick, Sutcliffe, & Obstfeld, 1999). Thus, the capability for NASA to measure, monitor, and maintain good team-work interactions for flight crews and mission control teams is essential.

One of the key challenges of conducting human research for NASA is that the population of astronauts (and other relevant mission personnel) is not very large. Moreover, opportunities to study space teams *in situ* are extremely limited. Thus, NASA has identified a set of analog environments that emulate aspects of space missions, their extremity, and/or personnel that are used as primary research contexts for studying team interaction processes relevant to space flight crews who will one day embark on long duration missions outside of near-Earth orbit (see Figure 10.3). The analogs of interest—in rough order of realism—include the NASA Extreme Environment Mission Operations (NEEMO; an undersea habitat), Human Exploration Research Analog (HERA; a transit mission simulation), the Hawai'i Space Exploration Analog and Simulation (HI-SEAS; a Mars surface exploration simulation), and real ICE teams that conduct scientific research (summer deployments) or winter-over in the Antarctic.[5]

FIGURE 10.3

NASA spaceflight research analog environments

HERA (photo by C. -H. Chang) HI-SEAS mission 2: day and night (photos by Ross Lockwood)

NEEMO mission 16 (Photo courtesy of NASA) Antarctic science teams camped on the ice

Targeted design. The targeted big data aspects of the project have two primary foci. First, we are collaborating with an engineering team to develop an unobtrusive team interaction assessment technology. Essentially, it is a sensor platform—a wearable social interaction badge—that captures dynamic, multimodal data streams in real time (i.e., physical, physiological, and behavioral), capturing team member and teamwork interactions. This technology generates copious data. Second, we are using experience sampling methods (ESM) to collect data designed to benchmark long-term team functioning in NASA and ICE analogs. Depending on the analog, we use the badges and/or ESM to assess team process dynamics over a variety of mission durations, ranging from one week up to one year. Across all the research settings, the teams are small—typically four to eight people—and the sample is often comprised of only one, and occasionally two or three, teams. In essence, the data collections assess the within-team dynamics and ecology of single teams. Hence, much of our research focus is on individual dynamics and interactions among team members. Although the teams are small, the data can be quite big. Next, we discuss each type of data collection—badge and ESM.

The wearable sensor system (Baard et al., 2012a, 2012b; Quwaider & Biswas, 2010) provides a continuous feed of multimodal data to capture teamwork interaction and process dynamics. The concept of the system is very similar to the sociometric badges developed by the MIT Media Lab.[6] However, the badge under development streams continuous multimodal data that can be distributed to other devices (e.g., smart phone, tablet, and/ or computer) for viewing in real time, whereas the Sociometric Solutions badge stores interaction data onboard for later upload and processing.[7] The sensor system consists of a wearable badge, which contains the sensor array, and a receiver and server to record the data streams and to distribute them via a web interface. The sensor package is roughly the size of a smart phone, although the sensors could be sewn directly into clothing. The sensors monitor the intensity of physical movement, vocal intensity, heart rate, and face time (interaction distance) with teammates who are also wearing sensors. Over time, one can identify the sequence, frequency, duration, and degree of arousal associated with patterns of interactions among team members. Structured team member interactions under highly controlled conditions have been used to validate the sensor data streams (Baard et al., 2012a, 2012b). Current research is evaluating the badges in a range of analog settings.

As highlighted previously, although there is considerable research on the relationship between teamwork processes that reflect the quality of team member interactions such as cohesion, conflict, and collaboration, most of the research is static. However, theory suggests that collaboration patterns and interaction quality vary over time as a team is assembled, undergoes developmental experiences, and works interactively together over lengthy time frames. It is a fact of life that team members have to manage work related problems and the challenges of social friction. However, relatively little is known about such dynamics because the majority of team process research has been cross-sectional (Kozlowski & Ilgen, 2006).

As you might imagine, the sensors collect copious amount of data. For example, teams of six in the HI-SEAS simulation generate approximately 250, 500, and 750 million data points across four-, eight-, and 12-month missions. Our use of the sensor technology for NASA is designed to develop protocols to infer the quality of team member interactions and when anomalies are assessed (i.e., meaningful departures from normative functioning), to trigger countermeasures to recover and restore cohesiveness. These technologies, however, have broad applicability. For example, one could use badge data to examine the dynamic interactions among members of research and development teams to see what type of network ties and network structures yield the most knowledge creation and innovation (e.g., Olguin, Gloor, & Pentland, 2009; Olguin, Waber, Kim, Mohan, Ara, & Pentland, 2009).

We use ESM to collect benchmarking data for ICE teams in the Antarctic. These data are intended to set normative standards for expected variation in team functioning for long duration missions. Many science field teams deploy to the Antarctic to conduct scientific study during the Antarctic summer, when conditions—although still quite challenging—enable them to deploy to the ice. The teams we are studying spend six weeks camped in the field seeking samples. In addition, permanent stations are an important part of the science infrastructure in the Antarctic. Stations have to be staffed and maintained, even during the difficult Antarctic winter. Crews who winter-over spend roughly nine months, mostly confined to the station, doing their work with teammates. In both settings, team members provide daily ESM ratings to assess the nature of the work (e.g., mental and physical workload), a variety of team process states (e.g., cohesion, conflict), and outcomes (e.g., performance, satisfaction).

We are also collecting benchmark ESM data from crews in NASA analogs that simulate transit and exploration missions. We have collected ESM and badge data from four-person crews during three HERA missions; this data collection is ongoing. In addition, we have collected ESM and badge data from a five-person crew at HI-SEAS during a four-month mission.

Two additional missions for two six-person crews are planned that will extend mission duration to eight and 12 months. Finally, we collected one week of ESM and badge data from the crew of NEEMO mission 18, which consisted of an international team of four astronauts and two habitat technicians.

It should be noted that our research team is just one among many who are studying team phenomena in NASA analogs. Other investigators are focusing on physiological monitoring, video recording, and communication (audio to text) as data sources. The discussion that follows centers on the badge and ESM data, but this setting provides a real big data integration opportunity across all the different data modalities.

Deduction—induction. One of the more interesting aspects of this project is the interplay between deduction and induction. For example, some of the mission simulations include workload and other manipulations (e.g., communication time lags) designed to stress team members. This is deductively oriented research in which we expect the stressors to influence the quality of team member interaction and exchange with effects on performance. But the research is also inductively oriented in two primary ways. First, our ESM data collections are building a descriptive research foundation of the longitudinal functioning of individuals and teams of different types, under different conditions, and across a range of durations. Although we have theoretically inspired notions about how shocks or disruptions to team members (e.g., bad weather, equipment failure, social conflict) may influence the variability of team processes and outcomes in the form of daily fluctuations, the data also enable exploratory analyses to identify time-lagged, reciprocal, and asymmetrical relationships. We are also examining different overall patterns of functioning that may be useful for classifying team profiles. Second, the badges stream a prodigious quantity of interaction data across several different sensing modalities. Again, although we have theoretically inspired ideas about how the data streams can be used to capture the quality of team interaction, it is also likely that such data contain non-linear patterns that do not conform to any current theory of individual and team interaction. Thus, one key aspect of developing the badge into a useful team regulation support system (i.e., assessment, diagnosis, and feedback) is the use of data mining techniques to quantify patterns across the sensor data streams that are predictive of individual and team process states and outcomes. For example, badge data can be coupled with frequent self-reports of affect (activation and valence) that can serve as criteria. As a simple example, one can create a 2 X 2 matrix of the orthogonal dimensions. Data mining tools (e.g., Weka[8], TDMiner[9]) can then be used to identify patterns among the data streams that classify the states of team members or teams into the 2 X 2 over given time frames (e.g., minutes, hours, days, etc.)

Alignment and analyses. As described by Beal (2015), ESM can be viewed as an umbrella term for a set of techniques (i.e., ecological momentary assessment, ambulatory assessment, everyday experience methods, and daily diary methods) that are all predicated on capturing experience *in situ* over meaningful time frames. They are intensive time series designs that enable an examination of research questions that are not amenable to investigation using conventional between subject research approaches. In that regard, they are idiographic in nature (i.e., within person), rather than nomothetic (i.e., between person). This raises issues regarding the generalization of findings about the dynamics of individuals to the broader population. However, looking across individuals in a common experience, across those exposed to different experiences, and identifying clusters with similar patterns represents a meaningful generalization target (Velicer & Molenaar, 2013).

Intensive longitudinal data at the person level enables an examination of process dynamics that are not amenable to traditional research designs (Iida, Shrout, Laurenceau, & Bolger, 2012). Primary foci include: the average states of a person and how much variability the person exhibits over time; the extent to which there is a systematic change in states over assessments, the nature of change (e.g., linear, quadratic, other), and whether the trajectories are similar or different between persons; and identification of cyclical, reciprocal, and lagged relationships among factors (e.g., workload), states (e.g., conflict, cohesion), and outcomes (e.g., satisfaction, performance).

As mentioned previously, the research goals regarding process dynamics need to be aligned with assessment frequency. In other words, the rates of change for the phenomenon of interest should be commensurate with the sampling frequency (Kozlowski, in press). This isn't an especially complicated observation. If one assesses on a daily basis but the phenomenon changes more rapidly, then you are going to miss those micro-dynamics. On the other hand, there are also pragmatic constraints such as how often you can ask respondents the same questions and expect to get meaningful answers (Beal, 2015). One way we have tried to address this trade-off is to recognize that the different ICE settings are useful for providing different team process insights. Thus, sampling frequency is shaped by both the degree of desired resolution in the data and what can reasonably be accomplished given pragmatic constraints.

For example, our ESM assessments for the Antarctic teams are conducted on a daily basis. More frequent assessments would be desirable, but the participants involved are in real ICE experiences and that is not pragmatically feasible. However, it is also the case that the factors that are likely to play a role in dynamics (e.g., work stress, fatigue, sleep deprivation, bad weather, interpersonal conflict) are likely to align with a daily sample rate, with lagged effects that manifest one or two days later. We have two different longitudinal durations ranging from approximately 45 daily assessments to roughly 270 daily assessments.

In contrast, our ESM assessments in the mission simulations are more frequent, on the order of three times per day. This allows for a more fine-grained examination of process dynamics (albeit under simulated conditions). Here the durations span 21 assessments (seven days) to over 1,000 (one year). Thus, part of the analytic strategy is to look for clusters of similar within person patterns across different settings and durations (Velicer & Molenarr, 2013) as a means to generalize the findings of these largely ideographic methods. If we find patterns that are robust across settings and that manifest across different durations, there will be more confidence that such patterns (e.g., weekly cycles; Beal, 2015) are likely to generalize.

Intensive time series data can be analyzed with a variety of approaches. According to Velicer and Molenarr (2013), the methodology most frequently used in psychology is a class of models labeled autoregressive integrated moving average models (ARIMA; Box & Jenkins, 1976). In OPB, such data are most often analyzed using multilevel or random coefficient modeling (Beal, 2015), although DeShon (2012) suggests that vector autoregressive (VAR) models may be more useful for unpacking the dynamics of multiple time series data. Consistent with Beal's (2015) advice, our general approach is to determine whether the targeted process states of interest are stable or exhibit trends, cycles, or lagged (autoregressive) effects. As this research is in progress, we have not conducted extensive analyses. However, based on the literature, we anticipate observing within day cycles (where the resolution allows it), daily trends, weekly cycles, and daily lags (Beal, 2015).

For example, we collected daily ESM data from 26 participants who wintered-over in the Antarctic for durations that ranged from nine to 15 months (Baard, Kermond, Pearce, Ayton, Chang, & Kozlowski, 2014). Participants rated their daily positive and negative mood, cohesion, conflict, conflict management, and performance. Overall, 2,333 daily measures were completed by the participants. Using the random coefficient modeling, we found that there were reciprocal relationships between daily cohesion and the subsequent day's performance ratings and vice versa, such that prior cohesion was predictive of subsequent performance and prior performance was also predictive of subsequent cohesion, after controlling for the autoregressive effects. Cohesion and performance were self-reinforcing. Reciprocal relationships between positive mood and conflict were also observed, such that prior positive mood predicted lower subsequent conflict and prior conflict predicted lower positive mood in the future, after controlling for the autoregressive effects. Asymmetrical relationships were also observed. In particular, prior positive mood predicted lower subsequent negative mood, but not the other way around. Conflict management was a positive predictor of subsequent cohesion, whereas prior cohesion was not a significant predictor of subsequent conflict management effectiveness.

Badge data constitute much more of a focus on micro-dynamics. Indeed, this is where the small world of one team becomes a very large world of big data. Such data can be scaled (filtered, aggregated) in any number of ways, which opens many interesting prospects for the investigation of team dynamics. We are interested in individual variability over time on the multimodal metrics, and those data (with appropriate filtering and aggregation) can be examined with the same types of analyses applied to ESM data. Moreover, the badges represent novel data that can be examined in novel ways. For example, work in clinical psychology is challenging the notion that psychopathic disorders (e.g., depression) are latent constructs represented by a set of manifest indicators (i.e., symptoms, diagnostic items). Instead, the disorder is conceptualized as a phenomenon that is a complex dynamic system of causally linked symptoms that self-reinforce (Borsboom & Cramer, 2013; Schmittmann, Cramer, Waldrop, Epskamp, Kievit, & Borsboom, 2013; Wichers, 2014). Data-based investigations of this conceptualization make use of network models and, again, intensive time series. This is an intriguing idea, because the concept of team cohesion, divorced from conventional survey assessment and aggregation, can also be considered a phenomenon that is a complex system of causally linked relations.

Consider, for example, a three-member team: Alpha, Bravo, and Charley. Alpha and Bravo have known each other for a long period of time and have many things in common, so they are close socially. Alpha and Charley, however, have very similar educational backgrounds and expertise, so they are close on taskwork. With this simple structure, one can easily imagine how patterns of interaction (i.e., frequency, duration), arousal (i.e., heart rate [HR], HR variability), and stress (i.e., vocal intensity modulation) could be indicative of a phenomenon called team cohesion.

Moreover, it is not difficult to conceptualize how events that are external (i.e., work load and tempo, equipment failures) or internal (i.e., interpersonal conflict) would play out dynamically in the frequency and duration of dyadic interactions, the degree of arousal when in proximity of others, and in the nature of their communications. This is a simple example, but the point is to draw attention to the idea that the dynamic relations among the different manifest indicators are representative of the state of the phenomenon—team cohesion.

There are a variety of candidate analyses that can be applied to such data. A detailed treatment is beyond our remit. However, the network approach described previously (Borsboom & Cramer, 2013) is one promising candidate. Another is the VAR model for handling multivariate time series data (DeShon, 2012). Besides description and forecasting, this approach is also useful for examining the causal impacts of shocks to specific variables in the time series and the effects of those shocks on the other variables in the system. Relational events analysis (REA; Butts, 2008) is another useful approach. It is:

> a highly flexible framework for modeling actions within social settings which permits likelihood-based inference for behavioral mechanisms with complex dependence . . . [and which can examine] base activity levels, recency, persistence, preferential attachment, transitive/cyclic interaction, and participation shifts with the relational event framework (p. 155).

And of course, as part of an inductive-deductive interplay, such data are amenable to a range of machine learning and data mining techniques as a way to identify non-linear patterns arising from the multimodal data that are predictive of effective team functioning.

Team Knowledge Emergence

Research focus and context. A patient visits his or her general physician and complains of pain in the region of the lower back. The pain could be due to a variety of maladies, so the physician schedules a functional magnetic resonance imaging (fMRI) scan. The radiologist reads the fMRI scan and reports. The patient, in consultation with the physician, radiologist, and potentially a surgeon, consider the best course of action to manage the discomfort.

Onboard a US Navy vessel, part of Combined Task Force 150 (a multinational coalition) that is off the Somali coast, messages are being received that report multiple possible sightings of Somali pirates. That information is being combined and coordinated by experts with data from aerial surveillance, radar, and underwater listening devices to decide where to vector the vessel's lone chopper to prevent a hijacking.

In the control room of a nuclear power plant, alarms suddenly trip indicating a cooling problem in the reactor. The control room crew is under time pressure to identify the source of the problem and to take effective action to prevent the power plant from becoming another pejorative term like Three Mile Island, Chernobyl, or Fukushima.

Teams are often used—in medicine, the military, and industry—in mission-critical decision-making situations where professionals with distinctively different expertise have to pull together information about a specific problem, share their knowledge to develop a common understanding, and then apply it to decide where to allocate limited resources to resolve the problem, often under tight time pressure and with high consequences for errors of judgment. The same team decision processes are also common in business organizations, although usually the outcomes are less time pressured and consequential in terms of human life.

Drawing on the human factors literature, Fiore and colleagues (Fiore, Rosen, Smith-Jentsch, Salas, Letsky, & Warner, 2010) describe this form of team collaborative learning and decision making for uncertain, complex, and consequential problems as "macrocognition." However, this conceptualization of team learning as a collective process and teams as information processors who are subject to biases and suboptimal decision making has deep roots in the psychological literature more broadly (see Bell, Kozlowski, & Blawaith, 2012; De Dreu, Nijstad, & van Knippenberg, 2008; Hinsz, Tindale, & Vollrath, 1997; Stasser, 1999; Stasser & Titus, 1985).

Targeted design. This type of distributed team information acquisition and decision making has been widely studied. For example, there are literally thousands of research studies using the "hidden profile" paradigm (Stasser, 1999; Stasser & Titus, 1985) in which decision makers have access to common (shared) information but also unique (privately assessable) information that represents distinctive expertise. A robust finding in this research is that team members spend far more time discussing common information and pay much less attention to unique information. Because the unique information is diagnostic for the optimal decision (the hidden profile), team decisions are typically suboptimal. Also, because teams usually only engage in one decision in such research, there is no feedback and learning. Our interests in this area of inquiry were less focused on the distribution of common and unique information and much more focused on issues relating to team dynamics that heretofore had received virtually no research attention. Those interests centered on how team-level knowledge emerged dynamically from individual learning processes, how it could be measured, and how it could be systematically examined as a longitudinal process.

The approach we developed is innovative in that it couples human research using a synthetic team task in a laboratory setting with virtual experimentation based on a computational model (CM) implemented in an agent-based simulation (ABS; Kozlowski, Chao, Grand, Braun, & Kuljanin, 2013; Kozlowski, Chao, Grand, Braun, & Kuljanin, in press). First, applying the principles of multilevel theory to the model of macrocognition (Fiore et al., 2010), we developed a set of metrics that could capture the dynamic patterns of team knowledge emergence (Kozlowski & Chao, 2012). Second, using the metrics as targeted outcomes to represent patterns of knowledge emergence, we developed a theoretical model of the learning and knowledge sharing mechanisms (Kozlowski et al., in press). This provided the basis for developing the CM of team knowledge emergence. A CM is a precise mathematical or logic-based model that specifies how a dynamic system changes from one time point to the next. The core process mechanisms—the drivers of system dynamics—of the CM were individual learning and knowledge sharing linked to the knowledge emergence metrics. These mechanisms were then instantiated in an ABS. We used the ABS to conduct virtual experiments by manipulating factors that were presumed to influence the process mechanisms of learning and sharing, and then observing the effects on the knowledge emergence metrics. That work provided insights regarding where and why teams developed bottlenecks in the knowledge emergence process. Third, in parallel with the CM and ABS development, we designed a synthetic team task that could be used for human experimentation. For example, in our ABS research, the knowledge emergence metrics were used to identify problematic points where agents plateaued or became bottlenecked. We then used that knowledge to design interventions for human teams that mitigated the bottlenecks, thereby enabling intervention teams to outperform control teams. Long term, the paradigm is designed to use the CM and ABS to conduct basic research. The CM and ABS can explore a meaningful theoretical space and identify interventions and/or process dynamics of interest. The agents do the heavy lifting. Human research, which is much more time and resource intensive, is then used to verify and validate interesting observations (Kozlowski et al., 2013, in press).

We have also embarked on a new research effort that will develop a more complex CM and ABS for studying formal and informal leadership mechanisms, team processes, and team effectiveness for multi-team systems. This new research effort will involve the development of a CM that emulates a broader range of team inputs (e.g., leadership, composition), process mechanisms (e.g., cognition, cohesion), and outcomes (e.g., performance); examines both within and between team interactions; and examines the effects of internal and external shocks on team adaptation and effectiveness. Modeling efforts of this sort generate massive, temporally sensitive data sets (i.e., approximately 22 million for the ABS).

Deduction—induction. This research paradigm explicitly builds in a linkage between inductive and deductive research approaches. For example, our initial research using the CM and ABS allowed us to examine input factors that were expected to influence the process of team knowledge emergence. We manipulated the distribution of common to unique information, agent cognitive ability (i.e., learning rate parameter), and agent extroversion (i.e., sharing rate parameter). We manipulated these factors to get wide variance on the emergence metrics as a means to validate both the CM and the metrics. However, interesting effects that we observed on the patterns of knowledge emergence via the metrics were then used to guide the design of "embedded agents" that were programmed into the human team simulation. Based on the bottlenecks and other anomalies we observed in the agent teams, the embedded agents were triggered when team member behavior fit an anomaly profile. The embedded agents provided dynamic advice or feedback to help improve human information acquisition, knowledge sharing, and decision making (Chao et al., 2013). This was a process of inductive to deductive research.

A similar interplay using modeling is described in research by Kennedy and McComb (2014), who video recorded laboratory teams working on a problem-solving task. They coded communication patterns to identify transition-action phase shifts (Marks et al., 2001). They then conducted virtual experiments to compare the observed lab (human) teams with simulated (agent) teams that received simulated interventions intended to improve communication patterns and simulated (agent) teams with optimal (based on a genetic algorithm) communication patterns. The findings from virtual experimentation were used to theorize about ways in which team communication patterns might be improved via interventions to enhance team effectiveness.

Alignment and analyses. This line of inquiry is really interesting because of its focus, scope, and ability to capture a wide range of process dynamics. The research design focus constitutes a well-defined, bounded context. It is a middle-range problem space that is highly generalizable to a wide range of teams and task contexts. Within that defined context, the amount of fine-grained behavioral data that is generated is astonishing. Moreover, it allows a scaling of the process focus that ranges from very precise micro-dynamics up to more molar, meso-, and macro-level dynamics. Finally, the behavioral data are exceptionally precise. Some might view such a well-defined research setting as too limited. It is a small world, but one with an enormous set of opportunities for inductive theory-building and deductive theory-testing (Kozlowski et al., 2013, in press). It provides a test-bed for investigating the process mechanisms of emergence and team process dynamics across scales that encompass micro, meso, and macro levels.

Consider, for example, the primary process mechanisms of team knowledge emergence—information acquisition or learning and knowledge sharing—that are the focus of the CM and the synthetic task, CRONUS.[10] The task is designed to track each behavioral act for each team member. The onset, execution, and closure of each act are time stamped. Thus, the precise timing, duration, sequencing, tempo, and pattern of acts across team members as they endeavor to extract information from the problem space and convey it to their teammates are coded in the data.[11] In a typical experiment, CRONUS generates approximately 500 million data points that capture the micro-dynamics of team knowledge emergence. The CM also tracks each act, although the world is much simpler for agents. This allows for an examination of the precise micro-dynamics of learning and sharing with respect to team knowledge emergence.

The data can also be scaled up into meaningful micro-meso chunks. For example, human experimentation is generally structured as a series of different but related scenarios (i.e., trials within team) with exposure to a context difference (i.e., between team manipulation). Because the data encode the most elemental of acts, it can be examined to capture the micro-dynamics of learning and sharing within teams, within scenarios. This was the scaling when we used the knowledge emergence metrics to infer from the CM agent (droids) data where human teams (noids) would have difficulties. As shown in Figure 10.4, the graphs compare the proportion of knowledge acquired for exemplar agent (droid) teams on the left, relative to human (noid) teams on the right. The top panes compare droid and noid teams with variable learning rates and cognitive ability. Note the characteristic plateau that denotes a shift from a primary emphasis on learning processes to an emphasis on sharing processes. The plateau is due to the slowest team member holding up the rest of the team. The bottom panes compare droid and noid teams with commensurate learning rates and cognitive ability. Note the absence of the plateau. Instead, the teams progress seamlessly from a primary emphasis on learning processes to sharing processes. Thus, the process mechanisms undergirding the plateaus were used to trigger interventions to advise human teams how to ameliorate the bottlenecks represented by the plateau effect in Figure 10.4. However, one can also scale up to a focus on repeated scenarios, where the focus is on within team trajectory patterns and the between team differences in trajectories over time due to the manipulations (embedded agents, no agents). Such a focus can be analyzed using conventional applications of multilevel random coefficient modeling (Chao et al., 2013).

It is also worth noting that both the CM and CRONUS data are amenable to modeling through the use of most of the analytic techniques discussed in the prior section including relational events analysis, dynamic network analyses, and machine learning and data mining techniques. For example, relational events analysis may be particularly insightful for the temporally precise CRONUS data because of its ability to model event sequences across different actors-receivers, handle complex temporal

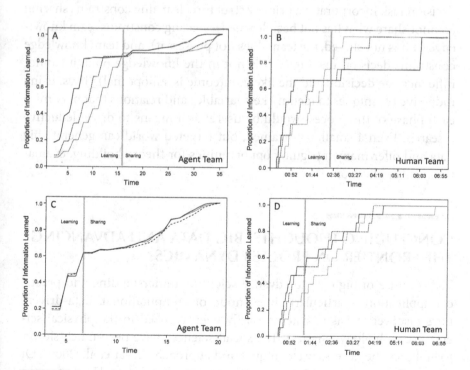

FIGURE 10.4

Comparison of agent (droid) and human (noid) team knowledge acquisition

Reprinted with permission from Kozlowski, Chao, Grand, Braun, & Kuljanin (in press)

dependencies, and provide a basis to estimate parameters and assess uncertainty (Butts, 2008). In addition to conceptualizing team knowledge building as a series of events, one could view the process as a dynamic pattern of exchanges among team member actors. In this conception, actors are nodes and exchanges of information are links or edges. Dynamic network analysis is potentially useful in its ability to detect four types of network changes including stability, evolution, shock, and mutation (McCulloh & Carley, 2009). An examination of stability would be akin to examining trajectories of the process over time and determining to what extent the changes vary between teams. Similarly, one would expect that teams would get better at managing exchanges over time, albeit differentially. The nature of this evolution could be examined. Shocks are external to the team and would represent manipulations that would require adaptation. If the shock prompted an adaptive change in the network, one would capture a mutation. Finally, as part of an inductive-deductive interplay, one could use machine learning and data mining techniques to search for patterns that are predictive of effective learning, sharing, and/or decision making. The decision task incorporates a priority structure: learning constrains sharing (cannot share what has not been learned), sharing constrains team knowledge (if it is not shared, the team does not possess it), and team knowledge constrains decision making (if it is not in the knowledge pool, it cannot influence the decision and the likely outcome is suboptimal). Thus, using inductive techniques to identify key variables and relations that maximize each phase of the process would be useful as a means to drive deductive research. Even a small, constrained, but targeted world can generate big data and offer many intriguing opportunities for theory building, evaluation, and application.

CONCLUDING THOUGHTS: BIG DATA AND ADVANCING THE FRONTIER ON PROCESS DYNAMICS

The promise of big data to advance scientific understanding and practical application—particularly in a mode of computational, data-driven, pure discovery—has to date primarily been realized in the physical sciences (e.g., biology, physics). The social sciences have been much slower to embrace the necessary techniques and approach (Lazar et al., 2009). Of course, there is also the issue of getting access to big data. Until recently, digital traces and other big data relevant to social interactions have been the province of nation states in cyberspace (e.g., China, Russia, the NSA[12]), large international technology firms (e.g., Google, IBM, Yahoo), and the retailer-credit card complex. Indeed, Lazar et al. (2009) warn that:

> Computational social science could easily become the almost exclusive domain of private companies and government agencies. Alternatively, there might emerge a "Dead Seas Scrolls" model, with a privileged set of academic researchers sitting on private data from which they produce papers that cannot be critiqued or replicated. Neither scenario will serve the long-term public interest in the accumulation, verification, and dissemination of knowledge. (p. 2)

However, this is changing, and it is changing rapidly. Lazar et al. (2009) also describe an array of technologies that promise to bring big data to social science research including extensive video recording, digital traces (e.g., email, chat, GPS, and Internet data), and sociometric sensors. The use of deployable, wearable sensors is exploding in the form of applications on smart phones and physical activity monitors. Technologies that seemed far-fetched not so long ago (Goodwin, Velicer, & Intille, 2008) are now an integral part of everyday modern life. There are rapidly emerging and maturing technologies that enable the relatively unobtrusive collection of big data on social interaction phenomena. The future is here!

The advent of multilevel theory and research methods (Kozlowski & Klein, 2000) has had a substantial influence on OPB research, particularly with energizing the widespread interest in linking micro, meso, and macro phenomena. Teams—at the meso level—are at the juncture of major systems forces: the macro context and micro-level of emergent phenomena. There has been an explosion of multilevel research over the last fifteen years, but a large majority of that research has continued to rely on conventional research design and measurement tools. It is largely based on cross-sectional, static designs with measurement mostly using retrospective self-reports of internal traits and states. This has not changed fundamentally for a century. But change is upon us now. The new technologies, tools, and techniques of a computational social science make it possible to directly study team process dynamics and emergent phenomena (Kozlowski & Chao, 2012). Process dynamics are the next frontier for the science of team effectiveness . . . and for multilevel OPB research more broadly.

Our focus in this chapter has been to describe how big data can be harnessed to unpack team dynamics. The data are not big in the sense of world wide web digital traces (which are very big but also very messy). Rather, the big data are intentionally targeted around a focal phenomenon. A typical medical team study we conduct yields approximately

10,000 data points (codes) across 60 teams for a 20- to 30-minute team process and performance scenario, and 20,000 data points when two scenarios are used. The magnitude of the data scales up from there very rapidly. The CM data are another order of magnitude higher. Our initial validation runs for a simple CM generated approximately 22.375 million targeted data points. The coupled human task simulation tracks 133 data points across approximately 3,800 time samples for each person in a typical experimental investigation. That generates approximately 500 million data points (e.g., about 240 teams of three people). The monitoring badges with their multimodal data sampling at high frequencies yield approximately 250 million data points for one HI-SEAS team of six members over a four month scenario, 500 million for eight months, and 750 million over 12 months. Compared to conventional team effectiveness studies conducted in the lab or field, these data sets are several orders of magnitude larger, but precisely targeted. This targeted big data approach holds great promise for unpacking the team process emergence and team dynamics.

The advent of new technologies and the big data they generate will fuel research on this new frontier. They promise to free researchers from the limitations of self-reported survey data as the primary measurement technology. Self-reports will still have utility, of course, but they will not be the primary or only observational method. The new measurement tools promise to be less obtrusive. Video and wearable sensors do not intrude and interfere with an ongoing stream of behavior. ESM is somewhat intrusive, but it is quick. Some tools hold the promise to collect behavior and interaction data at near continuous frequencies. Higher sampling rates mean that micro-process dynamics can be captured and scaled up to any higher-level meaningful aggregate, and the tools hold the promise of being more objective. You can be asked "to what extent" you feel aroused on a one (low) to seven (high) Likert scale, and you may be able to provide a reasonably reliable and valid self-report. But with a heart rate monitor assessing your heart rate and its variability across contexts and interactions, arousal can be established relative to baseline. It's not just a perception.

These tools, and the big data they generate, have much promise for enabling investigators to unpack process dynamics and emergent phenomena. However, challenges remain with respect to targeting research design on meaningful phenomena, balancing deductive and inductive approaches, and aligning research design, measurement, and analysis to enable solid inference. We do not envision a computational social science as a process of collecting big data willy-nilly, throwing it into a blind data mining analysis, and "discovering" new phenomena or relationships. Rather, big data techniques need to be targeted and appropriately harnessed to generate meaningful insights. The purpose of our chapter was to highlight these key research design considerations and to illustrate, using different research examples, ways in which these technologies, tools, and big data techniques can be used to study team process dynamics. We highlight the illustrations in Table 10.1. We hope the insights we shared are useful to other investigators.

Finally, we offer a closing thought. As investigators begin to use these tools and techniques more widely, theory will need to be more explicit about the nature of process dynamics (i.e., what types of dynamics), how processes evolve, and how they vary for particular substantive phenomena of interest. This advance in theoretical precision can only occur with the assistance of inductive methods that improve our descriptive understanding of process dynamics and the mechanisms that drive dynamic phenomena. Theory in OPB is light on process dynamics, and one cannot construct more precise theory without good descriptive data. Moreover, without good theory, one may not be able to make sense of dense, big, observational data sets (e.g., 270 days of ESM data coupled with 270 16-hour days of badge data). The multiple, continuous data streams and the end-of-day measures need to be fused and nonlinearities identified. This will likely necessitate the use of inductive data mining techniques to develop an understanding of the dynamic patterns characterizing phenomena. This sort of induction then needs to be coupled with deductive methods to verify that the inferred patterns are robust and replicate across multiple settings and samples. Big data call for an active interplay between theory building and theory testing—an interplay between induction and deduction.

Notice that in our description above we deliberately used the term "phenomena," rather than constructs. A focus on process dynamics and emergence will force theory to become more principled and system oriented (Kozlowski et al., 2013). Narrow "boxes" (i.e., constructs) and "arrows" (i.e., hypothetical linking mechanisms) models are tractable for making sense of static or very limited "chain-like unidirectional cause-effect relationships" (McGrath et al., 2000, p. 97), but they are not tractable for modeling dynamic phenomena (except over very short time slices). Investigators on the frontier are innovating how they conceptualize, measure, and make sense of dynamic behavioral phenomena. OPB as a field will need to innovate notions of theory, phenomena, and constructs too.

TABLE 10.1

Examples of big data in research on team process dynamics

Research Design and Example	Big Data	Deduction—Induction	Alignment and Analytics
High fidelity simulation Example: emergency medical teams	Coding HD audio and videos on SME validated behaviors related to teamwork and taskwork (medical care)	Deduction: apply OPB team process measurement to medical team context Induction: examine individual behaviors to identify appropriate leadership dimensions	Alignment: HD video provides rich stream of data that can be coded in multiple ways to capture temporal and team processes Analytics: structural equation modeling; regression-based pattern recognition analysis
Experience sampling methods Example: teams in isolated, confined, and extreme environments (NASA)	Physical, physiological, and behavioral data from wearable sensor system	Deduction: workload manipulations may stress quality of team member interactions Induction: data streams may identify new team profiles or non-linear patterns of team interactions	Alignment: intensive longitudinal data may identify team interaction patterns across different contexts and durations Analytics: autoregressive integrated moving average models; latent vector autoregressive models; relational events analysis
Simulation and computational modeling Example: teams learning and sharing information for decision making	Agent-based simulations (droids) allow virtual experiments on thousands of teams. Human teams (noids) operating in a computerized synthetic team task allow data capture at the click level.	Deduction: agents are designed to minimize errors and bottlenecks for human teams based on patterns observed in CM and ABS Induction: patterns of knowledge emergence were observed under different conditions of teammate characteristics	Alignment: team knowledge emergence results from CM and ABS can help design human experimentation. Knowledge emergence is tracked across scenarios within and between teams. Analytics: CM and ABS

NOTES

We gratefully acknowledge our research collaborators: J. Ayton, K. Binsted, S. Biswas, M. T. Braun, R. P. DeShon, J. A. Grand, R. Harvey, J. Karner, and G. Kuljanin.

We gratefully acknowledge our current and former graduate research assistants: S. K. Baard, D. Chatterjee, P. Curran, A. Dixon, S. Golden, J. Huang, C. Kermond, S. Mak, M. Pearce, D. Pickhardt, T. Rench, and J. Santoro.

We gratefully acknowledge the Agency for Health Research and Quality (AHRQ; 1R18HS020295–01, R. Fernandez, Principal Investigator, S. W. J. Kozlowski, Co-investigator and HS022458–01A1, R. Fernandez, Principal Investigator, G. T. Chao, Co-investigator), the Army Research Institute (ARI; W911NF-14-1-0026, S.W.J. Kozlowski and G. T. Chao, Principal Investigators), the National Aeronautics and Space Administration (NASA; NNX09AK47G, NNX12AR15G & NNX13AM77G, S.W.J. Kozlowski, Principal Investigator, S. Biswas and C. -H. Chang, Co-investigators), and the Office of Naval Research (ONR), Command Decision Making (CDM) Program (N00014–09–1–0519, S.W.J. Kozlowski and G. T. Chao, Principal Investigators) for support that, in part, assisted the composition of this chapter. Any opinions, findings, and conclusions or recommendations expressed are those of the authors and do not necessarily reflect the views of AHRQ, ARI, NASA, ONR, or the CDM Program.

1. http://www.nsf.gov/pubs/2014/nsf14543/nsf14543.pdf
2. http://fortune.com/2014/06/30/big-data-dirty-problem/; http://www.nytimes.com/2014/08/18/technology/for-big-data-scientists-hurdle-to-insights-is-janitor-work.html?_r=0
3. Although some scholars draw a sharp distinction between groups and teams as social units, we do not do so in this chapter and treat the units as equivalent for purposes of our discussion.
4. http://www.nasa.gov/exploration/systems/mpcv/#.U_tvKmM0-XM
5. The International Space Station (ISS) is the most realistic analog for long duration space missions, but access for team process data collection is, as one might expect, very limited.
6. http://hd.media.mit.edu/badges/publications.html
7. http://www.sociometricsolutions.com/
8. http://www.cs.waikato.ac.nz/ml/weka/index.html
9. minchu.ee.iisc.ernet.in/new/people/faculty/ . . . /TDMiner-User-Manual.doc
10. Crisis relief operation: naval unit simulation. Cronus is also the Greek god of time.
11. CRONUS also tracks a deliberation and decision-making process, but they are not described here to keep the discussion accessible.
12. http://www.nytimes.com/2011/11/04/world/us-report-accuses-china-and-russia-of-internet-spying.html?_r=0

REFERENCES

Baard, S. K., Braun, M. T., Rench, T. A., Pearce, M., Bo, D., Piolet, Y., . . . & Kozlowski, S. W. J. (2012a). Monitoring team collaboration and cohesion in real-time. Presented at the annual conference for INGRoup, Chicago, IL.

Baard, S. K., Kermond, C., Pearce, M., Ayton, J., Chang, C. -H., & Kozlowski, S. W. J. (2014). Understanding team affect, cohesion and performance dynamics in long duration Antarctic missions. In J. Ayton (Chair), *Human biology and Medicine*. Presented at 2014 Open Science Conference XXXIII SCAR Biennial Meetings, Auckland, New Zealand.

Baard, S. K., Kozlowski, S. W. J., DeShon, R. P., Biswas, S., Braun, M. T., Rench, T. A., . . . & Piolet, Y. (2012b). Assessing team process dynamics: An innovative methodology for team research. Presented at the annual conference for the Society for Industrial and Organizational Psychology, San Diego, CA.

Bales, R. F. (1950). *Interaction process analysis: A method for the study of small groups.* Oxford, England: Addison-Wesley.

Bales, R. F., & Cohen, S. P. (1979). *SYMLOG: A system for the multiple level observation of groups.* New York, NY: Free Press.

Barabási, A. L. (2012). The network takeover. *Nature Physics, 8*(1), 14–16.

Beal, D. J. (2015). ESM 2.0: State of the art and the future potential of experience sampling methods in organizational research. *Annual Review of Organizational Psychology and Behavior, 2,* 383–407.

Bell, B. S., Kozlowski, S. W. J., & Blawath, S. (2012). Team learning: An integration and review. In S. W. J. Kozlowski (Ed.), *The Oxford handbook of organizational psychology* (pp. 859–909). New York, NY: Oxford University Press.

Borsboom, D., & Cramer, A. O. J. (2013). Network analysis: An integrative approach to the structure of psychopathology. *Annual Review of Clinical Psychology, 9,* 91–121.

Box, G. E. P., & Jenkins, G. M. (1976). *Time series analysis: Forecasting and control.* San Francisco, CA: Holden-Day.

Butts, C. T. (2008). A relational event framework for social action. *Sociological Methodology, 38*(1), 155–200.

Chao, G. T., Kozlowski, S. W. J., Grand, J. A., Braun, M. T., Kuljanin, G., Pickhardt, D., & Mak, S. (2013). Macrocognition in teams: Agent-based interventions and emergence of team knowledge. In G. T. Chao & J. R. Rentsch (Chairs), *Building shared knowledge in teams: Shaping macrocognitive processes.* Presented at the annual conference of the Society for Industrial and Organizational Psychology, Houston, TX.

Cronin, M. A., Weingart, L. R., & Todorova, G. (2011). Dynamics in groups: Are we there yet? *The Academy of Management Annals, 5,* 571–612.

Davison, M. L., & Davenport Jr., E. C. (2002). Identifying criterion-related patterns of predictor scores using multiple regression. *Psychological Methods, 7*(4), 468–484.

DeDreu, C. K. W., Nijstad, B. A., & van Knippenberg, D. (2008). Motivated information processing in group judgment and decision making. *Personality and Social Psychology Review, 12*(1), 22–49.

DeShon, R. P. (2012). Multivariate dynamics in organizational science. In S. W. J. Kozlowski (Ed.), *The Oxford handbook of organizational psychology* (Vol. 1, pp. 117–142). New York, NY: Oxford University Press.

Fernandez, R., Pearce, M., Grand, J. A., Rench, T. A., Jones, K., Chao, G. T., & Kozlowski, S. W. J. (2013). Evaluation of a computer-based educational intervention to improve medical emergency teamwork and performance during simulated patient resuscitations. *Critical Care Medicine, 41*(11), 2551–2562.

Fernandez, R., Kozlowski, S. W. J., Shapiro, M., & Salas, E. (2008). Toward a definition of teamwork in emergency medicine. *Academic Emergency Medicine, 15,* 1104–1112.

Fiore, S. M., Rosen, M. A., Smith-Jentsch, K. A., Salas, E., Letsky, M., & Warner, N. (2010). Toward an understanding of macrocognition in teams: Predicting processes in complex collaborative contexts. *Human Factors, 52,* 203–224.

Goodwin, M. S., Velicer, W. F., & Intille, S. S. (2008). Telemetric monitoring in the behavioral sciences. *Behavioral Research Methods, 40,* 328–341.

Grand, J. A., Pearce, M., & Kozlowski, S. W. J. (2013). Investigating the episodic relationship between team processes and performance. In M. R. Kukenberger (Chair), *Modeling and understanding teams as dynamic entities.* Presented at the 73rd Annual Convention of the Academy of Management Association, Orlando, FL.

Grand, J. A., Pearce, M., Rench, T. A., Chao, G. T., Fernandez, R., & Kozlowski, S. W. J. (2013). Going DEEP: Guidelines for building simulation-based team assessments. *BMJ Quality & Safety, 22*(5), 436–448.

Hinsz, V. B., Tindale, R. S., & Vollrath, D. A. (1997). The emerging conceptualization of groups as information processors. *Psychological Bulletin, 121*, 43–64.

Iida, M., Shrout, P. E., Laurenceau, J. P., & Bolger, N. (2012). Using diary methods in psychological research. In H. Cooper, P. M. Camic, D. L. Long, A. T. Panter, D. Rindskopf & K. J. Sher (Eds.), *APA handbook of research methods in psychology, Vol. 1: Foundations, planning, measures, and psychometrics* (pp. 277–305). Washington, DC: American Psychological Association.

Ilgen, D. R., Hollenbeck, J. R., Johnson, M., & Jundt, D. (2005). Teams in organizations: From input-process-output models to IMOI models. *Annual Review of Psychology, 56*, 517–543.

Kennedy, D. M., & McComb, S. A. (2014). When teams shift among processes: Insights from simulation and optimization. *Journal of Applied Psychology, 99*, 784–815.

Klein, K. J., Ziegert, J. C., Knight, A. P., & Xiao, Y. (2007). Dynamic delegation: Shared, hierarchical, and deindividualized leadership in extreme action teams. *Administrative Science Quarterly, 51*, 590–621.

Kozlowski, S. W. J. (2012). Groups and teams in organizations: Studying the multilevel dynamics of emergence. In A. B. Hollingshead & M. S. Poole (Eds.), *Research methods for studying groups and teams: A guide to approaches, tools, and technologies* (pp. 260–283). New York, NY: Routledge.

Kozlowski, S. W. J. (in press). Advancing research on team process dynamics: Theoretical, methodological, and measurement considerations. *Organizational Psychology Review.*

Kozlowski, S. W. J., & Bell, B. S. (2003). Work groups and teams in organizations. In W. C. Borman, D. R. Ilgen & R. J. Klimoski (Eds.), *Handbook of psychology: Industrial and organizational psychology* (Vol. 12, pp. 333–375). London, England: Wiley.

Kozlowski, S. W. J., & Bell, B. S. (2013). Work groups and teams in organizations: Review update. In N. Schmitt & S. Highhouse (Eds.), *Handbook of psychology: Industrial and organizational psychology* (Vol. 12, 2nd ed., pp. 412–469). London, England: Wiley.

Kozlowski, S. W. J. & Chao, G. T. (2012). The dynamics of emergence: Cognition and cohesion in work teams. *Managerial and Decision Economics, 33*, 335–354.

Kozlowski, S. W. J., Chao, G. T., Grand, J. A., Braun, M. T., & Kuljanin, G. (2013). Advancing multilevel research design: Capturing the dynamics of emergence. *Organizational Research Methods, 16*(4), 581–615.

Kozlowski, S. W. J., Chao, G. T., Grand, J. A., Braun, M. T., & Kuljanin, G. (in press). Capturing the multilevel dynamics of emergence: Computational modeling, simulation, and virtual experimentation. *Organizational Psychology Review.*

Kozlowski, S. W. J., Gully, S. M., McHugh, P. P., Salas, E., & Cannon-Bowers, J. A. (1996). A dynamic theory of leadership and team effectiveness: Developmental and task contingent leader roles. In G. R. Ferris (Ed.), *Research in personnel and human resource management* (Vol. 14, pp. 253–305). Greenwich, CT: JAI Press.

Kozlowski, S. W. J., Gully, S. M., Nason, E. R., & Smith, E. M. (1999). Developing adaptive teams: A theory of compilation and performance across levels and time. In D. R. Ilgen & E. D. Pulakos (Eds.), *The changing nature of work performance: Implications for staffing, personnel actions, and development* (pp. 240–292). San Francisco, CA: Jossey-Bass.

Kozlowski, S. W. J., & Ilgen, D. R. (2006). Enhancing the effectiveness of work groups and teams. *Psychological Science in the Public Interest, 7*, 77–124.

Kozlowski, S. W. J., & Klein, K. J. (2000). A multilevel approach to theory and research in organizations: Contextual, temporal, and emergent processes. In K. J. Klein & S. W. J. Kozlowski (Eds.), *Multilevel theory, research and methods in organizations: Foundations, extensions, and new directions* (pp. 3–90). San Francisco, CA: Jossey-Bass.

Lazer, D., Pentland, A., Adamic, L., Aral, S., Barabási, A. L., Brewer, D., . . . & Van Alstyne, M. (2009). Life in the network: The coming age of computational social science. *Science, 323*(5915), 721–723.

Levine, J. M., & Moreland, R. L. (1990). Progress in small group research. *Annual Review of Psychology, 41*, 585–634.

Lewin, K. (1951) *Field theory in social science; selected theoretical papers*. D. Cartwright (Ed.). New York, NY: Harper & Row.

Marks, M. A., Mathieu, J. E., & Zaccaro, S. J. (2001). A temporally based framework and taxonomy of team processes. *Academy of Management Review, 26*, 356–376.

Mathieu, J. E., Maynard, M. T., Rapp, T., & Gilson, L. (2008). Team effectiveness 1997–2007: A review of recent advancements and a glimpse into the future. *Journal of Management, 34*, 410–476.

McCulloh, I., & Carley, K. M. (2009). Longitudinal dynamic network analysis: Using the over time viewer feature in ORA. *Carnegie Mellon University, School of Computer Science, Institute for Software Research, Technical Report CMU-ISR-09-115*.

McGrath, J. E. (1964). *Social psychology: A brief introduction*. New York, NY: Holt, Rinehart, & Winston.

McGrath, J. E., Arrow, H., & Berdahl, J. L. (2000). The study of groups: Past, present, and future. *Personality and Social Psychology Review, 4*(1), 95–105.

Olguin, D. O., Gloor, P. A., & Pentland, A. (2009, March). *Capturing individual and group behavior with wearable sensors. Proceedings at the AAAI Spring Symposium on Human Behavior Modeling*. Stanford, CA: AAAI Press.

Olguin, D. O., Waber, B. N., Kim, T., Mohan, A., Ara, K., & Pentland, A. (2009). Sensible organizations: Technology and methodology for automatically measuring organizational behavior. *IEEE Transactions on Systems, Man, and Cybernetics-Part B: Cybernetics, 39* (1), 43–55

Quwaider, M., & Biswas, S. (2010). *Wireless body area networks: A framework of network-integrated sensing and energy-aware protocols for resource-constrained applications in wireless body area networks*. Saarbrucken, Germany: VDM Verlag.

Salas, E., Stagl, K. C., & Burke, C. S. (2004). 25 years of team effectiveness in organizations: Research themes and emerging needs. *International Review of Industrial and Organizational Psychology, 19*, 47–91.

Schmittman, V. D., Cramer, A. O. J., Waldorp, L. J., Epskamp, S., Kievit, R. A., & Borsboom, D. (2013). Deconstructing the construct: A network perspective on psychological phenomena. *New Ideas in Psychology, 31*, 43–53.

Stasser, G. (1999). The uncertain role of unshared information in collective choice. In J. Levine & D. Messick (Eds.), *Shared cognition in organizations* (pp. 49–69). Mahwah, NJ: Lawrence Erlbaum.

Stasser, G., & Titus, W. (1985). Pooling of unshared information in group decision making: Biased information sampling during discussion. *Journal of Personality and Social Psychology, 48*, 1467–1478. Velicer, W. F., & Molenaar, P. C. (2013). Time series analysis for psychological research. In I. B. Weiner, J. A. Schinka & W. F. Velicer (Eds.), *Handbook of psychology, volume 2: Research methods in psychology* (2nd ed., pp. 628–660). Hoboken, NJ: John Wiley & Sons.

Weick, K. E., Sutcliffe, K. M., & Obstfeld, D. (1999). Organizing for high reliability: Processes of collective mindfulness. In R. S. Sutton & B. M. Staw (Eds.), *Research in organizational behavior* (pp. 81–123). Greenwich, CT: JAI Press.

Wichers, M. (2014). The dynamic nature of depression: A new micro-level perspective of mental disorder that meets current challenges. *Psychological Medicine, 44,* 1349–1360.

11

Using Big Data to Create Diversity and Inclusion in Organizations

Whitney Botsford Morgan, Eric Dunleavy, and
Peter D. DeVries

Big data affords organizations the capability to analyze every transaction, exchange, click, and movement, creating new possibilities for organizing, evaluating, and, ultimately, adding insight to pressing organizational challenges. The primary goal of big data analytics is to help companies make better business decisions by enabling users to analyze huge volumes of transaction data as well as other data sources that may be left untapped by conventional business intelligence programs (Rouse, 2012). Big data analytics is the process of examining large amounts of data of a variety of types to uncover hidden patterns, unknown correlations and other useful information. Such information can provide competitive advantages over rival organizations and result in business benefits.

Demand has also grown significantly for data scientists who can not only write software and manage data, but also find a story in the data and effectively communicate that insight (Davenport & Patil, 2012). Others have echoed this sentiment in blogs and online forums with specific focus on how big data can have a social impact (see Harvard Business Review's *Blog Network* and Skoll World Forum's *Up For Debate*). For example, Mr. Jim Fruchterman (2013), President and CEO of Benetech, stated that he believes big data "could help provide a pathway to maximize our human potential, instead of maximizing profits." This is precisely where we suggest industrial-organizational psychologists, in collaboration with data scientists, may add value. Regardless of area of expertise, the fundamental purpose of an industrial-organizational psychologist is to maximize human performance. We hope the following ideas will inspire collaboration among organizational researchers and practitioners to identify methods for discovering data-driven insights that move organizations closer to supporting diversity and inclusion.

Diversity and inclusion are two sides of the same coin. Diversity pertains to the representation of people from different ethnic, gender, religious, sexual orientation, socioeconomic, and parental status groups. Inclusion means that we create work environments where all are welcome (Thomas & Ely, 1996) and unique individuals feel a sense of belongingness (Shore et al., 2011). Whereas efforts around diversity focus on equal employment opportunities, Ferdman (2014) proposed that "inclusion is a *practice*—an interacting set of structures, values, norms, group and organizational climates, and individual and collective behaviors, all connected with inclusion experiences in a mutually reinforcing and dynamic system" (p. 16).

Big data may offer insights on such complex practices that are characteristic of inclusion, involving both individual experiences and patterns of behavior, as well as organizational structures and processes. We propose big data may aid in building both diversity (i.e., equal employment opportunities) and inclusion in organizations, as it provides organizations with new ways to capture and analyze unstructured, dynamic data from a variety of sources that may inform and redress incidents and systems of injustice that challenge the complete integration of diverse social identity groups into the fabric of organizations.

The chapter first presents the rationale for why characteristics that describe big data may be ideal for identifying both formal and informal forms of discrimination and answering unexplored questions related to diversity and inclusion. Second, we discuss EEO issues that may arise in big data scenarios. Third, we identify current inclusion challenges and discuss how existing practices related to big data could be adapted or translated to develop and maintain diverse talent at various stages in the career pipeline. Specifically, we offer possibilities for leveraging big data to create inclusive (1) recruitment practices, (2) interpersonal behaviors, (3) leadership practices, and (4) organizational practices. Finally, we discuss how big data may inform the scientific study of diversity and inclusion.

WHY BIG DATA MAY SUPPORT DIVERSITY AND INCLUSION

Data are now being generated and collected in a growing number of ways. Use of traditional transactional databases has been supplemented by multimedia content, social media, and myriad types of sensors (Manyika et al., 2011). Advances in information technology allow users to capture, communicate, aggregate, store, and analyze enormous pools of data, known as big data (Manyika et al., 2011). Data have been aggregating in every industry and business function and are now an important factor of production, alongside labor and capital (Manyika et al., 2011). We suggest that big data may provide organizations with strategic advantage in the increasingly competitive environment, especially considering the demographic shifts of the contemporary workforce, which has been labeled the war for talent (Michaels, Handfield-Jones, & Axelrod, 2001). Specifically, we propose that big data may be useful in building diverse and inclusive organizations because it uses (1) a variety of available resources, (2) large volumes of data, and (3) velocity when analyzing that may inform organizational initiatives.

Variety

First, there are three main classifications when describing the variety of big data: (1) structured data, (2) semi-structured data, and (3) unstructured. Structured data are formatted to allow storage, use, and generation of information (Coronel, Morris, & Rob, 2013). Traditional transactional databases store structured data (Manyika et al., 2011). Semi-structured data have been processed to some extent (Coronel, Morris, & Rob, 2013). XML or HTML tagged text are examples of semi-structured data (Manyika et al., 2011). Unstructured data are data in the format in which they were collected; no formatting is used (Coronel, Morris, & Rob, 2013). Some examples of unstructured data are PDFs, emails, and documents (Baltzan, 2012). Some people exclusively associate big data and big data analytics with unstructured data of that sort, but consulting firms like Gartner, Inc. and Forrester Research, Inc. also consider transactions and other structured data to be valid forms of big data (Rouse, 2012). Given that a voluminous amount of varied data is available, business executives with traditional database management systems need to broaden their data horizons to include collection, storage, and processing of unstructured and semi-structured data (Purcell, 2013).

Big data analytics may be good for analyzing semi-structured or unstructured data that describe diversity and inclusion challenges because such communications often contain subtle biases that are captured in less structured forms such as emails, sound clips, texts, blogs, Web 2.0 content, and click streams. Given that big data affords the possibility to monitor a variety of data sources—structured, semi-structured, and unstructured—it provides a way for organizations to combine and make sense of patterns that lie in a variety of sources when examined in combination with one another. Chen, Chiang, and Storey (2012) discuss how analysis of varied data (e.g., sensor content, customer transactions, search logs) can lead to big impact in a range of fields (e.g., government, health, science and technology, security). For example, content and text analysis combined with social network analysis can lead to improved transparency, participation, and equity in the government. Thus, it is the variety of data sources that likely provides organizations with information that allows them to uncover new patterns among the data and insight that may support or guide practices that increase diversity and build inclusion. Indeed, this may be particularly important in the context of diversity given that the employment life cycle involves a host of diverse decisions like hiring, promotion, termination, and various pay outcomes that are housed in separate databases that do not necessarily communicate with each other.

Volume

Second, big data analytics allow researchers and practitioners to analyze large volumes of data that may aid in building diverse and inclusive organizations. The data that organizations have traditionally collected, or had access to, only allowed for a snapshot of what was occurring on daily basis, forcing organizational practitioners and researchers to make judgments from a sample or examples, and undoubtedly missing information. A major advantage of big data analytics is that all data are analyzed; not just a sample.

Specific to the case of *diversity*, many personnel decision systems designed to improve work outcomes also result in substantial differences in employment outcomes across racial, ethnic, and gender groups. These statistical disparities are often referred to as adverse impact. Adverse impact statistics can serve as evidence in employment discrimination cases, establish diversity goals, and assess affirmative action programs. These EEO analytics—and more generally, inferences from statistical significance tests—take on new meaning in the world of big data. To the extent that big data sources involve actual populations rather than samples, traditional methods of detecting adverse impact and increasing diversity may be much less useful.

Specific to the focus on *inclusion*, big data approaches allow organizations to collect large volumes of robust information (e.g., conversation patterns, interaction time, and social networks through email correspondence), making it more likely to recognize patterns among the entire population of data points. For example, the health and medical field is using information from electronic medical records and similarities across patients to develop risk profiles that will guide proactive management of patients or build interventions, ultimately leading to a personalized approach to healthcare (Chawla & Davis, 2013). Such an approach may be advantageous for organizations when trying to identify subtle prejudices and unintended personal bias. For example, the lens of big data could be helpful in monitoring large volumes of employee interactions that may reveal pockets of exclusion or lack of inclusion and identify problems before they arise in the workplace. Based on this data, norms could be established for employees, and those falling below could be targeted for intervention before productivity suffers or turnover occurs. Thus, the analysis of large volumes of data may uncover pockets of subtle discrimination that may reveal patterns or relationships that provide new insights on theories of social identity, stigma, or discrimination, or inform organizational action.

Velocity

Finally, big data analytics allow researchers and practitioners to analyze the large volumes of varied data with great velocity—often real-time—which may assist in an organization's ability to respond to change or trigger proactive behaviors that may prevent the need for large-scale change. The characteristic of velocity provides organizations with a means to "develop continuous processes for gathering, analyzing, and interpreting data" (Davenport, Barth, & Bean, 2012). This is typically thought of as most helpful to organizations that are looking to remain ahead of competitors. An example discussed by McAfee (2012) is that MIT Media Lab used location data on mobile phones to determine how many customers were in a Macy's parking lot on Black Friday to predict the retailer's sales. Related to diversity, continuous monitoring of employment patterns may enable quicker detection of potential disparities before they actually occur. Related to inclusion, perhaps monitoring work teams' conversation length or the proportion of time individuals spend talking may inform organizations about the effectiveness of team creativity or decision-making. The velocity of data may also be useful to organizations seeking to optimize in-the-moment activities that may facilitate automatic or just-in-time decisions. This may be particularly helpful for organizations seeking to respond to "minor" incidents of exclusion or interpersonal discrimination (i.e., negative facial expressions) that often may accumulate to create major issues. Velocity, or the speed in which data are generated and analyzed, may provide organizations a competitive advantage, particularly when applied to building a diverse and inclusive workforce.

In sum, drawing upon its variety, volume, and velocity, big data allow for more robust analyses, which may lead to evidence-based interventions targeted at improving diversity and inclusion. Thus, through big data's variety, volume, and velocity, the organization can use predictive data analytics to save organizational resources and, ultimately, build inclusion for diverse employees.

UNDERSTANDING EEO ANALYTICS THROUGH THE LENS OF BIG DATA

In this section, we first describe the basic EEO landscape with particular emphasis on enforcement agencies and laws of interest. We then focus on basic adverse impact measurement, with particular focus on statistical significance testing and practical significance measurement. We next note the importance of data aggregation decisions in adverse impact measurement, particularly given big data scenarios. We conclude with some basic recommendations for the EEO analyst conducting research in the context of big data.

Introduction to the EEO Context

Adverse impact generally refers to disparities in employment decision rates between groups. These disparities may be of interest regardless of whether alleged discrimination is intentional or unintentional. Disparate treatment refers to intentional discrimination, and the typical allegation is that protected group status was used to make employment decisions. When intentional discrimination is alleged against a class of potential victims, disparities between favored and disfavored groups may be an important part of the evidence. This form of discrimination, called a pattern or practice, often involves unstructured and discretionary employment policies or practices. This form of discrimination is described in Title VII and was featured in the Supreme Court cases *International Teamsters v. U.S.* (1977) and *Hazelwood v. U.S.* (1977). For a more detailed review, please refer to Gutman, Koppes, and Vodvanovich (2010).

Unintentional discrimination, or disparate impact theory, was developed by the Supreme Court through rulings in *Griggs v. Duke Power* (1971) and *Albemarle Paper Co. v. Moody* (1975), and was refined in the

Civil Rights Act of 1991. The research question is usually whether facially neutral selection criteria disproportionately exclude higher percentages of one protected group relative to another. The identification of meaningful adverse impact does not necessarily imply illegal discrimination. In this scenario the use of a selection procedure with adverse impact may be justifiable if the employer can show that the procedure is job-related (i.e., valid), and the plaintiff cannot show that there are alternative selection procedures that are as valid but produce less adverse impact.

Impact analyses of employment decision outcomes are particularly useful to employers covered by laws and regulations administered by the Equal Employment Opportunity Commission (EEOC), the Office of Federal Contract Compliance Programs (OFCCP), and the Department of Justice (DOJ). These federal agencies are responsible for enforcing Title VII of the CRA, Executive Order (EO) 11246, and other statutes and regulations related to employment discrimination.

The EEOC is empowered by Title VII to evaluate claims of employment discrimination before a formal discrimination lawsuit is filed. Their investigations are reactive in the sense that they are conducted in response to a specific allegation. The DOJ generally specializes in Title VII enforcement for public entities and high profile cases that have led to complex litigation, and may partner with other agencies on a variety of issues. The OFCCP enforces EO 11246, which requires that federal contractors develop affirmative action plans to identify underrepresentation of women and racial and ethnic minorities in the workforce and provide equal employment opportunity in hiring, promotion, termination, and pay. Their investigations are proactive in the sense that they are audit-based and conducted without an allegation of discrimination. Analyses of adverse impact associated with employment decisions may be of interest to any of the three agencies depending on context.

Adverse Impact Measurement

As described by Dunleavy, Morris, and Howard (in press), statistical significance tests like the two sample Z test and Fisher's exact test are one way to measure adverse impact. In recent years, this method has become preferred by some courts (Esson & Hauenstein, 2006) and by federal agencies (Cohen & Dunleavy, 2009; 2010). Statistical significance tests use probability theory to evaluate the possibility that an observed difference in employment outcomes occurred due to chance. If chance is an unlikely explanation, then the difference is considered statistically significant. This framework is well established in the social scientific realm, and the criteria for identifying a statistically significant difference is generally similar across both social science and EEO contexts. In the legal realm, this standard was first endorsed in *Castaneda v. Partida* (1977), a jury selection case, and was later applied in in *Hazelwood v. US*, where the Supreme Court defined a significant result as one exceeding "two or three standard deviations." Using the lower bound of two, this standard is similar to the social scientific standard of using a two-tailed test and an alpha level of 0.05, which corresponds to about 1.96 standard errors.

The appeal of statistical significance tests is intuitive in that it assesses whether results could be due to chance and provides a "yes-or-no" outcome. However, statistical significance is not the only approach available to measure adverse impact, answers a narrow question, and does not directly assess the size of a difference.

Concerns about over-reliance on statistical significance tests have recently been described elsewhere (see Dunleavy, Morris, & Howard, in press; Dunleavy & Gutman, 2011; Jacobs, Murphy & Silva, 2012; Murphy & Jacobs, 2012), and in practice guidance (see Cohen, Aamodt & Dunleavy, 2010). Interestingly, the scholarly literature has often noted the limitations of statistical significance testing in small-sample scenarios (see Collins & Morris, 2008). However, researchers have only recently considered the limitations of statistical significance testing in large-sample scenarios (see Jacobs, Murphy, & Silva, 2012; Murphy & Jacobs, 2012). This contemporary research has demonstrated a long known fact, but one that has become more apparent in the era of big data: as sample size increases, any non-zero difference will become statistically significant eventually as a function of increasing sample size. Jacobs et al. (2012) frame this phenomenon as "being big is worse than being bad."

These criticisms are not new (see Cohen, 1994), and neither are endorsements of considering the magnitude of a finding in addition to statistical significance (see Kirk, 1996). Practically speaking, in some large-sample cases, statistical significance tests do not need to be computed; it would be shocking to find non-significant results regardless of the size of a difference. Dunleavy et al. (in press) demonstrated a scenario where a one percent difference in selection rates in an almost entirely inclusive selection system produces statistically significant results with an applicant pool of 2,400 individuals. In this scenario, the measures of magnitude lead to a different conclusion than the significance test results.

Assessing the size of variables relations involved in research is well-accepted in the area of industrial-organizational psychology. For example, in the 2010 publication manual of the American Psychological Association, a failure to report effect sizes (as practical significance measures) is considered a defect in the reporting of research:

> No approach to probability value directly reflects the magnitude of an effect or the strength of a relation. For the reader to fully understand the importance of your findings, it is almost always necessary to include some index of effect size or strength of relation in your Results section.

Additionally, the *Journal of Applied Psychology* requires authors to: "...indicate in the results section of the manuscript the complete outcome of statistical tests including significance levels, some index of effect size or strength of relation, and confidence intervals" (Zedeck, 2002, p. 141).

These guidelines essentially treat statistical significance as an initial standard to meet, followed by a consideration of the size of the variable relation of interest. A detailed review of practical significance is outside the scope of this chapter. The basic notion is that meaningful variable relationships are more useful than trivial non-zero relationships, regardless of whether they are statistically significant. This notion was recently endorsed in the adverse impact measurement context, where a technical advisory committee on adverse impact analyses (Cohen et al., 2010) noted that practical significance is an important addition to statistical significance in the consideration of potential adverse impact. For a detailed review of effect sizes as measures of practical significance and other considerations, refer to Dunleavy et al. (in press).

A Note on Data Aggregation

One other issue related to big data and properly modeling EEO analytics concerns data aggregation. Morris and Lobsenz (2000) demonstrated that when sample size is small, all tests for statistical significance have a low likelihood of finding a significant difference when differences exist. One potential response to this is to combine data across strata such as job, location, time period, etc., in order to increase the sample size. Combining data across strata will intuitively provide a larger sample size and increase the likelihood of finding a difference should it exist.

While the appeal of larger sample sizes is obvious from a statistical power perspective, care must be taken to properly account for systematic differences across data sets. If multiple strata are simply pooled together to form a larger data set, analyses may not mirror the reality of the system being analyzed, and a type of bias known as Simpson's Paradox can occur. Simpson's Paradox can occur when selection rates vary across samples and there is considerable variability in the size of those samples. Pooling strata together into a single analysis can ignore potentially meaningful differences from strata to strata, and thus can produce misleading results. Dunleavy et al. (in press) note an example of this.

It is important to operationalize the research questions being asked and consider whether those questions require some form of aggregation or disaggregation. In addition, there are more complex statistical approaches that evaluate disparities by strata to produce weighted results. These tests, which Dunleavy et al. (in press) broadly refer to as "multiple events tests," evaluate the degree of adverse impact within each strata and then combine these into an overall test statistic and associated effect size. Perhaps the most commonly used multiple events test is the Mantel-Haenszel statistical significance test (Mantel & Haenszel, 1959).

A separate and related question relates to whether results are similar across strata. As an example, a scenario where the highest selected group varies from strata to strata (e.g., men are highest selected in one year, and women are highest selected in another year) may be meaningfully different from a scenario where the highest selected group is always the same (e.g., men are highest selected in every year). If results are similar across strata, aggregation may be reasonable. Conversely, if results vary substantially by strata, it may be difficult to aggregate strata together and ignore existing differences.

In this context, the Breslow-Day statistical significance test (Breslow & Day, 1980) may be useful, as it assesses whether results vary by strata more than what would be expected due to chance. If results vary, assessing results at different strata is likely reasonable. As such, Biddle (2012) and others generally recommend that adverse impact is first assessed for similarity by strata using the Breslow-Day or a similar test, and if patterns are similar, the Mantel-Haenszel or a similar test can be used to assess the overall degree of adverse impact.

A Concluding Note on EEO Analytics in the Context of Big Data

As this section demonstrates, adverse impact analyses are often complex, particularly given the complexities of big data scenarios. We urge the EEO analyst to take away four messages from this section of the chapter. First, it is critical to consider theory to define and approach research questions and to use analytical approaches that mirror reality. Conceptual considerations can also be supplemented by empirical methods informing on a variety of topics.

Second, statistical significance testing may be limited in usefulness when big data essentially ensure significant results. Third, practical significance and the size of a difference between two groups should be evaluated as a separate and important criterion when a statistically significant disparity has been identified. Lastly, data aggregation and unit of analysis issues are often complex and should be considered in evaluating the usefulness of EEO analyses.

BUILDING INCLUSION THROUGH THE LENS OF BIG DATA

The following four sections discuss how big data may be used to build inclusion at various stages in the career pipeline. Specifically, we offer ideas for using big data to (1) develop recruitment practices that attract diverse individuals to organizations, (2) promote positive interpersonal interactions among employees, (3) encourage equitable approaches to leader development, and (4) create systematic organizational practices that seek to build inclusive organizations.

Inclusive Recruitment Practices

Contemporary organizations that seek to be competitive in today's environment likely have a recruiting strategy in order to enhance the diversity of the applicant pool (Kalev, Dobbin, & Kelly, 2006). Despite intentional approaches to increasing diversity in the workforce, recruiters may inadvertently and systematically discourage potential applicants due to their own unconscious biases. We propose that big data may afford new opportunity to attract diverse individuals to organizations that do not rely on recruiters actively pursuing candidates and possibly enacting their unconscious biases. Specifically, the following section discusses ideas for how big data may be used to (1) identify untapped potential talent for the pool, (2) specify individuals that should be targeted, and (3) develop advertisements that directly appeal to individuals from diverse (i.e., visible and invisible) backgrounds.

First, we propose that organizations may leverage big data to identify untapped potential markets. Many software (e.g., Google, Microsoft) and social media (e.g., Facebook) companies have well-established internet advertising networks where potential advertisers can submit ads to be shown to online users. The ad networks analyze information about which web pages users visit and which ads they click on (while ignoring personally identifiable information) in order to infer demographic information about a user, such as their age range and gender. For example, for those of you who have a Gmail account, you can view Google's estimates of your age range and gender in their ads preferences manager (www.google.com/ads/preferences). This demographic information is then used to serve ads that are relevant to users. Extending this existing practice to recruitment practices, we propose organizations may use a similar digital data approach (e.g., Kumar et al., 2013) to infer information about a user. For example, the digital footprint may allow organizations to infer personal characteristics about users such as parental status, sexual orientation, marital status, socioeconomic status, education, religious affiliation, or even hobbies. By capturing and examining the range of personal characteristics of users, organizations may then discover unexpected interest from new population(s), creating opportunity to identify an untapped potential talent pool. Big data allow for a proactive and ongoing approach to sourcing that may lead to attracting new, diverse individuals to the talent and, ultimately, applicant pool.

Second, once a new potential talent pool is identified, organizations may then specify the types of individuals that should be targeted either through advertising or other recruitment efforts. Targeted advertising is extremely successful: a Network Advertising Initiative study showed that users are 2.43 times more likely to buy a product or service from targeted ads than from randomly-shown ads (Beales, 2010). Extending this notion to recruitment, ads that are served to targeted individuals or types of individuals are more likely to generate interest in an organization than ads served to random, or untargeted, individuals. Research also suggests that there are two cues in recruitment ads that are effective with diverse populations: pictorial diversity and equal employment opportunity statements (see Avery & McKay, 2006). Therefore, through targeted pictorial or opportunity statement advertising, organizations have the possibility to attract new, and potentially diverse, individuals to their organization that otherwise may not have been targeted through traditional advertising efforts. For example, if an organization identified the LGBT community as an untapped potential talent pool, it could target its recruitment ads to include statements about resources (e.g., LGBT employee resource groups) or pictorial displays (e.g., ally or rainbow flag) that attract this population to join the applicant pool. Given that social media has come to the forefront of marketing campaigns, with 85 percent of marketers marketing on social network websites (Rogers & Sexton, 2012), this outlet could be ripe for organizations to explore serving targeted ads to newly identified populations that may, ultimately, increase the diversity of an organization's applicant pool.

Finally, current practice could be expanded to estimate further information on visible (e.g., ethnicity) and invisible (e.g., parental status) characteristics of users that could ultimately increase an organization's minority applicant pool. The effectiveness of the proposed targeted recruitment strategy could be enhanced by integrating equal employment opportunity statement information into the ad (e.g., word choice, images, information on diversity awards) that projects diversity or an organization's commitment to diversity (Avery & McKay, 2006; Born & Taris, 2010). For example, if an organization seeks to increase the number of mothers in the applicant pool, big data could afford organizations the capability not only to purchase ad space that is targeted towards this demographic group, but also to tailor the ads to include pictorial cues (e.g., woman dressed in business suit pushing a stroller) or factual statements about offerings or practices (e.g., on-site daycare) that would attract the population of interest to the organization. Given the success of targeted advertising, we believe there is both business promise and social value in expanding current uses of big data beyond age range and gender to attract individuals with visible and invisible characteristics of diversity to organizations.

Inclusive Interpersonal Behaviors

Creating a sense of belongingness for all unique individuals is extraordinarily challenging, in part because of naturally occurring in-groups and out-groups that develop over time in organizations. We are initially drawn to people who we perceive to be like us, and then share interactions and experiences that reinforce such liking, leading individuals within organizations to self-segregate (Tatum, 2003). Key elements of inclusive behavior include seeking out multiple perspectives and noticing when exclusion occurs. However, individuals may not possess the emotional intelligence to recognize these self-segregating trends or exert the extra effort required to intervene and interact with diverse individuals. We suggest that big data may (1) streamline an organization's ability to identify in-groups and out-groups and (2) assist in creating a culture of interaction among diverse individuals and identified in-groups and out-groups.

First, we propose that organizations may use big data to identify naturally occurring in-groups and out-groups that may serve as a barrier to inclusive cultures. Organizations could develop or adapt existing software that examines logs of email or instant messaging to determine social

networks, which provide visualizations or maps of the patterning of relationships within organizations (Tichy, Tushman, & Fombrun, 1979). Significant computer science research has been conducted in this area (see De
Choudhury, Hofman, Mason, & Watts, 2010). Social networks may include
both formal (i.e., work team or communication network) and informal
(i.e., regular lunch group or friendship network) relationships that vary in
terms of centrality (i.e., extent to which there is power, control, or access;
Brass, 1984, 1985) and density (i.e., extent to which there is close-knit relations or communication; Ahuja, 2000). Privacy concerns notwithstanding,
it is common practice for organizations to monitor and log all employees'
internet activity as well as electronic communications (e.g., email, instant
messaging) while using company property. This is usually done in an effort
to maintain information security as well as identify content that may inap-
propriately represent the organization (e.g., curse words). In fact, a study
showed that more than 40 percent of companies have deployed some form
of automatic email monitoring software, with that number expected to
continue to rise (Proofpoint, 2009).

At a medium- or large-size organization, one could examine social networks within departments to understand who interacts with whom, the
reason for the interaction (e.g., friendship, communication, advice, affect),
and the centrality and the density of the network. The resulting visualizations could integrate existing data on employment characteristics (e.g.,
ethnicity, gender, age) to determine frequency and nature of interactions
among visibly diverse individuals. The layering of employment characteristics on to these visualizations may then be used to, for example, identify who has the most (and least) frequent exchanges with individuals in
a formal network, detect cliques (i.e., groups of people who largely communicate only within their friendship network), determine the centrality
of networks comprised largely of minorities or diverse individuals, and
understand the density of homogeneous versus heterogeneous formal networks. Similarly, organizations that use video recordings in public spaces
(e.g., hallways, lounges) could use microexpression analysis to analyze
employees' facial expressions or body language to detect interpersonal discrimination (e.g., furrowed brow) or increase understanding of the density
of connections. The insights gained from such analyses and review could
be used in a number of ways to promote positive interpersonal interactions among employees (see below) or encourage equitable approaches to
leader development (see section on inclusive leadership practices).

Second, building upon the idea of understanding varied social networks as a function of diversity, we propose that organizations create

digital, data-driven systems that promote and foster interaction among diverse individuals to create a culture of inclusion within organizations. For example, algorithms that social applications like Facebook, LinkedIn, and email clients employ to identify "Friend Suggestions," "People You May Know," and "People You May Want to Add" could be adapted so that systems identify relevant coworkers with whom an employee interacts with the least. Perhaps the system identifies relevant coworkers with whom an employee usually only interacts within a communication (not social) network to suggest he or she be included in an informal social opportunity (e.g., lunch). We acknowledge this idea only addresses a limited number of visible characteristics of diversity and may not always be appropriate or efficient. However, we argue that through a technique called sentiment analysis, big data could allow organizations to understand the opinions of employees, therefore broadening organizations' understanding of the content of interactions within social networks.

Sentiment analysis allows organizations to monitor opinions (i.e., objective and subjective sentiments) of authors by analyzing a variety of documents (e.g., PDF, Word documents, etc.) using linguistic resources that then output sentiment scores or visualizations that leaders or decision-makers can use (Feldman, 2013). For example, sentiment analysis could be used to identify text that is social in nature (e.g., lunch, birthday, happy hour) and therefore increase the likelihood of appropriate suggestions for people you should include in the event. As previously discussed, algorithms could be trained to target individuals for inclusion who do not regularly engage in social interactions. Some researchers have argued creating a sense of belongingness is best accomplished by removing emphasis on identity groups and focusing on themes of diversity (Roberson, 2006; Thomas, Tran, & Dawson, 2010). In sum, big data could lend a hand in digitally identifying who is being excluded and encourage increased interaction among visibly diverse employees without explicitly identifying social identity groups.

Inclusive Leadership Practices

Despite an increasingly diverse workforce, senior leadership positions and board seats are overwhelmingly held by the dominant group (i.e., white males; Alliance for Board Diversity, 2013). Although there are multiple factors that account for such differentiation at the top of organizations, one reason is that social networks provide differential advancement opportunities for minorities, specifically ethnic minorities and women (Ibarra,

1995; Ibarra, Kilduff, & Tsai, 2005). In order combat this pervasive issue, organizations often support employee resource groups (ERG) or affinity groups to provide opportunities for minorities to interact with one another and facilitate connections across employees. In addition, organizations support formal career programs (e.g., Deloitte's Women's Initiative; Ernst & Young's Career Watch) designed to identify and develop high potential employees from diverse backgrounds. Although these initiatives are well-intended, unconscious biases of key decision-makers may lead to behaviors that negatively affect the experiences, and therefore the participation or inclusion rates, of diverse individuals. However, we propose big data may create opportunities for organizations to (1) understand existing interactions among dominant and non-dominant individuals or groups and (2) provide equitable identification of high potentials for leader development programs.

We previously discussed how big data could be used to identify formal and informal social networks (e.g., communication, friendship, advice) to more fully understand interactions among visibly diverse (e.g., ethnicity, gender, age) individuals and encourage increased interactions to create inclusive organizations. We also believe that the social network maps could be used to provide insight as to whether visibly diverse individuals are connected to central nodes or key decision makers (i.e., centrality) and the frequency of their interactions (i.e., density) that may, ultimately, influence diverse individuals' career trajectories. For example, in a study using big data analytics, conversation patterns and productivity (i.e., completing calls) were measured over six weeks through employees' sensor ID badges. Despite the fact that women were more productive (i.e., completing calls on average 24 seconds more quickly) than men and there were no differences in collaborative styles, women were not awarded promotions (Waber, 2014). Future research studies, like Waber's, may allow organizations to capture the density of heterogeneous formal networks (e.g., work team) as well as opinions or attitudes through sentiment analysis to more fully understand and explain complex phenomena contributing to the exclusion of diverse individuals in positions of leadership (e.g., lack of representation of women at upper echelons of organizations).

Second, we propose big data may provide equitable identification of high potentials for leader development programs that might otherwise be overlooked because of limited interactions or unconscious biases. For example, when shopping online at Target, Wal-Mart, Amazon, etc., you might receive suggestions for items you might like to purchase. Similar systems within Netflix and other media providers can recommend movies or music based on your previously shown preferences. Software companies build these so-called recommender systems that allow for organizations to predict which products or services would work well for customers. We propose that organizations could use a similar approach to identify employees for work teams or projects. Organizations could use analytics software to data mine all existing internal documents (e.g., progress reports, time logs, performance evaluations, employee profiles) for information on employees' areas of expertise, past work experience, or special skills, and then make recommendations to project managers or department heads as to whom is best suited to fill a role or need within a team. We believe this would reduce bias when identifying good or worthy candidates for developmental work experiences or high visibility projects where individuals from marginalized groups would be less likely to be nominated for a role. By examining how organizations identify and develop employees for management positions, they may retain minority individuals, as they are more likely to receive equitable objective outcomes that enhance their career progression. In summary, consumer products and services companies use big data to maximize revenue; however, we propose that organizations could adapt this technology to streamline which (and how) leaders assign employees to work teams or projects that would not only maximize profits, but also have social impact.

Inclusive Organizational Practices

A key organizational goal is to create systems that maintain inclusive climates through equitable processes and practices that are consistently applied across employees. However, a persistent challenge for organizations seeking systematically inclusive climates is the presence of subtle or interpersonal discrimination. Interpersonal discrimination is a pattern of social negativity (Hebl, Foster, Mannix, & Dovidio, 2002) that is similarly described as incivility (Cortina, 2008) or micro-aggressions (Sue et al., 2007). Interpersonal discrimination has been correlated with individuals' decreased performance (Singletary & Hebl, 2012) and satisfaction (Deitch et al., 2003), as well as organizational profits (King, Madera, Hebl, Knight, & Mendoza, 2006). The subtle nature of this form of hostility makes it difficult for organizational policies or practices to fully capture, and even more challenging for organizations to respond in a systematic fashion, which is a requirement of creating truly inclusive climates. We propose that big data may allow for (1) systematized approaches to capturing performance and (2) structured ways of redressing discriminatory communications.

First, we believe big data open the door to more refined measurement of organizationally desired and unbiased performance outcomes. For example, a service-based organization that wants to emphasize customer relations may currently use short Likert-type satisfaction surveys at the end of an interaction or perhaps a semi-annual client feedback form. Both tools use perceptual measures of performance that create opportunity for stereotyping in evaluation, as implicit biases are part of humans' normal psychological functioning. Big data allow organizations to capture a wider-range of behavior-based performance indicators on a much larger and finer-grain scale. Continuing with the example of the service-based organization, we propose such an organization may capture inquiry response times, length of transactions, and customer purchasing history when interacting with each employee or automatic coding of video surveillance. Big data remove the need for distal indicators of an employee's performance by capturing unbiased metrics of interpersonal interactions. For example, assume a stereotypical American customer calls technical support and connects with a customer service representative who is a non-native English speaker. At the close of the call, the customer's conscious or unconscious biases result in average ratings on a Likert-type satisfaction survey even though the customer's issue was resolved effectively and efficiently. In fact, Heckman et al. (2010) reveal that low-status (i.e., nonwhite and women) customer service employees receive lower customer satisfaction evaluations than high-status (i.e., white and men) employees, confirming discriminatory judgments of raters. However, using analytics software, the organization could aggregate the service data and train a regression model to output numeric performance scores (e.g., time to resolution) for each employee. These output statistics would supplement more traditional metrics for evaluating employees in an effort to provide unbiased views of their employees' job performance over time.

Second, we propose organizations adapt their existing communication monitoring software to identify prejudicial or discriminatory text that could serve as the foundation for developing structured systems of confrontation and/or problem resolution. Techniques from the field of natural language processing (NLP), which combines artificial intelligence and linguistics, could be used to automatically identify text that could be considered prejudicial or hostile in nature (e.g., fat, gay, ugly, accent) or use sentiment analysis, an aspect of NLP, to understand the nature or attitude of the language. It seems that we typically view prejudice confrontation as a face-to-face act that manifests as an in-the-moment response to a prejudicial comment or joke. However, using mathematical models trained on big data to identify more covert (i.e., written rather than spoken) forms of negativity may allow for organizations (rather than individuals) to absorb the burden of confronting, and responding to, prejudicial or anti-diversity statements. Moreover, this approach would allow for systematically identifying and responding to hostile or subtle discrimination. Great care would undoubtedly need to be taken in how this information is stored and addressed with offending individuals in order to avoid breaching confidentiality. However, big data may lay the groundwork for organizations to create structured approaches to identifying and redressing discriminatory communications and, ultimately, developing structured systems of confrontation and/or problem resolution.

ADVANCING THE SCIENTIFIC STUDY OF DIVERSITY AND INCLUSION

We propose that big data may aid both scholars and practitioners in advancing the scientific study of diversity and inclusion in diverse organizations. Thus, the following suggests how insights driven by big data may create opportunities for new theories of, and practical strategies for, building diverse and inclusive organizations.

Theoretical Advancements

We outline two possible frameworks for how big data analytics may allow scholars to theoretically advance understanding of building inclusion in organizations: (1) inclusion acceptance or adoption by critical mass and (2) adaptive or dynamic decision-making.

First, big data analytics may be used to capture and model an organization's readiness for, or adoption of, inclusion. Organizations are, ultimately, trying to create inclusive organizational cultures where all individuals feel valued and a sense of belongingness. In order to achieve this goal, organizations first need individuals to adopt or accept inclusive ideologies that will eventually spread, creating a culture of inclusion that is evident in employees' communications, leaders' decision-making, and organizational practices and policies. We propose that once there is a critical mass (Marwell & Oliver, 1984) of individuals within an organization who have adopted or accepted inclusive ideologies, the organization is ripe for a cultural shift toward inclusion.

This notion is akin to conceptual frameworks for individual and organizational innovation adoptions (see Frambach & Schillewaert, 2002). Specifically, the framework for individual innovation acceptance suggests that personal characteristics, individual differences, attitudes, and social networks influence an individual's innovation acceptance. We propose that an individual's inclusion acceptance may be influenced by a similar set of factors. Big data analytics (e.g., social network combined with personal and employment characteristics, sentiment analysis techniques, or facial/body language analysis) creates the possibility of capturing and therefore predicting individuals' inclusion acceptance, which would inform whether an organization has successfully achieved inclusion or, alternatively, how far it is from achieving inclusion. Drawing upon critical mass theory, big data analytics may then allow organizations to model collective action (see Marwell & Oliver, 1984) and possibly predict shifts in an organization's culture of inclusion.

Second, the velocity characteristic of big data may create opportunity for revised inclusion frameworks that address its dynamic nature. Although existing models of inclusion integrate the notion of dynamism (see Ferdman, 2014), where there "is a momentary, even evanescent creation, which depends on the particular people and the particular situation involved" (Davidson & Ferdman, 2002, p. 83), the real-time nature of big data analytics should encourage scholars to integrate the notion of velocity into frameworks of inclusion. This notion is akin to dynamic decision-making (DDM) that describes a decision-maker identifying the course of action at various points in time where the environment changes and prior decisions affect future scenarios (Brehmer, 1992). Organizational researchers have historically relied on simulations or models to evaluate complex environments that require adaptive changes in order to identify the types of experiences or decisions that lead to the most desirable outcomes. However, the velocity of big data provides organizations the opportunity to respond to an identified change or pattern that may allow for a decision that may not have otherwise been made, and possibly alter future interactions or behaviors. Thus, although diversity scholars have written about the dynamic nature of inclusion, the speed at which information can now be received has not fully been integrated into existing frameworks. In effect, we encourage diversity and inclusion frameworks to integrate real-time information gathering, analyzing, and decision-making. In sum, we propose that the velocity of big data encourages scholars to enhance inclusion frameworks, similar to those of dynamic decision-making, where real-time information alters decision-making.

Practical Advancements

We also propose that big data may assist in solving three widespread issues that challenge the advancement of comprehensive solutions for building diverse and inclusive organizations: (1) statistical significance testing, (2) pervasive, subtle discrimination, and (3) inconsistent or insufficient systems that enforce accuracy and accountability.

First, big data may also result in changes to the EEO realm related to adverse impact measurement. If big data scenarios become the norm, statistical significance testing may become a much less useful framework for assessing adverse impact. The concept of practical significance may become more critical, and EEO decision makers would need to reconsider the concept and frameworks for adverse impact measurement. Industrial and organizational psychologists working in this realm may have an opportunity to conduct research on practical significance metrics and corresponding decision rules and to educate the EEO community on adverse impact measurement best practices.

Second, a theme across theoretical and empirical diversity research is the decline in formal, overt, or hostile discrimination, and a rise in subtle manifestations characterized as interpersonal discrimination (Hebl, Foster, Mannix, & Dovidio, 2002), microaggressions (Sue et al., 2007), incivility (Cortina, 2008), or benevolence (Glick & Fiske, 1996). As previously discussed, recent research has begun to link these more subtle manifestations of discrimination to both individual and organizational outcomes, elevating the importance of studying verbal, nonverbal, and paraverbal displays in the workplace. Similarly, individuals with invisible social identities (e.g., homosexual, multiple sclerosis) experience personal and professional challenges (Clair, Beatty, & Maclean, 2005) that are often hidden from organizational stakeholders. The nature of invisible identities is such that to identify and consciously act to include these individuals in the organization places the burden of deciding whether to reveal or pass on those individuals with invisible identities, adding pressures to their already stigmatized status. Big data allow for organizations to capture not only what representatives see or hear, which is limited in scope and fraught with bias, but also subtle, implied, or unconscious behaviors that may negatively affect the experiences of diverse individuals in the workplace. Such incidents of subtle discrimination and interactions with invisible social identity groups are challenging to empirically capture, yet important to understand in order to develop comprehensive solutions that create inclusion in diverse organizations. Thus, we propose that organizational researchers can and should leverage big data in order to assist in the understanding, identification, and remediation of discrimination, particularly subtle discrimination.

Finally, a recurring challenge to the advancement of comprehensive inclusion solutions is reducing inconsistencies in the treatment of individuals and evaluations of performance, as well as developing structured systems that enhance accuracy and accountability across diverse individuals. A key criticism of some approaches (e.g., enhanced positivity; Miller, Rothblum, Felicio, & Brand, 1995) to remediating stigmatization or discrimination is that they place the burden on the victim. For example, if I am a member of a stigmatized group and perceive that I am continually excluded from social opportunities (e.g., coffee, lunch), I must take it upon myself to develop inroads with these social circles or, alternatively or simultaneously, alert organizational representatives who then may assist me in identifying opportunities for formal networking with key personnel. Regardless of approach, the burden is placed upon the target of discrimination, which some diversity scholars have argued is inappropriate and seeks only to remediate discrimination one person at a time. Big data create opportunity for the systematic collection of unbiased information that may aid in the creation of structured systems of prejudice confrontation, problem resolution, or inclusion strategies.

CONCLUSION

In conclusion, discussion on diversity and inclusion tends to take one of two perspectives: the business case (see Kilian, Hukai, & McCarty, 2005) or the values and ethics case (see Jones, King, Nelson, Geller, & Bowes-Sperry, 2013; van Dijk, van Engen, & Paauwe, 2012). However, we propose that big data may afford organizational scholars, practitioners, and scientists the luxury of fulfilling both perspectives by generating profit and social value. Almost every idea contained in this chapter remains untested, which opens up significant opportunity for researchers and practitioners. Moreover, it is likely that insights driven by big data will lead to new, untested questions or theories that may inform the scientific study and practice of diversity and inclusion, helping to make human resource departments strategic players in organizations.

NOTE

Acknowledgements: The authors thank Nick Bridle for his helpful comments on natural language processing and discussing relevant computer science research.

REFERENCES

Ahuja, G. (2000). Collaboration networks, structural holes, and innovations: A longitudinal study. *Administrative Science Quarterly, 45*, 425–455.

Alliance for Board Diversity (2013). Missing pieces: Women and minorities on Fortune 500 boards—fact sheet. Retrieved from http://theabd.org/Reports.html

American Psychological Association (2010). *Publication Manual of the American Psychological Association*. Washington, DC: American Psychological Association.

Avery, D. R., & McKay, P. F. (2006). Target practice: An organizational impression management approach to attracting minority and female job applicants. *Personnel Psychology, 59*, 157–187.

Baltzan, P. (2012). Business driven information systems (3rd ed.). New York, NY: McGraw-Hill.

Beales, H. (2010). The value of behavioral targeting. *Network Advertising Initiative*. Retrieved from http://www.networkadvertising.org/pdfs/Beales_NAI_Study.pdf

Biddle, D. A. (2012). *Adverse impact and test validation: A practitioner's handbook (3rd ed.)*. Folsom, CA: Infinity.

Born, M. P. H., & Taris, T. W. (2010). The impact of the wording of employment advertisements on students' inclination to apply for a job. *The Journal of Social Psychology, 150*, 485–502.

Brass, D. J. (1984). Being the in the right place: A structural analysis of individual influence in an organization. *Administrative Science Quarterly, 29*, 518–539.

Brass, D. J. (1985). Men's and women's networks: A study of interaction patterns and influence in an organization. *Academy of Management Journal, 28*, 327–343.

Brehmer, B. (1992). Dynamic decision making: Human control of complex systems. *Acta Psychologica, 81*, 211–241.

Breslow, N. E., & Day, N. E. (1980). *Statistical Methods in Cancer Research, Volume I: The Analysis of Case-Control Studies* (Vol. 32). Lyon, France: IARC Scientific Publications.

Chawla, N. V., & Davis, D. A. (2013). Bringing big data to personalized healthcare: A patient-centered framework. *Journal of General Internal Medicine, 28*, S660–665.

Chen, H., Chiang, R. H. L., & Storey, V. C. (2012). Business intelligence and analytics: From big data to big impact. *MIS Quarterly, 36*, 1165–1188.

Clair, J. A., Beatty, J. E., & Maclean, T. L., (2005). Out of sight but not out of mind: Managing invisible social identities in the workplace. *Academy of Management Review, 30*, 78–95.

Cohen, D., & Dunleavy, E. M. (2009). *A review of OFCCP enforcement statistics: A call for transparency in OFCCP reporting*. Washington, DC: The Center for Corporate Equality.

Cohen, D., Aamodt, M. G., & Dunleavy, E. M. (2010). Technical advisory committee report on best practices in adverse impact analyses. Washington, DC: Center for Corporate Equality.

Cohen, D., & Dunleavy, E. M. (2010). A review of OFCCP enforcement statistics for fiscal year 2008. Washington, DC: Center for Corporate Equality.

Cohen, J. (1994). The earth is round (p < .05). *American Psychologist, 49*, 997–1003.

Collins, M. W., & Morris, S. B. (2008). Testing for adverse impact when sample size is small. *Journal of Applied Psychology, 93*, 463–471.

Coronel, C., Morris, S., & Rob, P. (2013). Database systems: Design, implementation, and management (10th ed.). Boston, MA: Cengage Learning.

Cortina, L. M. (2008). Unseen injustice: Incivility as modern discrimination in organizations. *Academy of Management Review, 33*, 55–75.

Davenport, T. H., Barth, P., & Bean, R. (2012). How "big data" is different. *MIT Sloan Management Review, 54*(1).

Davenport, T. H., & Patil, D. J. (2012). Data scientist: The sexiest job of the 21st century. *Harvard Business Review, 90*, 70–76.

Davidson, M. N., & Ferdman, B. M. (2002, April). Inclusion: What can I and my organization do about it? *The Industrial-Organizational Psychologist, 39*(4) 80–85.

De Choudhury, M., Hofman, J. M., Mason, W. A., & Watts, D. J. (2010, April). Inferring relevant social networks from interpersonal communication. *Proceedings from the 19th international conference on World Wide Web*, 301–310.

Deitch, E. A., Barsky, A., Butz, R. M., Chan, S., Brief, A. P., & Bradley, J. C. (2003). Subtle yet significant: The existence and impact of everyday racial discrimination in the workplace. *Human Relations, 56*, 1299–1324.

Dunleavy, E. M., & Gutman, A. (2011). An update on the statistical versus practical significance debate: A review of Stagi v Amtrak (2010). *The Industrial Organizational Psychologist, 48*, 121–129.

Dunleavy, E. M., Morris, S. B., & Howard, E. (in press). Measuring adverse impact in employee selection systems. In C. Hanvey & K. Sady (Eds.), *A practitioner's guide to legal issues in organizations* (pp. 1–26). New York, NY: Springer.

Esson, P. L., & Hauenstein, N. M. (2006). *Exploring the use of the four-fifths rule and significance tests in adverse impact court case rulings*. Presented at the 21st annual conference of the Society for Industrial and Organizational Psychology, Dallas, TX.

Feldman, R. (2013). Techniques and applications for sentiment analysis. *Communications of the ACM, 56*, 82–89.

Ferdman, B. M. (2014). Diversity at work: The practice of inclusion. In B. M. Ferdman & B. R. Deane (Eds.), *Diversity at work: The practice of inclusion* (pp. 3–54). San Francisco, CA: Jossey-Bass.

Frambach, R. T., & Schillewaert, N. (2002). Organizational innovation adoption: A multilevel framework of determinants and opportunities for future research. *Journal of Business Research, 55*, 163–176.

Fruchterman, J. (2013, March 19). Big data means more than big profits. *Harvard Business Review*. Retrieved from https://hbr.org/2013/03/big-data-means-more-than-big-p

Glick, P., & Fiske, S. T. (1996). The ambivalent sexism inventory: Differentiating hostile and benevolent sexism. *Journal of Personality and Social Psychology, 70*, 491–512.

Gutman, A., Koppes, L., & Vodanovich, S. (2010). EEO law and personal practices (3rd ed.). New York, NY: Routledge/Taylor & Francis Group.

Hebl, M. R., Foster, J. B., Mannix, L. M., & Dovidio, J. F. (2002). Formal and interpersonal discrimination: A field study of bias toward homosexual applicants. *Personality and Social Psychology Bulletin, 28*, 815–825.

Heckman, D. R., Aquino, K., Owens, B. P., Mitchell, T. R., Schilpzand, P., & Leavitt, K. (2010). Examination of whether and how racial and gender biases influence customer satisfaction. *Academy of Management Journal, 53*, 238–264.

Ibarra, H. (1995). Race, opportunity, and diversity of social circles in managerial networks. *Academy of Management Journal, 38*, 673–703.

Ibarra, H., Kilduff, M., & Tsai, W. (2005). Zooming in and out: Connecting individuals and collectivities at the frontiers of organizational network research. *Organization Science, 16*, 359–371.

Jacobs, R., Murphy, K. R., & Silva R. (2012). Unintended consequences of EEO enforcement policies: Being big is worse than being bad. *Journal of Business and Psychology, 24*(4), 467–471.

Jones, K. P., King. E. B., Nelson, J. K., Geller, D. S., & Bowes-Sperry, L. (2013). Beyond the business case: An ethical perspective on diversity training. *Human Resource Management, 52*, 55–74.

Kalev A., Dobbin F., & Kelly E. (2006). Best practices or best guesses? Assessing the efficacy of corporate affirmative action and diversity policies. *American Sociological Review, 71*, 589–617.

Kilian, C. M., Hukai, C., & McCarty, E. (2005). Building diversity in the pipeline to corporate leadership. *Journal of Management Development, 24*, 155–168.

King, E. B., Madera, J. M., Hebl, M. R., Knight, J. L., & Mendoza, S. A. (2006). What's in a name? A multiracial investigation of the role of occupational stereotypes in selection decisions. *Journal of Applied Social Psychology, 36*, 1145–1159.

Kirk, R. E. (1996). Practical significance: A concept whose time has come. *Educational and Psychological Measurement, 56*, 746–759.

Kumar, V., Chattaraman, V., Neghina, C., Skiera, B., Aksoy, L., Buoye, A., & Hensler, J. (2013). Data-driven services marketing in a connected world. *Journal of Service Management, 24*, 330–352.

Mantel, N., & Haenszel, W. (1959). Statistical aspects of the analysis of data from retrospective studies of disease. *Journal of the National Cancer Institute, 22*, 719–748.

Manyika, J., Chui, M., Brown, B., Bughin, J., Dobbs, R., Roxburgh, C., & Byers, A. H. (2011). Big data: The next frontier for innovation, competition, and productivity. *McKinsey Global Institute.* Retrieved from http://www.mckinsey.com/insights/business_technology/big_data_the_next_frontier_for_innovation

Marwell, G., & Oliver, P. (1984). Collective action theory and social movements research. *Research in Social Movements, Conflicts and Change, 7*, 1–28.

McAfee, A., & Brynjolfsson, E. (2012). Big data: The management revolution. *Harvard Business Review, 90*, 60–68.

Michaels, E., Handfield-Jones, H., & Axelrod, B. (2001). *The war for talent.* Boston, MA: Harvard Business Press.

Miller, C. T., Rothblum, E. D., Felicio, D., & Brand, P. (1995). Compensating for stigma: Obese and nonobese women's reactions to being visible. *Personality and Social Psychology Bulletin, 21*, 1083–1106.

Morris, S. B., & Lobsenz, R. E. (2000). Significance tests and confidence intervals for the adverse impact ratio. *Personnel Psychology, 53*, 89–111.

Murphy, K., & Jacobs, R. (2012). Using effect size measures to reform the determination of adverse impact in equal employment litigation. Psychology, Public Policy and the Law.

Proofpoint, Inc. (2009). Outbound email and data loss prevention in today's enterprise. Retrieved from http://www.proofpoint.com/downloads/Proofpoint-Outbound-Email-and-Data-Loss-Prevention-2009.pdf

Purcell, B. (2013). The emergence of "big data" technology and analytics. *Journal of Technology Research, 4,* 1–7.

Roberson, Q. M. (2006). Disentangling the meanings of diversity and inclusion in organizations. *Group & Organization Management, 31,* 212–236.

Rogers, D., & Sexton, D. (2012). *Marketing ROI in the era of big data.* Retrieved from www.iab.net/media/file/2012-BRITE-NYAMA-Marketing-ROI-Study.pdf

Rouse, M., & Martinek, L. (2012, January 10). Big data analytics. *Essential Guide: Guide to Big Data trends and best practices.* Retrieved from http://searchbusinessanalytics.techtarget.com/definition/big-data-analytics

Shore, L. M., Randel, A. E., Chung, B. G., Dean, M. A., Erhart, K. H., & Singh, G. (2011). Inclusion and diversity in work groups: A review and model for future research. *Journal of Management, 37,* 1262–1289.

Singletary, S. L. & Hebl, M. R. (2009). Compensatory strategies for reducing interpersonal discrimination: The effectiveness of acknowledgments, increased positivity and individuating information. *Journal of Applied Psychology, 93,* 797–805.

Sue, D. W., Capodilupo, C. M., Torino, G. C., Bucceri, J. M., Holder, A. M. B., Nadal, K. L., & Esquilin, M. (2007). Racial microaggressions in everyday life: Implications for clinical practice. *American Psychologist, 62,* 271–286.

Tatum, B. R. (2003). *Why are all the black kids sitting together in the cafeteria? And other conversations about race.* New York, NY: Basic Books.

Thomas, D. A., & Ely, R. J. (1996). Making differences matter: A new paradigm for managing diversity. *Harvard Business Review, 74,* 79–90.

Thomas, K. M., Tran, N. M., & Dawson, B. L. (2010). An inclusive strategy of teaching diversity. *Advances in Developing Human Resources, 12,* 295–311.

Tichy, N. M., Tushman, M. L., & Fombrun, C. (1979). Social network analysis for organizations. *Academy of Management Review, 4,* 507–519.

Van Dijk, H., van Engen, M., & Paauwe, J. (2012). Reframing the business case for diversity: A values and virtues perspective. *Journal of Business Ethics, 111,* 73–84.

Waber, B. (2014, January 30). What data analytics says about gender inequality in the workplace. *Bloomberg Businessweek.* Retrieved from http://www.businessweek.com/articles/2014–01–30/gender-inequality-in-the-workplace-what-data-analytics-says

Zedeck, S. (2002, October). An expanded scope for the Journal of Applied Psychology. *The Industrial-Organizational Psychologist, 40*(2) 140–141.

Cases Cited

Albemarle Paper Company v. Moody, 422 US 405 (1975).

Castaneda v. Partida, 430 US 482 (1977).

Griggs v. Duke Power, 401 US 424 (1971).

Hazelwood School District v. United States, 433 US 299 (1977).

12

How Big Data Matter

Richard A. Guzzo

"What? I've never heard of that."
"Really? People can do that?"
"There's nothing new here."

Big data can elicit all manner of reactions, among them surprise, incredulity, excitement, dismissiveness, and insecurity. While engaged on the topic of big data in recent years, I have, at one time or another, felt each of these and reading the papers collected in this book brought them all back. Thankfully, my task here is not to emote. Rather, building on the trail-cutting work of the contributors to this book, this chapter offers an integrative perspective on the import of big data. It does so through six simple assertions.

BIG DATA TAKES US WHERE OUR THEORIES DON'T

Organizational psychology places a great premium on theories. We regard them as essential guides. They enable us to proclaim with confidence the not-so-directly-observable operation of such things as causes and mediators. The value of a good theory for practice has long been appreciated. And the emphasis on theory strongly influences what gets published in leading organizational research journals (as pointed out by Oswald and Putka in Chapter 3; Putka and Oswald in Chapter 7; and Hausknecht and Li in Chapter 9).

Our existing theories largely are products of an earlier era, an era without big data. Theories have been created and tested in a world marked by research projects of limited sample sizes and durations with data analyzed using statistical protocols well-suited to comparatively small numbers of observations. There is great excellence in this work, for sure. This excellence is safeguarded by mechanisms such as high standards of admission into programs of training for organizational researchers, heavy investment in those admitted few, well-developed standards of best practice in methods and measurement, and peer review of professional work throughout one's career.

Big data does not take away the value of existing theories. But it does expose their limitations. One of those limitations is the small number of conditionals cited. Generally speaking, our theories are quite good at asserting why relationships exist but are less good at articulating when they exist—for example, for what segments of a population, under what external conditions, with what dependencies on co-occurring events. Hausknecht and Li (Chapter 9) describe this state of affairs with regard to turnover where, they point out, much remains to be learned about the conditions under which antecedents of turnover are stronger or weaker and how big data can help illuminate the presence of conditional influences. Sometimes we build our theories to limit conditionals by design, such as when we randomly assign research participants to controlled experimental conditions to, in principle, nullify the impact of all other third variables. Such nullification surely strengthens our ability to assert why some effect was produced, but it often comes with a price of silence about potentially important conditionals thus limiting complexity and completeness. The more articulate and precise a theory is about when it applies—and when it does not—the more insightful, and useful, that theory will be. Further, being specific about how any one theory connects to another gives the theory more leverage for insight and action.

This is exactly where big data helps: high-volume and high-variety data create the opportunity to make our theories become far more fluent about when they apply, for whom, in what environments, with what other processes. Consider, for example, the investigation by Hernandez, Newman, and Jeon (Chapter 4) of job satisfaction and its capture of 301,595 spontaneous communications containing the word "job." That work invokes a long-standing theory of job satisfaction, namely Hulin's (1966) frame of reference effect, which asserts that affect about one's job is a result of social comparison processes. The researchers report evidence partially supporting the theory—namely, that the level of expressed job satisfaction is lower in communities where economic prosperity is greater (that is, I am less satisfied when I compare myself to others who are more favorably situated). It is a plausible theory, but not one that is fully developed with regard to articulating when it is most relevant. Big data can help here. Tweets can generate a high volume of relevant data in a short time, so let's consider them a source of big data. Tweets may be excellent carriers of facts that can be harnessed to test when, for example, social comparison theory is most powerful. To illustrate, perhaps social comparison processes are the strongest root cause of job satisfaction when the expression of job-related affect occurs in tweets that are replied to, especially when replies beget replies and an extended social exchange occurs involving job-related affect compared to, say, broadcast tweets that generate little response. Tweets also carry extensive embedded information about social networks that can be extracted by tracking who exchanges messages with whom. A network analysis based on exchanged tweets can yield a number of quantitative properties both of the network and of a person's position in it. The nature of a network and positions in it may be quite important to better understanding when social comparison processes are strong determinants of job-related affect. Information about the length of intervals between tweets might indicate the intensity of communication, another possibly important factor. One could imagine a series of programmatic small-sample studies to address each of these factors one at a time. The value of big data is that it so often gives us the ability to do all that research at once, with many observations to work with. That is, big data enable us to take our existing theories to new places and to become, almost immediately, far more articulate about the conditions and circumstances when a theory is most powerful and when not.

Organizational contexts present huge opportunities to use big data to enhance existing theories. Ryan (Chapter 2) describes this well. Many sources of relevant data exist, including systems of record, such as human resource information systems, that provide extensive facts about employee demographics, work experiences, performance, and compensation. Further, potentially useful data resides in technology platforms that support interaction among employees as well as in applicant tracking systems, learning management systems, performance management systems, and systems that track business performance. Such big data in the workplace offer the ability to test many theoretical conditionals simultaneously. Using the example of social comparison processes and job satisfaction, big data in the workplace can be used to test for individual differences (e.g., demographics, assessment scores), attributes of the social contexts of workplaces, and the nature of work performed.

Kozlowski, Chao, Chang, and Fernandez (Chapter 10) also describe how big data can add to current theories. Their research program makes clear how the volume, variety, and sometimes velocity of data that can be captured about team process and performance can be an engine of insights that complement and extend current theories. They make the point, too, that big data opens the door to more system-oriented theory—for example, theory that is more lucid about dynamic influences that change with time and circumstance, and with the operation of other influences.

Systems-oriented theory acknowledges situational complexity inherent in organizational dynamics; it is an alternative to more parsimonious "simple main effect" theories. The promise of complexity includes more accurate understanding, prediction with smaller errors, and more effective how-to guidance for interventions. Complex theory requires copious data, which now exists as never before. Another aspect of the systems-oriented theorizing is what is known in other sciences (e.g., ecology) as the "cumulative effects" problem (Weber, Krogman, & Antoniuk, 2012). The problem is in discerning the influence of combined factors (e.g., simultaneous changes happening in an organization) on multiple outcomes (e.g., employee attitudes, performance, and voluntary turnover). Tools for assessing cumulative effects include many that are associated with the analysis of big data, such as clustering algorithms and network analysis. Expertise in other domains about assessing cumulative effects may have great value when imported into the organizational sciences to advance system-oriented theory with data.

Expect big data to take our received theories to new places, especially in terms of from simpler to more complex and more complete. And expect it to do so with great speed because of the core characteristics of data volume, variety, and velocity.

THEORIZING IS AS IMPORTANT AS THEORY IN A BIG DATA WORLD

Related to the refinement of current theory is making new theory—theorizing—where there is little or none. Big data elevate the importance of theorizing. Some big data enthusiasts such as Mayer-Schonberger and Cukier (2013) argue that data-driven understanding will supplant hypothesis-driven understanding because existing theories are inadequate with regard to the possibilities of relationships discoverable in a big data world. To argue that hypothesis testing will disappear in a big data world seems an overstatement, but the rise of the importance of processes of theory creation seems certain. Indeed, the absence of theory can be a benefit, as Waijee, Higgins, and Singal (2013) describe in their discussion of predictive modeling in the medical sciences. The lack of predefined hypotheses, they assert, makes it less likely to overlook unexpected predictors and their interactions when building predictive models that not only predict future states but also become sources of new insight.

The process of generating theory will change with big data, as illustrated by Putka and Oswald's (Chapter 7) example of creating new theory where there is little in the selection and assessment context. The typical approach to establishing the validity of assessment scores in a selection context involves cataloging the evidence for validity through a single study or through the integration of multiple such studies. Each study, though, is a discrete-in-time entity. Putka and Oswald describe a big-data context in which there is continuously streaming data about applicants, their assessments, and post-hire performance and experiences. This continuous stream opens the door to new ways of conceptualizing the relationships between predictors and performance. In particular, the door is opened to understanding dynamic relationships, such as how changes in the organization influence the strength of the predictor-performance relationship. Such a dynamic relationship is mostly outside the scope of current thinking, and thus new theorizing is required to fill the void. Kozlowski et al. (Chapter 10) also make clear how high-variety, multi-channel data about teams can enable researchers to recognize and better understand emergent patterns important to team performance.

Theory creation involves the interplay of data and interpretation to support inductive thinking as well as deductive thinking. The use of evidence, which the big data world provides plenty of, is germane to both induction and deduction. Indeed, in organizational settings, big data almost force the inevitable interweaving of theory testing and theory generation, as illustrated with regard to research in organizational climate and culture (Guzzo, Nalbantian, & Parra, 2014). Data available today about climate and culture far exceeds the amount available to the originators of climate and culture theory. Researchers who are investigating those constructs in applied contexts now find themselves in a forest of facts relevant to each and in need of generating theory to delineate better what climate is, what culture is, and how their respective influences play out, all while still in a position to test hypotheses derived from existing climate and culture theory.

Big data bring with it new ways of displaying data to aid the process of theorizing. Using the ink-on-paper bar chart as the icon of traditional graphical displays, Stanton (Chapter 6) examines multimodal data representation, as when visual data displays are augmented by data-driven audio and touch sensations. Such multimodal representations may be able to convey the complexities of big data with greater fidelity than familiar graphics. During the exploratory, induction stages, such multimodal displays are likely to stimulate—literally—in new ways and create a distinct data experience that may in turn lead to distinct insights and interpretations. Perhaps we should consider multimodal displays as the big data embodiment of the spirit of Tukey's (1977) innovations in exploratory data analysis, although Tukey's innovations were understandably mostly graphical. Sinar (Chapter 5) goes deeply into alternative ways of visualizing big data, consistent with the spirit of Tufte's (1983) landmark work on communicating quantitative data visually. These visual alternatives can be useful not just for communicating to others but also for researchers' use in data exploration and hypothesis generation. Complementing these alternatives for data exploration, the chapter by Oswald and Putka (Chapter 3) examines an array of data analytic methods that originate in the big data world or are big data friendly. Some techniques would be considered uncommon in organizational research, such as the use machine learning algorithms and of ensembles of models to make inferences. Other techniques are more familiar, such as those rooted in Bayesian logic or in methods of cross-validation. In fact, the disciplined use of data to support the intertwined inductive and deductive work of researchers may be most effectively achieved through the simultaneous use of old and new data analysis techniques.

BIG DATA BLUR BOUNDARIES

Boundaries that big data change include those that exist between scientific disciplines, such as organizational psychology, labor economics, sociology and others that focus on work and organizations. This is not to say that the disciplines will disappear but rather that there will be a dramatic rise in the interdisciplinary and multidisciplinary application of science and practice to organizations.

One reason that big data make interdisciplinary research more likely is because professionals from many backgrounds have interests in accessing the same streamed and archived data. The variety inherent in such data makes it, or at least portions of it, appealing to multiple disciplines. Thus, researchers of diverse professional stripes can find themselves simultaneously drinking from the same well, so to speak, increasing the likelihood of interdisciplinary collaboration.

Another factor contributing to the dissolution of disciplinary boundaries is the nature of the talent being hired to analyze big data for commercial purposes. Employers that are seeking people who can manipulate and extract value from big data are casting a very wide interdisciplinary net in their recruiting. Job advertisements, for example, explicitly acknowledge a range of disciplines regarded as suitable for hire, including economics, engineering, epidemiology, finance, information technology, life sciences, marketing, mathematics, operations research, physics, psychology, and statistics—all disciplines which provide at least some its members in-depth training in relevant methods of data analysis. Populating in-house analytic teams with people from multiple disciplines will influence how big data work gets done, including the substantive interpretations made from data. This influence, in turn, can be expected to leave its mark in the activities of various professional societies and future research publications.

Data science is an emerging discipline. New graduate training programs in data science have sprung up in great numbers in recent years. Data science does not fit the mold of established organizational science disciplines. Many of the techniques described by Oswald and Putka (Chapter 3) are core topics in such data science curricula, as are topics related to the capture, storage, and integration of massive data sets. Data science is predominantly about technique. It does not have a strong reliance on existing research literatures in the same way that social science disciplines do and as such is more likely to emphasize data mining and prediction over explanation. Data scientists will increasingly add to the interdisciplinary mix but will contribute in ways different from established sciences.

Other boundaries that are softened by big data include those that sometimes guide research in the organizational sciences, such as the concept of levels of analysis. Levels of analysis are all about sorting and separating. The concept has been used to highlight differences in the professional identities among organizational researchers—"are you a micro type or a macro type?"—as well as to statistically assign variance to different sources, such as attributes of individuals versus attributes of the teams of which they are members. Big data provide information that comes at many levels of analysis all at once. Consider the array of sources of data in organizations described by Ryan (Chapter 2). An employer's big data platform is likely to contain information about employees as individuals, their work groups, an assortment of higher-order nested conditions in which individuals and their work groups are embedded (e.g., in a location, in a division, in a region), as well as organizational systems of practices (e.g., compensation, performance evaluation) to which employees are exposed. Indeed, such information is what makes possible more system-oriented theory, that is, theory that is articulate about the operation of multiple pathways of influence simultaneously. Consider equifinality, the systems-theory principle that a given outcome can be reached by many different paths. High rates of employee retention, for example, could be demonstrated to be a result that sits at the terminus of many active pathways of influence, pathways that may all be operating at different levels of analysis and in concert with one another (see Hausknecht and Li, Chapter 9). In this context, system-oriented theory about employee retention is less concerned with the reductionist-like assignment of the primacy of one path over others and is more concerned with communicating a holistic, multiple-pathway causal explanation.

NEW APPLICATIONS AND OPPORTUNITIES ABOUND

Big data enable organizational researches and practitioners to do more with more. Botsford Morgan, Dunleavy, and DeVries (Chapter 11) illustrate this nicely with regard to using big data to meet diversity and inclusion challenges in organizations. One of their examples illustrates a big data approach to recruiting diverse applicant pools. In it, research that joins demographic data with online search patterns may make it possible to identify and target under-accessed potential applicant pools that are more diverse than current applicants. Technologies that generate big data, such as email traffic, also capture workplace data that can provide a new window on where in organizations inclusive and exclusive behaviors are occurring, such as might be evidenced by communication patterns. Such insights can help target where interventions (e.g., training) may be most needed. The opportunities to apply big data to diversity and inclusion issues in organizations seem quite numerous. In addition to examples provided by Botsford Morgan, Dunleavy, and DeVries, data housed in human resource information systems can be a potentially rich source of insight into what may be subtle expressions of a lack of inclusiveness in an enterprise. To illustrate, such data can be used to identify patterns in the internal movement of employees from one job to another, including the identification of jobs that are especially good gateways to career paths full of future promotions. Differences in access to those critical jobs by gender or ethnicity, for example, can be detected with such data. Such differences in access, should they exist, could signal the need for corrective action. Other sources of data, too, may shed light on diversity and inclusion dynamics, such as data from employee relations records that can contain detailed facts about complaints and grievances filed by one employee about another.

Illingworth, Lippstreu, and Deprez-Sims (Chapter 8) speak to opportunities that big data bring in other realms, such as pre-employment assessments, coaching, and the impact of selection practices on organizational outcomes. Modern technologies, such as mobile computing, enable employers to deliver talent assessments fitted to the convenience of applicants. This not only can have the effect of increasing the number and diversity of applicants but also can open up new fields of inquiry, as Illingworth, Lippstreu, and Deprez-Sims describe in a case study. In a large-volume selection context (two million applicants per year), the opportunity is created to investigate the properties—such as construct and predictive validity—of assessments made via mobile devices. Combining types of devices with demographic data of applicants allows for a number of naturally occurring quasi-experiments from which a lot new can be learned. In short, big data expand the number of types of predictors in selection as well as expand the criterion space, creating new ways of carrying out selection and assessment and the new knowledge that comes with it.

Big data are creating many new opportunities for innovative research and practice in addition to those mentioned in this book. Some of those arise through the revitalization of long-standing areas of interest, such as work and health. Several aspects of work and health have been investigated for many years, such as work accidents and the link between job stress and affective and physical reactions. It is now possible, given the accumulation and storage of high-volume, high-variety data about employees, to investigate many additional work-health issues, especially those that have been difficult to address for want of measurements. Marmot's (2004) early research showing that working at lower levels of the British civil service hierarchy raises the risk of coronary heart disease relative to working at higher levels in the hierarchy is the sort of issue that can now be investigated with renewed vigor through the integration of workforce, organizational, and health data available in large organizations. That data can be used to perform analyses to more powerfully account for more third variables that may condition the impact of hierarchy on health than Marmot's data at the time could address, for example. Currently available data also opens up the possibility of testing new hypotheses in less-explored areas of work and health, such as the impact of patterns of career experiences—not just place in the hierarchy—on health. Available data, especially in large organizations, also make it possible to examine the productivity consequences of health by expanding the measures of productivity, thus getting away from the over-reliance on absenteeism as *the* productivity measure. Abundant data also make it easier to assess the impact of employer-sponsored health programs and benefits than has been the case previously. The mass of data now available would appear to be a solid foundation for enormous progress in knowledge and action with regard to health and work.

In addition to health, many other topics become amenable for research in new ways with big data. Retirement, for example, is a choice influenced by many possible factors, including financial preparedness, health, work experiences, attitudes and affect, family circumstances, and employer practices (see Wang, 2012). Expansive data that speak to each of these sets of issues are within reach, and the use of that data can lead to integrated, systemic theory in this area. Health and retirement are but two of several possible areas of research and practice fueled by big data, as are topics that are not yet imagined.

BIG DATA POSE ETHICAL AND INTEGRITY CHALLENGES

Sometimes in research it is important—and required—to protect the privacy and anonymity of those who are participants in or subjects of that research. Such protection in a big data world can be very problematic. Anonymized data, for example, may not stay that way for very long when other, outside data can be joined with it. In fact, re-identifying (or de-anonymizing) individuals in anonymized data sets can be accomplished "with astonishing ease" (Ohm, 2010, p. 1701). An early and famous demonstration of this was reported by Sweeney (2000), who obtained (for free) anonymized health records of Massachusetts state employees and then for $20 acquired the city of Cambridge's voter roll information, which contained basic facts essential to exercising the right to vote, including name, address, birth date, and gender. The two databases were then joined to identify health records. With a bit of flair, Sweeney promptly sent the governor of Massachusetts, a Cambridge resident, his health records. Keys to re-identification included that only six people in Cambridge shared the governor's birth date, three of the six were men, and only one lived in the governor's zip code. More generally, it has been reported that 87% of the US population can be identified by the combination of zip code, gender, and date of birth (Perry, 2010). Given the amount of useful data out there that is able to be joined with researcher-generated data, the simple act of anonymization may no longer be the pillar of protection that it has been. The big data world will force reconsideration of anonymization as a means of protecting research participants' interests.

Research conducted in organizational settings using employer-generated data (such as would be maintained in, say, workforce databases) involves, for obvious reasons, identified individuals who typically remain identifiable throughout analyses. Organization-based researchers may also find it useful to join such proprietary data with anonymized outside data. Because employers have very extensive personal and work-related information about employees, it is conceivable that employer-held data could be used to re-identify employees who are represented anonymously in outside data. Imagine this scenario: an employer is interested in finding out who is saying unkind things about the firm in social media messages, so the employer acquires an archived database of messages that comes with time and location markers and joins it with its proprietary data to identify which of its employees are the likely sources of the messages of interest.

Informed consent is another means of protecting research participants' interests that is challenged by big data. The American Psychological Association, for example, offers standards of ethical practice regarding obtaining informed consent. Circumstances when obtaining informed consent are generally not deemed to be a requirement include when data is collected anonymously, when it is collected via naturalistic observation (including the capture of voice and images), when archival data is utilized, and when employers conduct research internally. But big data can challenge such informed consent standards in several ways. One way concerns the ease with which anonymity can be stripped away in a big data world, as discussed above. Another way concerns the rapidly expanding amount and type of archived data captured via naturalistic observation and the potential downstream risks to individuals accruing from analyses of that data. To illustrate, consider the case of Uber, a transportation service provider, which caught a lot of flak when it reported that by analyzing ride patterns, it could identify likely incidences of its customers' sexual encounters (key data points included day of week and the time of an initial drop-off followed by a pick-up a few hours later within one-tenth of a mile of the drop off; Pagliery, 2014). There is no evidence to suggest that Uber did anything harmful with its findings, but the vignette illustrates the often short path between routinely collected data and its use in ways that could put individuals at risk. Uber users would not be expected to object to the company analyzing data routinely collected as a part of business operations—indeed, they may have explicitly given the company consent to do so when they opened their account—but it is difficult to imagine that all those users would agree specifically to be subjects of analyses of personal encounters. In summary, professional guidance regarding informed consent that originated in a small data world may well prove inadequate to the task in a big data world.

Data integrity also can be a challenge. Data coming from multiple sources via non-standardized means may result in observations with undesirable properties from a research perspective. The nature of much of what qualifies as big data is determined by such things as the constraints of technology and the forces of convenience rather than the skilled hand of the trained researcher. Fundamental concerns, such as the reliability and validity of measurement, still apply to such data but may be difficult to address in conventional ways. Volume, variety, and velocity are three often-mentioned properties that describe how big data varies in nature. Some discussions add a fourth V, veracity, which yet others consider to be an attribute of a fifth V, data value. Regardless of the number of Vs in big data, the essential point here is that big data can be expected to vary considerably in its trustworthiness and that a user of it for research purposes may encounter complications in assessing that trustworthiness, perhaps necessitating unconventional tactics of assessment. Another integrity-related issue concerns making proper inferences from big data. For example, extremely large sample sizes may rob meaning from statistical tests of significance that are widely relied on to guide inference-making.

THIS IS A PARADIGM CHANGE

I first read Thomas Kuhn's (1970) *The Structure of Scientific Revolutions* years ago. "Interesting," I thought, "worth keeping this book on the shelf. Not sure I believe it, though." Now I believe it. Big data are ushering in a paradigm change.

Is the magnitude of the paradigm change equal to that experienced when, say, scientists rejected the idea that the sun revolves around the earth with the knowledge that the earth revolves around the sun? No, probably not. Will this paradigm change happen in exactly the way that Kuhn describes—that is, a sufficient number of exceptions arise that cannot be explained by prevailing science and theory such that a crisis materializes, one that is resolved only through an entirely new paradigmatic way of understanding and seeing the world? No, the change probably will not unfold in just that way.

But there are unmistakable signs that a transformation is in the works for the organizational sciences such that "normal science," as Kuhn calls it, will not persist. Circumstances are quickly shifting because of big data. Collectively, we create more voluminous information with each passing year and that information has great variety and sometimes comes at us at high rates. The data available now for use in the conduct of organizational science are unlike anything that existed not so long ago. It is difficult to see this big-data-driven flood as anything other than irreversible and permeating all aspects of organizational science.

Simply put, big data bring many appealing intellectual options. With regard to theorizing, they enable the accelerated development of existing theories to account for more relevant factors and to become more complex, specific, and nuanced—and ideally more accurate and useful as a result. Big data also create an urgency to master the art of theorizing so as to quickly make sense of things not previously explored or of highly situated phenomena such as can emerge from big-data-driven analyses within a single organization (i.e., case studies that are deeply quantitative in nature). The era of big data introduces numerous techniques for analyzing and interpreting data, from visualizations to modeling, and those techniques will soon become essential topics in textbooks on research methods and on statistical analysis that are bedrock material for training in the organizational sciences. Perhaps it is textbooks on statistical analyses that will show the greatest change in the shortest time as they assimilate approaches that are core to big data, such as support vector machines for testing nonlinear relationships and ensemble techniques for integrating the results of different models (see Oswald and Putka, Chapter 3, for further details). An expansion of the breadth of interdisciplinary science also is a major departure from what normal science has been. These changes in methods, analysis, and perspectives will influence how the markers of good science evolve and ultimately influence what gets published in professional outlets. Big data also require re-examination of how we manage some of the supporting infrastructure of organizational research, such as protecting research participants and maintaining data integrity.

One other change that could rock normal science hinges on where the relevant big data are for the organizational sciences: in organizations. For-profit organizations are quite likely to regard that data as an asset, one that can be used to create competitive advantage. They may be disinclined to give it away and may restrict access to protect employee privacy. At the same time, organizations are also significantly increasing their own research and analytic capabilities. A combination of a large stock of data and in-house expertise to make use of it means that organizations are poised to become self-sufficient, primary producers of (and not just consumers of) organizational research. Thus, it is conceivable that the research center of gravity could shift away from academic institutions and research enterprises to where the data are. This would not be inconsequential. It could bring about unwanted conditions, such as a gap between big-data-based research and publication, since social scientists in business organizations do not have the same reasons to publish in professional journals as do those working in settings where professional publication is germane to the mission. Such unwanted consequences would seem to be preventable with a bit of careful professional monitoring and action. Change is happening because of big data; better to be masters than victims of the revolution.

REFERENCES

Guzzo, R. A., Nalbantian, H. R., & Parra, L. F. (2014). A big-data, say-do approach to climate and culture: A consulting perspective. In B. Schneider & K. M. Barbera (Eds.), *The Oxford handbook of organizational climate and culture* (pp. 197–211). New York, NY: Oxford University Press.

Hulin, C. L. (1966). Job satisfaction and turnover in a female clerical population. *Journal of Applied Psychology, 50*(4), 280–285.

Kuhn, T. S. (1970). *The structure of scientific revolutions* (2nd ed.). Chicago, IL: University of Chicago Press.

Marmot, M. (2004). *How social standing affects our health and longevity.* New York, NY: Owl Books.

Mayer-Schonberger, V., & Cukier, K. (2013). *Big data.* Boston, MA: Houghton Mifflin.

Ohm, P. (2010). Broken promises of privacy: Responding to the surprising failure of anonymization. *UCLA Law Review, 57,* 1701–1777.

Pagliery, J. (2014, November 25). Uber removes racy blog posts on prostitution, one-night stands. *CNN Money.* Retrieved from http://money.cnn.com/2014/11/25/technology/uber-prostitutes/index.html?hpt=hp_t4

Perry, C. (2010). You're not so anonymous. *Harvard Gazette.* Retrieved from: http://news.harvard.edu/gazette/story/2011/10/you%E2%80%99re-not-so-anonymous/

Sweeney, L. (2000). Uniqueness of simple demographics in the U.S. population. Laboratory for International Data Privacy, Working Paper LIDAP-WP4.

Tufte, E. R. (1983) *The visual display of quantitative information.* Cheshire, CT: Graphics Press.

Tukey, J. W. (1977). *Exploratory data analysis.* Boston, MA: Addison-Wesley.

Wang, M. (Ed.). (2012). *The Oxford handbook of retirement.* New York, NY: Oxford University Press.

Waijee, A. K., Higgins, P. D. R., & Singal, A. G. (2013). A primer on predictive models. *Clinical and Translational Gastroenterology, 4,* 1–4.

Weber, M., Krogman, N., & Antoniuk, T. (2012). Cumulative effects assessment: Linking social, ecological, and governance dimensions. *Ecology and Society, 17,* 22–28.

Contributors

Whitney Botsford Morgan, Ph.D., is an associate professor of management in the College of Business at the University of Houston-Downtown. She uses her training in industrial and organizational psychology as the foundation for examining interpersonal dynamics in the workplace, specifically how diversity with regard to gender and family status affect personal, professional, and organizational outcomes. Her research appears in outlets such as *Journal of Management, Journal of Applied Psychology*, and *Human Resource Management Review*. In addition, she sits on the editorial board for the *Journal of Business and Psychology*, and has consulted on applied projects including competency modeling, role clarification, workforce analysis, and entry-level selection systems.

Chu-Hsiang (Daisy) Chang, Ph.D. is an associate professor in the Department of Psychology at Michigan State University. Prior to joining Michigan State, she was a faculty member in the Department of Environmental and Occupational Health at the University of South Florida, and the Department of Psychology of Roosevelt University. She received her Ph.D. in industrial and organizational psychology from the University of Akron in 2005. Her research interests focus on occupational health and safety, leadership, and motivation. Specifically, she studies issues related to occupational stress, workplace violence, and how employee motivation and organizational leadership intersect with issues concerning employee health and well being. Her work has been published in *Academy of Management Review, Academy of Management Journal, Journal of Applied Psychology, Journal of Organizational Behavior, Organizational Behavior and Human Decision Processes, Psychological Bulletin*, and *Work & Stress*.

Georgia T. Chao, Ph.D. is an associate professor of management at the Eli Broad Graduate School of Management at Michigan State University. She has a B.S. in psychology from the University of Maryland and an M.S. and Ph.D. in industrial and organizational psychology from the Pennsylvania State University. Her research interests include teams, organizational socialization, career development, and international human resource management. She is also interested in early career expectations of emerging young adults. Recently, one of her 2013 publications in *Organizational Research Methods* won the Sage Best Paper Award in 2014 and SIOP's William A. Owens Scholarly Achievement Award in 2015. Currently, she serves on four editorial boards. She is a member of the Academy of Management, and a fellow of APA and SIOP.

Jose M. Cortina is a professor in the industrial and organizational psychology program at George Mason University. Professor Cortina received his Ph.D. in 1994 from Michigan State University. His recent research has involved topics in meta-analysis, structural equation modeling, significance testing, and philosophy of science as well as predictors and outcomes of emotions in the workplace. His work has been published in journals such as the *Journal of Applied Psychology*, *Personnel Psychology*, *Psychological Bulletin*, *Organizational Research Methods*, and *Psychological Methods*. He is a former editor of *Organizational Research Methods* and a former associate editor of the *Journal of Applied Psychology*. Dr. Cortina was honored by the Society for Industrial and Organizational Psychology (SIOP) with the 2001 Ernest J. McCormick Award for Distinguished Early Career Contributions, by the Research Methods Division of the Academy of Management with the 2004 Robert O. McDonald Best Paper Award and by the Organizational Research Methods Editorial Board with the 2012 Best Paper Award. He was also honored by George Mason University with a 2010 Teaching Excellence Award and by SIOP with the 2011 Distinguished Teaching Award. Dr. Cortina just finished serving as President of SIOP.

Anne-Sophie Deprez-Sims, Ph.D., is an associate director with APT-Metrics, Inc., where she provides consulting in the areas of job analysis, selection, litigation support, and competency modeling. Before working at APTMetrics, Anne-Sophie worked as a research and development specialist where she designed custom and off-the-shelf selection tests for public safety employers. She also worked in organizational development where she assisted with organizational surveys, processes improvements and data analysis. Anne-Sophie received her master's degree and Ph.D. from the Illinois Institute of Technology in industrial-organizational (I-O) psychology. She received her bachelor's degree in I-O psychology from DePaul University.

Peter D. DeVries, Ph.D., is a professor of EIS at the University of Houston-Downtown in the College of Business. DeVries earned an industrial engineering degree from Texas A&M, an MBA from Texas State, and a Ph.D.

in computer information systems and quantitative analysis from the University of Arkansas. Dr. DeVries has published in a variety of journals on topics including wireless networking, the Internet, website design, the eBay economy, RFID, online education, entrepreneurship, banking fraud, social media and cloud computing. Prior to academia, DeVries was an aerospace manufacturing engineer, KPMG Management Consultant and SAP Consultant implementing global corporate enterprise systems.

Eric Dunleavy, Ph.D., is a principal consultant at DCI Consulting Group, where he is involved in a wide variety of employee selection and equal employment opportunity/affirmative action (EEO/AA) consulting services. He also serves on staff with both the Center for Corporate Equality (CCE), a national nonprofit research group, and The OFCCP Institute, a national nonprofit employer association. Both focus on education and training related to EEO/AA issues. His primary areas of expertise are in employee selection, validation research, adverse impact analyses and other EEO analytics. Eric received his M.A. (2002) and Ph.D. (2004) in industrial/organizational psychology with a concentration in data analysis from the University of Houston. He received an honors B.A. (2000) in psychology from St. Anselm College. Eric has served as president, vice president, and legal chair of the Personnel Testing Council of Metropolitan Washington, D.C. (PTC/MW), and was on the editorial board of The Industrial-Organizational Psychologist for 7 years as co-author of the "On the Legal Front" column. In 2011, Dr. Dunleavy received the first Distinguished Early Career Contributions Award—Practice award from the Society for Industrial-Organizational Psychology. In 2015, he was elected as Fellow of the Society for Industrial-Organizational Psychology.

Rosemarie Fernandez, M.D., is an emergency medicine physician and associate professor and director of simulation in the Division of Emergency Medicine at the University of Washington. Dr. Fernandez's research focuses on developing simulation-based training and assessment systems for the purpose of evaluating team and individual skills during resuscitation and acute patient care events. Her work has been funded by the Agency for Healthcare Research and Quality, the Emergency Medicine Patient Safety Foundation, and the Washington State Department of Labor and Industry.

Alexis A. Fink, PhD., is currently the Director of Talent Intelligence Analytics at Intel. Her organization provides original organizational effectiveness research, HR analytics, talent marketplace analytics, and HR systems and tools. Prior to Intel, Alexis spent 7 years at Microsoft, where her roles included Director of Talent Management Infrastructure. Her career has been characterized by an integrative approach to HR, including developing and implementing competency systems and integrated talent management systems. Her background also includes work in large-scale organizational transformation. Alexis received her Ph.D. in industrial/organizational psychology from Old Dominion University. In addition to practicing and leading in organizations, she continues to teach, is a frequent SIOP contributor, and an occasional author and journal editor.

Richard A. Guzzo co-leads Mercer's Workforce Sciences Institute, a research and innovation center, and is based in Washington, D.C. In addition to R&D responsibilities, Rick delivers data-driven advisory work primarily to large, global clients on a wide range of strategic workforce issues. He has published four books and many professional articles in outlets such as *Journal of Applied Psychology*, *Personnel Psychology*, and *Harvard Business Review*. Prior to joining Mercer Rick was a professor of psychology at the University of Maryland (1989–97) and New York University (1980–89). His B.S. degree is from The Ohio State University and his Ph.D. is from Yale University. He is a Fellow of the Society for Industrial-Organizational Psychology.

John P. Hausknecht is an associate professor of human resource studies at Cornell University. He earned his Ph.D. in 2003 from Penn State University with a major in industrial/organizational psychology and minor in management. He teaches undergraduate and graduate-level courses on human resource management, staffing organizations, and HR analytics. Professor Hausknecht's research primarily falls within the domain of staffing and has appeared in the *Academy of Management Journal*, *Journal of Applied Psychology*, and *Personnel Psychology*. He currently serves on the editorial board of *Academy of Management Journal* and is an associate editor for *Personnel Psychology*.

Hailey Herleman, Ph.D., is an IBM Smarter Workforce Executive for North America. The Smarter Workforce business includes IBM's talent management software, behavioral sciences, workforce consulting and analytics solutions that improve HCM effectiveness and drive business performance. Hailey is responsible for advising CHROs and delivering

Smarter Workforce Workshops as well as supporting our clients delivering improved business outcomes across the broader Smarter Workforce solutions portfolio. Hailey also serves as an executive sponsor to certain strategic partnerships. In addition, Hailey is a nationally recognized thought leader in the field with multiple peer reviewed research publications and regular presentations at international HR conferences. Hailey also has held positions at the American Institutes for Research, Deloitte, and Clemson University. She holds a Ph.D. in industrial and organizational psychology, a M.S. in applied psychology, and a B.A. in psychology from Clemson University in Clemson, SC.

Ivan Hernandez, Ph.D., is a collaborative post-doctoral researcher in the SONIC lab at Northwestern University and the DELTA lab at the Georgia Institute of Technology. His research interests include computational social science (agent-based modeling, text mining, spatial methods), language cognition (fluency, cultural differences), and group behavior (regional variation, social networks, multi-team systems).

A. James Illingworth, Ph.D., provides talent management consulting services to public sector organizations and Fortune 100 and 500 companies in the areas of job analysis and competency modeling; selection and assessment; performance management, evaluation, and development; and legal compliance and defensibility. He works with clients across a wide range of industries to develop, validate, and implement talent management programs at all organizational levels and provide guidance on the use of technology-enhanced assessment. James earned his master's degree and Ph.D. in industrial-organizational (I-O) psychology from The University of Akron and has previously worked at APTMetrics and Personnel Decisions Research Institute (PDRI) providing consulting services in the areas of performance management and selection and assessment.

Gahyun Jeon, Ph.D., is a collaborative post-doctoral researcher in the SONIC lab at Northwestern University and the DELTA lab at the Georgia Institute of Technology. Her research interests include changes in job satisfaction across time and levels (i.e., within-persons, across the life course, and in response to job changes and work events), counterproductive work behavior from the perspective of multiple rating sources (self-ratings vs. coworker-ratings vs. supervisor-ratings), and statistics/research methods (social networks, multilevel modeling, meta-analysis, and modern missing data routines).

Eden B. King, Ph.D., joined the faculty of the industrial-organizational psychology program at George Mason University after earning her Ph.D. from Rice University in 2006. Dr. King is pursuing a program of research that seeks to guide the equitable and effective management of diverse organizations.

Richard J. Klimoski holds a dual appointment as professor of psychology and management in the School of Business at George Mason University, Fairfax, Virginia. His teaching and research interests center on managing the human side of work organizations, especially through effective leadership and the involvement of work teams. His numerous original research contributions have appeared in such publications as the *Academy of Management Journal, Academy of Management Learning and Education, Administrative Science Quarterly, Journal of Applied Psychology, Personnel Psychology,* and many other well respected journals. He is a past editor of the *Academy of Management Review* and served as an associate editor of the *Academy of Management Learning and Education journal.* He is a member of numerous journal editorial boards. Klimoski has co-authored several books, including *Research Methods in Human Resource Management* (1992), *The Nature of Organizational Leadership* (2002), *Emotions in Work Organizations* (2002), *The Handbook of Psychology (Volume 12): Industrial and Organizational Psychology* (2003), and *Research Companion to the Dysfunctional Workplace: Management Challenges and Symptoms* (2007). Most recently he co-edited the volume *Advancing Human Resource Project Management* (2014) published by Wiley on behalf of the SIOP Practice series.

Steve W.J. Kozlowski, Ph.D., is a professor of organizational psychology at Michigan State University. He is an authority on multilevel theory, team effectiveness, learning and adaptation. The goal of his programmatic research is to generate actionable theory, research-based principles, and applications to develop effective and adaptive individuals, teams, and organizations. His research is, or has been, supported by the Agency for Health Research and Quality (AHRQ), the Air Force Office of Scientific Research (AFOSR), the Army Research Institute for the Behavioral and Social Sciences (ARI), the National Aeronautics and Space Administration (NASA), and the Office of Naval Research (ONR), among others. Dr. Kozlowski is the associate editor for the *Archives of Scientific Psychology*, series editor for the *Oxford Series on Organizational Psychology and Behavior*, and former editor and associate editor for the *Journal of Applied Psychology*. He is an editorial board member for the *Journal of Management* and has served on the editorial boards of the *Academy of Management Journal, Human Factors,* the *Journal of Applied Psychology,* and *Organizational Behavior and Human Decision Processes.* He has published over 100 books, chapters, and articles and made over 300 invited and refereed presentations. He is a fellow of the American Psychological Association, the Association for Psychological Science, the International Association for Applied Psychology, and the Society for Industrial and Organizational Psychology (SIOP). He is President of SIOP (2015–2016). Dr. Kozlowski received his B.A. in psychology from the University of Rhode Island, and his M.S. and Ph.D. degrees in organizational psychology from The Pennsylvania State University.

Huisi (Jessica) Li is a doctoral student of human resource studies at Cornell University. She earned her M.A. in international comparative education in 2013 from Stanford University and her M.S. in industrial/organizational psychology in 2012 from Peking University. She studies employee turnover and its effects on team stability and performance, as well as communication processes within multinational teams.

Michael Lippstreu, Ph.D., is a project manager with APTMetrics. He provides consulting services in the areas of job analysis, competency modeling, employee selection and assessment, statistical analyses and quantitative methods, litigation support, and performance management. He has consulted for Fortune 500 companies from a variety of industries as well as public sector organizations. Michael earned his master's degree and Ph.D. in industrial-organizational (I-O) psychology from the Georgia Institute of Technology. Michael joined APTMetrics in 2004, where he completed a one-year internship before accepting a full-time position on the consulting staff. Prior to APTMetrics, Michael worked with various other organizations on a contract basis to provide consulting in the areas of statistical analyses, research methods, employee development, and performance assessment and feedback.

Daniel A. Newman, Ph.D., is an associate professor of psychology and labor and employment relations at the University of Illinois at Urbana-Champaign. His research deals with diversity/adverse impact in HR hiring practices, emotional intelligence, narcissism in the workplace, job satisfaction and work withdrawal/work engagement, and research methods (multilevel and social network approaches, missing data).

Frederick L. Oswald, Ph.D., is a professor in the Department of Psychology at Rice University. His research collaborations and grants center around personnel selection and test development issues within organizational, educational and military settings. Currently, Dr. Oswald serves as an associate editor for four journals (*Journal of Management, Psychological Methods, Research Synthesis Methods,* and *Journal of Research in Personality*) and for nine editorial boards. He is a fellow of APS, APA, and two APA divisions (Div. 5 and SIOP, Div. 14). He received his Ph.D. in industrial-organizational psychology with an emphasis in psychometrics and statistics from the University of Minnesota in 1999.

Dan J. Putka, Ph.D., is a principal staff scientist at the Human Resources Research Organization (HumRRO) in Alexandria, Virginia. He has over a decade of hands-on experience developing and evaluating assessments for selection and promotion, and managing and modeling large, messy archival datasets for purposes of predicting and understanding key outcomes such as job performance, turnover, counterproductive work behavior, and job satisfaction. Aside from his client centered work, Dan has maintained an active presence in the I-O psychology scientific community having authored numerous book chapters and journals articles on a variety of methods-related topics, and serving on the editorial boards of four journals. He is a past-president of the Personnel Testing Council of Metropolitan Washington, and a fellow of APA and three of its divisions (5, 14, and 19). Dan received his Ph.D. in I-O psychology with a specialization in quantitative methods from Ohio University.

Jacqueline Ryan is the Director of Science & Analytics for IBM Smarter Workforce Product Management. She is responsible for IBM's Smarter Workforce talent analytics business that improves employee and business performance through evidence-based decisions based on big data, advanced analytics and workforce sciences. With over 20 years experience in information management, analytics, and big data technologies, Jackie has led worldwide software development, product management, and marketing teams that have led the market in client value and innovation.

Evan F. Sinar, Ph.D., is Development Dimensions International's (DDI's) chief scientist and director of the Center for Analytics and Behavioral Research (CABER), a team of analytical specialists deploying its expertise globally across DDI's solutions portfolio. Evan partners with client organizations to build and execute analytic initiatives to demonstrate the impact of assessment and development programs on individual-level behavior change and organizational-level business objectives. Evan is also the lead author of DDI's *Global Leadership Forecast*, a major trend research study providing deep and actionable insights on how organizations can optimize their management of leadership talent in alignment with strategic priorities. Prior to his role as chief scientist Evan held the role of Manager of Assessment and Selection Analytics, leading design, development, and technology integrity for DDI's screening and testing solutions. Evan is an editorial board member of *Journal of Applied Psychology* and *Journal of Business and Psychology* and has also authored over 60 professional presentations and publications for major journals and professional conferences. He is a thought leader for DDI on topics such as data visualization, leadership development, generational differences, social media, and pre-employment assessment.

Jeffrey Stanton, Ph.D. (psychology, University of Connecticut, 1997), is professor and interim dean at Syracuse University's School of Information Studies. Stanton is an active scholar who has received more than $5.5M in extramural support including the National Science Foundation's CAREER award for early career researchers as well as funding from the Institute for Museum and Library Services, NASA, the Department of Homeland Security, the KeyBank Foundation, and the SIOP Foundation. His research expertise is in research methods, psychometrics, and survey design. He is the author of three books, dozens of scholarly articles in peer-reviewed behavioral science and technology journals as well as numerous book chapters on data science, privacy, research methods, and program evaluation. He has won several best paper awards and several awards for graduate student mentoring. Stanton's background also includes more than a decade of business experience in start-ups and established companies.

Scott Tonidandel, Ph.D., is the Wayne M. and Carolyn A. Watson Professor of Psychology at Davidson College and a faculty affiliate of the organizational science program at the University of North Carolina-Charlotte. He earned his Ph.D. in industrial-organizational psychology from Rice University. His research spans a variety of topics including reactions to selection procedures, leadership, mentoring, diversity, and statistical techniques. Dr. Tonidandel currently serves as the associate editor for both the *Journal of Business and Psychology* and *Organizational Research Methods*, and he is a fellow of the Society for Industrial and Organizational Psychology (APA div. 14).

Index

ability: cognitive 22, 218, 297–8; organization's 314, 322

absenteeism 92–3, 188, 193, 345

accuracy 49–50, 110, 121, 149, 152, 193, 196, 214, 219, 330–1; levels 110

activation 47, 290

adverse impact 313, 315–17, 319, 330; allegation 315; measurement 315–16, 330

agent-based simulation (ABS) 296–7

agents, embedded 297, 299

aggregation 65–7, 112, 245, 293, 312, 319

algorithmic modeling methods, modern 206

algorithms 6, 8, 45, 49, 51–3, 70–1, 107, 169, 184, 199, 217, 234, 238, 324

American Psychological Association 219, 243, 245, 318, 346

analytics 14, 38, 189, 192, 272, 283, 285; movement 183, 187, 202, 205, 207, 209; processes 28, 32, 35, 37–8; projects, multiple workforce 29, 32; team 186, 190, 198, 201

animated data visualizations 141–2

annotations 150–3

applicants: large number of 221–2; pool 223, 229, 317, 320–2

applicant tracking system (ATS) 23, 188, 221, 227, 235, 338

application programming interface (API) 76–8, 99–100, 105, 174; streaming 99–100

artificial neural networks (ANNs) 46–8

assessment processes 213–14, 220–1, 223, 226, 231, 234, 238, 242, 244–5; 360-degree 230; internal talent 220, 222–3; organization's talent 229

assessments 8–9, 12, 191–2, 194, 213–23, 225–9, 231, 233, 235, 237–46, 278,

280, 285, 290–2, 344; context 218, 237, 241, 340; daily 292; data 217, 227–8, 241–2; improving of 194; practices 214, 219–20, 237, 241–2; principles 214–15; procedures 222; scores 192, 194, 338, 340; situation 216; systems 23; work 214–16, 218, 220

ATS *see* applicant tracking system

badge data 289–90, 293, 303

badges 288, 290, 293

bar graphs 158–9, 161, 171

behavioral data 20, 22–3, 40, 298

behaviors 4–5, 10, 23, 64–5, 76, 96, 193–4, 232, 239–41, 272, 284, 302, 311, 325, 329; counterproductive work 58; individual 8, 217

bias, unconscious 320, 325

big data 7, 43, 45, 47, 49, 51, 53, 55, 57, 59, 101–2, 225, 230, 233, 243–4; availability of 233, 236–7; benefits 228, 232, 236; challenges 227, 231, 234–5; for diversity and inclusion 311, 313, 315, 317, 319, 321, 323, 325, 327, 329, 331; movement 181, 183, 185, 187, 189, 191, 193, 195, 197, 199, 201, 203, 205, 207, 209; potential applications 3, 6–7, 124, 250; reactions to 244; in selection and assessment 213, 215, 217, 219, 221, 223, 225, 227, 229, 231, 233, 235, 237, 239, 245–7; sensing 158–9, 161, 163, 165, 167, 169, 171, 173; and team effectiveness 273, 275, 277, 279, 281, 283, 285, 287, 289, 291, 293, 295, 297, 299, 301; in turnover and retention 250–1, 257, 259, 261, 263, 265, 267; types of 230; velocity of 65, 120, 329

biodata measures 194–5

bubble plot 136, 150

Printed in the United States
by Baker & Taylor Publisher Services